The Victorian Novel

Blackwell Guides to Criticism
Editor Michael O'Neill

'I very much like the way this general approach to the specific volumes has been formulated. The *Critical Heritage* volumes were so good, so useful. But I think your idea to thicken the editorial commentary is important.' JEROME J. McGANN.

The aim of this new series is to provide undergraduates pursuing literary studies with collections of key critical work from an historical perspective. At the same time emphasis is placed upon recent and current work. In general, historic responses of importance are described and represented by short excerpts in an introductory narrative chapter. Thereafter landmark pieces and cutting edge contemporary work are extracted or provided in their entirety according to their potential value to the student. Some volumes in the series diverge from this model, but each volume seeks to enhance enjoyment of literature and to widen the individual student's critical repertoire. Critical approaches are treated as 'tools', rather than articles of faith, to enhance the pursuit of reading and study. At a time when critical bibliographies seem to swell by the hour and library holdings to wither year by year, Blackwell's *Guides to Criticism* series offers students privileged access to and careful guidance through those writings that have most conditioned the historic current of discussion and debate as it now informs contemporary scholarship.

Published volumes

Corinne Saunders: *Chaucer*
Francis O'Gorman: *The Victorian Novel*

Forthcoming volumes

Roger Dalrymple: *Middle English*
Uttara Natarajan: *Romantic Poetry*
John Niles: *Anglo-Saxon*
Michael O'Neill: *Twentieth-century British and Irish Poetry*
Gareth Reeves: *American Poetry from Whitman to the Present*
Emma Smith: *Shakespeare's Comedies*
Emma Smith: *Shakespeare's Histories*
Emma Smith: *Shakespeare's Tragedies*
Michael Whitworth: *Modernism*

For Jane, with love

I speak therefore of good novels only;
and our modern literature is particularly rich in
types of such.

John Ruskin (1864)

Contents

Acknowledgements

I owe thanks to my friends and colleagues for their sustaining intelligence, good humour and well-timed glasses of wine while I have been writing this book. I am fortunate to have an academic home in the School of English at the University of Leeds and offer gratitude and admiration to my hard-working colleagues there. I am especially grateful to Professor David Fairer, Professor Joyce Hill, Dr Vivien Jones, Professor Ed Larrissy, Professor David Lindley, Dr John McLeod, Dr Gail Marshall, Dr Richard Salmon, Dr John Whale and Dr Jane Wood. John McLeod and Jane Wood read the chapters on postcolonialism and science respectively, and suggested helpful changes. Friends in other departments and elsewhere have been invaluable, and I am grateful to Dr Dinah Birch, Dr Juliet John, Dr Clare Morgan, Dr Corinne Saunders and Dr Katherine Turner. I am also grateful for the advice of Andrew McNeillie at Blackwells. Staff in the Brotherton Library at the University of Leeds, the City Library in Leeds, the British Library Document Supply Centre at Boston Spa, and the Bodleian Library, University of Oxford have been courteous and helpful, and I thank Ann Farr in particular for her prompt and interested assistance in the first of these libraries. Thanks also go to Stella Pilling in the third.

I have served as Tutor for Undergraduate Admissions while writing this book and have been assisted by the deft administrative hand of Elizabeth Paget in the admissions office: thank you. Other administrative and secretarial staff have eased the path, and I thank Sue Baker, Sharron Kyriacou and Pam Rhodes in particular.

I am grateful to the British Academy for a Small Research Award in May 2001 which considerably facilitated the research for this book. Thank you to my two referees, Dr Dinah Birch (again) and Professor Elisabeth Jay, and for the hospitality of Trinity College, Oxford, and the help of Professor Jim Leheny of the University of Massachusetts.

A number of friends and colleagues kindly answered an e-mail question-naire that I sent around in the early stages of this project and gave me hints for lines of thought. In particular, I thank Professor Elisabeth Jay (again), Dr Catherine Maxwell and Dr Marion Thain. Dr Delia da Sousa Correa's help was especially welcome.

This book has been written for students of the Victorian novel. I am grateful to those students on my option modules 2000–2001 at Leeds on Victorian Self-writing, on the Idea of Italy in Victorian Literature and Culture, and on the Victorian Literature core module for their good sense and enthusiasm while I tested out some ideas for this book on them.

My parents, John and Joyce O'Gorman, and my brother, Chris O'Gorman, have been interested listeners to my accounts of the progress of this collection, and I thank them. And to Jane, for unfailing faith in this book, for reading every word and suggesting improvements, and for much else besides: thank you.

All remaining errors and graceless expressions are mine.

Francis O'Gorman

School of English, University of Leeds

The editor and publishers wish to thank the following for permission to reprint copyright material:

Chapter 1:
Extract from George Saintsbury, *The English Novel* (London: J. M. Dent, 1913), pp. 237–44.
Extract from Lord David Cecil, *Early Victorian Novelists: Essays in Revaluation* (London: Constable and Robinson Publishing Ltd, 1934), pp. 3–23.

Chapter 2:
Extract from F. R. Leavis, *The Great Tradition* (London: Chatto and Windus, 1960), pp. 5–21. Reprinted by permission of The Random House Group Ltd.

Chapter 3:
Extract from Elaine Showalter, *A Literature of their Own: British Women Novelists from Brontë to Lessing*, pp. 19–32. © 1977 (Princeton University Press). Reprinted by permission of Princeton University Press.
Extract from Sandra S. Gilbert and Susan Gubar, *The Madwoman in the Attic: The Woman Writer and the Nineteenth-century Literary Imagination* (New Haven, Conn.: Yale University Press, 1979), pp. 356–62.

Chapter 4:
Extract from George Levine, *The Realistic Imagination: English Fiction from Frankenstein to Lady Chatterley* (Chicago: University of Chicago Press, 1981), pp. 3–22.
Extract from Catherine Belsey, *Critical Practice* (London: Routledge, 1980), pp. 67–82.
Extract from Penny Boumehla, 'Realism and the Ends of Feminism', in Susan Sheridan, ed., *Grafts: Feminist Cultural Criticism* (London: Verso, 1988), pp. 323–9.

Chapter 5:
Extract from Raymond Williams, *The English Novel* (London: Chatto and Windus, 1970), pp. 9–17. Reprinted by permission of The Random House Group Ltd.
Extract from Mary Poovey, *Making a Social Body: British Cultural Formation, 1830–1864* (Chicago: University of Chicago Press, 1995), pp. 132–4, 143–53.
Extract from Josephine Guy, *The Victorian Social-problem Novel* (Basingstoke: Macmillan, 1996), pp. 110–16. Reproduced by permission of Palgrave.

Chapter 6:
Extract from Patricia Ingham, *The Language of Gender and Class: Transformation in the Victorian Novel* (London: Routledge, 1996), pp. 20–30.
Extract from Dorothy Van Ghent, *The English Novel: Form and Function* (New York: Harper and Row, 1961, originally published 1953, New York: Rinehart), pp. 3–7. Reprinted by permission of the Thomson Corporation.
Extract from Peter Garrett, *The Victorian Multiplot Novel: Studies in Dialogical Form* (New Haven, Conn.: Yale University Press, 1980), pp. 16–21.

Chapter 7:
Extract from Gillian Beer, *Darwin's Plots: Evolutionary Narrative in Darwin, George Eliot and Nineteenth-century Fiction* (London: Routledge and Kegan Paul, 1983), pp. 149–56.
Extract from George Levine, *Darwin and the Novelists: Patterns of Science in Victorian Fiction* (Cambridge, Mass.: Harvard University Press, 1988), pp. 13–20. Reprinted by permission of the publishers. © 1988 by the President and Fellows of Harvard College.

Chapter 8:
Extract from John Sutherland, *Victorian Novelists and Publishers* (London: Athlone Press, 1976), pp. 20–40. Reprinted by kind permission of John Sutherland.

Extract from Catherine A. Judd, 'Male Pseudonyms and Female Authority in Victorian England', from John O. Jordan and Robert L. Patten, eds, *Literature in the Marketplace: Nineteenth-century British Publishing and Reading Practices* (Cambridge: Cambridge University Press, 1955), pp. 250–68.

Chapter 9:
Extract from Gayatri Chakravorty Spivak, 'Three Women's Texts and a Critique of Imperialism', *Critical Inquiry*, 12 (1) (1985), pp. 243–9. By permission of the author.
Extract from Firdous Azim, *The Colonial Rise of the Novel* (London: Routledge, 1993), pp. 29–31.
Extract from Susan Meyer, *Imperialism at Home: Race and Victorian Women's Fiction* (Ithaca, NY: Cornell University Press, 1996), pp. 60–66. © 1996 by Cornell University. Reprinted by permission of the publisher, Cornell University Press.

Every effort has been made to trace all the copyright holders, but if any has been inadvertently overlooked, the publishers will be pleased to make the necessary arrangement at the first opportunity.

Textual Note

All extracts have been edited. Omissions and insertions are signified with square brackets. Many extracts, in their original form, include long notes and references. For reasons of space, these have, regrettably, been shortened or omitted. Readers are recommended to consult the original versions, details of which are given in the text, for full notes. It is clear when the notes are editorial as distinct from authorial.

Introduction

Renaissance drama, Romantic period verse, and Victorian fiction: the three undisputed forms of literary greatness in English literature. These were genres of comparable stature, but differently popular in their own day. The original audience for Renaissance drama was small; for Romantic period verse, it was larger though not vast. But the original readers of the Victorian novel formed a sizeable portion of the middle class in a massively enlarged population with ever-increasing levels of literacy. The market for fiction in the nineteenth century became huge. In it, fortunes could be made, literary fame of a new, modern sort obtained. Dickens's lionization was an early form of the celebrity status that features prominently – and sometimes with similarly disastrous consequences – in our own cultural life. George Eliot courted a different, intellectual image. Henry James satirized literary adulation.[1] But each was a public figure, a novelist who achieved renown in his or her own lifetime through writing fiction. The Victorian novel, sustained by an enormous number of practitioners, some with an international fame, blossomed as a literary genre. It was a key medium for word art in a way not previously seen in English literature. The period was, and is, for many, the *age* of the novel.

But, paradoxically, it was not an age that universally approved of fiction. Even Anthony Trollope, a prolific contributor to the genre, once remarked: 'Fond as most of us are of novels, it has to be confessed that they have had a bad name among us.'[2] Many anxious critics agreed. Some of the debates about the ethics of novel reading were trenchant and included claims about the deleterious affects of fiction that were cognate with contemporary anxieties about the consequences of television and movie images in our own culture. This concern is clearly visible in the early works of criticism surveyed in the first chapter here. Such anxiety, looked at from a positive angle, indicated something of the importance the Victorian novel had, its capacity to generate comment and debate, as it proliferated in middle-class culture. Fiction was a live subject.

THE RANGE OF
VICTORIAN
FICTION

Such diversity of view is partly due to the fact that the category 'Victorian novel' covers so much literary writing. Beneath its ample mantle is work by authors from William Harrison Ainsworth (1805–82) to Israel Zangwill (1864–1926), from the provincial to the metropolitan, from the most judiciously moral to the daringly *risqué*, from the 1830s to the *fin de siècle*, from the enduring to the transitory, from realism to fantasy, from the runaway success to the unfortunately stillborn. Its practitioners are at once household names to us – Charles Dickens, George Eliot, Thomas Hardy – and, at the other end, deeply obscure, lost in the oubliette of literary history and familiar only to those whose professional scholarly work concerns the fiction of the Victorians. How many readers know W. G. Collingwood's *Thorstein of the Mere: A Saga of the Northmen in Lakeland* (1895) or Richard St John Tyrwhitt's *Hugh Heron, Ch. Ch.* (1880)? To be a serious student of the 'Victorian novel' is to set before oneself a diverse and uncontainable multitude of literary work. It is a plurality that exhilarates – and overwhelms.

DIFFICULTIES
OF THE TERM
'VICTORIAN
NOVEL'

The range of the novel in this period, its irreducible and energetic variety, has led critics to declare that the 'Victorian novel' is too general a term to be useful. Kathleen Tillotson's *Novels of the Eighteen-forties* (1954) made this point early on: she argued that 'It is now, I think, too late to talk about "Victorian novels"; their range is too vast and vague to lead to any useful generalization.'[3] Tillotson was right, and, now more than ever, in these days of academic specialism, only the foolhardy would venture general statements across the spectrum of nearly seventy years' worth of fiction. This *Guide* is not

DEFINITION
USED IN THIS
BOOK

about to commit such folly. The 'Victorian novel' in my title is a limited category. As it is used in this book, it refers principally to the acknowledged great names of Victorian fiction – Charlotte and Emily Brontë, Charles Dickens, George Eliot, Elizabeth Gaskell, Thomas Hardy, Henry James, William Makepeace Thackeray and Anthony Trollope – who have been and continue to be admired and continuously read, to be the subject of academic criticism, the focus of university and school courses, and consistently present in new editions on publishers' lists. It is with the critical history of this remarkable corpus of writing (and cognate, less well-known writers) that I am concerned in this survey of a hundred years of fertile critical investigation. That critical history is immense, and, squeezed with shrieks of protest into the pages of a single book, it reveals the changing face of our understanding of the major works of Victorian fiction, our altering areas of interest, and shifting sense of the nineteenth century itself across one hundred years.

THE
CHANGING
FACE OF
CRITICISM

It also reveals the changing face of English literary criticism. Here is a large slice of the development of literary studies in the Anglo-American academy from the literary history of the beginning of the twentieth century to the liberal humanism of the mid-years, to the radical political movements of the 1960s and 1970s, the post-structuralism of the 1970s and 1980s, the New

Historicism of the 1980s and 1990s, and the postcolonialism and feminist revisionism of the last years of the century. The rise of interdisciplinarity is visible here, including the emergence of visual studies in the 1990s; the shift from universalist postures in the early years to the interest in marginalized subjectivities in the later is apparent too; so is the change in the language and implied audience of criticism from the general reader of the Edwardian period to the highly educated specialist of the present, able to comprehend complex formulations of a now significantly professionalized subject area; the pressure of modern identity politics is evident as well as the increasing self-consciousness among critics in the twentieth century about the political commitments of their criticism. Visible across this slice of writing is the changing expectation of where meaning is located in literature, from the assumption that meaning is recognized or disinterred by the critic to the more contemporary assumption that it is produced by the reader. The shifting understanding of literature's relationship with history can also be seen here, the different answers to the question of how literature relates to its cultural context, and the developing ideas of literature's relation to ideology.

This last subject is, like all of them, a complex area. But it is one particularly prominent in this book's coverage. Put crudely, there is a pattern visible in this *Guide* of increasing sophistication from the beginning of the century to the end. Literary historians in the first decades were usually uninterested in fiction's relationship with ideas, history and society: the New Criticism that took over in the middle period ruled out literature's connection with its context as a matter of principle. In the 1960s, radical critics, beginning with Raymond Williams, upturned this assumption and investigated how literature engaged with its ideological environment. Fiction was often described from this point and into the following decades, in a reversal of the previous position, as a mode through which ideology was propagated. In recent years, however, critics have dissolved the binary and attended to ways fiction both upheld and subverted ruling ideologies. This is particularly evident in recent developments in feminist and postcolonial criticism.

Other patterns emerge in this survey of the elaborate texture of literary criticism's transformations over one hundred years. But mapping these transformations is only the secondary task of this book. Its primary interest is in Victorian fiction, how it has been and is read. Nineteenth-century fiction was popular in its own day and now sponsors an enormous range of criticism as diverse in character as itself. The first object of this *Guide* is to provide examples of the significant themes of that criticism, contextualized in an historical narrative, and placed in relation to continuing debates in the field. The first two chapters deal with historical movements necessary for understanding modern developments; the next seven are concerned with the themes that continue to occupy critics' attention today. From these seven, collectively,

OUTLINE OF THE BOOK

a general overview of where Victorian novel criticism is, at the present moment, should be clear. Reading these chapters should be like looking down from a tower on the contemporary critical terrain. This is not, of course, to say that the coverage is complete. Some things have disappeared beyond the horizon. A number of important critics are, for reasons of space, omitted, or merely referenced in the Further Reading sections, and some productive themes are passed by. I hardly, for instance, touch on the multifarious debates about Victorian fiction and religion (see the Further Reading section at the end of this Introduction) in my narratives. And these narratives, naturally, tidy up a diverse and non-linear history of criticism into an orderly progression, a shaped account, which readers who want to go further in the study of Victorian fiction will problematize and supplement. But, none the less, a picture of the principal features of the landscape does, I hope, emerge, a view from the bridge, an account of how it strikes a contemporary. Constructing such a reliable view of the recent and current critical debates as a starting-point for serious, informed reading of the Victorian novel is the principal aim of this *Guide*.

OUTLINE OF CHAPTER 1   A fuller outline is as follows. Chapter 1 considers criticism written at the beginning of the twentieth century, as the Victorian period was given its first *post hoc* definitions, its first posthumous assessments, and at a time when the novel was not held in high regard. This initial interest is compared to the academic study of the Victorian novel, such that it was, in the universities of the early twentieth century. The dominant critical mode of the time was literary history and its historical and appreciative purposes are analysed. Literary history's rupturing by E. M. Forster – author of, among other novels, *A Room with a View* (1908) and *Howards End* (1910) – in his popular *Aspects of the Novel* (1927) is also considered. The conclusion discusses the influential, genial criticism of Lord David Cecil, who taught several generations of undergraduates at Oxford, many of whom are still in teaching careers today. Cecil's views of the Victorian novel, its incoherent form and its avoidance of sexuality, remained peculiarly tenacious despite the work of subsequent critics and historians who upturned them.

OUTLINE OF CHAPTER 2   Like Cecil's, F. R. Leavis's work endured and continued to be a force in the academy into the 1970s. But Leavis's strongly held views on literary criticism and literary greatness came under attack in the 1970s and 1980s from those hostile to liberal humanism, especially Marxists, deconstructionists and feminists. Leavis became the *bête noire* of the intellectual Left and his work never fully recovered. None the less, at a greater distance from the 1970s, it is possible to re-evaluate his contribution to the study of Victorian fiction and to admire his insistence on the cultural and moral importance of literary criticism and his belief in the novel as a serious form of word art. Chapter 2 discusses Leavis's contribution and considers *The Great Tradition* (1948) in particular.

Leavis's influence continued into the 1970s, but, elsewhere, the woman's movement, as it had defined itself in the 1960s, had a considerable influence on the shape of intellectual projects across a range of disciplines in universities, polytechnics and institutes of higher education. Germaine Greer's *The Female Eunuch* (1970), Kate Millett's *Sexual Politics* (1970), Ellen Moers's *Literary Women* (1977), Sheila Robotham's *Hidden from History: 300 Years of Women's Oppression and the Fight Against It* (1977), Patricia Caplan's and Janet M. Bujra's collection *Women United, Women Divided: Cross-cultural Perspectives on Female Solidarity* (1978), and Mary Daly's *Gyn/ecology: The Metaethics of Radical Feminism* (1979) were just some of the important interventions in different disciplines, including the literary, which helped spread the radical feminist agenda across the academy's critical enterprise. For readers of Victorian fiction, the most significant works to have been written at this time, both from the United States, were Elaine Showalter's *A Literature of their Own: British Women Novelists from Brontë to Lessing* (1977) and Sandra M. Gilbert and Susan Gubar's *The Madwoman in the Attic: The Woman Writer and the Nineteenth-century Literary Imagination* (1979). These are discussed and their relation to their cultural moment evaluated in chapter 3.

Chapter 4 is dedicated to a subject that has prompted controversy since the Victorian novelists themselves: nineteenth-century fiction's understanding of 'realism'.[4] This contentious area, on which George Eliot and Henry James wrote directly, has involved widely differing views about nineteenth-century knowledge and faith, and stirred arguments over the epistemological and political assumptions of the classic novels of Victorian England. Discussions of realism in the 1970s and 1980s were strongly influenced by post-structuralist theory, especially the work of Roland Barthes and Jacques Derrida, and those years saw a reaction against practices of language that appeared to assume a naïve relationship with the real. The history of criticism of the Victorian novel reveals the marks of this reaction as well as the subsequent recuperations of the realist project by feminism in the 1990s, and the current interest in historicizing the real by New Historicists.

As with the question of realism, there has been a remarkable divergence of approach and range of critical and theoretical models in reading Victorian social-problem fiction. These form the topic of chapter 5. Together, chapters 4 and 5 survey the most contentious territory in this book. The genre or subgenre of Victorian social-problem fiction, including novels by Charlotte Brontë, Charles Dickens, Benjamin Disraeli, Elizabeth Gaskell and Charles Kingsley, interested critics working with a politicized critical methodology, especially Marxism, and has recently seen important interpretations by New Historicists and feminists. The debates about social-problem fiction involved discussion of the more widely applicable questions of the relationship of fiction to gender, politics and history. More particularly, the subject of Victorian social-problem fiction has recently become an arena for testing New Historicism's claims about fiction and social discourse.

OUTLINE OF
CHAPTER 6

Feminist scholarship added to the debate about social-problem fiction and also contributed to the study of the language of Victorian fiction. Chapter 6 considers recent work on literary language, including language and gender, and on form. It includes an examination of the impact of Bakhtinian models of fictional discourse on the study of the Victorian multi-plot novel. Henry James's impatient description of capacious nineteenth-century novels as 'large loose baggy monsters' provides the starting-point, as a range of critics across the twentieth century argued against it and thought more creatively about the ways in which the Victorian novel signified at a formal level.

OUTLINE OF
CHAPTER 7

The novel's relationship with the New Science, emerging to prominence in the middle of the nineteenth century, is the subject of chapter 7. Although the relationship between literary writing and Charles Darwin's evolutionary theory had been explored at the end of the nineteenth century and in the first decades of the twentieth, the 1980s saw a flourishing of interest in the topic. This criticism, from historicist and interdisciplinary perspectives, climaxed in the 1980s in Gillian Beer's study *Darwin's Plots: Evolutionary Narrative in Darwin, George Eliot and Nineteenth-century Fiction* (1983, 2nd edn 2000). Where Victorian life sciences intrigued writers in the 1980s, the 1990s saw an engagement with the mind sciences and medicine. Pathology in different forms was in the foreground of the critical debate here. These developments are all discussed.

OUTLINE OF
CHAPTER 8

In chapter 8, examples of critical writing on Victorian fiction are presented from one of the increasingly prominent fields in the current academy, the History of the Book. This, too, is a wide area, but I have given a flavour of its range. I include well-received discussions of the material conditions of publication and the circulation of the Victorian novel, Marxist re-readings of this topic, and some feminist revisions of earlier views of publishing history. The chapter also discusses feminist reconsideration of common assumptions about the role of women in the literary marketplace and about the use of male (and female) pseudonyms in the period.

FICTION AND
THE LAW

Correspondences between literary writing and science comprise the most active area of contextual research in Victorian fiction. But the study of fiction and the law, the relationship between novelistic writing and legal discourse, may gain future prominence. This would be highly appropriate: Victorian fiction frequently deals with matters of law or involves legal characters or settings, and around one in five Victorian novelists worked as lawyers or were legally connected at some time in their lives. There are signs that this subject is rising in importance in contemporary criticism though there is not yet enough to justify a separate chapter in this *Guide*. Randall Craig's study of the legal debates about the promise to marry, *Promising Language: Betrothal in*

Victorian Law and Fiction (2000), is an example. Craig examined how a range of classic Victorian texts, including Charlotte Brontë's *Jane Eyre*, George Eliot's *The Mill on the Floss*, Anthony Trollope's *Can You Forgive Her?* and Henry James's *The Wings of the Dove*, explored the implications of a broken engagement to marry, and how this related to the changing practices of law courts in actual cases. Connections between law, fiction and theology were pursued in Jan-Melissa Schramm's *Testimony and Advocacy in Victorian Law, Literature, and Theology* (2000), a book that related examples of Victorian fiction to the consequences of legislation in 1836 allowing barristers to address the jury on behalf of prisoners. Schramm argued that novelists fashioned a style of advocacy for fictional speakers that at once imitated, but also contested, the procedures increasingly prominent at the Bar. Kieran Dolin's *Fiction and the Law: Legal Discourse in Victorian and Modernist Literature* (1999) claimed ambitiously that part of the cultural authority of the Victorian novel was attributable to its critical engagement with the transforming practices of the law. Connections between law and nineteenth-century fiction, two cultural practices particularly concerned with the possibilities of language, its truthfulness or fictivity, its capacity to bear witness and persuade, look as if they may prove a new area of significance for scholars examining the historical situatedness of the Victorian novel.

The final chapter surveys responses to the nineteenth-century novel from critics working in postcolonialism, the field that has provided the most recent addition to the coverage and theoretical scope of English Literature as an academic discipline. While postcolonialism's literary focus has tended to be on the new literatures of postcolonial cultures, a number of significant new readings of Victorian fiction have appeared. These have characteristically explored the relation of novelistic discourse to ideologies of empire and colonialism understood to be circulating, even if covertly, in Victorian culture. I give instances of critical readings that have emphasized the complicity of Victorian fiction with these discourses, including an argument that the form of the nineteenth-century novel was saturated by the logic of imperialism. Once again, this chapter concludes by showing how feminism in the 1990s rethought previous critical positions and, here, offered a more complicated idea of the Victorian novel's transactions with ideologies of empire.

OUTLINE OF CHAPTER 9

Feminism, as will be clear, appears in many chapters. Chapter 3 is solely dedicated to a powerful manifestation of feminist literary criticism, but feminist readings of realism, social-problem fiction, language, the History of the Book, and postcolonialism are each considered. With its multiplicity of theoretical and political positions, feminism is no longer a discrete category in the Anglo-American academy and it would be misleading to imply that it remained a separable discourse, the developments of which could be plotted without reference to other areas of activity. As George Henry Lewes said of

FEMINISM AND THE CON-TEMPORARY ACADEMY

modern empirical science in the Victorian period, feminism has now penetrated everywhere: it informs all branches of critical investigation. The present
book reflects this condition of the modern academy as there is no single,
separate chapter surveying the multiple presence of feminism in the Victorian
fiction studies today, beyond the 1970s. The whole *Guide* testifies to the
ubiquity of its contemporary voices.

MASCULINITY
STUDIES   But feminism is not everything in gender studies. It is true that issues of
gender in literary criticism are still often assumed to refer exclusively to the
female or to feminism. Higher education examination questions in Victorian
literature that invite answers on 'gender and ...' normally precipitate answers
on representations of women or the work of female writers. But masculinities,
which have already attracted the attention of other disciplines such as anthropology, sociology and classics, grew as a topic of interest in nineteenth-
century literary studies in the 1990s and there is every sign that this subject
will further enrich understandings of gender in the Victorian period. Answers
to examination questions on gender that focus on masculinity may soon be a
small but significant indication of the extent to which this new intellectual
engagement has established itself in the academy.

On male desire, an early, ground-making book was Eve Kosofsky Sedgwick's *Between Men: English Literature and Male Homosocial Desire* (1985),
which had a chapter on Charles Dickens's *Edwin Drood* and the homophobia
of empire. For other texts on Victorian homosexuality, see the Further
Reading section at the end of this Introduction. In the 1990s, Annette
Federico considered the representation of male characters and what they
revealed about cultural gender politics in *Masculine Identity in Hardy and
Gissing* (1991). She adopted four stereotypes to investigate changes in male
identity at the end of the century: the virile man; the chaste man (or the seducer
and the saint); the idealist, the 'romantic fantasizer who seeks the woman of his
dreams'; and the realist, 'who recognizes the presence of the New Woman and
must try to deal with her as practically he can'.[5] Other work in the decade
included Herbert Sussman's *Victorian Masculinities: Manhood and Masculine
Poetics in Early Victorian Literature and Art* (1995), and James Eli Adams's
Dandies and Desert Saints: Styles of Victorian Masculinity (1995). Adams's study
aimed to 'underscore the importance of masculinity as a central problematic in
literary and cultural change',[6] and it is a key work in the field. Looking
specifically at fiction, Karen Volland Waters's *The Perfect Gentleman: Masculine
Control in Victorian Men's Fiction 1870–1901* (1997) considered a subject
tackled by Robin Gilmour (see Further Reading) and investigated the idea of
the gentleman and its role in the dynamics of Victorian gender politics. Waters
concentrated on fiction by Kipling, Gissing, Collins and Stevenson. There have
also been some individual studies of Victorian novels and manliness in essay
form, including Simon Petch's 'Robert Audley's Profession' in *Studies in the*

Novel (2000), which examined masculinity and the representation of the idle lawyer in Mary Elizabeth Braddon's *Lady Audley's Secret* (1862). (For more on masculinity and social-problem fiction, see pp. 165–7 below.) The area of Victorian masculinity studies is beginning to grow, and future surveys of Victorian fiction criticism will be able to plot its development more extensively.

Where Victorian masculinity does not yet have a substantial critical heritage, other areas of fiction criticism that do are none the less unrepresented in this book. One subject that has seen a major contribution from feminist scholars, from Elaine Showalter's *A Literature of their Own* onwards, is, because of the parameters of my project, hardly discussed here. Canon revision has been a widespread feature of modern literary studies, and the Victorian period is no exception. The present book concentrates on the classic fiction of the Victorians, and does not stray significantly beyond this boundary. But work in the past two decades in nineteenth-century fiction has recuperated and celebrated substantial areas of novel writing that have been occluded by the classic canon, hidden by the roll of 'great literature' (now in scare quotes). Feminism has been the biggest influence on this, but revisionary pressure has also come from the growing interest in the body, pathologies, the culturally marginalized, popular fiction, popular culture, and from the New Historicists' emphasis on the relevance of all cultural documents to reading literature (for an outline of New Historicism, see p. 162). Collectively, these forces have led to the increasing study of: sensation fiction, Gothic fiction, New Woman fiction, detective fiction, working-class writing, and popular fiction in general. The canon of the Victorian novel is strikingly different even from twenty years ago.

CANON REVISION IN RECENT VICTORIAN FICTION STUDIES

Feminist critics have been active in work on sensation fiction, a popular form of literature in the mid-Victorian period, and have explored the ways in which Victorian women novelists used the conventions of sensation to debate feminist themes that were less easy for a woman (or a man) to confront in the realist mode. Sensation fiction has emerged as a significant literary form in which women critiqued aspects of Victorian gender politics. Examples of recent criticism on sensation fiction include Winifred Hughes's *The Maniac in the Cellar: Sensation Novels of the 1860s* (1980), Lyn Pykett's *The 'Improper' Feminine: The Women's Sensation Novel and the New Woman Writing* (1992), Jenny Bourne Taylor's *In the Secret Theatre of Home: Wilkie Collins, Sensation Narrative, and Nineteenth Century Psychology* (1998), and Barbara Leckie's *Culture and Adultery: The Novel, the Newspaper, and the Law, 1857–1914* (1999), which includes a chapter on some less well-known novels such as Caroline Norton's *Lost and Saved* (1863) and Mary Elizabeth Braddon's *The Doctor's Wife* (1864). (For Leckie's interest in the law, see Further Reading.) These critics, proposing feminist modes for reading sensation fiction and

SENSATION FICTION

comprehending its cultural significance, have all contributed to arguments about canon revision and helped to ensure that the genre is now widely represented on courses on the Victorian novel in higher education.

GOTHIC
FICTION

Connected with sensation fiction is Gothic fiction which has also seen a rise in critical interest. The turn against realism in the 1980s propelled Gothic into the centre of fiction studies (see pp. 133–5 below), and the 1990s continued to investigate it. Marie Mulvey-Roberts's *The Handbook to Gothic Literature* (1998) brought together eminent critics in a survey of the mode across all periods, while recent monographs on Victorian Gothic include Kelly Hurley's *The Gothic Body: Sexuality, Materialism, and Degeneration at the Fin de Siècle* (1996), which grew partly from the 1980s' and 1990s' interest in how ideology was written on the body. Hurley accounted for the resurgence of the Gothic during the *fin de siècle* and examined a key scenario that haunted Gothic fiction: the loss of a unified, stable human identity, and the emergence of a chaotic and transformative 'abhuman' identity in its place. Robert Mighall's *A Geography of Victorian Gothic Fiction: Mapping History's Nightmares* (1999) offered a new, contextual way of thinking about the Gothic, 'an historicist alternative to the psychological, ontological, and "symbolic" approaches which dominate criticism of [it]'.[7]

NEW WOMAN
FICTION

Feminism brought the study of 'New Woman' novels to prominence as well as sensation fiction, urging a different form of canon revision by changing the conventional perception of literature in the *fin de siècle*. New Woman writing comprises a diverse group (some dispute the usefulness of gathering it under a general heading at all) from the end of the nineteenth century and beginning of the twentieth. It includes work in drama, fiction and non-fictional prose by Grant Allen, Mona Caird, George Egerton, George Gissing, Sarah Grand, Thomas Hardy, Henrik Ibsen, Olive Schreiner, G. B. Shaw and Rebecca West. New Woman writing challenged, or explored challenges to, oppressive understandings of female behaviour, sexuality and domestic responsibility. Recent critical work on the area of New Woman fiction includes Gail Cunningham's *The New Woman in the Victorian Novel* (1978), which contextualized the fiction and indicated its main radical ideas; Elaine Showalter's *Sexual Anarchy: Gender and Culture at the Fin de Siècle* (1991); and Sally Ledger's accessible survey *The New Woman: Fiction and Feminism at the* Fin de Siècle (1997).[8]

POPULAR
FICTION

Popular fiction has received recent critical attention too (though it had not been without investigation earlier in the century),[9] and this is also likely to develop as the study of popular culture gains in academic status. R. C. Terry's *Victorian Popular Fiction, 1860–1880* (1983) investigated middle-class popular fiction, including novels by the 'Queen of Popular Fiction', as he called her, Margaret Oliphant, whose reputation has significantly revived in the past few years.[10] More recent work, which has opened up an area of writing hitherto excluded from serious academic consideration, includes Pamela K. Gilbert's *Disease, Desire, and the Body in Victorian Women's Popular Novels* (1997) and Laurie Langbauer's *Novels of Everyday Life: The Series in English Fiction, 1850–1930* (1999). Juliet John's *Dickens' Villains: Melodrama, Character, Popular Culture* (2001) merged the canonical with the non-canonical by situating Dickens in the context of popular culture, especially the tradition and conventions of stage melodrama. John argued for an acknowledgement of Dickens's political commitment to the principle of cultural inclusivity, and her strategy of considering the relationship between canonical fiction and forms of popular culture was a distinctive contribution to Victorian literary studies.[11]

'THE VICTORIAN NOVEL' NOT 'VICTORIAN NOVELISTS'

In addition to the question of canonicity and the changing understandings of what the Victorian novel is, a further point needs to be made about the organization of this book. I have considered criticism that addresses the Victorian novel. But not individual Victorian novelists. This has had a significant consequence on the overall shape of this study, and the way it should be read. It is true that tracing the critical histories of, say, George Eliot, Charles Dickens and Thomas Hardy, would give a sample of the development of criticism of Victorian fiction more generally. But such a procedure would hardly be helpful to readers of Charles Kingsley or Anthony Trollope. So the critical texts discussed in this book are almost always studies of aspects of Victorian fiction, as I have defined it, in general. Only on a small number of occasions have I included criticism that concentrates on a single fictional text because it best exemplifies a particular critical trend: I have, periodically, assumed the reader's knowledge of the plot of George Eliot's *Middlemarch* (1871–2) and Charlotte Brontë's *Jane Eyre* (1847). Although other texts are, of course, constantly referenced, no other single novel emerges as privileged.

THE EMBEDDED-NESS OF CRITICISM

This book offers an introduction to the critical history of the Victorian novel over the past one hundred years, and a survey of the main fields of debate in contemporary criticism. It also provides a sample of how and in what pattern the discourses of English literary criticism have developed during that time. It works, in these respects, on several levels of generality. The *Guide* also has one other general ambition. Despite the valuable work of theory, there is still often, in my view, an insufficient recognition in student writing of the situatedness of criticism. Criticism speaks from its cultural moment and is as embedded in the terms of its own intellectual and social location as the literature it seeks to explicate. It matters whether the author is pre-war or post-war, 1970s or 1980s, David Cecil or Catherine Belsey. And yet criticism is often read as an innocent discourse, as a peculiar mode of authoritative utterance outside the logic of the culture from which it emerged and not susceptible to the same kind of critical analysis as a literary text. I have tried to problematize this mode of reading by discussing, throughout this book, aspects of the embeddedness of the voices anthologized. Much more of this could have been done than space permitted, but it is an important feature of the text. The *Guide* may thus appear to be involved in a sort of Platonic distancing from the original: it deals not with the original forms (the classic Victorian novels themselves), but with the criticism of them, and, at a third remove, it critiques the discourses of that criticism. The fiction itself, like Plato's Ideal forms, may seem a long way off. But I hope the material surveyed here, the historical development of novel criticism and the raft of contemporary concerns, will send readers, as it has sent me, back to that fiction, back to the origin and occasion of all this explicatory and analytical work, with renewed vitality. An enthusiasm for reading the Victorian novel is where criticism of it should start.

Chapter Notes

1   A well-received recent discussion of Henry James and literary fame is Richard Salmon, *Henry James and the Culture of Publicity* (Cambridge: Cambridge University Press, 1997).

2   Anthony Trollope, quoted in John Charles Olmsted, ed., *A Victorian Art of Fiction: Essays on the Novel in British Periodicals 1870–1900*, 3 vols (New York: Garland, 1979), iii. 113.

3   Kathleen Tillotson, *Novels of the Eighteen-forties* (Oxford: Clarendon, 1954), 1.

4   I use the term 'nineteenth century' throughout this book to refer to the 'Victorian period' unless it is clear from the context that I mean otherwise. Although this is not ideal, it provides a different way of referring to 'Victorian fiction' or the 'Victorian novel', terms that need to be varied for the sake of euphony.

5   Annette Federico, *Masculine Identity in Hardy and Gissing* (London and Toronto: Associated University Presses, 1991), 16.

6   James Eli Adams, *Dandies and Desert Saints: Styles of Victorian Masculinity* (Ithaca and London: Cornell University Press, 1995), 3.

7   Robert Mighall, *A Geography of Victorian Gothic Fiction: Mapping History's Nightmares* (Oxford: Oxford University Press, 1999), xix.

8   A recent dimension to criticism of late-Victorian literature and the representation of the actress was offered by Gail Marshall in *Actresses on the Victorian Stage: Feminine Performance and the Galatea Myth* (Cambridge: Cambridge University Press, 1998).

9   See Margaret Dalziel, *Popular Fiction 100 Years Ago: An Unexplored Tract of Literary History* (London: Cohen and West, 1957) which includes discussion of 'Penny Dreadfuls'.

10 A revival partly due to the work of Elisabeth Jay; see Jay, ed., *The Autobiography of Margaret Oliphant: The Complete Text* (Oxford: Oxford University Press, 1990); *Mrs Oliphant: 'A Fiction to Herself': A Literary Life* (Oxford: Clarendon, 1995), and *Women's Writing: Margaret Oliphant Special Edition*, vol. 6, no. 2 (1999), ed. Elisabeth Jay and Francis O'Gorman.

11 For a recent and fresh example of the recuperation of popular forms of narrative, see Brian Maidment, 'Re-arranging the Year: The Almanac, the Day Book and the Year Book as Popular Literary Forms, 1789–1860', in Juliet John and Alice Jenkins, eds, *Rethinking Victorian Culture* (Basingstoke: Macmillan, 2000), 91–113.

Further Reading

Books on the Victorian novel generally:

David Amigoni, *The English Novel and Prose Narrative* (Edinburgh: Edinburgh University Press, 2000): stimulating introduction to methodological issues in studying fiction which traces critical debates about the relation of the Victorian novel to biography, autobiography and ideas of 'self-culture'; also considers the formal innovations of Victorian fiction.

Deirdre David, ed., *The Cambridge Companion to the Victorian Novel* (Cambridge: Cambridge University Press, 2001): emphasis on North American approaches; an accessible overview by leading scholars on the state of modern criticism of the Victorian novel; some problems of accuracy.

Barbara Dennis, *The Victorian Novel* (Cambridge: Cambridge University Press, 2000): a brief introductory survey for beginners in the Cambridge Contexts in Literature series.

Robin Gilmour, *The Novel in the Victorian Age: A Modern Introduction* (London: Arnold, 1986): discusses middle-class fiction, its composite form, and links the novel with the transformations of British society. 'The story of the Victorian novel is the story of the novelists' attempts to interpret their changing world, and to hold on to a hopeful vision of the future until the pressure of pessimistic insight at the end of the period could no longer be contained within the reconciling mixed form.'

Jeremy Hawthorn, ed., *The Nineteenth-century British Novel* (London: Arnold, 1986): a collection of essays with an emphasis on theory, including one on 'Dickens and the New Historicism'.

Alan Horsman, *The Victorian Novel* (Oxford: Clarendon, 1990): in the Oxford History of English Literature series, a solid, unrepentantly old-fashioned survey of major novelists with a glance at minor ones: no acknowledgement of modern critical developments. Includes an individual chapter on Meredith.

Alice Jenkins and Juliet John, eds, *Rereading Victorian Fiction* (Basingstoke: Macmillan, 2000): a stimulating and well-received collection of essays by eminent scholars.

Kathleen Tillotson, *Novels of the Eighteen-forties* (Oxford: Clarendon, 1954): important in its scholarship and focus on detail; a new stage in the professionalization of the study of Victorian fiction.

Michael Wheeler, *English Fiction of the Victorian Period, 1830–1890*, 2nd edn (London: Longman, 1994): includes excellent bibliographical material. Wheeler argues that the 'movement of Victorian fiction' is 'away from the mediation of social reality through the consciousness of a hero or heroine, whose fate is ultimately secure in the hands of a God-like author–narrator' towards 'tragic schemes in which the universe is either neutral or hostile'; this reflects 'a decline in both individualism and the possibility of social salvation'.

Nineteenth-century views of, or documents relating to, the novel:

Edwin M. Eigner and George J. Worth, eds, *Victorian Criticism of the Novel* (Cambridge: Cambridge University Press, 1985): useful resource of contemporary statements about the novel.

Josephine M. Guy, *The Victorian Age: An Anthology of Sources and Documents* (London: Routledge, 1998): multifarious collection of documents covering ethics, economics and politics, science and religion, art and culture, sex and gender. It provides a context for 'some of the contemporary intellectual issues which inform [Victorian literature]'.

Ann Heilmann, ed., *The Late-Victorian Marriage Question: A Collection of Key New Woman Texts*, 5 vols (London: Routledge/Thoemmes, 1998): vol. 1 Marriage and Motherhood; vol. 2 The New Woman and Female Independence; vol. 3 New Woman Fiction I: Marriage, Motherhood and Work; vol. 4 New Woman Fiction II: Gender and Sexuality; vol. 5 Literary Degenerates.

John Charles Olmsted, ed., *A Victorian Art of Fiction: Essays on the Novel in British Periodicals 1870–1900*, 3 vols (New York: Garland, 1979): invaluable resource for Victorian comments on the novel.

Stephen Regan, ed., *The Nineteenth-century Novel: A Critical Reader* (London: Routledge, 2001): contains critical responses to a wide variety of nineteenth-century fiction and a good selection of Victorian documents relevant to the art of the novel, including ones by George Eliot, Nietzsche, R. L. Stevenson, and Zola. Designed for the Open University.

Reference book:

John Sutherland, *The Longman Companion to Victorian Fiction* (London: Longman, 1988): indispensable on individual novels and novelists, and all aspects of the fiction industry.

More on masculinity:

Diana Barsham, *Arthur Conan Doyle and the Meaning of Masculinity* (Aldershot: Ashgate, 2000): 'Doyle was committed to finding solutions to some of the most difficult cultural problematics of late Victorian masculinity. As novelist, war correspondent, historian, legal campaigner, propagandist and religious leader, he used his fame as the creator of Sherlock Holmes to refigure the spirit of British Imperialism.'

Joseph Bristow, *Effeminate England: Homoerotic Writing after 1885* (Buckingham: Open University Press, 1995).

Joseph Bristow, *Empire Boys: Adventures in a Man's World* (London: HarperCollins Academic, 1991): on late Victorian adventure fiction for boys and its relationship with empire and masculinity.

Andrew Dowling, *Manliness and the Male Novelist in Victorian Literature* (Aldershot and Burlington VT: Ashgate, 2001).

Robin Gilmour, *The Idea of the Gentleman in the Victorian Novel* (London: Allen and Unwin, 1981): especially on Dickens, Thackeray, and Trollope, with an emphasis on the eighteenth-century context of gentlemanliness.

Simon Petch, 'Robert Audley's Profession', *Studies in the Novel*, 32 (2000), 1–13.

Dianne F. Sadoff, *Monsters of Affection: Dickens, Eliot and Brontë on Fatherhood* (Baltimore: Johns Hopkins, 1982): Freudian reading of the primal scene, seduction, and castration as they apply to Dickens, Eliot, and Charlotte Brontë respectively.

More on expanding areas of the canon:

Barbara Leah Harman and Susan Meyer, ed., *The New Nineteenth Century: Feminist Readings of Underread Victorian Fiction* (New York and London: Garland, 1996): includes essays on Anne Brontë, Geraldine Jewsbury, Collins, Reade, Oliphant, Le Fanu, Stoker, Eliza Linton, Walter Besant, George Moore, Gissing, Sarah Grand, George Egerton, Mrs Humphry Ward, Flora Annie Steel.

K. D. M. Snell, ed., *The Regional Novel in Britain and Ireland, 1800–1990* (Cambridge: Cambridge University Press, 1998): interdisciplinary study that considers this much neglected area, though most of the authors studied are canonical (in the Victorian period, they are Gaskell and Manchester; Hardy and Wessex; Kingsley and Cornwall).

On law:

Barbara Leckie, *Culture and Adultery: The Novel, the Newspaper, and the Law, 1857–1914* (Philadelphia: University of Pennsylvania Press, 1999): highly theoretical investigation interested in 'the role that the novel and the institution of the novel plays in shaping what counts as taboo and in negotiating a social and political field in which certain subjects, like adultery, are targeted as transgressive and, therefore, outside the boundary of permissible literary representation'. See also p. 9 above.

Jeff Nunokawa, *The Afterlife of Property: Domestic Security and the Victorian Novel* (Princeton, NJ: Princeton University Press, 1994): considers the loss of property in Dickens and Eliot, and the acknowledgement in the fiction that the origin of such losses are in the market, not in the will or weakness of individuals.

Marlene Tromp, *The Private Rod: Marital Violence, Sensation, and the Law in Victorian Britain* (Charlottesville and London: University Press of Virginia, 2000): feminist investigation of literary and legal negotiations of marital violence in Dickens, Eliot and sensation writing.

On religion and the novel:

Valentine Cunningham, *Everywhere Spoken Against: Dissent in the Victorian Novel* (Oxford: Clarendon, 1975): prickly but learned study of dissent, valuing its sympathetic treatment.

Elisabeth Jay, *The Religion of the Heart: Anglican Evangelicalism and the Nineteenth-century Novel* (Oxford: Clarendon, 1979): widely read investigation of fiction and Evangelical movements; good on theological context.

Michael Wheeler, *Death and the Future Life in Victorian Literature and Theology* (Cambridge: Cambridge University Press, 1990): richly researched account of heaven, hell and the Victorian novel.

Consideration of the changes in criticism over the past 50 years:

Frank Kermode, F. W. Bateson Memorial Lecture: 'Literary Criticism: Old and New Styles', *Essays in Criticism*, 51 (2001), 191–207: '[criticism today] has much broader interests than the criticism of fifty years ago, and the "quaint rigour" of the young has taken a different and less pious form, but it has marked disadvantages: its principles actually prevent it from attending closely to the language of major works (in so far as that description is regarded as acceptable) – to the work itself, rather than to something more congenial, and to something more interesting, that can be put in its place. Nobody, I think, would want to go back; but it is reasonable to be apprehensive about the future, and the possibility that literature itself, let alone literary criticism, may not easily survive the onslaught of undisciplined interdisciplinarity.'

1

Early Criticism of the Victorian Novel from James Oliphant to David Cecil

James Oliphant – George Saintsbury – E. M. Forster – David Cecil

Criticism of the Victorian novel in the last decades of the twentieth century was unimaginably different from the critical practices of its first years. In form, consideration of literature's relationship with history, understanding of the canon, conception of the authority of the literary critic, in principles of evaluation, and perception of what characterized the Victorian period, early twentieth-century critics spoke a language different from today. Seeing the Victorian novel now though their eyes requires a strenuous task of imaginative sympathy. But, none the less, readers need to know their most important characteristics because the late twentieth-century understanding of Victorian fiction grew through negotiations and challenges to their critical assumptions. Many writers discussed in this book were arguing with their grandparents. This chapter discusses the criticism of the most significant of early twentieth-century writers on the Victorian novel, including E. M. Forster and *Aspects of the Novel* (1927). Forster, though he did not focus on the Victorian period, assumed universalist truths about fiction that provided the context for much debate about the Victorian novel and history in the later twentieth century.

I begin by considering the first writers on Victorian fiction at the beginning of the 1900s. The context for their criticism, the low status of the novel, the cultural anxieties about popular fiction, and the slowness of the universities to consider Victorian fiction as an appropriate subject in a degree in English Literature are outlined. I then discuss the importance of canon formation for the early critics and examine the principles of literary history and the literary survey with its prioritization of 'appreciation' and the idea of tradition. Forster's *Aspects* repudiated the historical assumptions of the survey and resisted the form of authority assumed by its authors; this, and Forster's consequential convictions about the novel and history are examined. Bloomsbury and Modernism in the 1920s urged a rejection of the Victorian, and the next major critic of Victorian fiction, David Cecil, wrote in a climate unsympathetic to the nineteenth century. I conclude by considering Cecil's evaluative approach to fiction before George Eliot, his views on historicization, and his provocative conclusions about the imperfect form of early Victorian novels.

THE STATE OF
THE NOVEL IN
1900

Looking around him in 1899, James Oliphant thought the British regard for art was low. 'There is very little idea in this country as yet', he said, 'that the pursuit of art in any form, unless as a means of livelihood, may be a serious occupation of one's time.'[1] Just before the beginning of a new century, it was a gloomy diagnosis of the nation's artistic health. One of the forms of art whose practitioners were most liable to criticism, Oliphant continued, was the novel, the literary genre that had developed and expanded most during the preceding period. It is, he said solemnly, 'depressed even below the other arts in the public esteem'.[2] Attending concerts or visiting art galleries was respectable enough; poetry was acceptable as far as any literary art was. But reading a novel shared with theatre-going the same response from the pragmatic and level-headed British public: it incurred 'the suspicion of levity'.[3] Prestigious journals agreed. The *Saturday Review* remarked in 1887 that the novel was certainly not for the serious-minded. All a reader of fiction requires, it declared, is 'that he may be amused and interested without taxing his own brains'.[4]

Reading novels had been regarded as a suspect or dispensable activity since the genre began. James Oliphant was not describing a phenomenon unique to the end of the nineteenth century, although controversies over the literature of the Aesthetic Movement and the decadence of the *fin de siècle* gave additional impetus to those concerned about the healthiness of pursuing art, in Oliphant's words, as a 'serious occupation of one's time'. This state of fiction was an issue with which late-nineteenth and early twentieth-century literary critics of the Victorian novel had to negotiate. Accordingly, they defended the claims of the novel for serious readers before they discussed the texts. Their writing exuded awareness of the contested ground on which they were treading. Oliphant called the first chapter of his *Victorian Novelists* (1899) 'The Novel as an Art-form', and he assumed this would be a polemical statement. The novel, he said, making as modest a claim as he could, was unable to compete with the highest of the arts, music, which was the 'most ethereal of all', for it did not have the same spiritual power: it struck no 'mysterious chords in the soul'.[5] But it did have a wider if less profound role to play as literature of realism. It was the form of art that could 'reflect the significant elements of life with peculiar fullness and fidelity', and it was the genre addressed most amply to our daily experience: it corresponded with our knowledge of life as we lived it, speaking 'a universal language [...] because it rest[ed] on a basis of experience which is in some degree common to all'.[6]

The notion that the novel expressed a universal language and spoke of and to the human condition was a tenacious one in the history of novel criticism in the twentieth century, not least because of E. M. Forster's critical work, discussed below (pp. 29–31). It remained a force with which critics engaged in complex ways for years, and this *Guide* illustrates the querying, unpacking and multiple dissolution of the assumption that the novel spoke with peculiar authority about the human condition, to and on behalf of a generalized human subject. In this, the history of the criticism of the Victorian novel shares in the broader narrative of the history of English literary criticism over the past one hundred years, with its movement away from univeralist postures. But it does so with a special force because the Victorian realist novel was constructed for a long time in English criticism as *the* universalist genre of the modern period, the form that most amply illustrated what human life was like.

Early in the twentieth century, some who were positive about the nature of the novel thought that it could even take the place of religion in teaching men and women about life. Ramsden Balmforth said this in his moralizing study *The Ethical and Religious Values of the Novel* (1912), when he argued, transforming a claim made for poetry by Matthew Arnold, that:

> It is the function of the novelist, by the portrayal of a multitude of experiences working on character or personality, to give definite shape and direction to [human beings'] blind and almost unconscious emotional forces, to widen and deepen feeling, to link us to the large life of humanity and of the universe, and so give a definite meaning and purpose to our life.[7]

Fiction at its best was a discourse of general humanity and acted like a religion in instructing readers about their proper development, making them aware of the condition of humanity at large.[8]

But Balmforth's confidence in fiction was not common among critics at the end of the nineteenth century and beginning of the twentieth. Part of the problem for those doubtful of the merits of fiction was the large number of novels on the market that did not seem to have any literary value. For the art and social critic, John Ruskin, in his only work of literary criticism, *Fiction, Fair and Foul* (1880–1), the content of most modern novels was so unwholesome that he thought they must be woven out of cobwebs.[9] Others felt the same about the popular fiction that many ordinary men and women were reading with relish. William Watson, speaking of H. Rider Haggard's fiction, declared in 1888 that it was incredible that so many readers could be found to read such rubbish. How could they, he asked, intemperately, but with a real concern about the moral health of the population, 'besot themselves with a thick, raw concoction, destitute of fragrance, destitute of sparkle, destitute of everything but the power to induce a crude inebriety of mind and a morbid state of the intellectual peptics[?]'[10] Other intellectuals greeted the expanding market for popular fiction with dismay. Arthur Quiller-Couch, in his inaugural lecture as King Edward VII Professor of English Literature at Cambridge University in January 1913, looked on the popular novel's rise to prominence as a regrettable cultural problem, admitting reluctantly that it was now the favoured reading matter of ordinary men and women and that intellectuals had to accept this 'whether [they] like it or not'.[11]

UNIVERSITY
STUDY OF
VICTORIAN
LITERATURE

Rarely accepted into the fold of good literature as the nineteenth century became the twentieth, the novel was in an uncertain state. Correspondingly, in the academy, the nineteenth-century novel took some time to become a subject for formal study, a topic for examination for any part of an undergraduate degree in the new university discipline of English Literature. So, although critics, a number of them based in university English departments, were writing on the Victorian novel in the first years of the new century, the university curriculum did not to reflect this. The Victorian novel was not a component of a twentieth-century degree course in English at the ancient universities until well into the second decade. The Oxford University Faculty of English, founded in 1895, set terms for many subsequent assumptions in the teaching of English Literature. It stopped on its English Literature syllabus at Sir Walter Scott until after the beginning of the Great War.[12] Walter Raleigh, the first Oxford Professor of English Literature, published a book on *The English Novel* in 1894 before he took up the Oxford chair. But its coverage appropriately coincided with the first range of the Oxford course, as its subtitle indicated: *A Short Sketch of its History from the Earliest Times to the Appearance of* [Sir Walter Scott's] *'Waverley'*. Oxford University introduced the formal study of the Victorian period (joined with the Romantic period in a paper called the 'History of English Literature, 1784–1901') only in the academic year 1915–16 (and it was later abolished). And in that course, which aimed to cover two major periods of literary creativity in a single paper, the Victorian novel did not feature prominently.

On the examination paper of 1916 for the 1784–1901 period, there was only one question specifically on a novelist ('Examine the attempt of Dickens to employ the novel as an instrument for effecting social reform'), and one other that could have been answered with material on fiction ('To what extent has the development of science influenced English nineteenth-century literature?').[13] The special paper corresponding to the Victorian part of the period, 'Tennyson and Browning', was on poetry. With regards to generic specialization in the period, verse was clearly being declared the prestigious form of nineteenth-century English letters by the architects of the first curriculum at Oxford.

Criticism of the Victorian novel was being written, nevertheless. Not everyone stopped where Walter Raleigh stopped, and James Oliphant was not a solitary pioneer, though an important one. By the time the Victorian novel made it on to the examination papers of the Oxford Faculty of English Language and Literature, there was a growing corpus of criticism. The word 'criticism', however, is problematic, for its meaning in 1910 was different from today. In fact, the criticism of the first few years of the century did not call itself such, using the title literary history (as in the Oxford University examination paper). This was not a practice of critical writing that proposed interpretation, nor, *a fortiori*, introduced new perspectives on fiction and fresh ways of looking at texts. It was not based on research that recovered lost contexts or offered new material that changed readers' understanding. It was criticism that assumed that the meaning of the novels was clear and it was predicated, at this level, on consensus. Literary history, assuming familiarity with the primary texts, surveyed instead how novelists related to each other topically, generically and stylistically, and encouraged literary appreciation.

There was an encyclopaedic dimension to these books on the Victorian novel. Leslie Stephen's *Dictionary of National Biography* (1882–1900) aimed to include entries on all the great men and women of British history. It was a panoramic survey of British history and national character, a kind of textual version of a similar project in British commemoration, the National Portrait Gallery, founded in 1856. This desire to embrace the fullness of achievement, to offer the reader an overview of literary history, was true of the first critics of the Victorian novel as they surveyed the range of British novelists they believed worthy of inclusion, writers whom they took to be valuable. Like other critics in the early part of the twentieth century, indeed, they were engaged in canon formation, in selecting, on grounds of quality, worthwhile authors for the general reader.

The Survey: George Saintsbury (1845–1933)

The major figure of English literary history to write on the Victorian novel was George Saintsbury. His work exemplified the elements outlined above and included other important features of early twentieth-century critical practice. Saintsbury began his professional life as a schoolteacher in Guernsey. After a period as a journalist in London, he became, with an ease of migration between professions more readily accomplished then than now, Professor of Rhetoric and English Literature at the University of Edinburgh, where he remained for some twenty years. He wrote prolifically, and his publications included *A History of Nineteenth Century Literature, 1780–1895* (1896) and *The English Novel* (1913). These were long appreciations and essays in

PRINCIPLES OF LITERARY HISTORY

historical placing. Their guiding motto was breadth over depth, a general culture over a specialist learning.

In the chapters on the Victorian novel in *The English Novel*, Saintsbury offered an account of the literary traditions that connected the nineteenth-century novelists, and brisk, evaluative summaries of the characteristics of each writer in a panoramic overview of a period marked by 'a very remarkable wind of refreshment and new endeavour' (he did not explain at length what he saw as the cause of this).[14] He did not dwell on specific novels, and barely quoted at all (the New Criticism with its emphasis on close textual reading eclipsed Saintsbury's method in the mid-century). His manner was patrician, writing with the confidence of a man assured that his readers would accept his judgement. He assumed that the typical member of his audience was the interested, non-specialist reader seeking guidance from an authoritative figure. He wrote accessibly and the language of his literary history, like most criticism of the first half of the century, eschewed the complexities of conceptualization, terminology and syntax that Samuel Taylor Coleridge had memorably introduced into literary criticism with *Biographia Literaria* (1817) and which became a prominent and sometimes intrusive feature of later twentieth-century critical debate.

THE
APPROACH OF
GEORGE
SAINTSBURY

Saintsbury's approach to the Victorian novel was to defuse its political or social force (see also Cecil, below, pp. 32–3): he was not interested in the novel of ideas and he did not consider that Victorian novels intervened in contemporary debates in and about society. The novel, he said in 1887, 'has nothing to do with any beliefs, with any convictions, with any thoughts in the strict sense, except as mere garnishings. Its substance must always be life.'[15] By this he meant that readers should approach fiction as if it were descriptive of universalized personal experience but did not relate to local historical or political circumstances. Saintsbury read Victorian fiction as separate from more or less all contexts except literary tradition and as a genre that described 'life' recognizable to all right-feeling readers.

Saintsbury was also concerned with canon formation, telling his readers what Victorian fiction was the best. His canon was based on quality judgement and his criticism was highly evaluative (in the extract given below, *Vanity Fair* is a 'supreme work', *Pendennis* a work of 'genius', Lever's *Charles O'Malley* is 'a distinctly delectable composition'). And a persistent feature of this critical practice was assertion over argument. If Saintsbury's work was predicated on a consensus about the meaning of the novels – everyone knows what they mean, or will when they have read them – it was also consensual in its assumption that readers would share Saintsbury's value judgements. Or, certainly, that they would accept his statements without needing explanation because of a general acknowledgement of his authority as a professional critic to make such judgements. Saintsbury was confident in the public role of the university intellectual as an arbiter of aesthetic taste. As far as knowledge was concerned, however, there were problems. Saintsbury did not always provide factually reliable information (this is evident in the extract that follows), and reviewers of his books thought that this undid part of his claim to authority as a trustworthy guide.[16]

The major factor controlling Saintbury's depiction of the terrain of Victorian fiction in the following extract is the identification of literary connections, descendencies and influences in the relations between novels and novelists. Saintsbury offered a map of literary history that privileged, in an aristocratic manner, the notion of inheritance, the idea of traditions and influences, and proposed how different nineteenth-century novelists – major and minor – related to each other generically. In this extract, the influence of Jane Austen and Sir Walter Scott, exponents of the domestic novel and the romance respectively, help Saintsbury organize his history. He sees the work of the Brontë sisters as the product of a cross between the traditions of Austen and Scott, and imagines Charlotte Brontë's writing in terms of her (formulaically expressed) relation to Thackeray and Dickens. Thackeray is placed in another tradition, with his roots in the eighteenth century. *Pendennis* is neither a 'press' novel about journalism nor a university novel, but a distinctive combination of both, a creative handling of traditional elements in a new form. Thackeray's mixture of domestic incident and drama (exemplified in *Vanity Fair*) strikes Saintsbury as the chief element of yet another generic strand of Victorian fiction: a tradition of novels that aspired to the 'domestic–dramatic' fusion. Networks of influences, links between forms of writing, are privileged in Saintsbury's depiction of Victorian novels, emphasizing that the most significant influence on the shape of Victorian fiction was fiction itself. The idea of a tradition became the central element, though differently understood, in F. R. Leavis's mapping of the history of the Victorian novel (see pp. 46–64 for Leavis and tradition; for a feminist approach, see pp. 187–8).

Extract from George Saintsbury, *The English Novel* (London: Dent, 1913), 237–44.

At about the very middle of the nineteenth century – say from 1845 to 1855 in each direction, but almost increasingly towards the actual dividing line of 1850 – there came upon the English novel a very remarkable wind of refreshment and new endeavour. Thackeray and Dickens themselves are examples of it, with Lever and others, before this dividing line: many others yet come to join them. A list of books written out just as they occur to the memory, and without any attempt to marshal them in strict chronological order, would show this beyond all reasonable possibility of gainsaying. Thackeray's own best accomplished work from *Vanity Fair* (1846)[1] itself through *Pendennis* (1849)[2] and *Esmond* (1852) to *The Newcomes* (1854);[3] the brilliant centre of Dickens's work in *David Copperfield* (1850)[4] – stand at the head and have been already noticed by anticipation or implication, while Lever had almost completed the first division of his work, which began with *Harry Lorrequer* as early as the year of *Pickwick*. But such books as *Yeast* (1848), *Westward Ho!* (1855); as *The Warden* (1855); as *Jane Eyre* (1847) and its too few successors; as *Scenes of Clerical Life* (1857); as *Mary Barton* (1848) and the novels which followed it, with others which it is perhaps almost unfair to leave out even in this allusive summary by sample, betokened a stirring of the waters, a rattling among the bones, such as is not common in literature. Death removed Thackeray early and Dickens somewhat less prematurely, but after a period rather barren in direct novel work. The others continued and were constantly reinforced: nor was it till well on in the seventies that any distinct drop from first- to second-growth quality could be observed in the general vintage of English fiction.

One is not quite driven, on this occasion, to the pusillanimous explanation that this remarkable variety and number of good novels was simply due to the simultaneous existence of an equally remarkable number of good novelists. The fact is that, by this time, the great example of Scott and Miss Austen – the great wave of progress which exemplified itself first and most eminently in these two writers – had had time to work upon and permeate another generation of practitioners. The novelists who have just been cited were as a rule born in the second decade of the century, just before, about, or after the time at which Scott and Miss Austen began to publish. They had therefore – as their elders, even though they may have had time to read the pair, had not – time to assimilate thoroughly and early the results which that pair had produced or which they had first expressed. And they had even greater advantages than this. They had had time to assimilate, likewise, the results of all the rest of that great literary generation of which Scott and Miss Austen were themselves but members. They profited by thirty years more of constant historical exploration and realising of former days. One need not say, for it is question-begging, that they also *profited* by, but they could at least avail themselves of, the immense change of manners and society which made 1850 differ more from 1800 than 1800 had differed, not merely from 1750 but from 1700. They had, even though all of them may not have been sufficiently grateful for it, the stimulus of that premier position in Europe which the country had gained in the Napoleonic wars, and which she had not yet wholly lost or even begun to lose. They had wider travel, more extended occupations and interests, many other new things to draw upon. And, lastly, they had some important special incidents and movements – the new arrangement of political parties, the Oxford awakening,[5] and others – to give suggestion and impetus to novels of the specialist kind. Nay, they had not only the great writers, in other kinds, of the immediate past, but those of the present, Carlyle, Tennyson, latterly Ruskin, and others still to complete their education and the machinery of its development.

The most remarkable feature of this *renouveau*,[6] as has been both directly and indirectly observed before, is the resumption, the immense extension, and the extraordinary improvement of the domestic novel. Not that this had not been practised during the thirty years since Miss Austen's death. But the external advantages just enumerated had failed it: and it had enlisted none of the chief talents which were at the service of fiction generally. A little more gift and a good deal more taste might have enabled Mrs Trollope to do really great things in it: but she left them for her son to accomplish. Attempts and 'tries' at it had been made constantly, and the goal had been very nearly reached, especially, perhaps, in that now much forgotten but remarkable *Emilia Wyndham* (1846) by Anne Caldwell (Mrs Marsh), which was wickedly described by a sister novelist as the 'book where the woman breaks her desk open with her head', but which has real power and exercised real influence for no short time.

This new domestic novel followed Miss Austen in that it did not necessarily avail itself of anything but perfectly ordinary life, and relied chiefly on artistic presentment – on treatment rather than on subject. It departed from her in that it admitted a much wider range and variety of subject itself; and by no means excluded the passions and emotions which, though she had not been so prudish as to ignore their results, she had never chosen to represent in much actual exercise, or to make the mainsprings of her books.

The first supreme work of the kind was perhaps in *Vanity Fair* and *Pendennis*, the former admitting exceptional and irregular developments as an integral part of its plot and general appeal, the latter doing for the most part without them. But *Pendennis* exhibited in itself, and taught to other novelists, if not an absolutely new, a hitherto little worked, and clumsily worked, source of novel interest. We have seen how, as early as Head or Kirkman, the possibility of making such a source out of the ways of special trades, professions, employments, and vocations had been partly seen and utilised. Defoe did it more; Smollett more still; and since the great war there had been naval and military novels in abundance, as well as novels political, clerical, sporting, and what not.

But these special interests had been as a rule drawn upon too onesidedly. The eighteenth century found its mistaken fondness for episodes, inset stories, and the like, particularly convenient here: the naval, military, sporting, and other novels of the nineteenth were apt to rely too exclusively on these differences. Such things as the Oxbridge scenes and the journalism scenes of *Pendennis* – both among the most effective and popular, perhaps *the* most effective and popular, parts of the book – were almost, if not entirely, new. There had been before, and have since been, plenty of university novels, and their record has been a record of almost uninterrupted failure; there have since, if not before, *Pendennis* been several 'press' novels, and their record has certainly not been a record of unbroken success. But the employment here, by genius, of such subjects for substantial *parts* of a novel was a success pure and unmixed. So, in the earlier book, the same author had shown how the most humdrum incident and the minutest painting of ordinary character could be combined with historic tragedy like that furnished by Waterloo, with domestic *drame* of the most exciting kind like the discovery of Lord Steyne's relations with Becky, or the at least suggested later crime of that ingenious and rather hardly treated little person.

Most of the writers mentioned and glanced at above took – not of course always, often, or perhaps ever in conscious following of Thackeray, but in consequence of the same 'skiey influences' which worked on him – to this mixed domestic-dramatic line. And what is still more interesting, men who had already made their mark for years, in styles quite different, turned to it and adopted it. We have seen this of Bulwer, and the evidences of the change in him which are given by the 'Caxton' novels. We have not yet directly dealt with another instance of almost as great interest and distinction, Charles Lever, though we have named him and glanced at his work.

Lever, who was born as early as 1806, had, it has been said, begun to write novels as early as his junior, Dickens, and had at once developed, in *Harry Lorrequer*, a pretty distinct style of his own. This style was a kind of humour-novel with abundant incident, generally with a somewhat 'promiscuous' plot and with lively but externally drawn characters – the humours being furnished partly by Lever's native country, Ireland, and partly by the traditions of the great war of which he had collected a store in his capacity of physician to the Embassy at Brussels. He had kept up this style, the capital example of which is *Charles O'Malley* (1840), with unabated *verve* and with great popular success for a dozen years before 1850. But about that time, or rather earlier, the general 'suck' of the current towards a different kind (assisted no doubt by the feeling that the public might be getting tired of the other style) made him change it into studies of a less specialised kind – of foreign travel, home life, and the like – sketches which, in his later days still, he brought even closer to actuality. It is true that in the long run his popularity has depended, and will probably always depend, on the early 'rollicking' adventure books: not only because of their natural appeal, but because there is plenty of the other thing elsewhere, and hardly any of this particular thing anywhere. To almost anybody, for instance, except a very great milksop or a pedant of construction, *Charles O'Malley* with its love-making and its fighting, its horsemanship and its horse-play, its 'devilled kidneys'* and its devil-may-care-ness, is a distinctly delectable composition; and if a reasonable interval be allowed between the readings, may be read over and over again, at all times of life, with satisfaction. But the fact of the author's change remains not the less historically and symptomatically important, in connection with the larger change of which we are now taking notice, and with the similar phenomena observable in the work of Bulwer.

At the same time it has been pointed out that the following of Miss Austen by no means excluded the following of Scott: and that the new development included 'crosses' of novel and romance, sometimes of the historical kind, sometimes not, which are of the highest, or all but the highest, interest. Early and good examples of these may be found in the work of the Brontës, Charlotte and Emily (the third sister Anne is but a pale reflection of her elders), and of Charles Kingsley. Charlotte (*b.* 1816) and Charles (*b.* 1819) were separated in their birth by but three years, Emily (*b.* 1818) and Kingsley by but one.

The curious story of the struggles of the Brontë girls to get published hardly concerns us, and Emily's work, *Wuthering Heights*,[†] is one of those isolated books which, whatever their merit, are rather ornaments than essential parts in novel history. But this is not the case with *Jane Eyre* (1847), *Shirley* (1849), *Villette* (1852), and *The Professor* (1857) (but written much earlier). These are all examples of the determination to base novels on actual life and experience. Few novelists have ever kept so close to their own part in these as Charlotte Brontë did, though she accompanied, permeated, and to a certain extent transformed her autobiography and observation by a strong romantic and fantastic imaginative element. Deprive Thackeray and Dickens of nearly all their humour and geniality, take a portion only of the remaining genius of each in the ratio of about 2 *Th.* to 1 *D.*, add a certain dash of the old terror-novel and the

---

* Edgar Poe has a perfectly serious and very characteristic explosion at the prominence of these agreeable viands in the book.
† Some will have it that this was really Charlotte's: but not with much probability.

German fantastic tale, moisten with feminine spirit and water, and mix thoroughly: and you have something very like Charlotte Brontë. But it is necessary to add further, and it is her great glory, the perfume and atmosphere of the Yorkshire moors, which she had in not quite such perfection as her sister Emily, but in combination with more general novel-gift. Her actual course of writing was short, and it could probably in no case have been long; she wanted wider and, perhaps, happier experience, more literature, more man- and-woman-of-the-worldliness, perhaps a sweeter and more genial temper. But the English novel would have been incomplete without her and her sister; they are, as wholes, unlike anybody else, and if they are not exactly great they have the quality of greatness. Above all, they kept novel and romance together – a deed which is great without any qualification or drawback. [. . .]

Notes

1   Saintsbury's use of dates is to be treated cautiously. I correct a number here as an example. *Vanity Fair*'s serialization began in 1847.
2   *Pendennis*, 1848–50.
3   *The Newcomes*, 1853–5.
4   *David Copperfield*, 1849–50.
5   The Oxford Movement, begun in 1833, aimed to reconnect the Church of England to its Catholic inheritance. The defection of John Henry Newman to the Roman Catholic church in 1845 dealt the movement a serious blow, but it continued (and continues) to have an influence on the Church of England.
6   Renewal.

The survey, with its key aspects of evaluation and the description of traditions, was paralleled in miniature by James Oliphant's book to which I have already referred (he presented a canon consisting of Scott, Austen, Dickens, Thackeray, Charlotte Brontë, George Eliot, Meredith, Stevenson, Kipling, and Israel Zangwill[17]), and by many others. It was the chief mode of writing on the Victorian novel for some thirty years. The prolific novelist Margaret Oliphant (not related to James) had, with F. R. Oliphant (her son), published a two-volume guide called *The Victorian Age of English Literature* (1892), in which she attempted, while aware of the considerable difficulties, to 'determine the final place in literature of contemporary writers'.[18] Her task was explicitly the construction of a canon of worthwhile authors. William James Dawson, in *The Makers of English Fiction* (1905), inflected his approach to tradition in his survey with Darwinian notions of evolutionary development, seeing novelists linked in an organically developing tradition given conceptual legitimacy by modern scientific thought. The French critic Louis Cazamian confined his attention to what he called the 'social novel', the *roman social*, in his *Le Roman Social en Angleterre (1830–1850)* (1903). He offered a major review of what are now referred to as social-problem novels, chiefly works by Dickens, Disraeli, Elizabeth Gaskell and Charles Kingsley (for more on his criticism of social-problem fiction, see chapter 5, pp. 151–2 below). Cazamian's understanding of the relationship between literary writing and its historical and political context was a significant effort, distinct from Saintsbury's assumptions, to historicize literature as an object for criticism (see also pp. 149–95 below).

The survey mode continued well into the twentieth century. Louis Cazamian joined Pierre Legouis to complete an account of the whole of English literature from the Anglo-Saxon period to modern times, published in two volumes in 1926 and 1927 respectively, and then in a single volume as *A History of English Literature* (1930). It was reprinted in an updated edition (discussing literature up to 1950) as late as 1971. Oliver Elton, Professor of English at the University of Liverpool, published his *A Survey of English Literature 1830–1880* in two volumes in 1920. The survey format reached two peaks in the first part of the twentieth century: in general literature, in the *Cambridge History of English Literature* (15 volumes, 1907–27), and, on the novel specifically, the exhaustive work of Ernest A. Baker, whose *The History of the English Novel* was published in ten volumes between 1924 and 1939.

Edwin Morgan Forster's *Aspects of the Novel* (1927)

The book that stoutly contested the assumptions of the survey was not exclusively about the Victorian novel. But it had much to say of consequence for the fiction of the nineteenth century. It deserves consideration in this *Guide* because of this, and also because it took Saintsbury's view of the novel further to affirm an ahistorical approach to fiction as a universalist humanist discourse separate from its historical environment. E. M. Forster's *Aspects of the Novel* comprised the Clark lectures at the University of Cambridge, January to March 1927, and promoted a conception of fiction as a practice of writing set apart from history, both literary and non-literary. Forster's confident ahistoricality, his belief in literature's timeless values, was a prominent articulation of the principles critiqued by Marxists, feminists, post-structuralists, New Historicists, queer theorists, and postcolonialists in the last four decades of the twentieth century, who argued that literature was always embedded in the ideologies of its culture.

E. M. Forster contested the kind of authority Saintsbury had assumed. Where Saintsbury considered his authority conferred on him by his university position, Edwin Morgan Forster claimed that most men in academic employment in universities were really 'pseudo-scholars'.[19] These were men who paid the tribute of ignorance to learning, and who were 'pernicious' as literary critics because they 'follow[ed] the method of the true scholar without having his equipment':[20] they catalogued books without having read them. Forster, repositioning the centre of authority in literary criticism, deposed most of the university intellectuals (he allowed for the existence of some real scholars) from the seat of power and made a claim for a different sort of criticism, predicated on common sense and the ordinary affections of the general reader. He approached the novel simply, 'with the human heart [. . .]. The final test of a novel will be our affection for it, as it is the test of our friends, and of anything else which we cannot define.'[21] He declared criticism's guiding force was nothing more unusual than the right thinking and right feeling human heart, a notion that assumed humanity's common moral identity and collective values. This view of a tension between academic critics and non-academic readers, incidentally, continued to be a theme through the century and reached a polemical climax in a study of Modernist writing by John Carey, both professional literary critic and journalist, entitled *The Intellectuals and the Masses: Pride and Prejudice among the Literary Intelligentsia 1880–1939* (1992). Ironically enough, this criticized Forster's intellectual elitism.[22]

E. M.
FORSTER AND
CRITIQUING
LITERARY
HISTORY

Forster, in opposition to literary history, had no patience with criticism that imposed taxonomies, dividing books up into categories, especially categories of chronology. The development hypothesis, moreover, the notion that litera-ture evolved or progressed, was entirely false, he said. Great novelists and great novels always transcended local temporality, the limits of their own culture, and the specifics of their moment in literary history. 'History de-velops', Forster said, with an aphorism such as those he used as motto truths in his own novels, 'Art stands still':

> Time, all the way through, is to be our enemy. We are to visualize the English novelists not as floating down that stream which bears all its sons away unless they are careful, but as seated together in a room, a circular room, a sort of British Museum reading-room – all writing their novels simultaneously. They do not, as they sit there, think: 'I live under Queen Victoria, I under Anne, I carry on the tradition of Trollope, I am reacting against Aldous Huxley'. The fact that their pens are in their hands is far more vivid to them.[23]

Forster's approach to fiction was to extract it from time and to imagine that it lived independently from its circumstances and history, rising above the particular conditions of its own day and its moment in the literary tradition. When great, it expressed values and truths that were immutable. This assur-ance was increasingly entrenched in the English education system in the 1920s and 1930s. Great literature was presented in educational rhetoric as a crucible of human values, and reading imagined as a civilizing force that could teach men and women, boys and girls, what it meant to be properly human. A similar conviction – it is usually assumed to have its roots in the work of Matthew Arnold in the middle of the Victorian period – had been officially enshrined in the Newbolt Report on *The Teaching of English in England* (1921), a government document from the Board of Education, published only a few years before Forster's *Aspects* (for more on the civilizing mission of English literary criticism, see pp. 46–50 below).

Lord David Cecil and *Early Victorian Novelists* (1934)

Where Forster extracted the Victorian novel from history, the next significant figure in the history of the criticism of Victorian literature saw nineteenth-century fiction's connection with its own times as a drawback. When Lord David Cecil delivered his lectures on the Victorian novel, not, like E. M. Forster, to the University of Cambridge, but to the University of Oxford, the intellectual climate was inhospitable to Victorian literature and society. Cecil was fully aware of this disapproval. His lectures, published in 1934 with his intention declared in his subtitle, as *Early Victorian Novelists: Essays in Revaluation*, took as an *a priori* truth the fact that Victorian novels were languishing on shelves, 'sallow with exposure to dust and daylight' (see p. 34 below).

Cecil's view of the state of the Victorian novel and Victorian society was widely held in the 1920s and 1930s. Bloomsbury and the Modernists, encouraging a rejection of the Victorian, heavily influenced this lack of enthusiasm as the *avant garde* writers and theorists of the inter-war years distinguished themselves from their predecessors. Deep though the division between the Modernist and the Victorian was, however, it was never straightforward: Victorian fiction has often suffered from the misleading assumption – promoted by Modernists themselves – that Modernism simply rejected it out of hand and absorbed nothing from the nineteenth century. But the relationship was more complex, and Modernism reconfigured and transformed a substantial part of its Victorian inheritance. As Giovanni Cianci and Peter Nicholls said in 2001, 'while Modernism defines itself in terms of a definitive break with the nineteenth-century past, it habitually reworks and reinvents the legacy from which it recoils.'[24] This more involved relationship is only now beginning to be explored.

THE MODERNIST CONSTRUCTION OF VICTORIAN FICTION

But it was true in the 1920s and 1930s that an enthusiasm for Modernist fiction tended to go hand in hand among younger readers with a dislike of the conventions of Victorian fictional prose. Sir Arthur Quiller-Couch (1863–1944), while Professor of English at Cambridge, considered the situation unfortunate. He told his undergraduate audience in a lecture published in *Studies in Literature: Second Series* (1922) that the Victorian period was indeed, as many people were saying, one of 'many oddities and certain glaring sins', but it was not therefore to be 'despised'. There should be no 'sneering at the Victorian age', he said: objective and compassionate thinking and reading would uncover literature of stature and substance.[25] Quiller-Couch's acknowledgement that nineteenth-century literature did not suit the taste of the generation who were newly enthusiastic for the writing of the Moderns was identical to Cecil's.

DAVID CECIL'S VIEW OF VICTORIAN NOVELS AND CULTURE
Cecil had no doubt that the Victorians were not being read with enjoyment. The fate of the Victorian novel was on a knife edge, he thought, though there was a glimmer of hope for the revival of Victorian literature in a returned enthusiasm for Tennyson. Cecil's lecture course was intended to give an objective evaluation of whether Victorian fiction was worth reading or not. Like Margaret Oliphant, Saintsbury and Forster, Cecil was preoccupied with evaluation (for F. R. Leavis and the principles of evaluation, see pp. 46–63, below). Edward Christian David Gascoyne Cecil (1902–86), whose career as an Oxford academic culminated in his long tenure of the Goldsmith's Chair of English Literature at the university from 1948 to 1969, disseminated ideas about literature and critical practice to generations of English graduates, many of whom continued to transmit versions of them as teachers themselves. Like F. R. Leavis at Cambridge, his evaluative principles permeated widely. More specifically, some of his ideas about the form of early Victorian fiction, its representations of sexuality, its comic nature, lack of political critique, and the evangelical nature of early Victorian society became critical commonplaces. They have been dislodged only with difficulty, and some remain clinging, to the regret of many modern scholars.

Evaluations, predicated on an ahistorical sense of what features were necessary to make a good novel, dominated Cecil's approach. Like Saintsbury, he relied on his position as a university don to give authority to his judgements: his mode privileged assertion over argument, pronouncement over debate. He assumed agreement about his aesthetic claims, so that when he declared Dickens's plots to be bad (see below p. 35) because they lacked organic connections, he took for granted his readers' agreement that organic plots were a *sine qua non* of good fiction through all time. He certainly did not accept the historically contingent nature of taste. When he read 'sentiment' in Dickens, he assumed everyone would agree it must be 'false', and when melodrama, he assumed it 'flashy' (contemporary criticism on the role of melodrama in Dickens's creative imagination is referenced on p. 11 above).

Cecil's manner was neither polemical nor iconoclastic but always urbane and civilized. Literary criticism was envisaged as a pursuit of a refined pleasure, a superior enjoyment. F. R. Leavis would upturn this gentlemanly conception of the critic's task with his belief in the moral importance of literary criticism. And refinement, for Cecil, was socially specific. The books that he described at the beginning of this lecture were not only situated in space (in a bookcase) but in a classed and gendered space (a gentleman's library). The critic's voice emerged from the male upper classes (literally from the aristocracy)[26] and resonated with a sense of owning the literature, of literature as a possession of the gentleman, and as a subject for discussion in cultured society. Reading English Literature as a university subject was inextricably connected with the preservation of the *status quo*, and its study constructed as a politically conservative activity. Radical or subversive elements of the critic's business were inconceivable.

Although Cecil's aesthetic principles were ahistorical, he did not read Victorian fiction as separate from its culture. He historicized matters of content and authorial attitudes, but only to find grounds for more evaluation. Early Victorian fiction suffered, he claimed, from the fact that the society from which it emerged was evangelical and parochial and that the period was one of sexual repression. This view of the society as Philistine, narrow-minded and sexually repressive still persists in popular conceptions of the period and its fiction (see the Further Reading section for re-evaluations of the relation of the novel to sexuality). Cecil thought that the limits of society restricted even its best novels, arguing that early Victorian novelists were partial in their presentation of human life because silent on matters of sexuality and 'the animal side of human nature'. Cecil's approach to early Victorian fiction was also characterized by the firm belief that fiction before George Eliot could be regarded in general terms as a whole, as 'very definitely one school'. He thought that the early Victorian novel was a taxonomical group in literary history about which generalizations could be made, proposing chiefly that their plots were more or less identical: 'The main outline of their novels is the same.' Early Victorian fiction was characterized by an absence of organic plotting, he said, a lack of formal coherence: 'their books are aggregations of brilliant passages rather than coherent wholes.' The incoherence of the plots of the Victorian novel became a topic of sustained literary debate through the rest of the twentieth century to the present and Cecil's view was radically revised (see pp. 213–29 below for more discussion of the form of Victorian fiction).

Extract from Lord David Cecil, *Early Victorian Novelists: Essays in Revaluation* (London: Constable, 1934), 3–23.

They crowd the shelves of every gentleman's library. *Editions de luxe*, heavy with gilding and the best rag paper, standard reprints clothed in an honourable and linen simplicity, dim behind glass doors, or sallow with exposure to dust and daylight, the serried lines confront one, Dickens, Thackeray, Trollope, George Eliot, lawful and undisputed monarchs of literature. At least so they were; else how should they have attained their majestic position on the shelves, rubbing shoulders on equal terms, as it were, with Milton and Gibbon and Boswell's *Life of Johnson*? But no author's reputation is certain for fifty years at least after his death. Will these novelists keep their high place? The experience of the last few years might lead one to doubt it.

For one thing people do not read most of them as they used. As often as not when one tries to open the glass book-case the lock sticks, stiff with disuse. And those that have read them have not all done it in a respectful spirit. The learned and Olympian kind of critic speaks of them less often than of French or Russian novelists; while the bright young people of the literary world, if they mention them at all, do so with boredom and contempt and disgust.

[...] Let us unlock the glass doors and pull down the books and see what they look like.

Well, they do not look at all the same as they used. The first thing that strikes one is that there is no Victorian Novel in the sense of a school with common conventions and traditions conterminous with the reign of Queen Victoria. There is one sort of novel before George Eliot and another after her.[1] On the other hand the earlier sort is not peculiar to the Victorian age. Our grandfathers, naturally enough, were chiefly struck by the differences between their own contemporaries and the writers preceding them. And, of course, there is a large difference in moral point of view and some smaller differences in subject: for every great writer in his turn extended the range of subject matter. But from the literary point of view, the point of view of form, the differences are much less than the likenesses. Between 1750 and 1860 the broad conception of what a novel should be did not change. *Tom Jones, Roderick Random, Waverley, Nicholas Nickleby,* are constructed on the same lines, composed within the same convention.

For, and this is the second feature that strikes us as we turn afresh the dusty pages, up till George Eliot the English novel is very definitely one school. Not a conscious school, with consciously common style and subject matter, like the fifteenth-century Italian painters, or the Elizabethan lyrical poets. The novel, the expression of the individual's view of the world, is always predominantly individualistic: the English, the wilful, eccentric, self-confident English, are the most individualistic of mankind: and the nineteenth century is the most individualistic of periods. *Laisser faire*[2] ruled the roost as triumphantly in the realm of art as in those of economics. No generalisation that one makes about these writers will be equally true of all. But of all, except Emily Brontë, certain generalisations are true. The main outline of their novels is the same. Their stories consist of a large variety of character and incident clustering round the figure of a hero, bound together loosely or less loosely by an intrigue and ending with wedding bells. Compared with the French, for instance, or the Russians, they seem an independent national growth with its own conventions, its own idiosyncrasies; strong in the same way, in the same way weak.

And here we come to the third outstanding fact about them. They are an extraordinary mixture of strength and weakness. There is no denying that the greatest English novelists are often downright bad; and in their greatest novels. At any moment and without a word of warning the reader may fall like a stone from a high flight of inspiration into a bog of ineptitude. There is hardly a book of Dickens which is not deformed by false sentiment, flashy melodrama, wooden characters; as often as not the hero is one of them; Thackeray's heroes are not much better; while whole passages of Charlotte Brontë could be incorporated without any effect of incongruity of style or sentiment in any penny novelette about pure maidens and purple passions.

Their faults of form are as bad as the faults of matter. It is very rare for a Victorian novelist before George Eliot to conceive the story as an organic whole of which every incident and character forms a contributory and integral part. Dickens chooses a conventional plot, generally a highly unlikely one, and then crams it as by physical violence on to a setting and character with which it has no organic connection; so that the main interest of the book lies in characters and scenes irrelevant to the story. In *Shirley* Charlotte Brontë suddenly changes the centre of the interest from Caroline to Shirley herself, half-way through the book. Thackeray had more idea of maintaining unity of interest; but his grasp on the development of the plot is very slack; in *Pendennis* and *The Newcomes* it drifts along in a succession of episodes to be cut short or extended as the author's caprice dictates. And both he and Trollope think nothing of having two or three plots devoid of any essential connection, flowing on in happy parallel independence at the same time.

But over and above the actual faults of these books one is struck by their limitations. They miss out so much of life, and so much of the important parts of it. They avoid – have we not heard it from the infuriated lips of a hundred earnest young students – any detailed treatment of the animal side of human nature. To those whose austere task it is to study the masterpieces of contemporary fiction this may seem a recommendation: and it is true that aesthetically it is not nearly so disastrous an inhibition as that which modern novelists seem to feel against the pathetic and heroic emotions. But a picture of human life which gives us hardly anything of its primary passion, or of those classes and types of people whose chief concern it is, must be a scrappy affair. The male novelists – the women seem more robust about emotion – shrink from passion even in its respectable manifestations. It is often a major motive in their plots as it has been in all plots since stories first began; but they pat the beast gingerly with fingers protected by a thick glove of sentimental reverence, and then hastily pass on.

But sex is not the only important omission from their books. We find little about the broader, more impersonal objects that occupy mankind; his relation to thought, to art, to public affairs. And though Dickens and Thackeray like to sprinkle their emotional scenes with a few drops of undenominational piety, to play a little soft music on the organ, as it were, to give solemnity to a death-bed, religion is never the chief preoccupation of their characters as it is that of Alyosha Karamazov.[3] This limitation of subject matter limits in its turn their range of characters. Their most successful creations, Mr Micawber, Becky Sharp, Mrs Proudie, Madam Beck, are all what actors call 'character parts', marked individual types whose interest lies in their comic or picturesque idiosyncrasy of speech and manner rather than in their relation to any general problems or interests of human nature. They are of the family of the Aguecheeks and Dame Quicklys; there are no Hamlets among them; no intellectuals, statesmen, or artists. For those deeper issues of human life which are the main interests of such characters do not form any part of the Victorian subject matter.

And as a result they hardly ever stir those profounder feelings to which the very greatest art appeals. The great Russians were to make the novel rouse the same emotions as tragedy or epic. Except for Emily Brontë, the Victorian novelists did not. And her emotional quality, for all its splendour, is too remote from the normal experience of mankind to bring her into the circle of great tragedians. Anna Karenina is a tragic figure as Othello is a tragic figure; Heathcliff is rather the demon lover of a border ballad.

And yet in spite of all these sins of omission and commission, to re-read these books is not to be disappointed. For their defects are more than counterbalanced by their extraordinary merits, merits all the more dazzling to us from the fact that they are so noticeably absent from the novels of our contemporaries. Apart from anything else, they tell the story so well. And though this may not be the highest merit of the novelist, it is, in some sort, the first: for it satisfies the primary object for which novels were first written. Mankind, like a child, wanted to be told a story. It is noticeable that people still give Dickens and Thackeray to children; and this is not, as some critics seem to suggest, because they are infantile, but because they make the story immediately and easily interesting. Improbable though the plot may be, it keeps one on tenterhooks so that one cannot put down the book at the end of a chapter, but must look over the next leaf to see what is going to happen. The most ardent admirer has never turned the next leaf of *Ulysses*[4] in order to see what was going to happen. Nor, even from a higher point of view, is the power to tell a story unimportant. For unless his interest is thoroughly engaged, how can a reader warm to that heightened, softened, acceptant condition of mind in which alone he is receptive of aesthetic impression? We turn once more to *Ulysses*, and repeat, how indeed!

And though from one aspect these novelists' range is limited, from another it is very large; much larger than that of most writers to-day. *Vanity Fair, Martin Chuzzlewit*, are not, like most modern novels, concentrated wholly on the fortunes of that handful of individuals who are its chief characters: they are also panoramas of whole societies. Now, as we read their pages, we are rubbing shoulders with kings and statesmen at Waterloo or Brussels, now huddling in an emigrant ship across the Atlantic, listening now to sharpers exchanging their plans across the sordid table of a gin palace, to schoolboys stridently teasing, to the genteel malice of a provincial drawing-room, to footmen relaxing over their beer; now we share the murmured confidences of two girls as the candle burns blue on the dressing-table and the ball-dress rustles from smooth shoulders to the floor. A hundred different types and classes, persons and nationalities, jostle each other across the shadow screen of our imagination. The Victorian novelists may miss the heights and depths, but they cast their net very wide. [. . .]

Now the great Victorian novels are all pictures. Sometimes they are fanciful and romantic, connected with reality only by a frail thread: more often they, too, stick close to the facts of actual existence. But these facts are never merely reproduced, they are always fired and coloured by a new and electric individuality. The act of creation is always performed. A street in London described by Dickens is very like a street in London; but it is still more like a street in Dickens. For Dickens has used the real world to create his own world, to add a country to the geography of the imagination. And so have Trollope and Thackeray and Charlotte Brontë and the rest of them. To read a paragraph of any of their books is to feel blowing into one's mental lungs unmistakably and invigoratingly a new and living air, the air of Dickensland, Thackerayland, Brontëland. For these authors possess in a supreme degree the quality of creative imagination.

It shows itself in the setting of their stories. Each has his characteristic, unforgettable scenery: Dickens' London, hazed with fog, livid with gaslight, with its shabby, clamorous, cheerful streets, its cosy and its squalid interiors, its stagnant waterside: and the different London of Thackeray: the west end of London on a summer afternoon, with its clubs and parks and pot-houses, mellow, modish and a little dusty, full of bustle and idleness: and Mrs Gaskell's countryside, so pastoral and sequestered and domesticated: and the elemental moorland of the Brontës.

It shows itself in their actual conception of incident. Mr Lockwood's first haunted night in the little room in Wuthering Heights, Lucy Snowe's drugged roaming through midnight Villette, garish with carnival, Bill Sykes, trapped in that sordid island by the river, Esmond come home after ten years' absence to the cathedral where Lady Castlewood's face gleams pale in the candleshine and the handful of worshippers mutter the weekly evensong: these stir the heart and stick in the memory, not because they are especially true to life, nor because of the characters – the picture remains in our minds when the very names involved in it are long forgotten – but because in themselves they are dramatic and picturesque. As a picture is an 'invention' of line and colour, so are these, brilliant 'inventions' of scene and action.

Imagination shows itself still more in their humour. Indeed the very fact that they have humour shows that they are creative; for humour is not a record of facts but a comment on them. To make a joke of something means, by definition, to make something new of it; not just to leave it where it is. The masterpieces of contemporary fiction, one may note, have little humour: there are few jokes in *Sons and Lovers, Portrait of the Artist as a Young Man*. But in *Vanity Fair* and *David Copperfield* and *Barchester Towers* there are hundreds. All the great Victorian novelists are humorists. And humorists each in a style of his own. Mr Micawber, Captain Costigan, Mrs Proudie, Miss Matty Jenkins, Paul Emanuel, are all comic in different ways.

But, of course, the most important expression of the creative imagination lies in the most important part of any novel, in the characters. The Victorians are all able to make their characters live. They do not always do it, they are as unequal about this as they are about everything else. And even when they do the result is often, from the realist's point of view, preposterous. What real human being ever acted like Mr Rochester or talked like Mr F.'s aunt? But Mr Rochester and Mr F.'s aunt are none the less alive for that. We should recognise them if they came into the room, we could imagine how they would behave if we were not there to see; their words and gestures and tricks of speech are their own and no one else's. Nor are the normal average characters, Johnny Eames or Molly Gibson, less individual. They are not types. If they do something characteristic one's first feeling is not 'How like a girl, how like a young man!' but 'How like Molly Gibson, how like Johnny Eames!' Within the limits the Victorians' range of character might seem inexhaustible. Their books linger in the memory, not as stories or theses, but as crowds; crowds of breathing, crying, laughing, living people. As long as they live, the books that house them will never die.

This extraordinary mixture of strength and weakness, then, is the second startling characteristic of the English novel. It is the striking characteristic of most English literature. The Elizabethan dramatists, the Caroline lyric poets, are as sensationally bad at one time as they are sensationally good at another. But in the Victorian novel a natural predisposition was intensified by two circumstances. For one thing the form was so new. We have seen that the broad conception of the novel form held by Dickens and Thackeray was still the same as that held by Fielding and Smollett, the creators of the novel; so that the Victorian novel is still the novel in its first stage. Nor had it yet achieved its present lofty position in the hierarchy of letters. [...]

[The Victorians] were remarkable people – how else indeed could they have done what they did? – with their insatiable appetite for life, their huge capacity for laughter and tears, their passionate conviction on every subject under heaven, full of inspiration and enterprise and eccentricity and determination. At the same time they were conceited, didactic and obstinate. And, like all people who have had to make their own way in the world, they had no traditions of taste and thought and conduct; if their achievements were sometimes cosmic, their outlook was often parochial. They were not men of the world; they did not value the things of the mind for themselves: they were the great English Philistines. Nor were they broadened by the fact that the predominant religious temper of their day was set by the narrow creed and relentless morality of the Evangelicals.

These circumstances inevitably accentuated any tendency to inequality in the novel. Because it was in its first stage, it was bound to be technically faulty. It had not yet evolved its own laws; it was still bound to the conventions of the comic stage and heroic romance from which it took its origin, with their artificial intrigues and stock situations and forced happy endings. Because it was looked on as light reading its readers did not expect a high standard of craft, nor mind if it had occasional lapses; especially as they themselves had no traditions of taste by which to estimate it. On the other hand they strongly objected to spending their hours of light reading on themes that were distressing or an intellectual strain. They did not read a novel for the same reason that they read *Hamlet*, they did not want it to be like *Hamlet*. While their moral views made any frank or detailed treatment of the physical side of life simply and finally impossible.

It is to be noted that here the Victorians show a definite decline from earlier novelists. The growing strength of the middle classes made them less cultivated and more puritanical than their predecessors. Technically, for instance, Scott is as defective as any of them, but he looked at life from the standpoint of a far more civilised tradition. He understands a man of another period like Dryden as triumphantly as Thackeray fails to understand a man of another period like Swift; he can write on France with the educated appreciation of a man of the world, while Dickens writes on Italy with the disapproving self-complacency of a provincial schoolmaster. And though Scott was a man of orthodox moral views, with a strong natural distaste to speaking of what he felt to be indelicate, if he has to, he does it straightforwardly and without fuss. Effie Deans'[5] lapse from virtue is referred to without any of that atmosphere of drawing the blinds and lowering the voice and getting out the pocket-handkerchief, in which Dickens has seen fit to enshroud the similar fate of little Em'ly. Moreover, Effie is ultimately permitted to marry a baronet and live out the remainder of her life in comparative peace; while poor Em'ly is shipped off to Australia to spend her remaining days there, single and in low spirits. For a crime so heinous as hers, poetic justice could with decency demand no lesser punishment.

But if the peculiar circumstances of their age encouraged the Victorians' peculiar faults, they are equally responsible for most of their peculiar merits. It was because the novelist had to entertain that he learnt to tell the story so well. If it did not engage the reader's attention he would not trouble to finish it; and because he had to entertain, not a literary coterie but the general reading public, the novelist learnt to cover a wide range of subject and mood; a range further extended by the fact that the public, though not seriously interested in art, were seriously interested in life and held strongly moral views about it. He had to be Mr Galsworthy, Mr Huxley, Mrs Woolf, Mrs Christie and Mr Wodehouse in one, for his readers would not have been satisfied with so narrow a field of experience as each of these authors separately appeals to. [...]

What, then, is our final impression of these novels? We have opened the glass book-cases and dragged the books down and read them. Shall we return them to their honourable places, tested and worthy peers of Milton and Boswell; are they the undisputed masterpieces of fiction that their contemporaries thought them? Not altogether. I have compared them to the Elizabethan drama.* And with intention. For they have a great deal in common; each the first, irresistible outcome of a new and major channel of literary expression, vital and imaginative in the highest degree, but inevitably stained by immaturity and inefficiency and ignorance. So that with a few wonderful exceptions, *Vanity Fair* and *Wuthering Heights*, their books are aggregations of brilliant passages rather than coherent wholes. And for this reason they are not among the very greatest novels, they do not attain that minute, final circle of the paradise of fiction, the circle of *War and Peace* and *Fathers and Children* and *Emma*.[6]

But though they are not the very greatest, they are great. For their merits are of so superlative a kind, forged in the central heat of the creative imagination, rich in the essential precious stuff from which the art of the novel is made. Here again they are like the Elizabethans; and to be truly appreciated must be approached in the same spirit. One must make up one's mind to their imperfections; to condemn them for improbable plots or conventional endings is as foolish as to condemn *Dr Faustus* or *The Duchess of Malfi*[7] for the same reason. On the other hand one must accustom one's eye to discern and concentrate on their splendid merits. [...]

Notes

1 For a criticism of this assumption, see p. 50 below.
2 *Laisser faire* = non-intervention.
3 In Fyodor Mikhailovich Dostoevsky's *The Brothers Karamazov* (1880).
4 James Joyce's *Ulysses* was serialized from 1918, and published as a book in 1922.
5 A character in Sir Walter Scott's *The Heart of Midlothian* (1818)
6 Tolstoy, *War and Peace* (1863–9); Turgenev, *Fathers and Sons* (1862); Jane Austen, *Emma* (1816).
7 Christopher Marlowe, *Dr Faustus* (1604); John Webster, *The Duchess of Malfi* (1623).

Chapter Notes

1 James Oliphant, *Victorian Novelists* (London: Blackie, 1899), [1].
2 Ibid.
3 Ibid.

* Of course, I do not mean Shakespeare; alas, the nineteenth century produced no supreme genius to organise the splendid chaos of the novel into a richer order.

4   Quoted in Kate Flint, 'The Victorian Novel and its Readers', in Deirdre David, ed., *The Cambridge Companion to the Victorian Novel* (Cambridge: Cambridge University Press, 2001), 20.

5   Oliphant, *Victorian Novelists*, 5.

6   Ibid.

7   Ramsden Balmforth, *The Ethical and Religious Value of the Novel* (London: Allen, 1912), xi–xii. Balmforth's principal subjects are Eliot, Eliza Lynn Linton, Dickens, Oliver Wendell Holmes and Mrs Humphry Ward.

8   Leslie Stephen had given the argument about the novel's universal appeal and scope in a lecture in 1880. His view was already a familiar one, and would become more so in the next few decades. The novelist, he said, 'tries to show us, as clearly as his powers allow, the real moving forces in the great tragic-comedy of human life'; John Charles Olmsted, ed., *A Victorian Art of Fiction: Essays on the Novel in British Periodicals 1870–1900* (New York: Garland, 1979), iii. 172.

9   *The Library Edition of the Complete Works of John Ruskin*, eds. E. T. Cook and Alexander Wedderburn, 39 vols (London: Allen, 1903–12), xxxiv. 284.

10 Olmsted, *Victorian Art of Fiction*, iii. 461.

11 Sir Arthur Quiller-Couch, *On the Art of Writing* (Cambridge: Cambridge University Press, 1928), 15.

12 It was not possible to take a degree in English alone at the University of Cambridge until 1926.

13 Quoted from the Oxford University examination paper in English Language and Literature, 1916.

14 See extract from Saintsbury, *The English Novel* on p. 23 of this *Guide*.

15 Olmsted, *Victorian Art of Fiction*, iii. 397.

16 Consider, for instance, the response of the *Saturday Review* to Saintsbury's *A History of Nineteenth Century Literature, 1780–1895* (1896). The reviewer remarked that it contained much that 'is offensive' (p. 423) and that it was full of errors. 'There is scarcely a chapter in it', the reviewer declared, 'which does not teem with blunders and misrepresentations, some having their origin in simple carelessness, many indicating that Professor Saintsbury is very imperfectly equipped in point of information for the task he has undertaken'; *Saturday Review*, 81 (1896), 424.

17 Israel Zangwill (1864–1926) was a writer on Jewish matters whose novel *Children of the Ghetto* (1892) was a searching portrayal of poor Jews in London.

18 Mrs [Margaret] Oliphant and F. R. Oliphant, *The Victorian Age of English Literature*, 2 vols (London: Percival, 1892), i. [v].

19 E. M. Forster, *Aspects of the Novel* (Harmondsworth: Penguin, 1962), 28.

20 Ibid., 29.

21 Ibid., 38.

22 See John Carey, *The Intellectuals and the Masses: Pride and Prejudice among the Literary Intelligentsia 1880–1939* (London: Faber, 1992), 18–19.

23 Forster, *Aspects of the Novel*, 27.

24 Giovanni Cianci and Peter Nicholls, eds, *Ruskin and Modernism* (Basingstoke: Palgrave, 2001), xvii.

25   Sir Arthur Quiller-Couch, *Studies in Literature: Second Series* (Cambridge: Cambridge University Press, 1922), 288.
26   See David Cecil, *The Cecils of Hatfield House* (London: Constable, 1973).

Further Reading

Discussions of early twentieth-century criticism:
Chris Baldick, *The Social Mission of English Criticism, 1848–1932* (Oxford: Clarendon, 1983): useful, measured critique of the arguments about literary criticism and morals from Arnold to Leavis.
Franklin E. Court, *Institutionalizing English Literature: The Culture and Politics of Literary Study, 1750–1900* (Stanford: Stanford University Press, 1992).
Franklin E Court, 'The Social and Historical Significance of the First English Literature Professorship in England', *Proceedings of the Modern Language Association*, 103 (1988): 796–807: about the appointment of Thomas Dale to the first professorship of English Literature at London University and the desire to 'democratize literature and encourage national literacy by popularising and legitimising the "reading habit"' this appointment represented.
Terry Eagleton, *The Function of Criticism: From* The Spectator *to Post-Structuralism* (London: Verso, 1984): Habermas-influenced Marxist approach to the role of criticism from the eighteenth century onwards during the decline of the 'public sphere'; chapter 3 considers criticism in the nineteenth and early twentieth centuries.
John Gross, *The Rise and Fall of the Man of Letters: Aspects of English Literary Life since 1800* (Harmondsworth: Penguin, 1973): treats the belletrists of the nineteenth century rather derogatorily.
Noel King, '"Teacher Must Exist Before the Pupil": The Newbolt Report on *The Teaching of English in England, 1921*', *Literature and History*, 13 (1987): 14–37: argues that class is central to the Newbolt Report and that it outlines a means for monitoring the conduct of a life.
Harold Orel, *Victorian Literary Critics* (Basingstoke: Macmillan, 1984): includes an account of Saintsbury (pp. 151–76) which is mostly summary with little critique; concentrates on Saintsbury's massive *A History of Criticism* (1901–4).
D. J. Palmer, *The Rise of English Studies: An Account of the Study of English Language and Literature from its Origins to the Making of the Oxford English School* (London: Oxford University Press, 1965): includes an historical account of the formation and principles of the Oxford English Faculty and its wider implications for the university teaching of English Literature.
René Wellek, *The Rise of English Literary History* (London: McGraw-Hill, [1966]): gives some background to the idea of literary history and comprises a history of English literary history, including Thomas Warton's *History of English Poetry* (1774–81); Wellek said his book 'not only satisfy[ies] the instructive desire of men to commemorate the achievements of their predecessors, but [...] help[s] to show by what ways the present vantage-point, or *impasse*, of literary studies has been reached'.

Peter Widdowson, *Literature* (London: Routledge, 1999): in The New Critical Idiom Series, includes accessible first chapter (pp. 36–59) covering early twentieth-century definitions of literature and the function of literary criticism.

Reading practices in the nineteenth century:
Richard D. Altick, *The English Common Reader: A Social History of the Mass Reading Public 1800–1900* (Chicago: University of Chicago Press, 1957): an important account of literacy and reading habits in the period (see p. 264 below for more on Altick).
Patrick Brantlinger, *The Reading Lesson: The Threat of Mass Literacy in Nineteenth-century British Fiction* (Bloomington, Ind.: Indiana University Press, 1998): useful if unoriginal survey of anxieties about the novel at the end of the century.

Books on or by individual critics discussed:
Lord David Cecil, *Hardy the Novelist: An Essay in Criticism* (London: Constable, 1954): another example of Cecil's evaluative approach to a major Victorian novelist.
Hannah Cranbourne, ed., *David Cecil: A Portrait* (Wimborne: Dovecote, 1990): affectionate and non-critical account of Cecil by many who knew him; useful for acquiring a sense of Cecil's milieu and his approach as a tutor.
Dorothy Richardson Jones, *'King of Critics': George Saintsbury, 1845–1933, Critic, Journalist, Historian, Professor* (Ann Arbor: University of Michigan Press, 1992): sympathetic biography of this private man and revealing account of the prevalence of literary history in education between the wars. Jones also asks why students should go back to read Saintsbury: because 'he may help them cultivate appreciation, develop an ear and a sensitivity to feeling and mood. He will give them access to and encourage them to sample the vast range of European literature and its pleasures, especially French.'

Challenges to Cecil's view of Victorian sexuality:
Dennis W. Allen, *Sexuality in Victorian Fiction* (Norman and London: University of Oklahoma Press, 1993): 'This study was generated by some of the implications of Michel Foucault's rejection of the "repressive hypothesis," namely, the notion that the Victorians simply and unilaterally refused to consider the sexual. On the contrary, Foucault argues, the proliferation of scientific and social discourses on sex and sexuality during the Victorian era demonstrates a vast enterprise designed to articulate – in effect to produce – the "truth" of the sexual. Although Foucault argues that we can no longer consider the Victorians as "Victorian," as impossibly prudish in the popular sense of the term, he does not claim that public discourse on sexuality in the nineteenth century was as explicit as in our own time. Foucault's analysis thus radically complicates out understanding of the representation of sex and sexuality in Victorian fiction. Erotically discreet, the Victorian novel nonetheless subtly constructs the sexual. As such, the erotic discretion of Victorian fiction cannot be seen simply as an unproblematic instance of sexual prudery'. Concentrates on *Cranford*, *Bleak House* and *The Picture of Dorian Gray*.

Michel Foucault, *The History of Sexuality*, vol. 1 (Harmondsworth: Penguin, 1990, translation): the nineteenth century saw an explosion in discourses about sexuality.

Other surveys:

G. K. Chesterton, *The Victorian Age in Literature* (London: Williams and Norgate, n.d.): typically lively effort to determine the characteristics of Victorian fiction, including its humour, and to justify the claim that 'The novel of the nineteenth century was female.'

Oliver Elton, *A Survey of English Literature 1830–1880*, 2 vols (London: Arnold, 1920): another influential and popular survey.

Frederic Harrison, *Studies in Early Victorian Literature* (London: Edward Arnold, 1895): Positivist Harrison argues that the defining characteristic of nineteenth-century fiction was 'the dominant influence of Sociology, – enthusiasm for social truths as an instrument of social reform'. Separate chapters on Disraeli, Thackeray, Dickens, Charlotte Brontë, Kingsley, Trollope, and George Eliot.

Mrs [Margaret] Oliphant and F. R. Oliphant, *The Victorian Age of English Literature*, 2 vols (London: Percival, 1892): see above, p. 00.

Sir Arthur Quiller-Couch, *Charles Dickens and Other Victorians* (Cambridge: Cambridge University Press, 1925): defends the greatness of Dickens though deplores his 'singular poverty of invention' [!]; claims a greater status for Trollope than Quiller-Couch's contemporaries recognized.

Sir Arthur Quiller-Couch, *Studies in Literature: Second Series* (Cambridge: Cambridge University Press, 1922): contains the lecture on 'The "Victorian Age"'.

2

F. R. Leavis and *The Great Tradition*

[The English] school is based, if on anything, on an idea of criticism as a discipline – of the critical study of literature as a training of sensibility and intelligence.[1]

INTRODUC-
TION E. M. Forster's principal target in *Aspects of the Novel*, discussed in chapter 1, was the survey mode of literary history, exemplified by Louis Cazamian, Oliver Elton and George Saintsbury. But the most consequential critique of this procedure of literary criticism came not from Forster but from Frank Raymond Leavis (1895–1978). Leavis was the most significant of all English critics of the central years of the twentieth century. His name filled several generations of critics and university graduates in English Literature with a respect that was genuine and enduring: his authority in the discipline of English Literature was remarkable. Leavis's reputation lasted for more or less half a century and shows some sign of undergoing reassessment today. But it suffered badly in the 1970s and 1980s. The theorists of these decades, in particular Marxists, feminists and deconstructionists, rejected him on well-argued grounds as the quintessence of unacceptable liberal humanism that was conservative in its politics, elitist in its conception of the role of the intellectual and the audience of criticism, danger-ously narrow in its assumptions about gender, race and class, and naïve in its beliefs about the role of the author in the formation of literary meaning and the relation of texts to history and ideology. Leavis's position, like liberal human-ism, has never fully recovered from this onslaught. But his more positive contribution to contemporary literary studies, the more fruitful dimension of his legacy, is being reconsidered today. Contemporary readers of Victorian fiction profit from him because of his admiration for the Victorian novel as a major art form, and his conviction that *fiction* was generally a subject worthy of critical investigation (for details of the poor regard for fiction prior to Leavis, see pp. 18–20 above). At an even more general level, all literary critics in the

academy owe a debt to his energy because he helped in the establishment of their discipline as a serious business. His lifelong conviction that literary criticism was an exacting, morally important and culturally significant activity is one that even critics otherwise antagonistic to the principles of liberal humanism can respect.

F. R. Leavis invested literary criticism with prestige and moral gravity absent from the writing of his predecessors. He perceived the literary work of men such as Saintsbury and Elton, and his Cambridge colleague Sir Arthur Quiller-Couch, as merely the gentlemanly pursuit of a refined kind of pleasure. Leavis had no patience with the cigar-scented criticism David Cecil's work represented. Through his own approach to literary texts and his extensive theorizing about the business of criticism, Leavis transformed the practice of literary criticism in the academy into a serious moral activity. English, Leavis said, was a 'relevant and essential discipline' in university life, a key part of a liberal education and a good training for the mind. It was, he went on, 'a discipline of intelligence, the means of starting the student towards real and creative thinking'. English studies was central to university education as far as Leavis was concerned because it trained men and women in both intellectual and emotional refinement. 'The study of literature has its key place in liberal education', he declared, 'because, properly pursued, it involves a discipline of intelligence that is at the same time a training of sensibility – of perception, qualitative response and judgment.'[2] It helped create a whole person. Leavis's ideas were influential, and English studies in the academy from the middle of the first half of the century, 'emancipated', as he put it, from the residual nineteenth-century practices of 'linguistic[s] and philology',[3] came to matter in a way they had not mattered before. English began to assume a prestige once the preserve of Classics in the ancient universities.

LEAVIS'S INFLUENCE

The Marxist critic Terry Eagleton – no admirer of Leavis's critical position in general – explained his influence in the following terms: 'In the early 1920s it was desperately unclear why English was worth studying at all; by the early 1930s it had become a question of why it was worth wasting your time on anything else. English was not only a subject worth studying, but *the* supremely civilizing pursuit, the spiritual essence of the social formation.'[4] Eagleton, who has argued at length his own radical ideas of why criticism matters to the social formation, was correct in the main. None the less, Leavis's influence on the discipline, his endeavours to invest English studies with ethical gravity, were not so successful in his own university. Indeed, Leavis had a great deal of trouble in persuading Cambridge of the significance of English Literature as an academic discipline at all. His career there was fraught with disagreement, and, unlike Raymond Williams, he was never to be awarded a professorial chair despite his international status as a critic.

However, it was at the University of Cambridge that Leavis succeeded first in articulating, despite those who disagreed with him or who took against his prickly style of doing things, the necessity of teaching English as a vital part of a liberal education. And this had, as Eagleton rightly indicated, a major influence on the conceptualization of English studies.

THE
PRINCIPLES OF
LEAVIS'S
CRITICISM

F. R. Leavis imagined British liberal education as a bastion against the sham values of mass culture that he saw threatening high art, national spiritual and moral principles, and traditional civilization. English Literature, as a part of a university's liberal education, played a central role in resisting the hollowness of popular culture. It was a weapon against the 'meaninglessness of the technologico-Benthamite world',[5] with its intolerance of art and disregard of humane principles. Leavis spoke in opposition to such Benthamism and 'the desperate plight of culture to-day'[6] throughout his creative life, and his words became more urgent. In 1968, ten years before his death, he was particularly gloomy. He described young people, living in the contemporary world of falsity and artificiality, as detached from their own artistic heritage, the potential source of their spiritual and moral renewal. They were experiencing a disastrous 'cultural disinheritance'. There was only one way of resisting this, he continued, giving fresh impetus to a theme that had preoccupied him since before the Second World War. This was to create: 'an educated, well-informed, responsible and influential public – a public that statesmen, administrators, editors, and newspaper proprietors can respect and rely on as well as fear. Society's only conceivable organ for such an effort is the university, conceived as a creative centre of civilization.'[7] English studies was a major part of the civilizing mission of the university. Leavis's writing represented the most ample flourishing in the English academy in the twentieth century of the Arnoldian impulse to communicate moral values through the criticism of literature (see also the Newbolt Report, discussed on p. 31 above) and to contest, with the reading of fiction, poetry and drama, the benighted forces ranged against civilization.[8]

If Leavis was the most important mid-century critic in turning the study of English literature into a crucial business, he had a more local effect of significance for the subject of this book. The novel was infrequently regarded as a prestigious form in English letters at the turn of the century (see pp. 18–20 above for discussion of this). Modernism, especially the novels of James Joyce, D. H. Lawrence and Virginia Woolf, improved the general status of prose fiction for readers previously suspicious of its credentials as a serious vehicle for word art and helped to confer on it intellectual prestige. But the increased standing of the novel and the willingness of the critical community to consider it as a significant genre also owed much, in the middle years of the century, to F. R. Leavis's critical endeavours. In the face of scepticism about the artistic merits of fiction, Leavis argued that the genre was a form for sincere and significant ideas and for the detailed exploration of human subjectivities.[9] His influence on the shape of the history of criticism of the Victorian novel was, at this level alone, substantial.

But Leavis also contributed directly to the study of Victorian fiction. His most important (and controversial) book in this area was *The Great Tradition* (1948). An extract from the first chapter is reprinted below. Prior to this study, Leavis's work had been in poetry, from the Renaissance to the twentieth century, and in educational polemic. His writing on poetry provided an important context for *The Great Tradition*, however, because Leavis was concerned there with the identification of canons of great writing. In *New Bearings in English Poetry* (1932), he had identified Edward Thomas, T. S. Eliot and Ezra Pound as the main voices of early twentieth-century verse. In *Revaluation: Tradition and Development in English Poetry* (1936), he fixed the central features of the whole English poetic tradition in a corpus that included John Donne, Alexander Pope, Samuel Johnson and Gerard Manley Hopkins. *The Great Tradition* was a departure from Leavis's previous genre interests. But it continued to privilege the central idea of an English tradition.

The idea of a tradition, of important sustained literary continuities, had played a part in the surveys of literary history at the beginning of the twentieth century, as indicated in the discussion of George Saintsbury in chapter 1 (see pp. 21–3 above). Inheritance, descent and influence were significant concepts for Saintsbury as for Leavis. But Leavis, arguing that 'Literary study, properly pursued, gives an incomparable initiation into the idea of tradition',[10] interpreted tradition in a radically new way. His canon was partly built from judgements about the moral qualities of fiction. The English novelists in *The Great Tradition* were identified, in part, by the moral seriousness of their works, the 'human awareness they promote[d]', and their consciousness 'of the possibilities of life', together with their perfect handling of form. (It should not be overlooked that Leavis, in a politically revealing way, thought that *novelists* were great rather than just their books: he made judgements about the moral identity of men and women, not just literary texts.) Knowledge of 'life' and 'intense moral preoccupation[s]' were, for Leavis, defining features of great fiction and, with adept use of form, the essential elements of the tradition. Concepts of 'life' and moral seriousness were difficult to pin down in Leavis's work; they were terms resistant to rational analysis, inviting instead an intuitive understanding. He understood what was moral and what was life as ideas that all right-thinking readers would understand.

Many readers have been unhappy about this. Like Matthew Arnold in his use of the touchstones of great poetry, Leavis's deployment of such phrases as 'awareness of the possibilities of life' assumed the understanding and agreement of a particular implied audience, but, refusing further elucidation, deliberately excluded others. This practice has been seen as expressive of Leavis's suspicions of mass culture and readership, and of his belief that criticism was for an elite.

THE IDEA OF TRADITION

1980s' REACTIONS TO THE POLITICS OF LEAVIS'S CRITICISM

Leavis's practice of isolating great books, moreover, his ranking of literature and novelists in hierarchies of value, was seen to imply a comparable hierarchization of readers. Catherine Belsey, in 'Re-reading the Great Tradition' (1982), argued that Leavis's critical discourse promoted a politics of elitism. 'What is inscribed in the Leavisian model', Belsey said, in a collection of essays edited by Peter Widdowson, another prominent antagonist of Leavis in the 1970s and 1980s, 'is the making of hierarchies through judgements of relative human value, not just in literature but in life.'[11] Leavis's criticism, according to Belsey, was embedded in a dangerous politics of exclusion (for more on Widdowson's collection, see the Further Reading section at the end of the chapter). Other readers have found less to worry about and have accepted Leavis's belief that there were good books as well as bad, just as there were good and bad readers. They have regarded the 1970s' and 1980s' backlash as predicated on idealism and a misplaced sense of political correctness.

THE
PRINCIPLES OF
LEAVIS'S *THE
GREAT
TRADITION*
(1948)

There is no dispute, however, that hierarchization and judgements of value were central to Leavis's critical purposes. Leavis famously began *The Great Tradition* with a statement of evaluation. The writers of greatness in the English tradition were, he plainly declared, Jane Austen, George Eliot, Henry James and Joseph Conrad. The book concentrated on the last three, but, in the extract given here, I omit, for the obvious reason, most of the concluding discussion of Conrad, except that which refers, in fact, to Dickens. Repudiating with some acerbity Lord David Cecil's claim from *Early Victorian Novelists* (see p. 34 above) that George Eliot was the first modern novelist, Leavis stressed the continuities between Jane Austen and the other three authors in the tradition, describing Austen, in a way that can be compared to Saintsbury's privileging of her in the literary tradition (see p. 24 above), as the first great writer of fictional prose in the English canon. But, of course, Leavis's reasons for seeing Austen in this position were different from Saintsbury's. She was, he said, the first writer to display 'intense moral preoccupation' expressed in perfectly handled form. As such, she was a central figure for the development of the great Victorian novel.

Leavis concentrated in *The Great Tradition* on the relationships of novelists to other novelists and was not interested in the contexts of literary works. In his other books, he championed 'practical criticism', a mode of close reading of poetry that discounted the interpretative relevance of contextual material. He thought that an over-eager interest in such material – in the way literature negotiated with the culture from which it emerged – betrayed a morally deplorable lack of commitment to literature itself. 'If you propose', he said:

> to place the importance of literary criticism in some non-literary-critical function [including the investigation of the interpretive relevance of context], you betray your unbelief that literary criticism matters. And, if you don't believe in literary

criticism, then your belief that literature itself matters will have the support of an honoured convention, but must be suspect of resting very much on that.[12]

Historicist criticism was a slight on literature itself.

Leavis's privileging of moral seriousness meant the exclusion of many significant novelists from the canon of Victorian fiction, whose aims were different, whose morality was articulated differently, or whose aesthetic principles did not meet Leavis's approval. Charles Dickens was the most significant casualty of *The Great Tradition*. Leavis perceived him chiefly as an entertainer and a novelist lacking, except in *Hard Times* (1854), the moral stature necessary for inclusion within the tradition of seriousness begun by Austen. Leavis later changed this view. In the 'Preface' to *Dickens the Novelist* (1970), a book written by Leavis and his wife Queenie, the authors declared, with characteristic emphasis on evaluation, that they wished to 'enforce as unanswerably as possible the conviction that Dickens was one of the greatest of creative writers; that with the intelligence inherent in creative genius, he developed a fully conscious devotion to his art, becoming as a popular and fecund, but yet profound, serious and wonderfully resourceful practising novelist, a master of it.'[13] Dickens, the Leavises now argued, was far more than an entertainer; indeed, they repulsed any 'academic, journalist or both' who '[tells] us with the familiar easy assurance that Dickens was a genius, but that his line was entertainment'.[14] This was, paradoxically, exactly the statement Leavis himself had made in *The Great Tradition* (in the extract below, p. 62).

But Leavis did not acknowledge his own change of mind, refusing to negotiate with his own past. *Dickens the Novelist* ignored the existence of *The Great Tradition* altogether. What had happened since the first book was Leavis's recognition of an element in Dickens's work that he had previously overlooked. By 1970, he had seen in the novelist an antagonist of false societal values, a repudiator of sham. Believing in the hollowness of his own age's values, Leavis now perceived a figure who had shared some of his own principles a century earlier, and he was able to take a more sympathetic view. What was not different from *The Great Tradition* was the pursuit of judgement, the insistence on discriminating evaluation. With all its problematic politics, this lay at the heart of Leavis's critical enterprise.

ITS
TREATMENT
OF DICKENS
AND LEAVIS'S
LATER VIEWS
ON HIM

Extract from F. R. Leavis, *The Great Tradition* (London: Chatto and Windus, 1960), 5–21.

[…] Having, in examination-papers and undergraduate essays, come much too often on the proposition that 'George Eliot is the first modern novelist', I finally tracked it down to Lord David Cecil's *Early Victorian Novelists.*[1] In so far as it is possible to extract anything clear and coherent from the variety of things that Lord David Cecil says by way of explaining the phrase, it is this: that George Eliot, being concerned, not to offer 'primarily an entertainment', but to explore a significant theme – a theme significant in its bearing on the 'serious problems and preoccupations of mature life' – breaks with 'those fundamental conventions both of form and matter within which the English novel up till then had been constructed'. What account, then, are we to assume of Jane Austen? Clearly, one that appears to be the most commonly held: she creates delightful characters ('Compare Jane Austen's characterization with Scott's' * – a recurrent examination-question) and lets us forget our cares and moral tensions in the comedy of pre-eminently civilized life. The idea of 'civilization' invoked appears to be closely related to that expounded by Mr Clive Bell.[†]

Lord David Cecil actually compares George Eliot with Jane Austen. The passage is worth quoting because the inadequate ideas of form ('composition') and moral interest it implies – ideas of the relation between 'art' and 'life' as it concerns the novelist – are very representative. (Its consistency with what has been said about George Eliot earlier in the same essay isn't obvious, but that doesn't disturb the reader by the time he has got here.)

---

* Scott was primarily a kind of inspired folk-lorist, qualified to have done in fiction something analogous to the ballad-opera: the only live part of *Redgauntlet* now is 'Wandering Willie's Tale', and 'The Two Drovers' remains in esteem while the heroics of the historical novels can no longer command respect. He was a great and very intelligent man; but, not having the creative writer's interest in literature, he made no serious attempt to work out his own form and break away from the bad tradition of the eighteenth-century romance. Of his books, *The Heart of Midlothian* comes the nearest to being a great novel, but hardly *is* that: too many allowances and deductions have to be made. Out of Scott a bad tradition came. It spoiled Fenimore Cooper, who had new and first-hand interests and the makings of a distinguished novelist. And with Stevenson it took on 'literary' sophistication and fine writing.

† '"As for the revolt against Nature", he continued, "that, too, has its uses. If it conduces to the cult of the stylized, the conventionalized, the artificial, just for their own sakes, it also, more broadly, makes for civilization."'

'"Civilization?" I asked. "At what point between barbarism and decadence does civilization reign? If a civilized community be defined as one where you find aesthetic preoccupations, subtle thought, and polished intercourse, is civilization necessarily desirable? Aesthetic preoccupations are not inconsistent with a wholly inadequate conception of the range and power of art; thought may be subtle and yet trivial; and polished intercourse may be singularly uninteresting"'; L. H. Myers, *The Root and the Flower*, p. 418.

Myers hasn't the great novelist's technical interest in method and presentment; he slips very easily into using the novel as a *vehicle*. That is, we feel that he is not primarily a

It is also easy to see why her form doesn't satisfy us as Jane Austen's does. Life is chaotic, art is orderly. The novelist's problem is to evoke an orderly composition which is also a convincing picture of life. It is Jane Austen's triumph that she solves this problem perfectly, fully satisfies the rival claims of life and art. Now George Eliot does not. She sacrifices life to art. Her plots are too neat and symmetrical to be true. We do not feel them to have grown naturally from their situation like a flower, but to have been put together deliberately and calculatedly like a building.

Jane Austen's plots, and her novels in general, were put together very 'deliberately and calculatedly' (if not 'like a building').* But her interest in 'composition' is not something to be put over against her interest in life; nor does she offer an 'aesthetic' value that is separable from moral significance. The principle of organization, and the principle of development, in her work is an intense moral interest of her own in life that is in the first place a preoccupation with certain problems that life compels on her as personal ones. She is intelligent and serious enough to be able to impersonalize her moral tensions as she strives, in her art, to become more fully conscious of them, and to learn what, in the interests of life, she ought to do with them. Without her intense moral preoccupation she wouldn't have been a great novelist.

This account of her would, if I had cared to use the formula, have been my case for calling Jane Austen, and not anyone later, 'the first modern novelist'. In applying it to George Eliot, Lord David Cecil says: 'In fact, the laws conditioning the form of George Eliot's novels are the same laws that condition those of Henry James and Wells and Conrad and Arnold Bennett.' I don't know what Wells is doing in that sentence; there is an elementary distinction to be made between the *discussion* of problems and ideas, and what we find in the great novelists. And, for all the generous sense of common humanity to be found in his best work, Bennett seems to me never to have been disturbed enough by life to come anywhere near greatness. But it would certainly be reasonable to say that 'the laws conditioning the form of Jane Austen's novels are the same laws that condition those of George Eliot and Henry James and Conrad'.[2] Jane Austen, in fact, is the inaugurator of the great tradition of the English novel – and by 'great tradition' I mean the tradition to which what is great in English fiction belongs.

---

novelist. Yet he is sufficiently one to have made of *The Root and the Flower* a very remarkable novel. Anyone seriously interested in literature is likely to have found the first reading a memorable experience and to have found also that repeated re-readings have not exhausted the interest.

* See '*Lady Susan* into *Mansfield Park*' by Q. D. Leavis in *Scrutiny,* 10 (2).

The great novelists in that tradition are all very much concerned with 'form'; they are all very original technically, having turned their genius to the working out of their own appropriate methods and procedures. But the peculiar quality of their preoccupation with 'form' may be brought out by a contrasting reference to Flaubert. Reviewing Thomas Mann's *Der Tod in Venedig*, D. H. Lawrence* adduces Flaubert as figuring to the world the 'will of the writer to be greater than and undisputed lord over the stuff he writes'. This attitude in art, as Lawrence points out, is indicative of an attitude in life – or towards life. Flaubert, he comments, 'stood away from life as from a leprosy'. For the later Aesthetic writers, who, in general, represent in a weak kind of way the attitude that Flaubert maintained with a perverse heroism, 'form' and 'style' are ends to be sought for themselves, and the chief preoccupation is with elaborating a beautiful style to apply to the chosen subject. There is George Moore, who in the best circles, I gather (from a distance), is still held to be among the very greatest masters of prose, though – I give my own limited experience for what it is worth – it is very hard to find an admirer who, being pressed, will lay his hand on his heart and swear he has read one of the 'beautiful' novels through. 'The novelist's problem is to evolve an orderly composition which is also a convincing picture of life' – this is the way an admirer of George Moore sees it. Lord David Cecil, attributing this way to Jane Austen, and crediting her with a superiority over George Eliot in 'satisfying the rival claims of life and art', explains this superiority, we gather, by a freedom from moral preoccupations that he supposes her to enjoy. (George Eliot, he tells us, was a Puritan, and earnestly bent on instruction.)[†]

As a matter of fact, when we examine the formal perfection of *Emma*, we find that it can be appreciated only in terms of the moral preoccupations that characterize the novelist's peculiar interest in life. Those who suppose it to be an 'aesthetic matter', a beauty of 'composition' that is combined, miraculously, with 'truth to life', can give no adequate reason for the view that *Emma* is a great novel, and no intelligent account of its perfection of form. It is in the same way true of the other great English novelists that their interest in their art gives them the opposite of an affinity with Pater and George Moore; it is, brought to an intense focus, an unusually developed interest in life. For, far from having anything of Flaubert's disgust or disdain or boredom, they are all

---

[*]   *Phoenix*, p. 308.

[†]   She is a moralist and a highbrow, the two handicaps going together. 'Her humour is less affected by her intellectual approach. Jokes, thank heaven, need not be instructive'; *Early Victorian Novelists*, p. 299.

distinguished by a vital capacity for experience, a kind of reverent openness before life, and a marked moral intensity.

It might be commented that what I have said of Jane Austen and her successors is only what can be said of any novelist of unqualified greatness. That is true. But there *is* – and this is the point – an English tradition, and these great classics of English fiction belong to it; a tradition that, in the talk about 'creating characters' and 'creating worlds', and the appreciation of Trollope and Mrs Gaskell and Thackeray and Meredith and Hardy and Virginia Woolf, appears to go unrecognized. It is not merely that we have no Flaubert (and I hope I haven't seemed to suggest that a Flaubert is no more worth having than a George Moore). Positively, there is a continuity from Jane Austen. There is evidence enough that George Eliot admired her work profoundly. The writer whose intellectual weight and moral earnestness strike some critics as her handicap certainly saw in Jane Austen something more than an ideal contemporary of Lytton Strachey. What one great original artist learns from another, whose genius and problems are necessarily very different, is the hardest kind of 'influence' to define, even when we see it to have been of the profoundest importance. The obvious manifestation of influence is to be seen in this kind of passage:

> A little daily embroidery had been a constant element in Mrs Transome's life; that soothing occupation of taking stitches to produce what neither she nor any one else wanted, was then the resource of many a well-born and unhappy woman.

> In short, he felt himself to be in love in the right place, and was ready to endure a great deal of predominance, which, after all, a man could always put down when he liked. Sir James had no idea that he should ever like to put down the predominance of this handsome girl, in whose cleverness he delighted. Why not? A man's mind – what there is of it – has always the advantage of being masculine, – as the smallest birch-tree is of a higher kind than the most soaring palm – and even his ignorance is of a sounder quality. Sir James might not have originated this estimate; but a kind Providence furnishes the limpest personality with a little gum or starch in the form of tradition.

The kind of irony here is plainly akin to Jane Austen's – though it is characteristic enough of George Eliot; what she found was readily assimilated to her own needs. In Jane Austen herself the irony has a serious background, and is no mere display of 'civilization'. George Eliot wouldn't have been interested in it if she hadn't perceived its full significance – its relation to the essential moral interest offered by Jane Austen's art. And here we come to the profoundest kind of influence, that which is not manifested in likeness. One of the supreme debts one great writer can owe another is the realization of unlikeness (there is, of course, no significant unlikeness without the common concern – and the common seriousness of concern – with essential human issues). One way of putting the difference between George Eliot and the Trollopes whom we are invited to consider along with her is to say that she was capable of understanding Jane Austen's greatness and capable of learning from her. And except for Jane Austen there was no novelist to learn from – none whose work had any bearing on her own essential problems as a novelist.

Henry James also was a great admirer of Jane Austen,* and in his case too there is that obvious aspect of influence which can be brought out by quotation. And there is for him George Eliot as well, coming between. In seeing him in an English tradition I am not slighting the fact of his American origin; an origin that doesn't make him less of an English novelist, of the great tradition, than Conrad later. That he was an American is a fact of the first importance for the critic, as Mr Yvor Winters brings out admirably in his book, *Maule's Curse.*† Mr Winters discusses him as a product of the New England ethos in its last phase, when a habit of moral strenuousness remained after dogmatic Puritanism had evaporated and the vestigial moral code was evaporating too. This throws a good deal of light on the elusiveness that attends James's peculiar ethical sensibility. We have, characteristically, in reading him, a sense that important choices are in question and that our finest discrimination is being challenged, while at the same time we can't easily produce for discussion any issues that have moral substance to correspond.

It seems relevant also to note that James was actually a New Yorker. In any case, he belonged by birth and upbringing to that refined civilization of the old European America which we have learnt from Mrs Wharton to associate with New York. His bent was to find a field for his ethical sensibility in the appreciative study of such a civilization – the 'civilization' in question being a matter of personal relations between members of a mature and sophisticated Society. It is doubtful whether at any time in any place he could have found what would have satisfied his implicit

---

*   He can't have failed to note with interest that *Emma* fulfils, by anticipation, a prescription of his own: everything is presented through Emma's dramatized consciousness, and the essential effects depend on that.

†   New Directions, Norfolk, Conn. (1938). To insist that James is in the English tradition is not to deny that he is in an American tradition too. He is in the tradition that includes Hawthorne and Melville. He is related to Hawthorne even more closely than Mr Winters suggests. A study of the very early work shows Hawthorne as a major influence – as *the* major influence. The influence is apparent there in James's use of symbolism; and this use develops into something that characterizes his later work as a whole.

demand: the actual fine art of civilized social intercourse that would have justified the flattering intensity of expectation he brought to it in the form of his curiously transposed and subtilized ethical sensibility.

History, it is plain, was already leaving him *déraciné*[3] in his own country, so that it is absurd to censure him, as some American critics have done, for pulling up his roots. He could hardly become deeply rooted elsewhere, but the congenial soil and climate were in Europe rather than in the country of his birth. There is still some idealizing charm about his English country-house in *The Portrait of a Lady*, but that book is one of the classics of the language, and we can't simply regret the conditions that produced something so finely imagined. It is what *The Egoist* is supposed to be.[4] Compare the two books, and the greatness of Henry James as intellectual poet-novelist of 'high civilization' comes out in a way that, even for the most innocently deferential reader, should dispose of Meredith's pretensions for ever. James's wit is real and always natural, his poetry intelligent as well as truly rich, and there is nothing bogus, cheap or vulgar about his idealizations: certain human potentialities are nobly celebrated.

That he is a novelist who has closely studied his fellow-craftsmen is plain – and got from them more than lessons in the craft. It is plain, for instance, in *The Portrait of a Lady* that he sees England through literature. We know that he turned an attentive professional eye on the French masters. He has (in his early mature work) an easy and well-bred technical sophistication, a freedom from any marks of provinciality, and a quiet air of knowing his way about the world that distinguish him from among his contemporaries in the language. If from the English point of view he is unmistakably an American, he is also very much a European.

But there could be no question of his becoming a French master in English, and the help he could get from the Continent towards solving his peculiar problem was obviously limited. It was James who put his finger on the weakness in *Madame Bovary*: the discrepancy between the technical ('aesthetic') intensity, with the implied attribution of interest to the subject, and the actual moral and human paucity of this subject on any mature valuation. His own problem was to justify in terms of an intense interest in sophisticated 'civilization' his New England ethical sensibility. The author who offered a congenial study would have to be very different from Flaubert. It was, as a matter of fact, a very English novelist, the living representative of the great tradition – a writer as unlike Flaubert as George Eliot.

George Eliot's reputation being what it is, this suggestion won't recommend itself to everyone immediately. 'Like most writers, George Eliot could only create from the world of her personal experience – in her case middle- and lower-class rural England of the nineteenth-century Midlands.'* Moreover, she was confined by a Puritanism such as James (apart from the fact that he wasn't lower-middle-class) had left a generation or two behind him: 'the enlightened person of to-day must forget his dislike of Puritanism when he reads George Eliot.' Weighty, provincial, and pledged to the 'school-teacher's virtues', she was not qualified by nature or breeding to appreciate high civilization, even if she had been privileged to make its acquaintance. These seem to be accepted commonplaces – which shows how little even those who write about her have read her work.

Actually, though 'Puritan' is a word used with many intentions, it is misleading to call her a Puritan at all,† and utterly false to say that her 'imagination had to scrape what nourishment it could from the bare bones of Puritan ethics'. There was nothing restrictive or timid about her ethical habit; what she brought from her Evangelical background was a radically reverent attitude towards life, a profound seriousness of the kind that is a first condition of any real intelligence, and an interest in human nature that made her a great psychologist. Such a psychologist, with such a relation to Puritanism, was, of all the novelists open to his study, the one peculiarly relevant to James's interests and problems. That, at any rate, becomes an irresistible proposition when it is added that, in her most mature work, she deals and (in spite of the accepted common-places about her) deals consummately, with just that 'civilization' which was James's chosen field. To say this is to have the confident wisdom of hindsight, for it can be shown, with a conclusiveness rarely possible in these matters, that James did actually go to school to George Eliot.

That is a fair way of putting the significance of the relation between *The Portrait of a Lady* and *Daniel Deronda* that I discuss in my examination of

---

*   All the quotations in this paragraph are from Lord David Cecil.

†   Unless you specify that, of the definitions Lord David Cecil gives us to choose from, the one you have in mind is that given here: 'But the moral code founded on that Puritan theology had soaked itself too deeply into the fibre of her thought and feeling for her to give it up as well. She might not believe in heaven and hell and miracles, but she believed in right and wrong, and man's paramount obligation to follow right, as strictly as if she were Bunyan himself. And her standards of right and wrong were the Puritan standards. She admired truthfulness and chastity and industry and self-restraint, she disapproved of loose living and recklessness and deceit and self-indulgence.' I had better confess that I differ (apparently) from Lord David Cecil in sharing these beliefs, admirations and disapprovals, so that the reader knows my bias at once. And they seem to me favourable to the production of great literature. I will add (exposing myself completely) that the enlightenment or aestheticism or sophistication that feels an amused superiority to them leads, in my view, to triviality and boredom, and that out of triviality comes evil (as L. H. Myers notes in the preface to *The Root and the Flower*, and illustrates in the novel itself, especially in the sections dealing with the 'Camp').

the latter book. That relation demonstrated, nothing more is needed in order to establish the general relation I posit between the two novelists. James's distinctive bent proclaims itself uncompromisingly in what he does with *Daniel Deronda* (on the good part of which – I call it *Gwendolen Harleth*[5] – *The Portrait of a Lady* is a variation; for the plain fact I point out amounts to that). The moral substance of George Eliot's theme is subtilized into something going with the value James sets on 'high civilization'; her study of conscience has disappeared. A charming and intelligent girl, determined to live 'finely', confidently exercises her 'free ethical sensibility' (Mr Winters' phrase) and discovers that she is capable of disastrous misvaluation (which is not surprising, seeing not only how inexperienced she is, but how much an affair of inexplicitnesses, overtones and fine shades is the world of discourse she moves in). It is a tragedy in which, for her, neither remorse is involved, nor, in the ordinary sense, the painful growth of conscience, though no doubt her 'ethical sensibility' matures.

Along the line revealed by the contrast between the two novels James develops an art so unlike George Eliot's that, but for the fact (which seems to have escaped notice) of the relation of *The Portrait of a Lady* to *Daniel Deronda*, it would, argument being necessary, have been difficult to argue at all convincingly that there was the significant relation between the novelists. And I had better insist that I am not concerned to establish *indebtedness*. What I have in mind is the fact of the great tradition and the apartness of the two great novelists above the ruck of Gaskells and Trollopes and Merediths. Of the earlier novelists it was George Eliot alone (if we except the minor relevance of Jane Austen) whose work had a direct and significant bearing on his own problem. It had this bearing because she *was* a great novelist, and because in her maturest work she handled with unprecedented subtlety and refinement the personal relations of sophisticated characters exhibiting the 'civilization' of the 'best society', and used, in so doing, an original psychological notation corresponding to the fineness of her psychological and moral insight. Her moral seriousness was for James very far from a disqualification; it qualified her for a kind of influence that neither Flaubert nor the admired Turgenev could have.

Circumstances discussed above made James peculiarly dependent on literature; the contact with George Eliot's distinctive kind of greatness was correspondingly important for him. It is significant that *Madame de Mauves* (1874), the early story in which he uses something like the theme of *The Portrait of a Lady*, has a wordy quality premonitory (one can't help feeling) of the cobwebbiness that afflicted him in his late phase. We can't doubt that George Eliot counts for something in the incomparably superior concreteness of *The Portrait of a Lady*. In that book, and in its successor, *The Bostonians,* his art is at its most concrete, and least subject to the weakness attendant on his subtlety. It is not derivativeness that is in question, but the relation between two original geniuses. 'We cannot attempt to trace', says Mr Van Wyck Brooks in *The Pilgrimage of Henry James,* 'the astonishing development of a creative faculty which, in the course of a dozen years, transcended the simple plot-maker's art of *The American,* the factitious local-colourism of *Roderick Hudson,* and rendered itself capable of the serene beauty of *The Portrait of a Lady,* the masterly assurance of *The Bostonians,* the mature perfection of *Washington Square.*' – It is more than a guess that, in that development, George Eliot had some part.

The reader is likely to comment, I suppose, on the degree in which my treatment of James is taken up with discussing his limitations and the regrettable aspects of his later development. Since it will also be noted that, of my three novelists, he, in terms of space, gets least attention, it might be concluded that a corresponding relative valuation is implied. I had, then, perhaps better say that there is no such relation intended between valuation and length of treatment. I will not, however, deny that, of the three, James seems to me to give decidedly most cause for dissatisfaction and qualification. He is, all the same, one of the great. His registration of sophisticated human consciousness is one of the classical creative achievements: it *added* something as only genius can. And when he is at his best that something is seen to be of great human significance. He creates an ideal civilized sensibility; a humanity capable of communicating by the finest shades of inflection and implication: a nuance may engage a whole complex moral economy and the perceptive response be the index of a major valuation or choice. Even *The Awkward Age,* in which the extremely developed subtlety of treatment is not as remote as one would wish from the hypertrophy that finally overcame him, seems to me a classic; in no other work can we find anything like that astonishing – in so astonishing a measure successful – use of sophisticated 'society' dialogue.

In considering James's due status, in fact, it is not easy to say just where the interest of the classical artist turns into the interest of the classical 'case'. But it seems to me obvious that the 'case' becomes in some places boring to the point of unreadableness. Yet there is a tacit conspiracy to admire some of the works that fall, partly, at any rate (wholly, one must conclude, for the admirers who risk explanatory comment on them), under this description. And here is sufficient reason why an attempt to promote a due appreciation of James's genius should give a good deal of discriminatory attention to the tendencies that, as they develop, turn vital subtlety into something else.

When we come to Conrad we can't, by way of insisting that he is indeed significantly 'in' the tradition – in and of it, neatly and conclusively relate him to any one English novelist. Rather, we have to stress his foreignness – that he was a Pole, whose first other language was French. I remember remarking to André Chevrillon how surprising a choice it was on Conrad's part to write in English, especially seeing he was so clearly a student of the French masters. And I remember the reply, to the effect that it wasn't at all surprising, since Conrad's work couldn't have been written in French. M. Chevrillon, with the authority of a perfect bilingual, went on to explain in terms of the characteristics of the two languages why it had to be English. Conrad's themes and interests demanded the concreteness and action – the dramatic energy – of English. We might go further and say that Conrad chose to write his novels in English for the reasons that led him to become a British Master Mariner.

I am not, in making this point, concurring in the emphasis generally laid on the Prose Laureate of the Merchant Service. What needs to be stressed is the great novelist. Conrad's great novels, if they deal with the sea at all, deal with it only incidentally. But the Merchant Service is for him both a spiritual fact and a spiritual symbol, and the interests that made it so for him control and animate his art everywhere. Here, then, we have a master of the English language, who chose it for its distinctive qualities and because of the moral tradition associated with it, and whose concern with art – he being like Jane Austen and George Eliot and Henry James an innovator in 'form' and method – is the servant of a profoundly serious interest in life. To justify our speaking of such a novelist as in the tradition, that represented by those three, we are not called on to establish particular relations with any one of them. Like James, he brought a great deal from outside, but it was of the utmost importance to him that he found a serious art of fiction there in English, and that there *were*, in English, great novelists to study. He drew from English literature what he needed, and learnt in that peculiar way of genius which is so different from imitation. And for us, who have *him* as well as the others, there he is, unquestionably a constitutive part of the tradition, belonging in the full sense.

As being technically sophisticated he may be supposed to have found fortifying stimulus in James, whom he is quite unlike (though James, in his old age, was able to take a connoisseur's interest in *Chance* and appreciate with a professional eye the sophistication of the 'doing'). But actually, the one influence at all obvious is that of a writer at the other end of the scale from sophistication, Dickens. As I point out in my discussion of him, Conrad is in certain respects so like Dickens that it is difficult to say for just how much influence Dickens counts. He is undoubtedly there in the London of *The Secret Agent:* though – except for the extravagant *macabre* of the cab-journey, where the writer was in fact F. M. Ford, and (from the same hand – there was a desperate push to get the book finished) one or two minor instances of mannerism – he has been transmuted into Conrad. This co-presence of obvious influence with assimilation suggests that Dickens may have counted for more in Conrad's mature art than seems at first probable: it suggests that Dickens may have encouraged the development in Conrad's art of that energy of vision and registration in which they are akin. ('When people say that Dickens exaggerates', says Santayana, 'it seems to me that they can have no eyes and no ears. They probably have only *notions* of what things and people are; they accept them conventionally, at their diplomatic value.') We may reasonably, too, in the same way see some Dickensian influence in Conrad's use of melodrama, or what would have been melodrama in Dickens; for in Conrad the end is a total significance of a profoundly serious kind.

The reason for not including Dickens in the line of great novelists is implicit in this last phrase. The kind of greatness in question has been sufficiently defined. That Dickens was a great genius and is permanently among the classics is certain. But the genius was that of a great entertainer, and he had for the most part no profounder responsibility as a creative artist than this description suggests. Praising him warmly in *Soliloquies in England*, Santayana, in concluding, says: 'In every English-speaking home, in the four quarters of the globe, parents and children would do well to read Dickens aloud of a winter's evening.' The note is right and significant. The adult mind doesn't as a rule find in Dickens a challenge to an unusual and sustained seriousness. I can think of only one of his books in which his distinctive creative genius is controlled throughout to a unifying and organizing significance, and that is *Hard Times*, which seems, because of its unusualness and comparatively small scale, to have escaped recognition for the great thing it is.

It has a kind of perfection as a work of art that we don't associate with Dickens – a perfection that is one with the sustained and complete seriousness for which among his productions it is unique. Though in length it makes a good-sized modern novel, it is on a small scale for Dickens: it leaves no room for the usual repetitive over-doing and loose inclusiveness. It is plain that he felt no temptation to these, he was too urgently possessed by his themes; the themes were too rich, too tightly knit in their variety and too commanding. Certain key characteristics of Victorian civilization had clearly come home to him with overwhelming force, embodied in concrete manifestations that suggested to him connexions and significances he had never realized so fully before. The fable is perfect; the symbolic and representative values are inevitable, and, sufficiently plain at once, yield fresh subtleties as the action develops naturally in its convincing historical way.

In Gradgrind and Bounderby we have, in significant relation, two aspects of Victorian Utilitarianism. In Gradgrind it is a serious creed, devoutly held, and so, if repellent (as the name conveys), not wholly unrespectable; but we are shown Gradgrind as on the most intimate and uncritical terms with Josiah Bounderby, in whom we have the grossest and crassest, the most utterly unspiritual egotism, and the most blatant thrusting and bullying, to which a period of 'rugged individualism' gave scope. Gradgrind, in fact, marries his daughter to Bounderby. Yet he is represented as a kind of James Mill; an intellectual who gives his children, on theory, an education that reminds us in a very significant way of the *Autobiography* of the younger Mill. And it is hardly possible to question the justice of this vision of the tendency of James Mill's kind of Utilitarianism, so blind in its onesidedness, so unaware of its bent and its blindness. The generous uncalculating spontaneity, the warm flow of life, towards which Gradgrindery, practical and intellectual, must be hostile, is symbolized by Sleary's Horse-riding.

The richness in symbolic significance of *Hard Times* is far from adequately suggested by this account. The prose is that of one of the greatest masters of English, and the dialogue – very much a test in such an undertaking – is consummate; beautifully natural in its stylization. But there is only one *Hard Times* in the Dickensian *œuvre*.

Though the greatness of *Hard Times* passed unnoticed, Dickens couldn't fail to have a wide influence. We have remarked his presence in *The Secret Agent*. It is there again, in a minor way, in George Eliot, in some of her less felicitous characterization; and it is there in Henry James, most patently, perhaps, in *The Princess Casamassima*, but most importantly in *Roderick Hudson*. It is there once more, and even more interestingly, in D. H. Lawrence, in *The Lost Girl*. The ironic humour, and the presentation in general, in the first part of that book bear a clear relation to the Dickensian, but are incomparably more mature, and belong to a total serious significance. [...]

Notes

1   Cf. p. 34 above.
2   Austen, Eliot, James and Conrad – the four great novelists of *The Great Tradition*.
3   Rootless.
4   George Meredith, *The Egoist* (1879).

5   Leavis thought *Daniel Deronda* was two novels in one: a good novel about the life of Gwendolen, and a bad one about Jewish history.

Chapter Notes

1   F. R. Leavis, *Education and the University: A Sketch for an 'English School'* (London: Chatto and Windus, 1943), 40.
2   F. R. Leavis, *Valuation in Criticism and other Essays*, ed. G. Singh (Cambridge: Cambridge University Press, 1986), 173.
3   Leavis, *Education and the University*, 33.
4   Terry Eagleton, *Literary Theory: An Introduction* (Oxford: Blackwell, 1983), 31; italic is original.
5   Letter to *The Times*, 8 October 1968, printed in John Tasker, ed., *Letters in Criticism by F. R. Leavis* (London: Chatto and Windus, 1974), 130.
6   F. R. Leavis, *Mass Civilization and Minority Culture* (Cambridge: Minority, 1930), 3.
7   Tasker, ed., *Letters in Criticism by F. R. Leavis*, 130.
8   Leavis periodically drew comparisons between his own work as a critic and Arnold's. See, for instance, *Mass Civilization and Minority Culture*, 3.
9   For an important preliminary statement about the significance of the novel as a genre, see F. R. Leavis, 'The Novel as Dramatic Poem (I): *Hard Times*', *Scrutiny*, 14 (1946–7), 185–203.
10   Leavis, *Valuation in Criticism*, 175.
11   Catherine Belsey, 'Re-reading the Great Tradition', in Peter Widdowson, ed., *Re-reading English* (London: Methuen, 1982), 129.
12   F. R. Leavis, ed., *A Selection from 'Scrutiny'*, 2 vols (London: Cambridge University Press, 1968), ii. 299.
13   F. R. and Q. D. Leavis, *Dickens the Novelist* (New Brunswick, NJ: Rutgers University Press, 1979), ix.
14   Ibid.

Further Reading

Catherine Belsey, 'Re-reading the Great Tradition', pp. [121]–135 in Peter Widdowson, ed. (below): argues against the implied elitist politics of Leavis's critical practice, and proposes a feminist reading of George Eliot's *Daniel Deronda* to emphasize that meaning is produced rather than recognized in literary texts, depending on the ideological situation of the critic.

F. R. Leavis and Q. D. Leavis, *Dickens the Novelist* (London: Chatto and Windus, 1970): a discussion of *Dombey and Son, David Copperfield, Bleak House, Hard Times, Little Dorrit, Great Expectations*, and the illustrations to the novels.

Q. D. Leavis, *Collected Essays*, ed. G. Singh, 3 vols (Cambridge: Cambridge University Press, 1983–9): involves much discussion of nineteenth-century fiction, including, for instance, her prescient enthusiasm for Margaret Oliphant. Also her influential argument about Jane Austen's engagement with the wider world is here.

Q. D. Leavis, *Fiction and the Reading Public* (London: Chatto and Windus, 1965; first pub. 1932): ground-breaking study of the readers of fiction, arguing that 'the general reading public of the twentieth century is no longer in touch with the best literature of its own day or of the past' and that 'It is almost impossible for the novel which is an aesthetic experience to become popular.'

Ian MacKillop, *F. R. Leavis: A Life in Criticism* (London: Lane/Penguin, 1995): sympathetic biography, oddly abrupt and abbreviated in places, and fairly non-discursive, but useful on Leavis's tense relations with Cambridge as he endeavoured to forge a new identity for English studies.

Francis Mulhern, *The Moment of 'Scrutiny'* (London: New Left Books, 1979): trenchant Marxist approach to the '*mortmain*' [dead hand] of *Scrutiny* on English studies (p. 328), though argues that socialists should at least honour the fact that Leavis's critical practice was 'militant, committed, interventionist'. [The journal *Scrutiny*, in which Leavis had a leading role, began in May 1932, under the editorship of Donald Culver and L. C. Knights, as an effort to counter the 'general dissolution of standards' both in criticism and in life.]

Anne Samson, *F. R. Leavis* (Hemel Hempstead: Harvester Wheatsheaf, 1992): in the Modern Cultural Theorists series, a deft introduction considering Leavis and the growth of English studies, Leavis's world picture, English as a university subject, and literary theory and constituting the canon.

Peter Widdowson, ed., *Re-reading English* (London: Methuen, 1982): 'an attempt to take stock of the current state of that area in higher education traditionally referred to as "English" or "Literary Studies", and to redirect it in response to pressing social and political needs.' Evaluates Leavisite assumptions and Christopher Ricks's statement that 'it is our job to teach and uphold the canon of English literature.'

See also Further Reading for chapter 1.

3

Feminism and the Victorian Novel in the 1970s

Ellen Moers – Elaine Showalter – Sandra M. Gilbert and Susan Gubar

The nineteenth-century novel, with its key female practitioners and enormous terrain, proved particularly susceptible to the critical agenda of the New Feminism in North America in the 1960s and 1970s, and the Victorians were sufficiently close in time for critics in this field to read the female novelists as feminist precursors and to see in them admirable models of protest and dissent. The feminist critical work of the 1970s was energized by political commitment and was far-reaching in its influence on the practices of university literary criticism and its assumptions about gender, as well as in its more local effects on the study of the nineteenth-century novel. Indeed, it is almost impossible to read some individual Victorian novelists now, especially the work of the Brontës, without being conscious at some level of the critical approaches defined with vigour in the United States in the 1970s.

THE INFLUENCE OF 1970s' FEMINISM So extensive was the influence of this feminism on reading the Victorian novel and imagining the gender politics of the century that readers may now be familiar with the outlines of the arguments without having read the source texts at all. Some of the ideas of the North American movement, dynamized by Kate Millett's powerfully trenchant *Sexual Politics* (1970), have entered the general critical consciousness and its assumptions about the oppressed state of female creativity in the nineteenth century. The arguments have not gone without challenge – the most important critiques of the New Feminism's views of Victorian fiction came from post-structuralists in the 1980s, and postcolonialists, cultural historians and feminist revisionists in the 1990s – but they have proved tenacious. For some, too much so. Their main points of significance were as follows. They projected a view of the Victorian period as 'patriarchal', as ruled by men to their own advantage in all aspects of public life. They argued that women, accordingly, were multiply oppressed but concentrated on the oppression of artistic creativity and self-expression. They saw Victorian women writers struggling against the prohibitions of patriarchy and inventing strategies to overcome it. The New Feminism also argued that Victorian fiction by women authors was autobiographical in its reflection of female oppression, seeing episodes of conflict in the novels as dramatizations of the wider cultural scene of patriarchy's oppression of women. A lasting effect of North American feminism was to propel the question of female creativity and the notion of patriarchy into the centre of Victorian studies.

The two most consequential works of 1970s' feminism as far as Victorian fiction was concerned both became classics of innovative literary criticism (though their authors would point to the irony of books originally radical in aim becoming classics in the literary establishment). They were Elaine Showalter's *A Literature of their Own: British Woman Novelists from Brontë to Lessing* (1977) and Sandra M. Gilbert and Susan Gubar's co-authored *The Madwoman in the Attic: The Woman Writer and the Nineteenth-century Literary Imagination* (1979). The projects of these gynocritics (literary critics concerned with women writers) were distinct but had important common purposes in constructing a view of the Victorian period as one in which women writers struggled with the forces of patriarchy towards self-expression.

An important precursor of Showalter's book, and a high-profile text from the women's movement more generally, was Ellen Moers's *Literary Women* (1976). A witty and lively study, this ushered the notion of a woman's tradition, a canon consisting of female writers in negotiation with other female writers only and distinct from the tradition of men, into the critical community. *Literary Women* was a celebration of this corpus of women writers, concentrating on the eighteenth, nineteenth and twentieth centuries, in debate with each other across the centuries. Moers described her study as 'plainly a celebration of the great women who have spoken for us all'.[1] Moers's work, popular in its day, fell out of favour with later readers whose feminism was different from the distinctive ideas and needs of the 1970s. In seeking to recover lost voices of female experience, *Literary Women* took for granted a universal female subjectivity – 'spoken for us all' – and a straightforward relationship between text and author that feminist critics in the 1980s, under the influence of post-structuralism with its rejection of the author as central producer of meaning, found hard to take. Helen Taylor said in her 1986 preface to the reissued book (Moers died of cancer in 1979) that it was problematically a 'liberal humanist text which accepts as unproblematic the relationship of author and work, and uses biography and history in fairly simplistic and unmediated ways'.[2] Cognate problems were found in the 1980s in Showalter's study, discussed below. Critics working with the terms of identity politics in the 1990s also found difficulties with Moers's approach – as with much work from the women's movement of the 1970s – and deplored its ethnocentricity and heterosexism (see also the reception of Gilbert and Gubar, below).

ELLEN MOERS'S *LITERARY WOMEN* (1976)

Ellen Moers's conception of the female tradition contested previous constructions of the canon as patriarchal, as having excluded women from the ranks of prestigious literature, and insisted that the gender of the author played the determining role in literary production. The question of reconfiguring the canon provided the point of contact with Elaine Showalter's work. The impulse of *A Literature of their Own* was to challenge the notion of a tradition of British fiction dominated by men (or of a canon that did not acknowledge gender as a significant element). Taking a narrower chronological field than Moers, Showalter (b. 1941) presented the case for an explicitly female tradition in nineteenth and twentieth-century writing. George Saintsbury and the literary historians at the beginning of the twentieth century (see pp. 21–9 above) had, of course, considered the function of tradition, understood as generic relationships between literary texts extracted from their non-literary historical context, when mapping the Victorian novel. F. R. Leavis (see chapter 2) had invested the concept with serious moral gravity. But neither approaches had paid attention to gender and, more particularly, to the way in which traditions had habitually excluded most women writers. In the 1980s and 1990s, the literary canon would be challenged across the board for excluding colonial literature, gay literature, working-class writing, popular literature and regional writing. But in the 1970s, the most urgent task was to include the work of women.

ELAINE SHOWALTER AND THE FEMALE TRADITION

Elaine Showalter made gender a priority in revising the idea of tradition. She agreed with Ellen Moers, and more specifically with Patricia Meyer Spacks in *The Female Imagination* (1975), that there was a 'special female self-awareness [...] through literature in every period',[3] and endeavoured to show 'how the development of this tradition is similar to the development of any literary subculture'.[4] Showalter did not explicitly argue for an innate difference in female and male experience or imagination, but none the less said that there was a marked and continual difference between men's writing and women's. This was a fundamental feature of her gynocritical revisionism that helped change the map of Victorian fiction. But it seemed to fudge an important question. Feminist readers of the 1980s, having taken on board Foucauldian ideas about the formation of subjectivities, certainly found problems with exactly what Showalter's position on gender was, and – this was to happen to Gilbert and Gubar in the post-structuralist revolution also – asked whether she was hiding essentialist statements about differences between men and women. Concentrating on writers who were united by their gender alone, Showalter also conflated differences, contests of viewpoints, and the social and historical specificities of each author.

Showalter's criticism assumed a relationship between fiction and personal experience that was straightforward. Her work was thus open to criticism similar to that levelled in the 1980s and 1990s at the biographizing approach of Moers and Gibert and Gubar as the critical agenda in the academy changed to become suspicious of authorial presence. Showalter perceived nineteenth-century literature by women as expressing with eloquence the social and political situation of female writers in the reign of Queen Victoria and beyond. She was staking out a clear relationship between literature and the society from which it emerged, necessary because she was writing in the early stages of a radical movement's self-definition. Accordingly, she was not concerned to explore complex, ambiguous or contradictory relationships between literature and experience or between literature and ideology; nor was she interested in thinking of the reader as a producer of meaning. An example of her perception of the correspondence between literary productions and the position of female authors in society is the assumption in the extract below that the fate of Dorothea at the end of George Eliot's *Middlemarch* (1871–2) directly corresponded to Eliot's professional position and sense of compromise necessitated by her position as female author. By extension, Showalter made Dorothea's plight refer to the situation of female novelists through the whole of the early and mid-Victorian period (for a related view of *Middlemarch* as a novel about female authorship, see N. N. Feltes's work, pp. 284–5 below). Showalter's influential and often-repeated argument at the beginning of the extract that the adoption of the male pseudonym was a sign of patriarchal oppression and the role-playing required by women to succeed in the Victorian literary marketplace was problematized by Catherine Judd in 1995 (see pp. 289–302 below).

Showalter, now a professor at Princeton, divided the nineteenth-century female tradition into three categories which she saw common to all 'literary subcultures'.[5] 'First', she said:

> there is a prolonged phase of *imitation* of the prevailing modes of the dominant tradition, and *internalisation* of its standards of art and its views on social roles. Second, there is a phase of *protest* against these standards and values, and *advocacy* of minority rights and values, including a demand for autonomy. Finally, there is a phase of *self-discovery*, a turning inward freed from some of the dependency of opposition, a search for identity.[6]

For the female novelists of the nineteenth century, these stages were best labelled '*Feminine, Feminist*, and *Female*'.[7] This taxonomy determined her view of the century.

In the extract below, Showalter argues for the characteristics of the first two of these three categories in the 'subculture' of nineteenth-century literature by women (the third falls mostly outside the Victorian period). The *feminine* novelists of the period, including Elizabeth Gaskell, the Brontës and George Eliot, she proposes, were working against their society's understanding of what a woman should do and against their own internalized anxiety about social transgression. She divides this group itself into three, but, throughout,

DISCUSSION OF SHOWALTER'S *A LITERATURE OF THEIR OWN* (1977)

her model of the mid-Victorian period is one of the patriarchal oppression of female creativity (her view can be contrasted with David Cecil's view that inhibition was a product of Evangelicalism, see p. 39 above). As a consequence, the feminine novelists suffered guilt over their writing, and this found expression in their treatment of those female characters who were ambitious or independent. They habitually undermined, punished or married them (another kind of punishment) in an effort obliquely to resolve their own anxiety. Elizabeth Barrett Browning's *Aurora Leigh* (1857) evidenced this situation as Aurora, at the end of the autobiographical novel-in-verse, is unable to live, in Showalter's analysis, with the 'guilt of self-centred ambition'. She marries Romney to assuage it. The assumption that there is a link between the author's position in the matrix of power in mid-century society and the characters of her verse or fiction is again clear.

Showalter notes the censorship and restriction impinging on the *feminine* writer, and suggests that conflict in her literature is always really about gender. Representations of class struggle – such as in the work of Gaskell – are thought to be coded representations of gender conflict, of necessity disguised as something unlikely to endanger the novelist's position as womanly. Showalter was taking an interpretative assumption from Marxism – that all forms of opposition and antagonism can be related to a central form of conflict – and changing that central conflict from class to gender (for another example of this sort of Marxist manoeuvre, see pp. 284–5 below).

The literature of *feminism* commences, Showalter says, with the death of George Eliot. *Feminist* writers, including those now known as ' "New Woman" writers, are 'not important artists', she continues, but they were valuable in their contribution to female independence, and even in their 'outspoken hostility to men'. Showalter's regard for the value of the *feminist* writers' politics, their exploration of womanhood and their declaration of independence in the nineteenth century, reveals to what extent her evaluative criteria are determined by her political sympathies. Indeed, this question of evaluation touches on another challenging feature of Showalter's analysis evident throughout the book and visible to an extent in the extract given below, which is its position on history. Showalter arranged the history of Victorian literature in what was essentially a Whig narrative, a history that was progressive (though certainly not a *simple* progression). The movement was broadly from literary imitation to a greater freedom; it was a narrative that revealed increasing liberty in which early Victorians led up to the more liberal modern. Showalter was certain that even the feminist analysis improved: it was once 'naïve and incoherent', as she says below, but it became shrewder as it reached the twentieth century.

The appropriateness of this approach to history has been debated. One problem was that Showalter's understanding of history avoided asking the question whether the Victorians would have seen it in the same way. Her history marshalled the Victorian novel and Victorian feminism into a pattern but did not inquire whether that pattern would be comprehensible to the Victorians themselves (for more of this angle on criticism, historicism and Victorian social-problem fiction, see pp. 178–85). For example, what appeared to the 1970s' feminist as 'naïve and incoherent' feminism does not tell us whether it was in Victorian terms. Victorian feminism had, of course, different priorities and strategies from those of the 1970s, and seeing it only as inadequate ran the risk of anachronism, of mistakenly judging the past only by the terms and conditions of the present.

Later feminists who absorbed the implications of post-structuralism developed a rhetoric to defend themselves against these charges of ahistoricality. Feminists such as Catherine Belsey – whose approach to Leavis's *Great Tradition* was discussed in chapter 2 and whose reading of the politics of classic realism is analysed in chapter 4 – argued in 1982, under the banner of post-structuralism, that efforts to disinter 'authentic' meanings from texts were doomed and that all literary productions were interpreted first and foremost in the light of the culture in which they were read. Criticism was not a matter of recognizing meaning; it was rather about openly acknowledging how each reader produced meaning for himself or herself. If this argument is accepted, the question of ahistoricality vanishes.

Despite problems with Showalter's analysis and historiography, her influential study presented for many readers a persuasive way of perceiving Victorian women's fiction, and a clearly defined narrative that was attractive partly because of its clarity, in which to situate individual practitioners and their work. Showalter's championing of a female tradition, moreover, helped impel an enormous amount of literary recuperation, the scholarly recovery of lost female voices from the nineteenth century in all genres, which still continues. Showalter's *A Literature of their Own* was a vital force in the reconfiguration of the Victorian canon in modern times and in placing feminism in the foreground of the study of Victorian fiction.

1980s'
RESPONSE TO
SHOWALTER

Extract from Elaine Showalter, *A Literature of their Own: British Women Novelists from Brontë to Lessing* (Princeton, NJ: Princeton University Press, 1977), 19–32.

[…] Thus, in talking about the situation of the feminine novelists, I have begun with the women born after 1800, who began to publish fiction during the 1840s when the job of the novelist was becoming a

recognizable profession. One of the many indications that this generation saw the will to write as a vocation in direct conflict with their
status as women is the appearance of the male pseudonym.[1] Like Eve's
fig leaf, the male pseudonym signals the loss of innocence. In its radical
understanding of the role-playing required by women's effort to participate in the mainstream of literary culture, the pseudonym is a strong
marker of the historical shift.

There were three generations of nineteenth-century feminine novelists. The first, born between 1800 and 1820, included all the women
who are identified with the Golden Age of the Victorian authoress: the
Brontës, Mrs Gaskell, Elizabeth Barrett Browning, Harriet Martineau,
and George Eliot. The members of this group, whose coevals were
Florence Nightingale, Mary Carpenter, Angela Burdett, and other
pioneer professionals, were what sociologists call 'female role innov-
ators'; they were breaking new ground and creating new possibilities.
The second generation, born between 1820 and 1840, included Charlotte Yonge, Dinah Mulock Craik, Margaret Oliphant, and Elizabeth
Lynn Linton; these women followed in the footsteps of the great,
consolidating their gains, but were less dedicated and original. The
third generation, born between 1840 and 1860, included sensation
novelists and children's book writers. They seemed to cope effortlessly
with the double roles of woman and professional, and to enjoy sexual
fulfillment as well as literary success. Businesslike, unconventional,
efficient, and productive, they moved into editorial and publishing
positions as well as writing.

By the time the women of the first generation had entered upon their
careers, there was already a sense of what the 'feminine' novel meant in
terms of genres. By the 1840s women writers had adopted a variety of
popular genres, and were specializing in novels of fashionable life,
education, religion, and community, which Vineta Colby subsumes
under the heading 'domestic realism.' In all these novels, according to
Inga-Stina Ewbank, 'the central pre-occupation . . . is with the woman
as an influence on others within her domestic and social circle. It was
in this preoccupation that the typical woman novelist of the 1840s
found her proper sphere: in using the novel to demonstrate (by assumption rather than exploration of standards of womanliness) *woman's*
proper sphere.'* A double standard of literary criticism had also developed [. . .] with a special set of terms and requirements for fiction by
women.

---

* Inga-Stina Ewbank, *Their Proper Sphere: A Study of the Brontë Sisters as Early-Victorian
Female Novelists* (London, 1966), 41.

There was a place for such fiction, but even the most conservative and devout women novelists, such as Charlotte Yonge and Dinah Craik, were aware that the 'feminine' novel also stood for feebleness, ignorance, prudery, refinement, propriety, and sentimentality, while the feminine novelist was portrayed as vain, publicity-seeking, and self-assertive. At the same time that Victorian reviewers assumed that women readers and women writers were dictating the content of fiction, they deplored the pettiness and narrowness implied by a feminine value system. 'Surely it is very questionable,' wrote Fitzjames Stephen, 'whether it is desirable that no novels should be written except those fit for young ladies to read.'*

Victorian feminine novelists thus found themselves in a double bind. They felt humiliated by the condescension of male critics and spoke intensely of their desire to avoid special treatment and achieve genuine excellence, but they were deeply anxious about the possibility of appearing unwomanly. Part of the conflict came from the fact that, rather than confronting the values of their society, these women novelists were competing for its rewards. For women, as for other subcultures, literature became a symbol of achievement.

In the face of this dilemma, women novelists developed several strategies, both personal and artistic. Among the personal reactions was a persistent self-deprecation of themselves as women, sometimes expressed as humility, sometimes as coy assurance-seeking, and sometimes as the purest self-hatred. In a letter to John Blackwood, Mrs Oliphant expressed doubt about 'whether in your most manly and masculine of magazines a womanish story-teller like myself may not become wearisome.'† The novelists publicly proclaimed, and sincerely believed, their antifeminism. By working in the home, by preaching submission and self-sacrifice, and by denouncing female self-assertiveness, they worked to atone for their own will to write.

Vocation – the will to write – nonetheless required a genuine transcendence of female identity. Victorian women were not accustomed to *choosing* a vocation; womanhood was a vocation in itself. The evangelically inspired creed of work did affect women, even though it had not been primarily directed toward them. Like men, women were urged to 'bear their part in the *work* of life.'‡ Yet for men, the gospel of work

* *Saturday Review*, 4 (July 11, 1857), 40–1. See also David Masson, *British Novelists and their Styles* (Cambridge, 1859), 134.
† *Autobiography and Letters of Mrs M. O. W. Oliphant*, ed. Mrs Harry Cogshill (New York, 1899), 160.
‡ 'An Enquiry into the State of Girls' Fashionable Schools', *Fraser's*, 31 (1845), 703.

satisfied both self-interest and the public interest. In pursing their ambitions, they fulfilled social expectations.

For women, however, work meant labor for *others*. Work, in the sense of self-development, was in direct conflict with the subordination and repression inherent in the feminine ideal. The self-centeredness implicit in the act of writing made this career an especially threatening one; it required an engagement with feeling and a cultivation of the ego rather than its negation. The widely circulated treatises of Hannah More and Sarah Ellis translated the abstractions of 'women's mission' into concrete programs of activity, which made writing appear selfish, unwomanly, and unchristian. '"What shall I do to gratify myself – to be admired – or to vary the tenor of my existence?"' are not, according to Mrs Ellis, 'questions which a woman of right feelings asks on first awakening to the avocations of the day.' Instead she recommends visiting the sick, fixing breakfast for anyone setting on a journey in order to spare the servant, or general 'devotion to the good of the whole family.' 'Who can believe,' she asks fervently, 'that days, months, and years spent in a continual course of thought and action similar to this, will not produce a powerful effect upon the character?'* Of course it did; one notices first of all that feminine writers like Elizabeth Barrett, 'Charlotte Elizabeth,' Elizabeth M. Sewell, and Mrs Ellis herself had to overcome deep-seated guilt about authorship. Many found it necessary to justify their work by recourse to some external stimulus or ideology. In their novels, the heroine's aspirations for a full, independent life are undermined, punished, or replaced by marriage.

Elizabeth Barrett Browning's *Aurora Leigh* (1857) is one of the few autobiographical discussions of feminine role conflict. Aurora's struggle to become an artist is complicated by the self-hatred in which she has been educated, by her internalized convictions of her weakness and narcissism, and by the gentle scorn of her suitor Romney. She defies him, however, and invokes divine authority to reject his proposal that she become his helpmeet:

> You misconceive the question like a man
> Who sees the woman as the complement
> Of his sex merely. You forget too much
> That every creature, female as the male,
> Stands single in responsible act and thought . . .
> I too have my vocation, – work to do,
> The heavens and earth have set me.
>
> (Book II, 460–6)

---

* Sarah Ellis, *The Women of England* (New York, 1844), 9.

Aurora succeeds as a poet. But she marries Romney in the end, having learned that as a woman she cannot cope with the guilt of self-centered ambition.[2] It is significant that Romney has been blinded in an accident before she marries him, not only because he has thereby received first-hand knowledge of being handicapped and can empathize with her, but also because he then needs her help and can provide her with suitably feminine work. When Aurora tells Romney that 'No perfect artist is developed here / From any imperfect woman' (Book IX, 648–9) she means more than the perfection of love and motherhood; she means also the perfection of self-sacrifice. This conflict remains a significant one for English novelists up to the present; it is a major theme for women novelists from Charlotte Brontë to Penelope Mortimer. Male novelists like Thackeray, who came from an elite class, also felt uncomfortable with the aggressive self-promotion of the novelist's career. As Donald Stone points out:

> Thackeray's ambivalent feelings towards Becky Sharp indicate the degree to which he attempted to suppress or make light of his own literary talents. The energies which make her (for a time) a social success are akin to those which made him a creative artist. In the hands of a major woman novelist, like Jane Austen or George Eliot, the destructive moral and social implications of Becky's behavior would have been defined more clearly and more urgently. Jane Austen's dissection of Lydia Bennet, and George Eliot's demolition of Rosamond Vincy, for example, indicate both how and why the defense of the status quo – insofar as women of the nineteenth century were concerned – was most earnestly and elaborately performed by women writers. Their heroines are hardly concerned with self-fulfillment in the modern sense of the term, and if they have severely limited possibilities in life it is because their authors saw great danger in, plus a higher alternative to, the practice of self-assertiveness.*

The dilemma is stated by George Eliot in *Romola* as the question of where 'the duty of obedience ends and the duty of resistance begins.'† Yet this was the question any Victorian woman with the will to write would have had to ask herself: what did God intend her to do with her life? Where did obedience to her father and husband end, and the responsibility of self-fulfillment become paramount? The problem of obedience and resistance that women had to solve in their own lives before they could begin to write crops up in their novels as the heroine's

---

* Donald Stone, 'Victorian Feminism and the Nineteenth-century Novel', *Women's Studies*, 1 (1972), 69.
† *Romola* (New York, 1898), II, ch. XXIII, p. 157.

moral crisis. The forms that the crisis takes in feminine fiction are realistically mundane – should Margaret, in Mrs Gaskell's *North and South*, lie to protect her brother? Should Ethel May, in Charlotte Yonge's *Daisy Chain*, give up studying Greek to nurse her father? – but the sources were profound, and were connected to the women novelists' sense of epic life. At the same time that they recognized the modesty of their own struggles, women writers recognized their heroism. 'A new Theresa will hardly have the opportunity of reforming a conventual life,' wrote George Eliot in *Middlemarch*, 'any more than a new Antigone will spend her heroic piety in daring all for a brother's burial: the medium in which their ardent deeds took shape is forever gone. But we insignificant people with our daily words and acts are preparing the lives of many Dorotheas, some of which may present a far sadder sacrifice than that of the Dorothea whose story we know.'*

The training of Victorian girls in repression, concealment, and self-censorship was deeply inhibiting, especially for those who wanted to write. As one novelist commented in 1860, 'Women are greater dissemblers than men when they wish to conceal their own emotions. By habit, moral training, and modern education, they are obliged to do so. The very first lessons of infancy teach them to repress their feelings, control their very thoughts.'† The verbal range permitted to English gentlewomen amounted almost to a special language. The verbal inhibitions that were part of the upbringing of a lady were reinforced by the critics' vigilance. 'It is an immense loss,' lamented Alice James, 'to have all robust and sustaining expletives refined away from one.'‡ 'Coarseness' was the term Victorian readers used to rebuke unconventional language in women's literature. It could refer to the 'damns' in *Jane Eyre*, the dialect in *Wuthering Heights*, the slang of Rhoda Broughton's heroines, the colloquialisms in *Aurora Leigh*, or more generally to the moral tone of a work, such as the 'vein of perilous voluptuousness' one alert critic detected in *Adam Bede*.§ John Keble censored Charlotte Yonge's fiction, taking the greatest care 'that no hint of "coarseness" should sully the purity of Charlotte's writings. Thus he would not allow Theodora in *Heartsease* to say that "really she had a heart, though some people thought it was only a machine for pumping blood." He also transformed

* *Middlemarch*, ed. Gordon S. Haight (Boston, 1956), 'Finale,' p. 612.
† Jane Vaughan Pinckney, *Tacita Tacit*, 11, p. 276; quoted in Myron Brightfield, *Victorian England in its Novels* (Los Angeles, 1968), iv. 27.
‡ *The Diary of Alice James*, ed. Leon Edel (New York, 1934), 66.
§ *British Quarterly Review*, 45 (1867), 164. On the term 'coarseness,' see Ewbank, *Their Proper Sphere*, 46–7.

the "circle" of the setting sun into an "orb" and a "coxcomb" into a "jackanapes".* While verbal force, wit, and originality in women was criticized, a bland and gelatinous prose won applause. 'She writes as an English gentlewoman should write,' the *North British Review* complimented Anne Marsh in 1849; 'her pages are absolutely like green pastures.'† Reduced to a pastoral flatness, deprived of a language in which to describe their bodies or the events of their bodies, denied the expression of pain as well as the expression of pleasure, women writers appeared deficient in passion.

It is easy to understand why many readers took the absence of expression for the absence of feeling. In 'The False Morality of Lady Novelists,' W. R. Greg argued that woman's sexual innocence would prevent her ever writing a great novel:

> Many of the saddest and deepest truths in the strange science of sexual affection are to her mysteriously and mercifully veiled and can only be purchased at such a fearful cost that we cannot wish it otherwise. The inevitable consequence however is that in treating of that science she labours under all the disadvantages of partial study and superficial insight. She is describing a country of which she knows only the more frequented and the safer roads, with a few of the sweeter scenes and the prettier by-paths and more picturesque detours which be not far from the broad and beaten thoroughfares; while the rockier and loftier mountains, and more rugged tracts, the more sombre valleys, and the darker and more dangerous chasms, are never trodden by her feet, and scarcely ever dreamed of by her fancy.‡

The results of restrictive education and intensive conditioning were taken as innate evidence of natural preference. In an ironic twist, many reviewers who had paternally barred the way to the sombre valleys, the darker chasms, and the more rugged tracts also blamed women for the emasculation of male prose, finding, like the *Prospective Review*, that the 'writing of men is in danger of being marked' by 'the delicacy and even fastidiousness of expression which is *natural* to educated women' [my italics].§ When G. H. Lewes complained in 1852 that the literature of women was 'too much a literature of imitation' and demanded that women should express 'what they have really known, felt and suffered,'** he was asking

---

* Margaret Mare and Alicia C. Percival, *Victorian Best-seller: The World of Charlotte Yonge* (London, 1947), 133.

† James Lorimer, 'Noteworthy Novels,' *North British Review*, 11 (1849), 257.

‡ W. R. Greg, 'The False Morality of Lady Novelists', *National Review*, 7 (1859), 149.

§ 'Puseyite Novels', *Prospective Review*, 6 (1850), 498.

** 'The Lady Novelists', *Westminster Review*, 1 (1852), 132.

for something that Victorian society had made impossible. Feminine novelists had been deprived of the language and the consciousness for such an enterprise, and obviously their deprivation extended beyond Victoria's reign and into the twentieth century. The delicacy and verbal fastidiousness of Virginia Woolf is an extension of this feminized language.

Florence Nightingale thought the effort of repression itself drained off women's creative energy. 'Give us back our suffering,' she demanded in *Cassandra* (1852), 'for out of nothing comes nothing. But out of suffering may come the cure. Better have pain than paralysis.'* It does sometimes seem as if feminine writers are metaphorically paralyzed, as Alice James was literally paralyzed, by refinement and restraint, but the repression in which the feminine novel was situated also forced women to find innovative and covert ways to dramatize the inner life, and led to a fiction that was intense, compact, symbolic, and profound. There is Charlotte Brontë's extraordinary subversion of the Gothic in *Jane Eyre*, in which the mad wife locked in the attic symbolizes the passionate and sexual side of Jane's personality, an alter ego that her upbringing, her religion, and her society have commanded her to incarcerate.[3] There is the crippled artist heroine of Dinah Craik's *Olive* (1850), who identifies with Byron, and whose deformity represents her very womanhood. There are the murderous little wives of Mary Braddon's sensation novels, golden-haired killers whose actions are a sardonic commentary on the real feelings of the Angel in the House.

Many of the fantasies of feminine novels are related to money, mobility, and power. Although feminine novelists punished assertive heroines, they dealt with personal ambition by projecting the ideology of success onto male characters, whose initiative, thrift, industry, and perseverance came straight from the woman author's experience. The 'woman's man' [...] was often a more effective outlet for the 'deviant' aspects of the author's personality than were her heroines, and thus male role-playing extended beyond the pseudonym to imaginative content.

Protest fiction represented another projection of female experience onto another group; it translated the felt pain and oppression of women into the championship of mill-workers, child laborers, prostitutes, and slaves. Women were aware that protest fiction converted anger and frustration into an acceptable form of feminine and Christian expression. In the social novels of the 1840s and 1850s, and the problem novels of the 1860s and 1870s, women writers were pushing back the boundaries of their sphere, and presenting their profession as one that

---

* 'Cassandra', in *The Cause*, ed. Ray Strachey (Port Washington, NY, 1969), 398.

required not only freedom of language and thought, but also mobility and activity in the world.[4] The sensation novelists of the 1870s, including Mary Braddon, Rhoda Broughton, and Florence Marryat, used this new freedom in a transitional literature that explored genuinely radical female protest against marriage and women's economic oppression, although still in the framework of feminine conventions that demanded the erring heroine's destruction.

From Jane Austen to George Eliot, the woman's novel had moved, despite its restrictions, in the direction of an all-inclusive female realism, a broad, socially informed exploration of the daily lives and values of women within the family and the community. By 1880, the three-decker had become flexible enough to accommodate many of the formerly unprintable aspects of female experience. Yet with the death of George Eliot and the appearance of a new generation of writers, the woman's novel moved into a Feminist phase, a confrontation with male society that elevated Victorian sexual stereotypes into a cult. The feminists challenged many of the restrictions on women's self-expression, denounced the gospel of self-sacrifice, attacked patriarchal religion, and constructed a theoretical model of female oppression, but their anger with society and their need for self-justification often led them away from realism into oversimplification, emotionalism, and fantasy. Making their fiction the vehicle for a dramatization of wronged womanhood, they demanded changes in the social and political systems that would grant women male privileges and require chastity and fidelity from men. The profound sense of injustice that the feminine novelists had represented as class struggle in their novels of factory life becomes an all-out war of the sexes in the novels of the feminists. Even their pseudonyms show their sense of feminist pride and of matriarchal mission to their sisters one representative feminist called herself 'Sarah Grand.'[5] In its extreme form, feminist literature advocated the sexual separatism of Amazon utopias and suffragette sisterhoods.

In the lives of the feminists, the bonds of the female subculture were particularly strong. The feminists were intensely devoted to each other and needed the support of close, emotional friendships with other women as well as the loving adulation of a female audience. In this generation, which mainly comprises women born between 1860 and 1880, one finds sympathetically attuned women writing in teams; Edith Somerville and Violet Martin were even said to have continued the collaboration beyond the grave.* Although they preached individualism,

* See Maurice Collis, *Somerville and Ross* (London, 1968) for an account of the careers of Edith Somerville and Violet Martin. After Martin's death in 1915, the 'collaboration'

their need for association led to a staggering number of clubs, activities, and causes, culminating in the militant groups and the almost terrifying collectivity of the suffrage movement. They glorified and idealized the womanly values of chastity and maternal love, and believed that those values must be forced upon a degenerate male society.

In their lives and in their books, most feminist writers expressed both an awareness of, and a revulsion from, sexuality. Like the feminine novelists, they projected many of their own experiences onto male characters, creating, for example, the Scarlet Pimpernels, 'effeminate' fops by day and fearless heroes by night, semi-androgynous symbols of a generation in uneasy transition. To some degree these tactics were typical of the period in which they wrote; male novelists were creating 'masculine' independent women who, as Donald Stone puts it, 'could be used as a cover for those men who, for one reason or another, were anxious to proclaim their own standards and follow their own instincts.'*

As the feminists themselves often seem neurotic and divided in their roles, less productive than earlier generations, and subject to paralyzing psychosomatic illnesses, so their fiction seems to break down in its form. In the 1890s the three-decker novel abruptly disappeared due to changes in its marketability,[6] and women turned to short stories and fragments, which they called 'dreams,' 'keynotes,' and 'fantasias.' At the turn of the century came the purest examples of feminist literature, the novels, poems, and plays written as suffragette propaganda and distributed by the efficient and well-financed suffrage presses.

The feminist writers were not important artists. Yet in their insistence on exploring and defining womanhood, in their rejection of self-sacrifice, and even in their outspoken hostility to men, the feminist writers represented an important stage, a declaration of independence, in the female tradition. They did produce some interesting and original work, and they opened new subjects for other novelists. Sarah Grand's powerful studies of female psychology, George Egerton's bitter short stories, and Olive Schreiner's existential socialism were all best sellers in their own day and still hold attention. Through political campaigns for prostitutes and working women, and in the suffrage crusades, the feminists insisted on their right to use the male sexual vocabulary, and to use it forcefully and openly. The feminists also challenged the monopoly of male publishers and rebelled against the dictatorship of the male establishment. Men –

---

continued through psychic communications. Katherine Bradley and Edith Cooper wrote under the name of 'Michael Field;' the sisters Emily and Dorothea Gerard used the name 'E. D. Gerard' for such joint efforts as *Beggar My Neighbor* (1882).

* Stone, 'Victorian Feminism and the Nineteenth-century Novel', 79.

John Chapman, John Blackwood, Henry Blackent, George Smith – had published the works of feminine novelists and had exerted direct and enormous power over their contents. Sarah Grand parodied the masculine critical hegemony by describing a literary journal she called the *Patriarch*, and feminist journalists, writing in their own magazines, argued against the judgments of the men of letters. In the 1860s the sensation novelists had begun to retain their copyrights, work with printers on a commission basis, and edit their own magazines. The feminists continued to expand this economic control of publishing outlets. Virginia Woolf, printing her own novels at the Hogarth Press, owed much of her independence to the feminists' insistence on the need for women writers to be free of patriarchal commercialism.

In its early stages feminist analysis was naïve and incoherent, but by the turn of the century Mona Caird, Elizabeth Robins, and Olive Schreiner were producing cogent theories of women's relationship to work and production, to class structure, and to marriage and the family.* Robins and other members of the Women Writers Suffrage League were beginning to work out a theory of women's literature, making connections between the demands of the male publishing industry, the socialization of women, and the heroines, plots, conventions, and images of women's fiction. Finally, the militant suffrage movement forced women writers to confront their own beliefs about women's rights, and in the process to reexamine their own self-hatred and inhibition.

English women (or at least those women who were over thirty, householders, the wives of householders, occupiers of property of £5 or more annual value, or university graduates) were given the franchise in 1918 by a government grateful for their patriotism during World War I.[†] Ironically, the death of many young male writers and poets during the war left English women writers with a poignant sense of carrying on a national literary tradition that had, at its heart, excluded them. Women felt a responsibility to continue, to take the men's place, but they also felt a pitiful lack of confidence. Alice Meynell's poem 'A Father of Women' conveys some of the anxiety, as well as the guilt, of the survivors:

> Our father works in us,
> The daughters of his manhood. Not undone
> Is he, not wasted, though transmuted thus,
>   and though he left no son.

---

* Mona Caird, *The Morality of Marriage* (London, 1897); Elizabeth Robins, *Way Stations* (London, 1913); Olive Schreiner, *Women and Labour* (London, 1911).
† See Andrew Rosen, *Rise Up, Women!* (London, 1974), 266.

Meynell calls upon her father's spirit in the poem to arm her 'delicate mind,' give her 'courage to die,' and to crush in her nature 'the ungenerous art of the inferior.'

The literature of the last generation of Victorian women writers, born between 1880 and 1900, moved beyond feminism to a Female phase of courageous self-exploration, but it carried with it the double legacy of feminine self-hatred and feminist withdrawal. In their rejection of male society and masculine culture, feminist writers had retreated more and more toward a separatist literature of inner space. Psychologically rather than socially focused, this literature sought refuge from the harsh realities and vicious practices of the male world. Its favorite symbol, the enclosed and secret room, had been a potent image in women's novels since *Jane Eyre*, but by the end of the century it came to be identified with the womb and with female conflict. In children's books, such as Mrs Molesworth's *The Tapestry Room* (1879) and Dinah Craik's *The Little Lame Prince* (1886), women writers had explored and extended these fantasies of enclosure. After 1900, in dozens of novels from Frances Hodgson Burnett's *A Secret Garden* (1911) to May Sinclair's *The Tree of Heaven* (1917), the secret room, the attic hideaway, the suffragette cell came to stand for a separate world, a flight from men and from adult sexuality. [...]

Notes

1   For Catherine Judd's argument against this assertion, see pp. 289–302 below.
2   For a reply to this view, see Linda Peterson, 'Rewriting *A History of the Lyre*: Letitia Landon, Elizabeth Barrett Browning and the (Re)Construction of the Nineteenth-century Woman Poet', in Isobel Armstrong and Virginia Blain, eds, *Women's Poetry, Late Romantic to Late Victorian: Gender and Genre, 1830–1900* (Houndmills: Macmillan, 1999), 115–32.
3   This is the perception developed by Gilbert and Gubar, pp. 85–91 below.
4   For feminist discussions about female power in social-problem fiction, see pp. 186–90 below.
5   The New Woman novelist, Sarah Grand's real name was Frances Elizabeth Bellenden McFall, *née* Clarke.
6   For the history of the three-volume novel in the nineteenth century, see pp. 266–84 below.

Significance
of Gilbert
and Gubar's
The

Sandra M. Gilbert and Susan Gubar, now professors of English at the universities of California at Davis and Indiana respectively, join Elaine Showalter as key figures in the propulsion of feminism into the centre of Victorian fiction studies. Where Showalter provided readers of the Victorian novel with a well-defined history in which to situate individual texts, Gilbert and Gubar, who were more positive about a wider range of Victorian fiction than Showalter, offered a compelling model of female experience and protest, and a view of the consciousness of the woman novelist (and literary writer more generally) in the nineteenth century, struggling against the oppression of 'patriarchy'. *The Madwoman in the Attic: The Woman Writer and the Nineteenth-century Literary Imagination* (1979) articulated a view of the conditions in which nineteenth-century women wrote and the inventive strategies of mask-wearing they adopted to defeat those conditions. Like Showalter, Gilbert and Gubar read literature as expressive of authorial experience and saw gender as the central determinant of that experience. Again, like Showalter, they saw in episodes in individual Victorian texts dramatizations of wider truths about the experience of women and their struggle for self-expression. Their criticism extrapolated general arguments from local instances and again, sometimes, lost the specificity of the original in the trajectory to the general. Similarly, they perceived literature by women as distinctive *by definition* of it being by a woman; they offered their own version of a 'literature of their own'. They also encouraged readers to see women's writing in the period as *always* dissenting in some way. It was an assumption that has been hard to break.

Madwoman
in the
Attic (1979)

In *The Madwoman in the Attic*, Gilbert and Gubar argued that women writers in the West had been inhibited by a patriarchal literary culture that privileged male creativity and denigrated or denied the female. Women throughout that culture, they said, were constrained by the images men had of them, the 'mythic masks male artists have fastened over [a woman's] human face both to lessen their dread of "inconstancy" and – by identifying her with the "eternal types" they have themselves invented – to possess her more thoroughly'.[8] In the nineteenth century, the most deathly of these masks were the monster (madwoman) and the 'angel in the house', the phrase Gilbert and Gubar took from Coventry Patmore's poem *The Angel in the House* (1854–63) to express an aesthetic, moral and sexual ideal of Victorian domestic femininity. Gilbert and Gubar recalled Virginia Woolf's declaration of revolt against what she saw as the sexual politics of the Victorians. Woolf said that, before an early twentieth-century woman could write, she must rid herself of this inhibiting model of domesticity, she 'must "kill" the "angel in the house"'.[9] They argued that all constraining models of femaleness that hindered literary creativity had to be so killed. They were slain by Victorian novelists, Gilbert and Gubar proposed, through inventive duplicity, through the use of stereotypes that were subverted; employed, not to inhibit, but to articulate female writers' voices. *The Madwoman in the Attic* argued that Victorian female novelists engaged with patriarchy by subversively adopting patriarchy's own images of women and turning them to their own advantage (a comparison can be made here with the ideas of mimicry proposed by Luce Irigaray in the 1970s).

The
Madwoman
discussed

The title of *The Madwoman in the Attic* comes, obviously, from the plight of Bertha Mason, Rochester's mad wife, in Charlotte Brontë's *Jane Eyre* and an extract from the chapter on that novel is offered below as a way into Gilbert and Gubar's quasi-psychological, biographically based feminism. The approach to *Jane Eyre* is symptomatic of the book's critical method because it exemplifies what Gilbert and Gubar saw as a novelist's subversive handling of a common figure (the madwoman) from the so-called patriarchal descriptors of woman. In *Jane Eyre*, the madwoman served as an articulate expression of Jane's own condition, and, in the extract below, Gilbert and Gubar trace ways in which Bertha is an expression of part of Jane's (feminist) consciousness. Brontë, they claim, was making serviceable an instrument of female oppression to articulate Jane's selfhood and exemplifying the subversive mimicry exploited by Victorian female writers.

What needs to be emphasized in this extract, because it relates generally to the habit of mind expressed in *The Madwoman*, is its focus on Jane as on a life-pilgrimage about self-fulfilment and individual happiness, a search for 'maturity, independence, and true equality [in marriage]'. Gilbert and Gubar's emphasis, together with their resistance to commenting on self-control, self-denial or altruistic labour in the novel, hints that they were making of Jane Eyre a late twentieth-century woman, a figure whose aspirations for individual liberty and sexual equality were akin to the desires of generations born long after Charlotte Brontë. Gilbert and Gubar were producing meaning from the fiction of the nineteenth century that was influenced by the needs of their own cultural moment. This reading of *Jane Eyre* and the narration of the emergence of a modern feminist subject it enabled was challenged by postcolonialists in the 1980s and 1990s for its ethnocentricity, especially by Gayatri Chakravorty Spivak, in an influential essay in 1985 discussed on pp. 310–17 below.

GILBERT AND GUBAR'S APPRAISAL OF *THE MADWOMAN*

The Madwoman was not only a child of the broader social and political moment. In Gilbert and Gubar's own candid reflections on the conditions that produced *The Madwoman* in the 'Introduction' to the second edition (2000), they also acknowledged the personal nature of their enterprise, the connection between the intellectual project of the book and their own lives as young female academics and mothers in the 1970s. Both recalled arriving at the University of Indiana at Bloomington to be confronted by various forms of institutional sexism that denied their significance as professional critics. *The Madwoman*'s assault on the constraining powers of patriarchy grew out of this experience. And both recognized the significance of their own motherhood to the project. Indeed, Sandra Gilbert described the link between mothering and the book's interest in female creativity as a driving force. 'Mothering, motherhood, and mothers:' she wrote, 'as I look back on the years when we were researching and writing *The Madwoman*, I realise that maternity was always somehow central to our project. Resisting "patriarchal poetry" and poetics, we struggled, like all feminist critics of our generation, to find alternative tropes for creativity.'[10] Responsive to the needs of a feminist generation seeking independence in male-dominated professions and a recognition of sexual equality, Gilbert and Gubar, whose interest had always been in the links between written texts and authorial experience, encouraged their readers twenty-one years after *The Madwoman*'s publication, to see it inscribed by their own personal histories.

The 'Introduction' to the second edition of *The Madwoman* was generous in acknowledging how the feminist agenda had altered since its first publication, and how Gilbert and Gubar's approach seemed to many subsequent readers unsatisfactory. In the changing years following the completion of the book, Sandra Gilbert wrote, they were faulted 'for intellectual crimes whose lineaments most of us would never have recognized in that blissfully naïve dawn of the 1970s',[11] including that of 'essentialism, racism, heterosexism, phallogocentricism'.[12] Gilbert and Gubar acknowledged the extent that their assumptions about the connections between a literary text and its author in the 1970s did not suit 1980s' ideas about authorship or the identity politics of the 1990s. The second edition did not attempt to address these criticisms, and the body of the text was unaltered. Rather, Gilbert and Gubar modulated their reflections on the condition of the modern academy into a lament for the financially impoverished state of higher education in the United States, and then into a buoyant statement that enthusiasm for the writers with whom they had been concerned many years before – the Brontës, Barrett Browning, George Eliot, Emily Dickinson – would one day return. It was an elegantly silent acceptance of the many differences between the feminist critical agenda and canon of the 1970s and the 1990s and a quiet statement of hope for the return of more common-sense criticism that valued the author as creator. Its irony lay in its construction of late twentieth-century feminism, rather than patriarchy, as *The Madwoman*'s most energetic assailant.

Extract from Sandra M. Gilbert and Susan Gubar, *The Madwoman in the Attic: The Woman Writer and the Nineteenth-century Literary Imagination* (New Haven, Conn. and London: Yale University Press, 1979), 356–62.

That Rochester's character and life pose in themselves such substantial impediments to his marriage with Jane does not mean, however, that Jane herself generates none. For one thing, 'akin' as she is to Rochester, she suspects him of harboring all the secrets we know he does harbor, and raises defenses against them, manipulating her 'master' so as to keep him 'in reasonable check.' In a larger way, moreover, all the charades and masquerades – the secret messages – of patriarchy have had their effect upon her. Though she loves Rochester the man, Jane has doubts about Rochester the husband even before she learns about Bertha. In her world, she senses, even the equality of love between true minds leads to the inequalities and minor despotisms of marriage. 'For a little while,' she says cynically to Rochester, 'you will perhaps be as you are now, [but] ... I suppose your love will effervesce in six months, or less. I have observed in books written by men, that period assigned as the farthest to which a husband's ardor extends' (ch. 24). He, of course, vigorously repudiates this prediction, but his argument – 'Jane: you please me, and you master me [because] you seem to submit' – implies a kind of Lawrentian sexual tension and only makes things worse. For when he asks 'Why do you smile [at this], Jane? What does that inexplicable ... turn of countenance mean?' her peculiar, ironic smile, reminiscent of Bertha's mirthless laugh, signals an 'involuntary' and subtly hostile thought 'of Hercules and Samson with their charmers.' And that hostility becomes overt at the silk warehouse, where Jane notes that 'the more he bought me, the more my cheek burned with a sense of annoyance and degradation. ... I thought his smile was such as a sultan might, in a blissful and fond moment, bestow on a slave his gold and gems had enriched' (ch. 24).

Jane's whole life-pilgrimage has, of course, prepared her to be angry in this way at Rochester's, and society's, concept of marriage. Rochester's loving tyranny recalls John Reed's unloving depotism, and the erratic nature of Rochester's favors ('in my secret soul I knew that his great kindness to me was balanced by unjust severity to many others' [ch. 15]) recalls Brocklehurst's hypocrisy. But even the dreamlike paintings that Jane produced early in her stay at Thornfield – art works which brought her as close to her 'master' as Helen Graham (in *The Tenant of Wildfell Hall*) was to hers – functioned ambiguously, like Helen's, to predict strains in this relationship even while they seemed to be conventional Romantic fantasies. The first represented a drowned female corpse; the second a sort of avenging mother goddess rising (like Bertha Mason Rochester or Frankenstein's monster) in 'electric travail' (ch. 13); and the third a terrible paternal specter carefully designed to recall Milton's sinister image of Death. Indeed, this last, says Jane, quoting *Paradise Lost*, delineates 'the shape which shape had none,' the patriarchal shadow implicit even in the Father-hating gloom of hell.

Given such shadowings and foreshadowings, then, it is no wonder that as Jane's anger and fear about her marriage intensify, she begins to be symbolically drawn back into her own past, and specifically to reexperience the dangerous sense of doubleness that had begun in the red-room. The first sign that this is happening is the powerfully depicted, recurrent dream of a child she begins to have as she drifts into a romance with her master. She tells us that she was awakened 'from companionship with this baby-phantom' on the night Bertha attacked Richard Mason, and the next day she is literally called back into the past, back to Gateshead to see the dying Mrs Reed, who reminds her again of what she once was and potentially still is: 'Are you Jane Eyre? . . . I declare she talked to me once like something mad, or like a friend' (ch. 21). Even more significantly, the phantom-child reappears in two dramatic dreams Jane has on the night before her wedding eve, during which she experiences 'a strange regretful consciousness of some barrier dividing' her from Rochester. In the first, 'burdened' with the small wailing creature, she is 'following the windings of an unknown road' in cold rainy weather, straining to catch up with her future husband but unable to reach him. In the second, she is walking among the ruins of Thornfield, still carrying 'the unknown little child' and still following Rochester; as he disappears around 'an angle in the road,' she tells him, 'I bent forward to take a last look; the wall crumbled; I was shaken; the child rolled from my knee, I lost my balance, fell, and woke' (ch. 25).

What are we to make of these strange dreams, or – as Jane would call them – these 'presentiments'? To begin with, it seems clear that the wailing child who appears in all of them corresponds to 'the poor orphan child' of Bessie's song at Gateshead, and therefore to the child Jane herself, the wailing Cinderella whose pilgrimage began in anger and despair. That child's complaint – 'My feet they are sore, and my limbs they are weary; / Long is the way, and the mountains are wild' – is still Jane's, or at least the complaint of that part of her which resists a marriage of inequality. And though consciously Jane wishes to be rid of the heavy problem her orphan self presents, 'I might not lay it down anywhere, however tired were my arms, however much its weight impeded my progress.' In other words, until she reaches the goal of her pilgrimage – maturity, independence, true equality with Rochester (and therefore in a sense with the rest of the world) – she is doomed to carry her orphaned alter ego everywhere. The burden of the past cannot be sloughed off so easily – not, for instance, by glamorous lovemaking, silk dresses, jewelry, a new name. Jane's 'strange regretful consciousness of a barrier' dividing her from Rochester is, thus, a keen though disguised intuition of a problem she herself will pose.

Almost more interesting than the nature of the child image, however, is the *predictive* aspect of the last of the child dreams, the one about the ruin of Thornfield. As Jane correctly foresees, Thornfield *will* within a year become 'a dreary ruin, the retreat of bats and owls.' Have her own subtle and not-so-subtle hostilities to its master any connection with the catastrophe that is to befall the house? Is her clairvoyant dream in some sense a vision of wish-fulfilment? And why, specifically, is she freed from the burden of the wailing child at the moment *she* falls from Thornfield's ruined wall?

The answer to all these questions is closely related to events which follow upon the child dream. For the apparition of a child in these crucial weeks preceding her marriage is only one symptom of a dissolution of personality Jane seems to be experiencing at this time, a fragmentation of the self comparable to her 'syncope' in the red-room. Another symptom appears early in the chapter that begins, anxiously, 'there was no putting off the day that advanced – the bridal day' (ch. 25). It is her witty but nervous speculation about the nature of 'one Jane Rochester, a person whom as yet I knew not,' though 'in yonder closet... garments *said* to be hers had already displaced [mine]: *for not to me appertained that... strange wraith-like apparel*' (ch. 25 [ital. ours]). Again, a third symptom appears on the morning of her wedding: she turns toward the mirror and sees 'a robed and veiled figure, so unlike my usual self that it seemed almost the image of a stranger' (ch. 26), reminding us of the moment in the red-room when all had 'seemed colder and darker in that visionary hollow' of the looking glass 'than in reality.' In view of this frightening series of separations within the self – Jane Eyre splitting off from Jane Rochester, the child Jane splitting off from the adult Jane, and the image of Jane weirdly separating from the body of Jane – it is not surprising that another and most mysterious specter, a sort of 'vampyre,' should appear in the middle of the night to rend and trample the wedding veil of that unknown person, Jane Rochester.

Literally, of course, the nighttime specter is none other than Bertha Mason Rochester. But on a figurative and psychological level it seems suspiciously clear that the specter of Bertha is still another – indeed the most threatening – avatar of Jane. What Bertha now *does*, for instance, is what Jane wants to do. Disliking the 'vapoury veil' of Jane Rochester, Jane Eyre secretly wants to tear the garments up. Bertha does it for her. Fearing the inexorable 'bridal day,' Jane would like to put it off. Bertha does that for her too. Resenting the new mastery of Rochester, whom she sees as '*dread* but adored,' (ital. ours), she wishes to be his equal in size and strength, so that she can battle him in the contest of their marriage. Bertha, 'a big woman, in stature almost equalling her husband,' has the necessary 'virile force' (ch. 26). Bertha, in other words, is Jane's truest and darkest double: she is the angry aspect of the orphan child, the ferocious secret self Jane has been trying to repress ever since her days at Gateshead. For, as Claire Rosenfeld points out, 'the novelist who consciously or unconsciously exploits psychological Doubles' frequently juxtaposes 'two characters, the one representing the socially acceptable or conventional personality, the other externalizing the free, uninhibited, often criminal self.'[1]

It is only fitting, then, that the existence of this criminal self imprisoned in Thornfield's attic is the ultimate legal impediment to Jane's and Rochester's marriage, and that its existence is, paradoxically, an impediment raised by Jane as well as by Rochester. For it now begins to appear, if it did not earlier, that Bertha has functioned as Jane's dark double *throughout* the governess's stay at Thornfield. Specifically, every one of Bertha's appearances – or, more accurately, her manifestations – has been associated with an experience (or repression) of anger on Jane's part. Jane's feelings of 'hunger, rebellion, and rage' on the battlements, for instance, were accompanied by Bertha's 'low, slow ha! ha!' and 'eccentric murmurs.' Jane's apparently secure response to Rochester's apparently egalitarian sexual confidences was followed by Bertha's attempt to incinerate the master in his bed. Jane's unexpressed resentment at Rochester's manipulative gypsy-masquerade found expression in Bertha's terrible shriek and her even more terrible attack on Richard Mason. Jane's anxieties about her marriage, and in particular her fears of her own alien 'robed and veiled' bridal image, were objectified by the image of Bertha in a 'white and straight' dress, 'whether gown, sheet, or shroud I cannot tell.' Jane's profound desire to destroy Thornfield, the symbol of Rochester's mastery and of her own servitude, will be acted out by Bertha, who burns down the house and destroys *herself* in the process as if she were an agent of Jane's desire as well as her own. And finally, Jane's disguised hostility to Rochester, summarized in her terrifying prediction to herself that 'you shall, yourself, pluck out your right eye; yourself cut off your right hand' (ch. 27) comes strangely true through the intervention of Bertha, whose melodramatic death causes Rochester to lose both eye and hand.

These parallels between Jane and Bertha may at first seem somewhat strained. Jane, after all, is poor, plain, little, pale, neat, and quiet, while Bertha is rich, large, florid, sensual, and extravagant; indeed, she was once even beautiful, somewhat, Rochester notes, 'in the style of Blanche

Ingram.' Is she not, then, as many critics have suggested, a monitory image rather than a double for Jane? As Richard Chase puts it, 'May not Bertha, Jane seems to ask herself, be a living example of what happens to the woman who [tries] to be the fleshly vessel of the [masculine] *élan*?'[2] 'Just as [Jane's] instinct for self-preservation saves her from earlier temptations,' Adrienne Rich remarks, 'so it must save her from becoming this woman by curbing her imagination at the limits of what is bearable for a powerless woman in the England of the 1840s.'[3] Even Rochester himself provides a similar critical appraisal of the relationship between the two. 'That is *my wife*,' he says, pointing to mad Bertha,

> And *this* is what I wished to have... this young girl who stands so grave and quiet at the mouth of hell, looking collectedly at the gambols of a demon. I wanted her just as a change after that fierce ragout... Compare these clear eyes with the red balls yonder – this face with that mask – this form with that bulk... (ch. 26).

And of course, in one sense, the relationship between Jane and Bertha is a monitory one: while acting out Jane's secret fantasies, Bertha does (to say the least) provide the governess with an example of how not to act, teaching her a lesson more salutary than any Miss Temple ever taught.

Nevertheless, it is disturbingly clear from recurrent images in the novel that Bertha not only acts *for* Jane, she also acts *like* Jane. The imprisoned Bertha, running 'backwards and forwards' on all fours in the attic, for instance, recalls not only Jane the governess, whose only relief from mental pain was to pace 'backwards and forwards' in the third story, but also that 'bad animal' who was ten-year-old Jane, imprisoned in the red-room, howling and mad. Bertha's 'goblin appearance' – 'half dream, half reality,' says Rochester – recalls the lover's epithets for Jane: 'malicious elf,' 'sprite,' 'changeling,' as well as his playful accusation that she had magically downed his horse at their first meeting. Rochester's description of Bertha as a 'monster' ('a fearful voyage I had with such a monster in the vessel' [ch. 27]) ironically echoes Jane's own fear of being a monster ('Am I a monster?... is it impossible that Mr Rochester should have a sincere affection for me?' [ch. 24]). Bertha's fiendish madness recalls Mrs Reed's remark about Jane ('she talked to me once like something mad or like a fiend') as well as Jane's own estimate of her mental state ('I will hold to the principles received by me when I was sane, and not mad – as I am now [ch. 27]'). And most dramatic of all, Bertha's incendiary tendencies recall Jane's early flaming rages, at Lowood and at Gateshead, as well as that 'ridge of lighted heath' which she herself saw as emblematic of her mind in its rebellion against society. It is only fitting, therefore, that, as if to balance the child Jane's terrifying vision of herself as an alien figure in the 'visionary hollow' of the red-room looking glass, the adult Jane first clearly perceives her terrible double when Bertha puts on the wedding veil intended for the second Mrs Rochester, and turns to the mirror. At that moment, Jane sees 'the reflection of the visage and features quite distinctly in the dark oblong glass,' sees them as if they were her own (ch. 25).

For despite all the habits of harmony she gained in her years at Lowood, we must finally recognize, with Jane herself, that on her arrival at Thornfield she only *'appeared* a disciplined and subdued character' [ital. ours]. Crowned with thorns, finding that she is, in Emily Dickinson's words, 'The Wife – without the Sign,'[4] she represses her rage behind a subdued facade, but her soul's impulse to dance 'like a Bomb, abroad,' to quote Dickinson again,[5] has not been exorcised and will not be exorcised until the literal and symbolic death of Bertha frees her from the furies that torment her and makes possible a marriage of equality – makes possible, that is, wholeness within herself. At that point, significantly, when the Bertha in Jane falls from the ruined wall of Thornfield and is destroyed, the orphan child too, as her dream predicts, will roll from her knee – the burden of her past will be lifted – and she will wake. In the meantime, as Rochester says, 'never was anything at once so frail and so indomitable ... consider the resolute wild free thing looking out of [Jane's] eye ... Whatever I do with its cage, I cannot get at it – the savage, beautiful creature' (ch. 27).

Notes

1   Claire Rosenfeld, 'The Shadow Within: The Conscious and Unconscious Use of the Double', in Albert J. Guerard, ed., *Stories of the Double* (Philadelphia: Lippincott, 1967), 314.
2   Richard Chase, 'The Brontës, or Myth Domesticated', in Richard J. Dunn, ed., *Jane Eyre* (New York: Norton, 1971), 467.
3   Adrienne Rich, 'The Temptations of a Motherless Woman', *Ms.* 2 (1973): 69–70.
4   See Emily Dickinson, *Poems*, J. 1072.
5   Ibid., J. 512.

Chapter Notes

1   Ellen Moers, *Literary Women*, with an introduction by Helen Taylor (London: Women's Press, 1986, first pub. 1976), xvi.

2   Ibid., ix.
3   Quoted in Elaine Showalter, *A Literature of their Own: British Women Novelists from Brontë to Lessing* (Princeton, NJ: Princeton University Press, 1977), 8.
4   Ibid., 11.
5   Ibid., 13.
6   Ibid. (italic in original).
7   Ibid. (italic in original).
8   Sandra M. Gilbert and Susan Gubar, *The Madwoman in the Attic: The Woman Writer and the Nineteenth-century Literary Imagination* (New Haven, Conn. and London: Yale University Press, 1979), 17.
9   Ibid.
10 Sandra M. Gilbert and Susan Gubar, *The Madwoman in the Attic: The Woman Writer and the Nineteenth-century Literary Imagination*, 2nd edn (New Haven, Conn. and London: Yale University Press, 2000), xxii.
11 Ibid., xxiv–xxv.
12 Ibid., xxv.

Further Reading

Catherine Belsey and Jane Moore, eds, *The Feminist Reader*, 2nd edn (Basingstoke: Macmillan, 1997): a good spread of modern feminist criticism and a useful overview from editors on 'the story so far'. Toril Moi tackles the categories of 'Feminist, Female, Feminine' in her essay (pp. 104–16). Each piece has an adroit editorial summary.

William Cain, ed., *Making Feminist History: The Literary Scholarship of Sandra M. Gilbert and Susan Gubar* (New York and London: Garland, 1994): an important collection, including Nancy Miller's analysis of the initial attacks on *The Madwoman*. Carolyn Heilbrun's introduction resists the notion that there is a universal female subject, as the *Madwoman* assumed, but argues that there is still a community of interest among women internationally. The book also considers Gilbert and Gubar's work on Modernism.

Jenni Calder, *Women and Marriage in Victorian Fiction* (London: Thames and Hudson, 1976): links with some US feminism of the 1970s in chapter 3; argues that 'Quiescent, ambitious, immoral, peculiar, like dolls or like dragons, women are seen to be multifariously engaged in a contest with an over-whelmingly paternalistic society' particularly visible in the literary representation in marriages.

Vineta Colby, *Yesterday's Women: Domestic Realism in the English Novel* (Princeton, NJ: Princeton University Press, 1974): worth reading as evidence of the critical discourse on women's fiction prior to the feminist revolution. Colby considered that the early domestic fiction writers in the nineteenth century were worth considering 'for what they tell us about that glorious and seemingly miraculous rebirth of the great novel in the mid-nineteenth century'.

Sandra M. Gilbert and Susan Gubar, *The Madwoman in the Attic: The Woman Writer and the Nineteenth-century Literary Imagination*, 2nd edn (New Haven, Conn. and

London: Yale University Press, 2000): includes revealing new Introduction reflecting on the conditions that produced *The Madwoman* and its reception (see above pp. 84–5).

Toril Moi, *Sexual/Textual Politics: Feminist Literary Theory* (London: Methuen, 1985): chapter 3 of this valuable book contains a shrewd evaluation of the contribution to feminist literary criticism made by Showalter and Gilbert and Gubar in the two books extracted above. Considers their relationship with 'patriarchal' notions of aesthetics.

Elaine Showalter, *Daughters of Decadence: Women Writers of the Fin de Siècle* (London: Virago, 1993): short stories by Kate Chopin, Victoria Cross, Ada Leverson, George Egerton, 'Borgia Smudgiton', George Fleming, Charlotte Perkins Gilman, Charlotte Mew, Mabel E. Wotton, Constance Fenimore Woolson, Vernon Lee, Sarah Grand, Olive Schreiner and Edith Wharton.

Elaine Showalter, 'Family Secrets and Domestic Subversion: Rebellion in the Novels of the 1860s', in Anthony Wohl, ed., *The Victorian Family: Structures and Stresses* (London: Croom Helm, 1978), 101–16.

Elaine Showalter, *The Female Malady: Women, Madness and English Culture 1830– 1980* (London: Virago, 1987).

Elaine Showalter, *Sexual Anarchy: Gender and Culture at the Fin de Siècle* (London: Virago, 1992).

Signs: Journal of Women in Culture and Society, 24 (3) (1999): includes a forum 'Commemorating Literary Women: Ellen Moers and Feminist Criticism after Twenty Years', comprising assessments by Deborah Epstein Nord, Ellen Pollak, Sharon O'Brien and Maria DiBattista.

Patricia Meyer Spacks, *The Female Imagination: A Literary and Psychological Investigation of Women's Writing* (London: Allen and Unwin, 1976): answers the question 'What are the ways of female feeling, the modes of responding, that persist despite social change?' with discussion of canonical female Victorian novelists.

Tom Winnifrith, *Fallen Women in the Nineteenth-century Novel* (Basingstoke: Macmillan, 1994): argues that novelists accepted the 'conventional sexual code' on the surface 'if not to subvert it, at any rate to modify it by drawing different moral conclusions'. Discusses Austen, Charlotte Brontë, George Eliot, Thackeray, Dickens and Hardy.

4

Realism

Ian Watt – Ioan Williams – George Levine – Leo Bersani –
Catherine Belsey – D. A. Miller – Marxist Feminist Literature
Collective – Penny Boumehla – Lawrence Rothfield – Nancy
Armstrong – Kate Flint

What was realism in Victorian fiction? What truths did it assume about the real world? What political assumptions did it involve? By far the most debated area in the history of the criticism of Victorian fiction in the past decades has been the subject of realism, and the answers to these questions have been stimulatingly diverse. The whole topic has seen dramatic shifts and confrontations that involve both intellectual disagreement and sharp political variance, together with strikingly different understandings of Victorian culture and the purposes and achievements of the major novelists within it. The chief features of these variances are mapped in the present chapter.

The first approaches to realism were concerned with identifying its historical context and tracing its origin in philosophy and economics. Realism's roots in Cartesian thinking provided the focus of interest. Growing from this identification of the Cartesian certainties that lay behind realism, the critical debate in the 1970s and 1980s considered the epistemological assumptions of Victorian realism and the nature of those 'certainties' more thoroughly. Did the practice of realist representation involve naïve confidence in the knowability of the world beyond the page? Or were its practitioners, as George Levine argued in 1981, aware of, and self-conscious of, the limits of realism? These arguments about the assumptions of realism were occurring simultaneously in the late 1970s and early 1980s with a critique of realism's political implications, generated from the academy's immersion in theory. For the literary community that absorbed the arguments of post-structuralism, Barthesian theories of language and Althusserian concepts of ideology, and came to understand referentiality in language as illusory, the assumptions of the Victorian realists seemed naïve and dangerously conservative. I consider Catherine Belsey's Althusserian-influenced critique of 'classic realism' as a literary practice which did the work of ideology, and D. A. Miller's investigation of the novel and the police, as both typical of the 1980s' politicized response to realism.

Theory initially prompted a political reaction against realism and led other critics to value Victorian realist texts only for those parts that were not realist (for example, Gothic) or to focus their energies on the silences and absences in realist fiction. Such readers, either interested in what realism did not say or in those parts of the text that modulated out of realism, avoided the political implications perceived by Belsey and the like. The reaction to Belsey's ideas, when it came towards the end of the 1980s, was far-reaching. Ignoring the core of the realist project seemed to a new generation of feminists to be a dangerous act of silencing. The realist mode enabled Victorian women to speak in the public forum, and to repudiate this as merely a bourgeois practice of representation was to imitate the work of patriarchy in silencing women's voices. As a representative of this argument, I reproduce an essay by Penny Boumehla which articulated this repudiation theory with sophistication.

New Historicism in the 1990s insisted that what was important about reading realism was comprehending how the Victorian notion of the real was historically specific. Rather than pondering the politics of the mode, New Historicists identified the discourses circulating in the culture that claimed most authoritatively to represent reality. This new dimension of thinking, which particularly emphasized the visual and the relationship between seeing and knowing (visuality became a particular topic of interest in Victorian studies in the second half of the 1990s),[1] may continue to be the focus of work on realism in the next few years.

Histories of Realism

The first phase of the discussion of realism saw an effort to establish distinctly its identity as a practice of writing, and to account historically for its emergence as the dominant mode of fictional writing in the nineteenth century. Throughout the debate about realism, the first part of this project – to define realism with a watertight definition – has remained an unresolved issue. Realism, as a mode of Victorian fiction, has resisted being fixed to the satisfaction of all. One of the problematic features of many of the critical texts discussed below, prior to the 1990s, is the reluctance of any single Victorian novel to embody the particular definition of 'realism' being proposed. Victorian realism has, especially in these early stages of its recent critical history, been given a kind of Platonic identity, imagined as a form only imperfectly manifested in actual literary texts. The consequence of this Platonism has been to unsettle the authority of the critical analyses that rest on it (for other caveats about historical generalization, see p. 2 above).

IAN WATT'S
THE RISE OF
THE NOVEL
(1957)

Ian Watt's work on the history of the English novel remains the important starting-point of discussions of the realist tradition. His study of the eighteenth-century novel, *The Rise of the Novel: Studies in Defoe, Richardson and Fielding* was published first in 1957 and provided an account of the emergence of realism in fiction in England that naturally had implications for its development in the nineteenth century. It continues to be, along with Watt's other works on the novel, a widely read text on undergraduate novel courses.[2] Each of the features I draw out of Watt's discussion of the eighteenth century here has proved a matter of continued debate in Victorian studies. The context for the rise of realism that interested Watt was the philosophical developments of the seventeenth and eighteenth centuries and the influence of Descartes and Locke. In the first chapter of *The Rise of the Novel*, Watt identified the important correspondences between the philosophical context and the fiction, indicating the similarities between the emerging discourse of fictional realism and the dominant strands of eighteenth-century empirical philosophy. He was not proposing a clearly defined theory of the *relationship* between these discourses; he did not discuss exactly *why* those correspondences worked. His interest was in mapping the philosophical beside the literary.

THE
CARTESIAN
CERTAINTIES
OF REALISM

Watt argued that René Descartes's axiom in the *Discourse on Method* (1637), *cogito, ergo sum* [I am thinking, therefore I exist], and his pursuit of truth as an independent matter, separate from past tradition and mere authority, was reflected in the novel of the eighteenth century in its embrace of the individual as the centre of interest and its innovative, non-traditional plots and form. Likewise, Watt saw correspondences between fiction and philosophy in the novel's attention to the particularities of experience. This, paralleling the rejection of universals in philosophy, included the individuation of characters and the detailed presentation of their environment: the use of individual personal names in the new novels of the century (rather than generalized ones such as John Bunyan's Mr Badman or Mr Valiant-for-Truth) indicated at a micro-level the concentration of fiction on individuals who were discrete and had independent, psychologically credible life. Time was also significant. John Locke, Watt said, 'had defined personal identity as an identity of consciousness through duration in time; the individual was in touch with his own continuing identity through memory of his past thoughts and actions',[3] and this too was registered in fiction that, 'from Sterne to Proust', took as a subject 'the exploration of the personality as it is defined in the interpenetration of its past and present self-awareness'.[4]

WATT
CRITIQUED

Identifying realism chiefly as a particular mode of representation, and privileging the novel of human psychology, Watt concluded his preliminary discussion of the Cartesian history of realism with an analogy that has been much debated. Watt observed that he had summarized the ways in which the eighteenth-century novel's 'imitation of human life followed the procedures adopted by philosophical realism in its attempt to ascertain and report the truth', but then added:

> These procedures are by no means confined to philosophy; they tend, in fact, to be followed whenever the relation to reality of any report of an event is being investigated. The novel's mode of imitating reality may therefore be equally well summarized in terms of the procedures of another group of specialists in epistemology, the jury in a court of law. Their expectations, and those of the novel reader coincide in many ways: both want to know 'all of the particulars' of a given case – the time and place of the occurrence; both must be satisfied as to the identities of the parties concerns, and will refuse to accept evidence about anyone called Sir Toby Belch or Mr Badman – still less about a Chloe who has no surname and is 'common as the air'; and they also expect witnesses to tell the story 'in his own words'. The jury, in fact, takes the 'circumstantial view of life', which T. H. Green found to be the characteristic outlook of the novel.[5]

Watt's analogy with the practice of the legal profession – he was thinking more of the modern law than that of the eighteenth century – provided a memorable model for the empirical, imitative mode of realism. But it omitted a key aspect: the law itself. The jury is not, as many readers of Watt's analogy have observed, seeking a circumstantial view of life in the manner of a mythical objective observer, but trying to determine whether the defendant has committed a crime. The jury's reflections on evidence are situated in a particular contextual frame. This has a clear correspondence in fiction. Watt's emphasis on the realist novel's circumstantial view of life, and the representation of things as they are, excluded consideration of the role of contexts and conventions in writing and representation, the terms and ideologies that influence the literary production. Subsequent discussions of realism investigated the conventions, the particular characteristics of rhetoric, and the shaping forces, chiefly the political, that determined the fiction.

One other aspect of *The Rise of the Novel* needs to be mentioned. Watt's work as a literary historian was authoritative, and his book remains a useful account of the eighteenth-century philosophical parallels of the early realist project. As history, however, Watt's work has also been challenged and his identification of seventeenth and eighteenth-century philosophy as the major context for the realist novel has been disputed or supplemented. Elizabeth Deeds Ermarth, in her interdisciplinary study straddling literary criticism and art history, *Realism and Consensus in the English Novel* (1983), reminded her readers that key epistemological changes that enabled the assumptions of realism occurred much earlier than the eighteenth century in the transition from the medieval to the Renaissance. The adoption of the rules of perspective in Renaissance painting, for instance, that signalled the unification of space and the rationalization of sight, set the terms for the later unification of time

ALTER-
NATIVE
HISTORIES OF
REALISM

and rationalization of consciousness in realist fiction. Similarly, the abandonment of medieval historiography, in which the only meaningful distinctions were between time and eternity, in preference for a humanist historiography which found past and present mutually informative also contributed to the intellectual climate that eventually permitted realist fiction (see also the Further Reading section).

Epistemology of Realism

IOAN
WILLIAMS
AND
REALISM'S
CERTAINTIES

Watt saw realism emerging from a Cartesian philosophical climate. For critics of the Victorian novel in the 1970s and early 1980s, the question of what epistemology was assumed by the practices of realism, and what statements about the world and its underlying order were implied, were vexed ones. Cartesian certainties were debated. At one level, answers to the questions about the epistemological basis of nineteenth-century realism seemed self-evident. Realism involved the scrupulous attention to detail of actual life, it resisted idealism, and appeared to have faith in the human capacity to know the material world as daily experienced. Realism, philosophically, was taken by some critics as predicated on confidence about the cognitive powers of the mind. Ioan Williams, for instance, in *The Realist Novel in England: A Study in Development* (1974), said in her 'Introduction: The Basis of Realism', that Victorian realism was a discourse synonymous with certainty about reality as a matter of knowledge, and one that exuded confidence in underlying order. We 'have come', she said,

> to associate mid-Victorian literature with a naïve confidence that Reality consisted in the material and social world around them. There is no doubt that the mid-Victorian novel rested on a massive confidence as to what the nature of reality actually was, and that although it could not be identified with matter itself, it certainly lay in the material world.[6]

Such a position saw a rock-solid (and to Williams's mind 'naïve') connection between realism and a philosophy of epistemological assurance, a confidence in the powers of the mind suggestive of confidence about the values of the age. This understanding of realism can been seen from a different perspective in the work of linguists on the Victorian novel, discussed on pp. 198–200 (see also MacCabe in the Further Reading Section).

GEORGE
LEVINE'S VIEW
OF REALISM
AND SELF-

Williams's view was challenged in the early 1980s by the work of the North American critic George Levine in *The Realistic Imagination: English Fiction from Frankenstein to Lady Chatterley* (1981). I reproduce all the Introduction to this important book below (with the exception of the final paragraph). This

densely woven argument – related to the argument about realism's strategies   CONSCIOUS-
of containment in Leo Bersani's *A Future for Astyanax* (1976) discussed on   NESS
p. 120 below – explored the idea that realism in the nineteenth century was
not at all predicated on confidence but was part of a longing for it, that it was
built not on faith but on doubt, and that its showed throughout the signs of
the struggle to overcome uncertainty.

Levine started his first chapter with the acknowledgement that contemporary literary criticism in the early 1980s was strongly dominated by deconstruction and the challenge to the referential basis of language.[7] Theory, Levine
admitted, especially Barthesian and Derridean views, had encouraged many to
see Victorian realism as naïve (see Barthes in the Further Reading section). But
Levine did not simply reject this theoretical assumption, arguing that his own
understanding of realism was itself intimately and authoritatively connected to
the contemporary critical debates about the uncertainties of language and truth.
Deconstruction paradoxically gave him the entrée into the realist project because his approach was shaped by a continual interest in doubt and the realist
novelist's own pre-Barthesian, pre-Derridean awareness of the gap between
language's aspiration and achievement. Levine saw realist fiction arising out of a
struggle to make a credible fictional world in the face of language's intractability
and in the absence of secure confidence about the order of reality itself. 'No
major Victorian novelists', he said, arguing against Williams, 'were deluded into
believing that they were in fact offering an unmediated reality; but all of them
struggle to make contact with the world out there, and, even with their
knowledge of their own subjectivity, to break from the threatening limits of
solipsism, of convention, and of language'. Levine's view credited the realists
with awareness of the ideological dangers of their own mode of writing.

Extract from George Levine, *The Realistic Imagination: English Fiction from Frankenstein to Lady Chatterley* (Chicago: Chicago University Press, 1981), 3–22.

To take the word *realism* and the idea of representation seriously entails
a challenge to the antireferential bias of our criticism and to the method
of radical deconstruction that has become a commonplace.[1] It is to
challenge the assumptions about the status of literature variously held
by Roland Barthes and Jacques Derrida, and, in the area of Victorian
literature, J. Hillis Miller. It is to resist the now well established
convention that realism is at best a historically inevitable mistake. I do

not attempt anything like a full theoretical confrontation with this way of doing criticism, but choose to avoid extensive speculations on theory in order to keep my eye on the texts whose wonders are the occasion of this study.

Even that choice has important implications for literary theory, and I do not wish to avoid them. They are consonant with the attitude toward realism that I am trying to develop and with the overall argument, theoretically significant, that realism is itself intimately and authoritatively connected to the modernist position. This study, in any case, assumes that criticism has a responsibility both to explication and to history, and this despite powerful epistemological arguments denying the possibility of the referentiality of language, despite semiotic theories that show every sign significant only of other signs within an arbitrary code, despite the indeterminacy of texts. Willy-nilly, criticism addresses itself to something besides itself, even in its most dazzling regressions, and creates communities of meaning (if only to agree on unmeaning). At the risk of ideological and metaphysical complicity with things as they are, criticism must behave at times as though something is really out there after all. These are not questions of either/or: one is not either for realism or against it, as though this were a football game, or a war. Realism posits 'mixed' conditions. So do I.

Ironically, when I began this study it was to call Victorian realism into question, but as I proceeded I found the great Victorian realists to be immensely compatible. Their art and their commitments have driven me to see Victorian realism as an astonishing effort both of moral energy and of art, and one that must not be diminished by the historical distortions of contemporary critical method or by the Whiggish view of history (I used to share), that we know better now. Nevertheless, this study was made possible by the criticism it often attacks in notes, by the contemporary insistence on the sheer textuality of fiction and the consequent impossibility of external reference.

Modernist criticism has been invaluable in bringing to focus the fact, extensively argued by Gerald Graff,[2] that modernism is not so modern as it seems, but is at least two hundred years old. Part of my point throughout this study is that nineteenth-century writers were already self-conscious about the nature of their medium, and that there is a direct historical continuum between the realists who struggled to make narrative meaningful and modern critics who define themselves by virtue of their separation from realism and even from narrativity itself. In the face of arguments that where we have seen unity of vision there is only indeterminacy, where we have found reference there is only self-reference, I argue that the historical situation was too complex for such readings. The Victorians, surely, did write with the awareness of the possibilities of indeterminate meaning and of solipsism, but they wrote *against* the very indeterminacy they tended to reveal. Their narratives do not acquiesce in the conventions of order they inherit but struggle to reconstruct a world out of a world deconstructing, like modernist texts, all around them. With remarkable frequency, they are alert to the arbitrariness of the reconstructed order toward which they point as they imply the inadequacy of traditional texts and, through self-reference and parody, the tenuousness of their own. But they proceed to take the risk of believing in the possibility of fictions that bring us at least a little closer to what is not ourselves and not merely language.

The 'realism' with which this study is concerned is not that of the Scholastic philosophers.[3] And it is only minimally that once notorious kind with which late-nineteenth-century writers sought to sweep away the pieties and conventionalities of the mid-Victorians and of their popular imitators. Realism in England belongs, rather, to a much more affable and moderate tradition, focusing not on the dregs of society, not on the degradations and degenerations of humans in bondage to a social and cosmic determinism. It belongs, almost provincially, to a 'middling' condition and defines itself against the excesses, both stylistic and narrative, of various kinds of romantic, exotic, or sensational literatures. The programatic realism of the late century, with its pseudoscientific connections, its 'experimental novels,' its assumption that the norm of human experience is the extreme, was part of a rebellious movement against the mid-Victorian real and the art that projected it.

The mark of a less insular and more cynical culture was upon this later realism that Gissing explored, in which George Moore dabbled, and through which the great and not so great French and Russian novelists entered the mainstream of English fiction. But even it can be understood, within the terms I shall be finding for the whole tradition of English realism, as a self-conscious rejection of certain conventions of literary representation and of their implications. Purporting, like all realism, to speak the truth, it in fact invents a truth defined by its almost perfect inversion of mid-Victorian conventions. Thus, where earlier nineteenth-century realists found little incompatibility between 'sincere' representation and a conscious attempt to speak helpfully to a sympathetic audience, the later realists insisted, like their more aesthetically inclined contemporaries, on an artistic integrity that alienated them from the traditional novel-reading audience. They imagined that the truth would be offensive to that audience, and found confirmation of their fictions precisely in their offensiveness.

Thus Henry James, in his review of Zola's *Nana*, asks with uncharacteristic Jamesian bitterness, 'On what authority does [M. Zola] represent nature to us as a combination of the cesspool and the house of prostitution? On what authority does he represent foulness rather than fairness as the sign that we are to know her by?'[4] And in so speaking, James represents the implicit attitudes, not only of the late-century artists who were fostering a more highly aesthetic literary tradition, but of the earlier realists to whom, however far he developed their art and perhaps transcended it, he owed his primary allegiance. For in their inversion of the very tradition that James was trying to outgrow by a renewed partly Flaubertian preoccupation with the nature of his medium, the later realists rejected not only the predominantly middle class perception of reality that informed the moderate landscapes of the Victorian novel, but also the apparently rarefied and genteel emphasis on form and pattern, as opposed to the hard, cold 'truth,' in the aesthetic tradition to which, we might say, James, and Pater, and Wilde, and the later George Moore in their various ways belonged.

But the later realism, as an alternative to the earlier and apparently conventionalized realism, had few serious exponents in England, where there are no Maupassants or Zolas or Goncourts. Gissing, Hardy, James, Conrad, Moore himself – they all rejected the 'experimental novel': and, despite their great differences, they wrote recognizably within the English tradition and sought to reconcile form and art with an appeal both to truth and to their audiences. Nevertheless, the emergence of late-century realism marks an important stage in the breakdown of the realism with which I am primarily concerned; and that stage further complicates the word *realism*, making it an even more dangerously multivalent one.

It is, nevertheless, an inescapable word, and in what follows I risk the dangers because with all the divergent possibilities of meaning, the word, in its literary application, carries a consistent thrust through all its inconsistent history. Whatever else it means, it always implies an attempt to use language to get beyond language, to discover some non-verbal truth out there. The history of English realism obviously depended in large measure on changing notions of what *is* 'out there,' of how best to 'represent' it, and of whether, after all, representation is possible or the 'out there' knowable. The history was further complicated by the artist's sense of responsibility to the audience, by conventions of propriety, and by the nature of earlier literary imaginations of the 'real'. Moreover, there is the problem that 'realistic' did not become a label for novels until rather late, so that while Ian Watt can talk about the 'rise of realism' in the eighteenth century,[5] the word in ordinary usage is associated not so much with Jane Austen's kind of novel as with Arnold Bennett's or Gissing's, and even more, of course, with Zola's. Nevertheless, I assume a continuity from Defoe through to the nineteenth century, and I begin this study with Jane Austen.

Nineteenth-century realism was an international phenomenon, with its deepest roots in the transformations of culture and literature that we call by the name 'Romantic.' Realism presumes that the 'ordinary' (another difficult but persistent word) has a value hitherto ascribed almost exclusively to the experience of the select few. What was generically low and comic became, as Erich Auerbach's *Mimesis* has definitively shown, mixed and serious.[6] Realism tended to explode the distinctions between high and low in art, although the traces of a comic and 'low mimetic' tradition remain visible even now. In England, realism developed its own conventions as it recoiled from earlier 'misrepresentations,' so that there are easily recognizable similarities among fictions that are ostensibly shaped primarily by their commitment to plausibility and truthfulness rather than to generic conventions.

My concern here is primarily with the development and disruption and transformation of these similarities as they hardened into conventions that were recognized *as* conventions. That they did so harden is manifest, for example, in Gissing's casual dismissal of them in the midst of an attack on the later realism. Realism, Gissing says, 'merely contrasts with the habit of mind which assumes that a novel is written "to please people," that disagreeable facts must always be kept out of sight, that human nature must be systematically flattered, that the book must have a "plot," that the story should end on a cheerful note, and all the rest of it.'[7] That 'habit of mind,' ironically, was what had become of Victorian realism, so that the 'realism' Gissing evokes against it is apparently an altogether different thing. Actually however, this later realism is, in effect, using the earlier ideal of realism, the attempt to represent life sincerely, to dismiss its own hardened conventions.

The sticky self-contradictions latent in this relatively simple use of the word will get even stickier. The great novelists of the nineteenth century were never so naïve about narrative conventions or the problems of representation as later realists or modern critics have suggested. If we now can detect the conventionality of their admirable struggles to get at truth without imprisoning it in conventions, we can also see that the attempt allies them with the very writers and critics who defined themselves by rejecting them. The later realism is only one evidence of the self-contradictory nature of realism itself.

My concern then, is not with a definition of 'realism,' but with a study of its elusiveness. As an idea realism is one thing (or many things); as a literary practice, it is quite another (or others). I want to focus on the practice. In this case at least, our current emphasis on theory as opposed to practice, and the theoretical arguments against exegesis, are a danger to theory itself. No theory of the novel can stand that is not based firmly in a detailed consideration of what novelists actually did. A theory of realism, for instance, which fails to take into account the way particular novels radically change, in style and 'content,' the conventions of the past and present that realism is frequently said to affirm, can be no theory at all. The theory of this study is, thus, embedded in and inseparable from the exegeses of texts.

Writers and critics return to 'realism,' from generation to generation, because each culture's perception of reality changes and because literature requires ever new means to intimate the reality. As we may by now be tired of hearing, language, in representing reality, most forcefully demonstrates reality's absence. At best, language creates the illusion of reality so that our current definitions of realism swerve from implying the possibility of direct representation to focus on the difference between the medium and the reality whose absence it registers. Language, finally, can 'represent' only other language. Thus a convenient and slippery definition provided by David Lodge comes close to accommodating both our common sense notion that realism tries to represent reality and our sophisticated awareness that it cannot. Realism, he says, is 'the representation of experience in a manner which approximates closely to description of similar experience in non-literary texts of the same culture.'[8] The philosophical holes in this are large, but no definition of realism can be quite satisfactory. And insofar as this one attempts to get at the connection between nonfictional and fictional experience, it does good service.

But my focus will be on the struggle inherent in any 'realist' effort – the struggle to avoid the inevitable conventionality of language in pursuit of the unattainable unmediated reality. Realism, as a literary method, can in these terms be defined as a self-conscious effort, usually in the name of some moral enterprise of truth telling and extending the limits of human sympathy, to make literature appear to be describing directly not some other language but reality itself (whatever that may be taken to be); in this effort, the writer must self-contradictorily dismiss previous conventions of representation while, in effect, establishing new ones. No major Victorian novelists were deluded into believing that they were in fact offering an unmediated reality; but all of them struggled to make contact with the world out there, and, even with their knowledge of their own subjectivity, to break from the threatening limits of solipsism, of convention, and of language. Some aspects of their continuing struggle make the subject of this book.

Abstractly, their struggles follow the large-scale fate of the word *realism* itself. For realism begins, in Aristotelian and Scholastic philosophers, as the reification of the ideal, belief in the prior reality of universals and in the merely contingent reality of things. The idea exists outside the thinker and before the thing. Yet, by a well-known historical quirk, realism slides over to mean its opposite. The elements are the same: ideas and things. But now things are independent of conciousness, ideas empirically contingent upon things. In commonsense language, this way of imagining the world makes realism a grumpy suspicion of ideas, a hard-nosed facing of the facts and of the power of the external world over dream, desire, idea. Ironically, however, this realism edges back in modern thought and literature toward its beginnings, or toward its own entire elimination. For in the new relationship between idea and thing, they become incommensurate, as in nineteenth-century fiction. Neither can be contingent on the other. The idea is reified again, but phenomenally, as an idea, not as a prior reality or a means to reality. By virtue, then, of the very 'realistic' discourse that marks the connection between idea and thing, we are, in the modernist predicament, cut off from things. The idea becomes the clearest indication of the thing's absence. Language, as mediator, can be about only itself, for each predicate modifies not the thing, but another predicate, obeys the rules not of the idea but of its own ordering principles. What language attempts to possess by describing eludes, like Keats's fair maiden of the urn, our longing embrace.

But I do not want to dwell on the *abstraction*. Although my focus must be on realism as a convention, it is a mode that depends heavily on our commonsense expectation that there are direct connections between word and thing. And hence, of all literary movements, realism is most threatened by the contemporary severing of text from referent. Realism, after all, was initiated out of and against the severance. The coincidence of realism and parody is a well-established idea to which I shall be returning frequently, but that coincidence should remind us of the centrality to realism of a self-conscious rejection of literature. Like Don Quixote's friends, realism seems intent on burning libraries, recognizing the madness of taking what is only a text as though it had the authority of reality. Yet, like the Don's friends, realism never quite burns all the books: it claims for itself a special authority. Part of realism's complex fate has to do with the continuing struggle of its practitioners to avoid the implications of their own textuality, that they are merely part of the Don's library, deserving of burning. Much of the power of nineteenth-century realist fiction derives from the integrity of its pursuit of possibilities that would paradoxically deprive it of its authority and sever it from its responsibility to reality and audience. With the high Victorian ideal of Truth or Sincerity, novelists exposed the artificiality of their own conventions, tested the limits of their own exclusions, and as best they could kept their eyes on their objects.

It is no accident, therefore, that conventionally we speak of 'romance' as the most obvious alternative to realism. As we shall see with Austen and Thackeray, much nineteenth-century realism defined itself against romance because that form implied wish fulfillment rather than reality. And the romance/realism dichotomy, classically stated by Richard Chase, variously imagined by writers from Clara Reeve and Walter Scott to Nathaniel Hawthorne and Henry James to Northrop Frye and Leslie Fiedler, does require attention. But 'romance' has become almost as confused a term as 'realism.' At present, the conventional dichotomy may help to suggest an alternative to the way I am imagining the problem of realism. What I shall be calling 'contradictions' in the realist's program may be seen as more absolute differences in genre. Edward Eigner's recent study, for example, valuably extends this way of arguing. He distinguishes the predominantly mimetic writers from what he calls the 'metaphysical novelists,' who describe not so much the 'effect of experience on individuals,' as 'the nature of experience itself.'[9]

The value of such a generic distinction is evident in the details of Eigner's excellent study, but its elaboration also runs counter to the very mixed condition of Victorian thought. Victorian nonfiction is rich with instances of arguments, firmly based in the mimetic ideal, that make no distinction between what we might call scientific description and metaphysical speculation. One of the primary efforts of Victorian thought was to reconcile empirical science with metaphysical truth. We find such effort, although unsystematic, in most of Ruskin's work, as it is already implicit in Carlyle's. Moreover the great Victorian system maker, Herbert Spencer, the creator of 'The Unknowable,' claimed to be creating his system inductively. One of the most interesting and touching fragments of such an effort can be found in G. H. Lewes's five-volume *Problems of Life and Mind*, the last two volumes of which were published posthumously by George Eliot, and about which I shall have much to say later.[10]

As we look over the criticism that attached to realism from the start, we find recurring objections to what Hardy was later to attack as mere 'copyism.'[11] The antimimetic tradition most forcefully espoused by Bulwer never completely lost out, and in fact occupied an important position in the dominant realistic tradition. Although, retrospectively, we can find little important Victorian fiction validly subject to the complaint of copying, the possibility worried many writers. Reviewers in the *Quarterly*, early in the century, were lamenting the failure of novelists working the new field of the 'domestic' to throw over their narratives 'the colours of poetry.'[12] Ironically, late-century writers were finding Victorian realism too ideal, insufficiently real or faithful in its copying. The opposite of realism, Lewes had said around mid-century, was not idealism but 'Falsism.'

Lewes's defense of realism implies, nevertheless, a cultural consensus that realism tended to be *un*-poetic and *un*-ideal. But the very lateness with which the word appeared on the literary scene, and the difficulty it had surviving serious criticism from novelists themselves, suggest that in England at least the convention was a symptom not of a realistic school, but of a tendency among very different writers. The ease with which realism was reconciled with other objectives – the ideal, the beautiful – further implies not a single genre but a variety of ways of organizing some special historical perspectives. The isolation of a genre to be called the realistic novel entails a circular inductive method: the abstraction from novels we already presume to be realistic of the qualities that make them so. I prefer to keep the focus on the qualities nineteenth-century writers shared, without worrying about generic labels. [...]

Whatever qualities are abstracted to produce a definition of genre that would include, say, both James's *The Ambassadors* and Thackeray's *Vanity Fair*, formal differences would subvert the definition. The continuing literary problem that plagued realism from the start was the incompatibility of tight form with plausibility. 'The realistic writer soon finds,' says Northrop Frye, 'that the requirements of literary form and plausible content always fight against each other.'[13] James's disapproval of much Victorian fiction is partly a disapproval of the expansiveness of form required to produce a cumulatively effective plausibility.

Whatever its difficulties and contradictions, however, realism was a historical impulse that manifested itself as a literary method and imposed itself on almost every form of prose narrative. It was a method consonant with empirical science in that it was exploratory rather than definitive. The method of realism, Georg Lukács has argued, is a method of discovery, not of representation of preestablished realities.[14] The quest could lead in the direction of the 'metaphysical novelists,' but normally only through the exploration of the here and now; and although realism may make the particular typical, it resists using allegorical forms and prefers what we might call a Wordsworthian method of finding in the individual a common human appeal. The truth realism sought was replacing the transcendent reality that had dominated knowledge until the Renaissance,[15] but that truth could lead out from the particular once more to an alternative transcendence – as, say, in the

Feuerbachian ideal of George Eliot. In withdrawing a metaphysical sanction from reality, George Eliot immediately replaced it with a 'humanist' sanction by seeing the forms of human experience in a Wordsworthian light, as manifestations of a large, morally sanctified community. The secular truth might lead as well to a negative transcendence as in the structure of Hardy's fiction. There, the Providential patterns are exactly reversed to give to the defeated protagonist an almost transcendent dignity. The variety of possibilities reflects the way the realistic impulse is most precisely located in the historical context of a secularizing movement directed against the falsehoods of earlier imaginations of reality. Because it was an impulse particularly vulnerable to social, scientific, and epistemological transformation, its actual embodiments were polymorphous.

If it were possible to locate a single consistent characteristic of realism among its various rejections of traditional forms and ideals, it would be that antiliterary thrust I have already noted; and this thrust is also – inevitably – antigeneric in expression. The quest for unmediated experience becomes central to the dramatic tensions of most realistic fiction, even where the rhetorical strategy is to establish several layers of mediation – as in *Wuthering Heights*, which is generically a romance, or in *The Newcomes*, with Pendennis narrating a quintessentially realistic fiction. The fate of realism and its complicated relation to all those literary forms in which it confusedly manifests itself are intimately involved with the writer's and the culture's capacity to believe in the accessibility of experience beyond words.

If we agree to take realism in this way, as a historical phenomenon, we can discuss it with some precision, locate those qualities that mark it as anticonventional, and keep it unstably in process. For the label, 'realism,' sticks. In disentangling the threads that weave the label, I want to insist on three major points. First, realism *was* always in process as long as it was important to nineteenth-century fiction; second, there was no such thing as naïve realism – simple faith in the correspondence between word and thing – among serious Victorian novelists; and third and not quite contradictorily, Victorian realists, recognizing the difference between truth and the appearance of truth, did try to embrace the reality that stretched beyond the reach of language. Their eyes and hearts were on Keats's fair maiden.

Despite its appearance of solidity, realism implies a fundamental uneasiness about self, society, and art. It becomes a dominant way of seeing at the time J. Hillis Miller describes as marking 'the splitting apart of [the communion] of . . . verbal symbols with the reality they named.'[16] While 'Nature' had become for Carlyle a 'grand unnameable

Fact,'[17] poets and novelists were engaged in naming it. But the activity was self-conscious, and truth telling was raised to the level of doctrine. Such intensity of commitment to speaking the truth suggests difficulties where before none had been perceived. The mystery lay not beyond phenomena, but in them. Description, as Lukács argues, begins at the point where things are felt to be alienated from human activity. Realists take upon themselves a special role as mediator, and assume self-consciously a moral burden that takes a special form: their responsibility is to a reality that increasingly seems 'unnameable,' as Carlyle implies mockingly in the pseudo-science that opens *Sartor Resartus*; but it is also to an audience that requires to be weaned or freed from the misnaming literatures past and current. The quest for the world beyond words is deeply moral, suggesting the need to reorganize experience and reinvest it with value for a new audience reading from a new base of economic power.

The general disrepute into which novel writing had fallen by the beginning of the nineteenth century, although it does not imply disbelief in the power of language to engage reality, does express moral and intellectual outrage at the dominance of literature that trivialized human experience. We see this outrage in Carlyle's puritanical distrust of fiction as a form of lying (picked up and turned upside down by Oscar Wilde in 'The Decay of Lying'); in Macaulay's affectionate unease with the appeal of fiction to what is childish in us; in Thackeray's extensive ironies or Austen's amused defense. In the vigor of the dismissal of earlier literature, particularly of the popular novels by women at the end of the eighteenth century, of gothic, sentimental, and silver-fork novels, is an implicit consensus that literature had to be relocated. Although the novel remained an amusement, it often attempted to become (sometimes willy-nilly became) an instrument of knowledge as well.

The relocation entailed a shift of focus from the large to the small, from the general to the particular, and a diminishment of dramatic extremes, as from tragedy to pathos. It is a commonplace to say that realism does not stay at that reduced scale, but the criterion of plausibility requires at least that the beginnings be here, where the characteristic mid-century novel struggles to remain. The shift and the transience of the shift are captured as early as *Sketches by Boz*, where Dickens can be seen learning his craft by learning how to give to the particular and ordinary the resonances traditionally to be found in the universals of an earlier philosophy and literature.

In the first sketch, as published in book form, Dickens's opening words might be taken as a metaphor, or a thesis sentence, for realism's effort to make the ordinary significant: 'How much is conveyed in those two short words – "The Parish!" And with how many tales of distress and misery, of broken fortune and ruined hopes, too often of unrelieved wretchedness and successful knavery are they associated!'[18] Already, Dickensian melodrama is present, the impatience with limits; yet the means of transcending limits is 'the parish,' not a religious organization but a commonplace secular society – Austen's kind of geography. Crude as Dickens's method may be, the means of transcending limits is the exploration of the known as though it were unknown. Dickens will not merely copy the parish; he will see it with a freshness and clarity that will at once make it recognizable to the new popular audience who might take it seriously as a subject, and transform it. The particular, under the pressure of intense and original seeing, gives back the intensities normally associated with larger scale, traditional forms. That such a passage as this sounds now like a cliché and belongs to the 'Our Town' convention implies much about the fate of mid-century realism. In any case, by looking intensely at doorknobs, and walls, and old clothes, and cabmen, Dickens uses his *Sketches* to bring together the particular and the conventional, the ordinary and the extreme, making experience amusing, as George Eliot would say of art, by enlarging our sympathies and our knowledge.

Dickens, certainly, was less easy with the limits of realism than most of his contemporaries, but he shares here its mimetic and exploratory tendencies. And his example suggests, perhaps more than the examples of, say, Thackeray, Trollope, and George Eliot, that it is perverse to apply to realism a critical method that assumes the separation of language from its object and the irresistibly conventional nature of literary forms. In his essay on the *Sketches*, J. Hillis Miller attempts precisely to apply such a method: 'Any literary text is both self-referential and extra-referential, or rather it is open to being not seen as the former and mistakenly taken as the latter. All language is figurative, displaced. All language is beside itself.'[19] Yet surely the figurativeness of the *Sketches* appears to be asking to be taken as 'extra-referential.' Surely, too, to treat as conventions of literature such references as that to 'broken fortunes and ruined homes' does violence, if not to the experience of reading, then to the historical force of the language. Laurence Lerner speaks directly to this difficulty:

> To treat romance, fable, or comedy in terms of a set of literary conventions, devices for noticing some things and not others, is to say nothing unacceptable to the practitioners of these modes; but to treat realism in this way is to knock the bottom out of its programme.... To treat realism as merely

another set of conventions is to display such a lack of sympathy with its aims as to be virtually incapacitated from appreciating its products.[20]

Such sanely antitheoretical arguments belong in the tradition of realism they defend. Lerner, moreover, understands many of the difficulties of his position. Nevertheless, although Miller carries the argument beyond its historically justifiable place, and Lerner has a firm historical sense of the realist's position, no historical perspective that ignores the problems posed by modern epistemology and criticism can entirely sustain itself. E. H. Gombrich's classic discussion of this kind of problem demonstrates that in spite of a deep commitment to the external real, the artist must use conventions for the representation of reality from which nobody working the medium can too widely depart, and that representations of reality normally change through more or less subtle variations on other representations in the medium – like Constable's on Cozens's clouds, like Austen's on the gothic novel. All perception is mediated by the culture into which one is born so that the Heaven that 'lies about us in our infancy. . . fade[s] into the light of common day.' 'There is no reality,' says Roland Barthes, 'not already classified by man.'[21] And while every beginning, like Dickens's own, is a discontinuity, discontinuity produces, as Edward Said argues, a 'difference which is the result of combining the already-familiar with the fertile novelty of human work in language.'[22] Beginnings and discontinuities can be understood only by way of relationship. And the beginning, for writers in the tradition with which I am concerned, implies differences within a range so recognizably shared that they seem, in their very unconventionality, conventional. While Victorian realists strained to be extrareferential, and must be read as though they were, the nature of their 'references' or 'representations' is comprehensible only if we also see its conventionality.

We get close to the texture of realism, however, if we recognize that narratives touched by the realistic impulse try to resist or circumvent the '*formal*' conventions of narrative. The primary conventions of realism are its deflation of ambition and passion, its antiheroism, its tendency to see all people and things within large containing social organizations and, hence, its apparently digressive preoccupation with surfaces, things, particularities, social manners. Committed to treat 'things as they are and not as the story teller would like them to be for his convenience'[23] realists assume the possibility of making the distinction and thus save meaning at the sacrifice of pleasure. Realism further complicates itself because in requiring a continuing alertness to the secret lust of the spirit to impose itself on the world – if not as hero, then as martyr – and in resisting the romance forms that embody those lusts, it is always on the verge of another realism: the recognition that the reality it most adequately represents is a subtly disguised version of its own desires.

There is, then, a continuing tradition of self-consciousness in realistic fiction, a tradition formally initiated in *Don Quixote*. The self-consciousness marks realism's awareness both of other literature and of the strategies necessary to circumvent it, and – at last – its awareness of its own unreality. The complex fate of realism as it unfolds through the century is latent in that self-consciousness. Ironically, the self-consciousness itself becomes a convention, and we can detect it in realism's most overt anti-literary manifestos. A look at a few of these provides a useful starting point.

> If, among those who may be tempted to peruse my history, there should be any mere novel-readers, let me advise them to throw the book aside at the commencement of this chapter, for I have no more wonderful incidents to relate, no more charges at the muse, no more sudden turns of fortune. I am now become a plodding man of business . . . [Maria Edgeworth, 'Ennui, or Memoirs of the Earl of Glenthorne' (1804)]

> I do not invite my fair readers, whose sex and impatience gives them the greatest right to complain of these circumstances, into a flying chariot drawn by hippogriffs, or moved by enchantment. Mine is an humble English post-chaise, drawn upon four wheels, and keeping his Majesty's highway. Such as dislike the vehicle may leave it at the next halt, and wait for the conveyance of Prince Hussein's tapestry. [Scott, *Waverley* (1814)]

> All which details, I have no doubt, JONES, who reads this book at his Club, will pronounce to be excessively foolish, trivial, twaddling, and ultra-sentimental. Yes; I can see Jones at this minute (rather flushed with his joint of mutton and half-pint of wine), taking out his pencil and scoring under the words 'foolish, twaddling,' etc., and adding to them his own remark of '*quite true.*' Well, he is a lofty man of genius, and admires the great and heroic in life and novels; and so had better take warning and go elsewhere. [Thackeray, *Vanity Fair* (1847)]

> If you think from this prelude that anything like a romance is preparing for you, reader, you never were more mistaken. Do you anticipate sentiment, and poetry, and reverie? Do you expect passion and stimulus, and melodrama? Calm your expectations: reduce them to a lowly standard. Something real, cool, and solid lies before you; something as unromantic as Monday morning, when all who work wake with the consciousness that they must rise and betake themselves thereto. It is not positively affirmed that you shall not

have a taste of the exciting, perhaps towards the middle and close of the meal, but it is resolved that the first dish set upon the table shall be one that a Catholic – ay, even an Anglo-Catholic – might eat on Good Friday in Passion Week; it shall be cold lentils and vinegar without oil; it shall be unleavened bread with bitter herbs and no roast lamb. [Charlotte Brontë, *Shirley* (1849)]

The Rev. Amos Barton, whose sad fortunes I have undertaken to relate, was, you perceive, in no respect an ideal or exceptional character, and perhaps I am doing a bold thing to bespeak your sympathy on behalf of a man who was so very far from remarkable, – a man whose virtues were not heroic, and who had no undetected crime within his breast; who had not the slightest mystery hanging about him, but was palpably and unmistakably commonplace; who was not even in love, but had that complaint favourably many years ago. 'An utterly uninteresting character!' I think I hear a lady reader exclaim – Mrs Farthingale, for example, who prefers the ideal in fiction; to whom tragedy means ermine tippets, adultery, and murder; and comedy, the adventures of some personage who is quite a 'character.'...

Depend upon it, you would gain unspeakably if you would learn with me to see some of the poetry and the pathos, the tragedy and the comedy, lying in the experience of a human soul that looks out through dull, grey eyes, and that speaks in a voice of quite ordinary tones. [George Eliot, 'The Sad Fortunes of the Rev. Amos Barton,' *Scenes of Clerical Life* (1857)]

The family resemblances are remarkable, and these quotations are unquestionably characteristic of a tone and attitude that dominated in English fiction for the first fifty or sixty years of the nineteenth century. They are kin, for example, to the parodic opening of *Northanger Abbey*, in which Catherine Morland is defined by virtue of her qualities inappropriate to heroines; to Dickens's explanation of the naturalness of melodrama in *Oliver Twist* (chapter 17); to the mock-heroic language of some passages in *Barchester Towers*, and to Trollope's explanation there of why he abjures surprises in fiction, and has difficulties with happy endings; to the strategy of Mrs Gaskell in *Mary Barton* of attempting to force upon the reader a recognition of the 'hidden romances' in 'the lot of those who daily pass you by in the street.'[24]

Although such passages had become commonplace by the time of George Eliot, each writer, however sophisticated, writes as though the enterprise of the ordinary in fiction were new and difficult, and that in 1860 as well as 1804, the audience had to be warned and cajoled about it. Yet there are differences in the rhetorical strategies, suggesting that the stakes were getting higher. What light satire remains in the passage by George Eliot (compare Mrs Farthingale with Thackeray's Mr Jones) moves into a rhetoric of almost romantic intensity, so that the style insists on the seriousness which, in Austen, Scott, even Thackeray, is one of the immediate objects of derision. Even the awkward satirical thrust of the passage from *Shirley* is intense enough to belie the Thackerayan gestures in the metaphors of food. Thematically, that is to say, these passages all conventionally assert that fiction should shift its focus from the extreme to the ordinary, and that to do so is morally instructive; rhetorically, they imply that to do so is also to violate the dominant conventions of fiction (implicitly absurd, immoral, or both), but in fact to make fiction more, not less, intense, and to give back with greater authenticity by Wordsworthian strategies the very romantic powers taken away in the rejection of conventions.

The refusal of major realists to acknowledge the conventionality of these strategies has partly to do with the nature of much popular fiction of the time, but more important, the refusal was essential to the convention itself. It supported the special authenticity the realist novel claimed by emphasizing its primary allegiance to experience over art. But there is no need to think the emphasis disingenuous. In adopting the technique of the direct address to the audience in order to justify the treatment of ordinary experience, all these writers participate in a cultural project – moral, empirical, and self-conscious – that appears conventional only in retrospect.

The epistemology that lay behind realism was empiricist, with its tendency to value immediate experience over continuities or systems of order, and it was obviously related to the developments in empirical science as they ran through the century. These developments did not, of course, validate either the discontinuities empiricism would seem to imply, or the minimizing of imagination and intuition. Yet in requiring the validation of imagination in the visible world, recognizable to the audience that figures so prominently in these passages, realism posits a tension between imagination (with the faculty of reason, as well) and reality. Values are reversed in that the realistic method proceeds to what is not visible – the principles of order and meaning – through the visible; the *a priori* now requires validation.

But the process does not imply a mere literalism of reportage, or 'copyism.' The implication of each of these passages, most powerfully developed by George Eliot, is that the aim of the apparently dull record of the humdrum is to discover 'the poetry and the pathos, the tragedy and the comedy.' The writers all share a faith that the realist's exploration will reveal a comprehensible world. George Eliot requires that her narrative, attaining to tragedy, convey the impression of an empirically shareable experience. Its relation to reality may be mediated by consciousness, but it is authenticated by the appeal of consciousness to the shared consciousness of the community of readers. For the realistic method, it is a matter of balance.

One of the dominant theories about nineteenth-century English realism has pointed misleadingly to a reconciliation of these difficulties. If the reality observed is coherent and meaningful, so the theory runs, so too will be its represented form. Thus, the important distinction between realism of correspondence and realism of coherence, invented (used even by the Victorians) to cope with the difference between the text and its subject, between reality and art's appearance of reality, is lost. Ioan Williams, arguing the standard case, for example, says that 'there is no doubt that the mid-Victorian novel rested on a massive confidence as to what the nature of Reality actually was,' and that 'the most fundamental common element in the work of the mid-Victorian novelist . . . is probably the idea that human life, whatever the particular conditions, may ultimately be seen as unified and coherent.'[25] Generally, the quotations confirm this view: they do, after all, conclude with 'tragedy and comedy,' and the apparent confidence with which they imply the value of the trivial suggests an underlying organicism, characteristic of Victorian thought.

But reflection suggests that what is most striking in these passages is not their unquestioning confidence, but their self-consciousness about the difficulties of the arguments in favor of common sense. They are engaged in a battle parallel to that familiar one, most allegorically handled in *Hard Times*, between life, with all its emotion and vitality, and utilitarianism, with all its analytic calculation. The organic and the mechanical are opposed forces in Victorian fiction, and the deadliness of the struggle is most apparent in post-Darwinian thought: the faith was that science would reveal the organic, the secularist's last hope for meaning and the validation of morality; the fear was that it would yield only the mechanical. The distinction made by G. H. Lewes can make clear how important the struggle was if realism was to retain any contact with the values from which it had cut itself off:

> Theoretically taking the Organism to pieces to understand its separate parts, we fall into the error of supposing that Organism is a mere assemblage of organs, like a machine which is put together by juxtaposition of different parts. But this is radically to misunderstand its essential nature and the universal solidarity of its parts. The Organism is not made, not put together, but *evolved*; its parts are not juxtaposed, but differentiated; its organs are groups of minor organisms, all sharing in a common life.[26]

The mechanical reading of the organs is an implicit threat through much of nineteenth-century fiction. Metaphorically, it is foreshadowed by Victor Frankenstein's creation of his monster, and the terrible threat of the nonrational violence built into that machine lurks behind the human ideals that give meaning to the lives of fiction's protagonists, as Pip's ambitions are the reverse image of murderous, Orlick-like desires. For Lewes, the emphasis on organism is part of an argument that leads to metaphysics through science, necessary because common perception and common sense fail to yield the truth visible under the microscope.

None of the novelists uses a microscope, of course, although George Eliot is driven to the analogy herself; but the passages I have quoted all suggest an uneasiness about what unaided vision can yield. The self-consciousness manifests itself in the self-denigrating language with which they refer to the reality they are to describe: the production of 'a plodding man of business,' 'trivial, twaddling, and ultra-sentimental,' like 'cold lentils and vinegar,' or 'an utterly uninteresting character.'

We need to shift the balance in our appraisal of realism. It was not a solidly self-satisfied vision based in a misguided objectivity and faith in representation, but a highly self-conscious attempt to explore or create a new reality. Its massive self-confidence implied a radical doubt, its strategies of truth telling, a profound self-consciousness. In a culture whose experience included the Romantic poets and the philosophical radicals; Carlyle and Newman attempting to define their faiths; Charles Lyell telling it that the world reveals 'no vestige of a beginning, no prospect of an end'; the Higher Criticism of the Bible from Germany; Hume, Kant, Goethe, Comte, and Spencer, with their varying systems or antisystems; non-Euclidean geometry and a new anthropology made possible by a morally dubious imperialism; John Stuart Mill urging liberty and women's equality; Darwin, Huxley, and the agnostics; Tennyson struggling to reimagine faith; Browning, Arnold, Swinburne, Pater – in such a culture it is more than a little difficult to imagine a serious literary mode based on a 'massive confidence as to what the nature of Reality actually was.' In *Dombey and Son* the railroad produces an 'earthquake' and opens up new realities to the insular Dombey (but more important, to his insular audience). In *The French Revolution* Carlyle describes a world in constant process, always burning, and warns of the possible consummation for English society. And Mrs Gaskell – in *Mary Barton* and *North and South* – maneuvers carefully against what she feared correctly to be a growing breach between the classes.

The confident moralism of which the great Victorian writers are frequently accused turns out almost invariably to be an attempt to rediscover moral order after their primary energies have been devoted to disrupting conventions of moral judgment. The tradition reflected in the passages I have quoted belongs with Wordsworth's attempt to 'choose incidents and situations from common life, and...to throw over them a certain coloring of the imagination,' and with Carlyle's attempt to persuade us to see every drawing room as the crossroads of the infinite. Nineteenth-century realism, far from apologizing for what is, deliberately subverts judgments based on dogma, convention, or limited perception and imagination. Mr Podsnap is the enemy not only of Dickens, but of all the Victorian novelists. For Stephen Blackpool and Mr Tulliver it's a 'puzzle' or a 'muddle.' What seems clear becomes cloudy as we see more and from different perspectives. Even as they articulate the social codes, these novels complicate them, engaging our sympathy with lost women, tyrannical husbands, murderers, revolutionaries, moral weaklings, rebellious girls, spendthrifts, and dilettantes. When George Eliot dismisses the 'men of maxims,' she only articulates what is implicit in the realistic impulse, and when by shifting perspectives she reimagines the nature and worth of her characters, she only acts out formally what Thackeray constantly talked about and what she had already discovered in Scott's novels, as they treated sympathetically both sides of every historical conflict.

The disruptions of moral judgment, of aesthetic patterning, of common sense perceptions have a serious import that we can too easily solemnize. After all, despite the disappearance of God, the potential disappearance of meaning, the mysteries and disruptions, the primary form in which most nineteenth-century English realism manifests itself is comedy. Even these highly moral passages, urging upon us what seems an ascetic renunciation of the glamorous, are partly comic performances. They seem to take pleasure in the details they invoke from outside the patterning conventions of romance. And the great realistic fictions are exuberant with details, even when they are melancholy thematically. The alienation implied by description is partially compensated for by the sheer pleasure of being able to *see*, as though for the first time, the clutter of furniture, the cut of clothing, the mutton chop and the mug of hot rum, the flushed cheeks of Mr Jones, and the dull grey eyes of Amos Barton. This very vitality of detail is part of the realist's gestures at life, for they will not succumb to the conventions of patterning. James Kincaid finds in Trollope, for example, 'a sense that genuine life is to be found only outside all pattern.'[27] It is just possible that – as I shall argue in my discussion of Thackeray – the realist's self-conscious rejection of form represents a viable alternative to the Jamesian self-conscious restriction and purification of form. There is a violence implied in the conventions of narrative that wrests resolution from the muddle of experience. If nineteenth-century realism normally succumbs to these wishful thrusts, it also typically indulges in the satisfaction of anticlimactic wisdom, pretending that life extends beyond its pages, that life is only partially reflected in the novel's multitudinous disregard. There is a pleasure in knowing life, and a pleasure in the power to seduce an audience into believing it has seen life too.

As we explore even the most conservative of the classic novels of the nineteenth century, we find continuing experiments with forms, styles, modes of valuing. Those experiments are not aberrations from some realistic norm, but intrinsic to its nature. Resisting forms, it explores reality to find them; denying excess, it deserts the commonplace self-consciously asserted as its subject. Positing the reality of an external world, it self-consciously examines its own fictionality. Even as we watch the apparently confident assimilation of reality to comic patterns, we find fissures, and merely 'literary' conventions required to imply the reality of those patterns. The realistic novel persistently drives itself to question not only the nature of artificially imposed social relations, but the nature of nature, and the nature of the novel.

Realism exists as a process, responsive to the changing nature of reality as the culture understood it, and evoking with each question another question to be questioned, each threatening to destroy that quest beyond words, against literature, that is its most distinguishing mark. What consistency there may be in the fate of realism is no greater than that we can find among the implications of these passages: pre-occupation with the nature of their own materials; willingness to violate narrative conventions to call attention to themselves; implicit comparison between the falsities and pleasures of literature and the truths and rigors of life; concern with audience and the moral consequences of the activities of reading and writing; the moral urgency of seeing with disenchanted clarity and valuing the ordinary as the touchstone of human experience. The impelling energy in the quest for the world beyond words is that the world be there, and that it be meaningful and good; the persistent fear is that it is merely monstrous and mechanical, beyond the control of human meaning. Realism risks that reality and its powers of disruption. And while it represses the dreams and desires of the self with the cumulative, formless energies of the ordinary, it seeks also the self's release – sometimes in the very formlessness of the ordinary, sometimes in the increasingly complicated elaborations of the conventions and forms of the novel (which need, as Frank Kermode has noted, to become more difficult and less fairy-talish in order to be convincingly satisfying).[28] In the integrity of its explorations, realism increasingly imagined the limits of its power to reform, the monstrous possibility of the unnameable, the likelihood that the monstrous lurked in its very desire to see and to make the world good. [...]

Notes

1   One must not forget that this book was published in 1981, in the heart of the deconstruction phase of North American academia.
2   Gerald Graff, *Literature against Itself* (Chicago, 1979), esp. ch. 2.
3   Realism in medieval philosophy had a meaning that conflicted with its usage in the nineteenth century: it referred to a belief in universals as the objective reality. See p. 105 above for more of Levine's discussion of this.
4   Leon Edel, ed., *The House of Fiction* (Westport, Conn., 1973), 276.
5   See pp. 96–7 above.
6   See the Further Reading section.
7   George Gissing, 'The Place of Realism in Fiction', *Selections Autobiographical and Imaginative from the Works of George Gissing* (London, 1929), 221.
8   David Lodge, *The Modes of Modern Writing* (Ithaca, 1977), 25.
9   Edward Eiguer, *The Metaphysical Novel in England and America: Dickens, Bulwer, Hawthorne, Melville* (Berkeley, 1978), 2–3.
10 For Levine on science in Victorian culture more amply, see pp. 244–52 below.
11 'The Science of Fiction', *Life and* Art (New York, 1925), 87.
12 See 'Periodical Criticism: Reviewers Reviewed. The *Quarterly*', *Athenaeum*, 1 (2) (January 1828), 11.
13 Northrop Frye, *Fables of Identity* (New York, 1963), 36.
14 See, for example, Georg Lukács, *Studies in European Realism* (New York, 1964).
15 See Ermarth (pp. 97–8 above) for another perspective on this.
16 J. Hillis Miller, *The Disappearance of God* (New York, 1965), 3.
17 Thomas Carlyle, *Past and Present* (Boston, 1965), ch. 2, p. 13.
18 Charles Dickens, *Sketches by Boz, The Works of Charles Dickens*, 36 vols (Gadshill Edition; London: Chapman and Hall, 1877–1908), ch. 1, p. 1.
19 J. Hillis Miller, 'The Fiction of Realism', in Ada Nisbet, ed., *Dickens Centennial Essays* (Berkeley, Calif.: University of California Press, 1971), 124.
20 Laurence Lerner, 'Daniel Deronda: George Eliot's Struggle with Realism', in Alice Shalvi, ed., *Daniel Deronda: A Centenary Symposium* (Jerusalem, 1976), 92.
21 Roland Barthes, *Critical Essays*, trans, R. Howard (Evanston, 1972), xvii.
22 Edward Saïd, *Beginnings* (New York, 1975), xiii.
23 Frye, *Fables of Identity*, 27.
24 Elizabeth Gaskell, *Mary Barton* (London, 1906), ch. 6, p. 70.
25 Ioan Williams, *The Realist Novel in England: A Study in Development* (Pittsburgh, 1974), x, 13. Also, see above, p. 98.
26 G. H. Lewes, *The Problems of Life and Mind* (London, 1890), i. 113–14.
27 James Kincaid, *The Novels of Anthony Trollope* (New York, 1977), 40.
28 Frank Kermode, *The Sense of an Ending* (New York, 1967).

PSYCHOLOGIC-
AL COHERENCE
IN REALISM:
BERSANI'S *A
FUTURE FOR
ASTYANAX*
(1976)

The debate about realism's epistemological basis was not the only area of discussion on the implications of realism in the 1980s. What also proved controversial was the related matter of the link, variously understood, between the practice of nineteenth-century realism and its confidence in moral and political order. What kind of *politics* did Victorian realism involve? What were its dominant ideologies? Levine, in the extract above, contributed to this debate because he perceived the Victorian novelists imagining alternative fictional worlds of greater harmony than those they perceived in actuality. Realism was conceived as political in so far as it was an effort imaginatively to resist the unsatisfactory order of the world *out there*. Levine's approach to this aspect of the realist enterprise, as already mentioned, related to the ideas of Leo Bersani's *A Future for Astyanax: Character and Desire in Literature* (1976).[8] Bersani, working outside Derridean theory and inside the field of comparative literature, conceived of realism as embedded within a politics of reassurance and containment.

In 'Realism and the Fear of Desire' from *A Future for Astyanax*, Bersani argued that the nineteenth-century realist novel aimed to contain social fragmentation. It was a practice of writing that prioritized the ordering of elements disordered in the world beyond the page. But, in all the most interesting realists of the century, that effort failed. Ordering the world in fiction was a doomed project, scarred with a confession of failure. Realists counterpointed this awareness of the absence of wholeness with another myth: the notion of the unified nature of the human personality. Realism, Bersani said, was a pan-European practice of writing that offered its readers representations of psychological unity, persuading them of the knowableness of the human self. It presented models of selves who were harmonious and undisturbed by contradictory or inconsistent desires. For Bersani, the realist novels seldom subverted the coherent wholeness of personality however complex and fraught their fictional characters: 'Psychological complexity is tolerated as long as it doesn't threaten an ideology of the self as a fundamentally intelligible structure unaffected by a history of fragmented, discontinuous desires'[9] (for more on the emergence of the psychological in Victorian fiction, see Mary Poovey's work, discussed on pp. 164–79). The myth of the unified self, Bersani argued, was offered as a reassuring consolation in a world otherwise perceived as splintered and fragmentary. It was the essential restorative idea of nineteenth-century realism.

POLITICS OF
CLASSIC
REALISM AND
COHERENCE
CRITICIZED IN
THE 1980s

Both Levine and Bersani, though they differed in other respects and in their evaluation of the novelists' achievements, viewed the realist novel as struggling at an imaginative level to repair fractures. The efforts of the realist to present coherence was admired by Levine, but Catherine Belsey at the beginning of the 1980s saw this articulation of mythical wholeness as dangerous. More significantly, it was Bersani's notion of the unified self, the coherent, comprehensible human personality, which Belsey deplored in the texts of 'classic realism', a mode of representation she defined to include, among other forms, the canon of classic fiction of the nineteenth century and contemporary popular fiction. Bersani identified the unified self as the consoling myth offered by realist fiction, but Belsey saw a capitalist illusion in this argument. Her *Critical Practice* (1980), a widely read undergraduate introduction to modern theories of literature and reading, owed much to the Marxist Louis Althusser's conception of ideology as the general name for forces at work in society that fashion and 'interpellate' the individual and impart to him or her a sense of selfhood and identity.[10] *Critical Practice* argued that the texts of classic realism (no single text exemplifies all the qualities embraced in this term) invoked the notion of the coherent personality, of the whole psychology. But, unlike Bersani, Belsey read this from her Marxist viewpoint as a bourgeois strategy, seeing realism as smoothing over the cracks and flaws in the human personality that were always the product of life under capitalism. Belsey argued that the classic realist novel also addressed and interpellated the reader as a unified subject, flattered him or her as a coherent, non-contradictory self, and as the privileged individual who perceived the meaning of the text from a superior vantage point of knowledge. In reassuring the reader of his or her own psychological coherence, classic realism did more of the work of ideology because it papered over the contradictions of the reader's real self, the inevitable product of the dehumanizing conditions of modern capitalism.

Extract from Catherine Belsey, *Critical Practice* (London: Methuen, 1980), 67–82.

Classic realism, still the dominant popular mode in literature, film and television drama, roughly coincides chronologically with the epoch of industrial capitalism. It performs, I wish to suggest, the work of ideology, not only in its representation of a world of consistent subjects who are the origin of meaning, knowledge and action, but also in offering the reader, as the position from which the text is most readily intelligible, the position of subject as the origin both of understanding and of action in accordance with that understanding.

It is readily apparent that Romantic and post-Romantic poetry, from Wordsworth through the Victorian period at least to Eliot and Yeats, takes subjectivity as its central theme. The developing self of the poet, his consciousness of himself as poet, his struggle against the constraints of an outer reality, constitute the preoccupations of *The Prelude, In*

Memoriam or *Meditations in Time of Civil War*. The 'I' of these poems is a kind of super-subject, experiencing life at a higher level of intensity than ordinary people and absorbed in a world of selfhood which the phenomenal world, perceived as external and antithetical, either nourishes or constrains. This transcendence of the subject in poetry is not presented as unproblematic [...] but it is entirely overt in the poetry of this period. The 'I' of the poem directly addresses an individual reader who is invited to respond equally directly to this interpellation.

Fiction, however, in this same period, frequently appears to deal rather in social relationships, the interaction between the individual and society, to the increasing exclusion of the subjectivity of the author. Direct intrusion by the author comes to seem an impropriety; impersonal narration, 'showing' (the truth) rather than 'telling' it, is a requirement of prose fiction by the end of the nineteenth century. In drama too the author is apparently absent from the self-contained fictional world on the stage. Even the text effaces its own existence as text: unlike poetry, which clearly announces itself as formal, if only in terms of the shape of the text on the page, the novel seems merely to transcribe a series of events, to report on a palpable world, however fictional. Classic realist drama displays transparently and from the outside how people speak and behave.

Nevertheless, as we know while we read or watch, the author is present as a shadowy authority and as source of the fiction, and the author's presence is substantiated by the name on the cover or the programme: 'a novel by Thomas Hardy', 'a new play by Ibsen'. And at the same time, as I shall suggest in this section, the *form* of the classic realist text acts in conjunction with the expressive theory and with ideology by interpellating the reader as subject. The reader is invited to perceive and judge the 'truth' of the text, the coherent, non-contradictory interpretation of the world as it is perceived by an author whose autonomy is the source and evidence of the truth of the interpretation. This model of intersubjective communication, of shared understanding of a text which re-presents the world, is the guarantee not only of the truth of the text but of the reader's existence as an autonomous and knowing subject in a world of knowing subjects. In this way classic realism constitutes an ideological practice in addressing itself to readers as subjects, interpellating them in order that they freely accept their subjectivity and their subjection.

It is important to reiterate, of course, that this process is not inevitable, in the sense that texts do not determine like fate the ways in which they *must* be read. I am concerned at this stage primarily with ways in which they are conventionally read: conventionally, since language is conventional, and since modes of writing as well as ways of reading are conventional, but conventionally also in that new conventions of reading are available [...]. In this sense meaning is never a fixed essence inherent in the text but is always constructed by the reader, the result of a 'circulation' between social formation, reader and text (Health, 1977–8: 74). In the same way, 'inscribed subject positions are never hermetically sealed into a text, but are always positions in ideologies' (Willemen, 1978: 63). To argue that classic realism interpellates subjects in certain ways is not to propose that this process is ineluctable: on the contrary it is a matter of choice. But the choice is ideological: certain ranges of meaning (there is always room for debate) are 'obvious' within the currently dominant ideology, and certain subject-positions are equally 'obviously' the positions from which these meanings are apparent. [...]

Classic realism is characterized by *illusionism*, narrative which leads to *closure*, and a *hierarchy of discourses* which establishes the 'truth' of the story. *Illusionism* is by now, I hope, self-explanatory. The other two defining characteristics of classic realism need some discussion. Narrative tends to follow certain recurrent patterns. Classic realist narrative, as Barthes demonstrates in *S/Z*, turns on the creation of enigma through the precipitation of disorder which throws into disarray the conventional cultural and signifying systems. Among the commonest sources of disorder at the level of plot in classic realism are murder, war, a journey or love. But the story moves inevitably towards *closure* which is also disclosure, the dissolution of enigma through the re-establishment of order, recognizable as a reinstatement or a development of the order which is understood to have preceded the events of the story itself.

The moment of closure is the point at which the events of the story become fully intelligible to the reader. The most obvious instance is the detective story where, in the final pages, the murderer is revealed and the motive made plain. But a high degree of intelligibility is sustained throughout the narrative as a result of the *hierarchy of discourses* in the text. The hierarchy works above all by means of a privileged discourse which places as subordinate all the discourses that are literally or figuratively between inverted commas. Colin MacCabe illustrates this point by quoting a passage from George Eliot (MacCabe, 1974: 9–10). Here is another. It concerns Mr Tulliver, who has determined to call in the money he has lent his sister, Mrs Moss. They are discussing Mrs Moss's four daughters who have, as she puts it, 'a brother a-piece':

'Ah, but they must turn out and fend for themselves,' said Mr Tulliver, feeling that his severity was relaxing, and trying to brace it by throwing out a wholesome hint. 'They mustn't look to hanging on their brothers.'

'No; but I hope their brothers 'ull love the poor things, and remember they came o' one father and mother: the lads 'ull never be the poorer for that,' said Mrs Moss, flashing out with hurried timidity, like a half-smothered fire.

Mr Tulliver gave his horse a little stroke on the flank, then checked it, and said angrily, 'Stand still with you!' much to the astonishment of that innocent animal.

'And the more there is of 'em, the more they must love one another,' Mrs Moss went on, looking at her children with a didactic purpose. But she turned towards her brother again to say, 'Not but what I hope your boy 'ull allays be good to his sister, though there's but two of 'em, like you and me, brother.'

That arrow went straight to Mr Tulliver's heart. He had not a rapid imagination, but the thought of Maggie was very near to him, and he was not long in seeing his relation to his own sister side by side with Tom's relation to Maggie. Would the little wench ever be poorly off, and Tom rather hard upon her?

'Ay, ay, Gritty,' said the miller, with a new softness in his tone; 'but I've allays done what I could for you,' he added, as if vindicating himself from a reproach. (*The Mill on the Floss*, ch. 8)

The distinction here between the dialogue and the authorial and therefore authoritative exposition of its psychological import illustrates the distinction made by Benveniste between 'discourse' and 'history' (*histoire*) (Benveniste, 1971: 205–15). History narrates events apparently without the intervention of a speaker. In history there is no mention of 'you' and 'I'; 'the events seem to narrate themselves' (Benveniste, 1971: 208). Discourse on the other hand, assumes a speaker and a hearer, the 'you' and 'I' of dialogue. In third person narrative fiction like *The Mill on the Floss* the discourses are placed for the reader by a privileged, historic narration which is the source of coherence of the story as a whole. Here Mr Tulliver is more aware of the 'truth' of the situation than Mrs Moss – we know this because the fact has previously been related as history: 'If Mrs Moss had been one of the most astute women in the world, instead of being one of the simplest, she could have thought of nothing more likely to propitiate her brother . . .'. But he has less access to the 'truth' than the reader, whose comprehensive understanding is guaranteed by the historic narration: 'he was not long in seeing his relation to his own sister side by side with Tom's relation to Maggie.' The authority of this impersonal narration springs from its effacement of its own status as discourse.

At the same time the passage is interesting as an example of the way in which the reader is invited to *construct* a 'history' which is more comprehensive still. The gently ironic account of Mr Tulliver's treatment of his horse is presented without overt authorial comment. The context, however, points more or less irresistibly to a single interpretation which appears as the product of an intersubjective communication between the author and the reader in which the role of language has become invisible. Irony is no less authoritative because its meanings are implicit rather than explicit. Indeed, the frequent overt authorial intrusions and generalizations of George Eliot are much easier to resist since they draw attention to themselves as propositions. First person narration, therefore, or the presentation of events through the perceptions of centres of consciousness within the fiction, however 'unreliable', are not necessarily ways of evading authorial authority. But they seem to offer the reader a meaning which is apparently not in the words on the page. Through the presentation of an intelligible history which effaces its own status as discourse, classic realism proposes a model in which author and reader are subjects who are the source of shared meanings, the origin of which is mysteriously extra-discursive. It thus does the work of ideology in suppressing the relationship between language and subjectivity.

Classic realism, then, is what Barthes in *S/Z* defines as the readable (*lisible*), the dominant literary form of the nineteenth century, no longer 'pertinent' in the twentieth and yet still the prevailing form of popular fiction, the accomplice of ideology in its attempt to arrest the productivity of literary practice. Classic realism tends to offer as the 'obvious' basis of its intelligibility the assumption that character, unified and coherent, is the source of action. Subjectivity is a major – perhaps the major – theme of classic realism. Insight into character and psychological processes is declared to be one of the marks of serious literature: 'it is largely the victory of character over action that distinguishes the high literature of modern times' (Langbaum, 1963: 210). Conversely, inconsistency of character or the inappropriateness of particular actions to particular characters is seen as a weakness. It is because Emma is the kind of person she is that she behaves as she does; Sir Willoughby Patterne acts as he does because he is an egoist. Whether influenced by family relationships and upbringing, or simply mysteriously given, character begins to manifest itself in the earliest years of Maggie Tulliver, Jane Eyre and Paul Morel, for instance, and it proves a major constraint on their future development, on the choices they make and the courses they pursue. In the more arbitrary world portrayed in earlier literary forms, pairs of characters, barely distinguishable from each other except by name, demonstrate the differences that result from circumstances and accidents of choice. Palamon and Arcite, Helena and Hermia, Rosalind and Celia seem to have everything in common except their destinies (and in the last two cases their physical heights).

When pairs of characters appear in classic realist texts, however, it is more often with the effect of showing how the differences of character between them are the source of their differing destinies. When Dorothea rejects Sir James Chettam and Celia marries him their respective actions are seen as consistent with the character-patterns established for them at length in the opening pages of *Middlemarch*. Elinor and Marianne Dashwood are naturally different, and if Marianne acquires at nineteen the sense that she lacked at seventeen it is at the price of a considerable period of illness and convalescence.

The illness marking such adjustments of character was to become a convention of nineteenth-century fiction and the problem of change it symbolizes forms a striking contrast to the rapid transformation of, for instance, Shakespeare's erring prodigals, Prince Hal, Angelo and Bertram, who are able to enter so promptly into the possession of virtue, a quantity equally and readily available to all repentant sinners. Their tragic counterparts in Renaissance drama fall equally readily into vice: Faustus, Beatrice-Joanna and Macbeth need not be understood as *characteristically* depraved, though a mode of criticism based on the dominance of classic realist literature has until recently been inclined to analyse them in terms appropriate to the novel. If Lawrence did indeed do away with 'the old stable ego of the character', it was in search of a deeper form of subjectivity that he did so. It is difficult to imagine Miriam becoming like Clara, Gudrun like Ursula or Gerald like Birkin. Equally, the overt project of *The Mill on the Floss* is most 'obviously' intelligible in terms of an essential difference between Tom and Maggie.

Classic realism presents individuals whose traits of character, understood as essential and predominantly given, constrain the choices they make, and whose potential for development depends on what is given. Human nature is thus seen as a system of character-differences existing in the world, but one which nonetheless permits the reader to share the hopes and fears of a wide range of kinds of characters. This contradiction – that readers, like the central figures of fiction, are unique, and that so many readers can identify with so many protagonists – is accommodated in ideology as a paradox. There is no character in *Middlemarch* with whom we cannot have some sense of shared humanity. In *Heart of Darkness*, Marlow is appalled to find in the jungles of the Congo a recognition of his own remote kinship with primeval savagery: 'And why not? The mind of man is capable of anything – because everything is in it, all the past as well as all the future' (section 2). 'The mind of man', infinite and infinitely mysterious, homogeneous system of differences, unchangeable in its essence however manifold its forms, is shown in classic realism to be the source of understanding, of action and of history.

The consistency and continuity of the subject provides the conceptual framework of classic realism, but it is characteristic of the action of the story, the narrative process itself, to disrupt subjectivity, to disturb the pattern of relationships between subject-positions which is presented as normal in the text. In many cases the action itself represents a test of identity, putting identity in question by confronting the protagonist with alternative possible actions. In others a murder, marital infidelity, a journey, or the arrival of a stranger commonly disrupts the existing system of differences which constitutes human nature as represented in the microcosm of the text. To this extent classic realism recognizes the precariousness of the ego and offers the reader the sense of danger and excitement which results from that recognition.

But the movement of classic realist narrative towards closure ensures the reinstatement of order, sometimes a new order, sometimes the old restored, but always intelligible because familiar. Decisive choices are made, identity is established, the murderer is exposed, or marriage generates a new set of subject-positions. The epilogue common in nineteenth-century novels describes the new order, now understood to be static, and thus isolates and emphasizes a structural feature which is left implicit in other classic realist texts. Jane Eyre tells her readers, 'My tale draws to its close: one word respecting my experience of married life, and one brief glance at the fortunes of those whose names have most frequently recurred in this narrative, and I have done' (ch. 38). Harmony has been re-established through the redistribution of the signifiers into a new system of differences which closes off the threat to subjectivity, and it remains only to make this harmonious and coherent world intelligible to the reader, closing off in the process the sense of danger to the reader's subjectivity. This characteristic narrative structure, which deserves more detailed exposition, is discussed in the context of a full analysis of the film, *Touch of Evil*, in Stephen Heath's 'Film and System: Terms of Analysis' (1975).

Jane Eyre addresses itself to the reader, directly interpellates the reader as subject, as the 'you' who is addressed by the 'I' of discourse. This interpellation (address) in turn facilitates the interpolation (inclusion) of the reader in the narrative through the presentation of events from a specific and unified point of view. The meeting between Odysseus and Nausicaa in *The Odyssey* or the death of Priam in *The Aeneid* provides no specific position in the scene for the reader. But classic realism locates the reader *in* the events: we seem to 'see' Mr Brocklehurst through the eyes of Jane as a child: 'I looked up at – a black pillar!

– such, at least, appeared to me, at first sight, the straight, narrow, sable-clad shape standing erect on the rug: the grim face at the top was like a carved mask, placed above the shaft by way of capital' (ch. 4). Besides emphasizing the concern of the text with subjectivity, this technique also limits the play of meaning for the reader by installing him or her in a single position from which the scene is intelligible. This is not an inevitable consequence of first person narrative – Aeneas recounts the death of Priam – nor is it confined to that particular form. Here is an episode from *Oliver Twist*:

> The undertaker, who had just put up the shutters of his shop, was making some entries in his day-book by the light of a most dismal candle, when Mr Bumble entered.
>
> 'Aha!' said the undertaker, looking up from the book, and pausing in the middle of a word; 'is that you, Bumble?'
>
> 'No one else, Mr Sowerberry,' replied the beadle. 'Here. I've brought the boy.' Oliver made a bow.
>
> 'Oh! that's the boy, is it?' said the undertaker, raising the candle above his head, to get a better view of Oliver. 'Mrs Sowerberry, will you have the goodness to come here a moment, my dear?'
>
> Mrs Sowerberry emerged from a little room behind the shop, and presented the form of a short, thin, squeezed-up woman with a vixenish countenance.
>
> 'My dear,' said Mr Sowerberry deferentially, 'this is the boy from the workhouse that I told you of.' Oliver bowed again.
>
> 'Dear me!' said the undertaker's wife, 'he's very small.' (ch. 4)

The scene (since again the narrative is full of visual detail) is viewed from a quite specific point of view, just inside the door of the shop. The raising of the candle, the emergence of Mrs Sowerberry and her appearance are all 'presented' to this single place, the place of Oliver, who is the centre of consciousness of the episode. We 'see' what Oliver sees, and to this extent we identify with him. But we also see more than Oliver sees: we are aware of his bow, narrated in the third person; we also know that the undertaker has just put up the shutters, and that he pauses in the middle of a word. This information has no obvious place in Oliver's consciousness, and the more comprehensive point of view that it permits the reader sets up a tripartite relationship between the reader, the fictional character and the implied author. The reader participates not only in the point of view of the subject of the *énoncé*, the subject inscribed *in* the utterance, Oliver, but also in the point of view of the subject of the enunciation, the subject who narrates, who 'shows' Oliver's experience to the reader, the implied author. In a similar way the conventional tenses of classic realism tend to align the position of the reader with that of the omniscient narrator who is looking back on a series of past events. Thus, while each episode seems to be happening 'now' as we read, and the reader is given clear indications of what is already past in relation to this 'now', nonetheless each apparently present episode is contained in a single, intelligible and all-embracing vision of what from the point of view of the subject of the enunciation is past and completed.

In this way heterogeneity – variety of points of view and temporal locations – is contained in homogeneity. The text interpellates the reader as a transcendent and non-contradictory subject by positioning him or her as 'the unified and unifying subject of its vision' (Heath, 1976: 85).

This construction of a position for the reader, which is a position of identification with the subject of the enunciation, is by no means confined to third person narrative, where authorial omniscience is so readily apparent. In distinguishing between 'reliable' and 'unreliable' first person narrators, the reader assumes a position of knowledge – of a history, a 'truth' of the story which may not be accessible to a dramatized narrator who, as a character in the text, is a subject of the *énoncé*. Jane Eyre as a child often has less understanding of the implications of her experience than the reader does. In *Wuthering Heights* the inadequacies of the perceptions of Lockwood or Nellie Dean do not prevent the reader from seeming to apprehend the real nature of the relationship between Catherine and Heathcliff. Browning's dramatic monologues, to cite an extreme example, invite the reader to make judgements and draw conclusions not available to the speaker. Robert Langbaum perfectly describes the common reading experience in which the knowledge of the reader seems to surpass the knowledge of the speaker, but to be a knowledge shared with the author, so that author and reader independently produce a shared meaning which confirms the transcendence of each:

> It can be said of the dramatic monologue generally that there is at work in it a consciousness, whether intellectual or historical, beyond what the speaker can lay claim to. This consciousness is the mark of the poet's projection into the poem; and it is also the pole which attracts our projection, since we find in it the counterpart of our own consciousness. (Langbaum, 1963: 94)

Irony thus guarantees still more effectively than overt authorial omnis-cience the subjectivity of the reader as a source of meaning.

The dramatic monologue is compelled by the logic of its form to leave the recognition of irony to the reader. The classic realist novel, however, has a surer way of establishing its harmonious 'truth'. Perhaps the commonest pattern in the novel is the gradual convergence of the discourses of the subject of the *énoncé* and the subject of the enunciation until they merge triumphantly at the point of closure. At the end of the detective story, reader, author and detective all 'know' everything necessary to the intelligibility of the story. Nineteenth-century protagonists learn by experience until they achieve the wisdom author and reader now seem to have possessed all along. (Paradoxically the protagonist's discovery also has the effect of confirming the wisdom of the reader.) Wayne Booth describes the position of the reader who has completed *Emma*:

> 'Jane Austen' has learned nothing at the end of the novel that she did not know at the beginning. She needed to learn nothing. She knew everything of importance already. We have been privileged to watch with her as she observes her favorite character climb from a considerably lower platform to join the exalted company of Knightley, 'Jane Austen', and those of us readers who are wise enough, good enough, and perceptive enough to belong up there too. (Booth, 1961: 265)

Bleak House must be one of the most interesting instances of converging discourses. The story itself concerns social and ideological contradictions – that the law of property set up in the interests of society benefits only lawyers and destroys the members of society who invoke it in their defence; that the social conception of virtue promotes hypocrisy or distress. The narrative mode of *Bleak House* also functions contradictorily, initially liberating the reader to produce meaning but finally proving to be a constraint on the process of production. The novel has two narrators, Esther Summerson, innocent, generous, unassuming and sentimental, and an anonymous third person narrator, detached, ironic, rendered cynical by what he knows about the Court of Chancery. Neither is omniscient. The anonymous narration is in the present tense, and claims little knowledge of feeling. At the beginning of *Bleak House* the two narratives form a striking contrast. The first section is by the worldly, knowing narrator, and is succeeded by Esther's immediate insistence on her own lack of cleverness but strength of feeling: 'I have not by any means a quick understanding. When I love a person very tenderly indeed, it seems to brighten...' (ch. 3).

The reader is constantly prompted to supply the deficiencies of each narrative. The third person narration, confining itself largely to behaviour, is strongly enigmatic, but provides enough clues for the reader to make guesses at the 'truth' before the story reveals it; Esther's narrative frequently invites an ironic reading: we are encouraged to trust her account of the 'facts' but not necessarily her judgement:

She was a good, good woman. She went to church three times every Sunday, and to morning prayers on Wednesdays and Fridays, and to lectures whenever there were lectures; and never missed. She was handsome; and if she had ever smiled, would have been (I used to think) like an angel – but she never smiled. She was always grave, and strict. She was so very good herself, I thought, that the badness of other people made her frown all her life . . . It made me very sorry to consider how good she was, and how unworthy of her I was. (ch. 3)

Thus, a third and privileged but literally unwritten discourse begins to emerge, the discourse of the reader which grasps a history and judges soundly.

Gradually, however, the three discourses converge. The childlike spontaneity of Mr Skimpole, which enchanted Esther in chapter 6, and which rapidly emerges as irresponsibility in the discourse of the reader, is dismissed by Esther in chapter 61 with a briskness worthy of the ironic narrator:

He died some five years afterwards, and left a diary behind him, with letters and other material towards his Life; which was published, and which showed him to have been the victim of a combination on the part of mankind against an amiable child. It was considered very pleasant reading, but I never read more of it myself than the sentence on which I chanced to light on opening the book. It was this. 'Jarndyce, in common with most other men I have known, is the Incarnation of Selfishness.'

It is Esther, and not the ironic narrator, who recounts the black comedy of the completion of the case of Jarndyce and Jarndyce, while the anonymous narrative softens, as if as a result of its encounters with the innocence of Jo, the crossing-sweeper, the Bagnet family and Mr George:

A goodly sight it is to see the grand old housekeeper (harder of hearing now) going to church on the arm of her son, and to observe – which few do, for the house is scant of company in these times – the relations of both towards Sir Leicester, and his towards them. (ch. 66)

The three discourses thus converge to confirm the reader's apparently extra-discursive interpretation and judgement.

By this means, *Bleak House* constructs a reality which appears to be many-sided, too complex to be contained within a single point of view, but which is in fact so contained within the single and non-contradictory invisible discourse of the reader, a discourse which is confirmed and ratified as Esther and the ironic narrator come to share with the reader a 'recognition' of the true complexity of things. By thus smoothing over the contradictions it has so powerfully dramatized in the interests of a single, unified, coherent 'truth', *Bleak House*, however critical of the world it describes, offers the reader a position, an attitude which is given as non-contradictory, fixed in 'knowing' subjectivity.

Classic realism cannot foreground contradiction. The logic of its structure – the movement towards closure – precludes the possibility of leaving the reader simply to confront the contradictions which the text may have defined. The hierarchy of discourses ensures that a transcendent level of knowledge 'recognizes' the contradictions in the world as tragic (inevitable), as is predominantly the case in Hardy, or ironic, as in *Bleak House*, or resolved as in *Sybil* or *Jane Eyre*. When contradiction exists in classic realism it does so in the margins of a text which, as Pierre Macherey argues in *A Theory of Literary Production* (1978), is unable in spite of itself to achieve the coherence which is the project of classic realism. [. . .]

References

Benveniste, Emile (1971) *Problems in General Linguistics* (Miami: University of Miami Press).

Booth, Wayne C. (1961) *The Rhetoric of Fiction* (Chicago: University of Chicago Press).

Heath, Stephen (1975) 'Film and System: Terms of Analysis', *Screen*, 16 (1): 7–77; 16 (2): 91–113.

Heath, Stephen (1976) 'Narrative Space', *Screen*, 17 (3): 68–112.

Heath, Stephen (1977–8) 'Notes on Suture', *Screen*, 18: 48–76.

Langbaum, Robert (1963) *The Poetry of Experience* (New York: Norton).

MacCabe, Colin (1974) 'Realism and the Cinema: Notes on Some Brechtian Theses', *Screen*, 15: 7–27.

Macherey, Paul (1978) *A Theory of Literary Production* (London: Routledge and Kegan Paul); trans. of *Pour une théorie de la production littéraire* (1966).

Willemen, Paul (1978) 'Notes of Subjectivity – on Reading "Subjectivity under Siege"', *Screen*, 19: 41–69.

BELSEY
CRITIQUED

Belsey's approach to classic realism was a product of its theoretical moment. It was also determined by her scholarly interests in the Renaissance and an underlying preference for non-naturalistic modes of characterization that generated dissatisfaction with what she saw in homogeneous terms as the 'classic realist' procedure. Indeed, her presentation of this realist mode was difficult precisely in terms of its definition: Belsey deployed 'classic realism' as a portmanteau category, declaring it a general mode of writing that covered a wide period of history, and collapsed generic categories from contemporary cinema film to popular fiction to nineteenth- and twentieth-century detective fiction to Dickens's *Bleak House* (1852–3) in the term. She lost textual, generic and historical specificity in the process. Belsey also homogenized the ideological trajectories of the texts themselves, seeing works of classic realism as operating in the service of a single logic, reading them as coherent in their ideological identities. She did not allow that nineteenth-century fiction was complex, dialogic or multi-voiced in its relationship with ideologies. These perspectives have been argued eloquently elsewhere (see, for instance, pp. 220–24 and 325–30). Her description of the order that was established by the realist narrative at its point of closure, moreover, involved difficulties, as her account did not correspond to that corpus of Victorian fiction that was self-conscious about closure, or left gaps and openings and elements unresolved. The end of Dickens's *Great Expectations* (1860–1) is an obvious example.

Belsey's influential critique of realism expressed the principal difficulties the mode presented to critics working with theory in the late 1970s and 1980s. But she was not the only major writer to explore the embeddedness of the Victorian realist novel in the ideology of the ruling classes. Where Belsey had indicated the dangerous politics of the unified psychology in 1980, the political identity of the Victorian novel, and its capacity to shape subjectivities, was given a more dramatic slant in D. A. Miller's *The Novel and the Police* in 1988. This was not about the realist novel alone. It discussed detective fiction, sensation fiction and Newgate fiction as well. But Miller's ideas about the disciplinary implications of fiction profoundly concerned the Victorian realist novel. Miller's idea of the relationship between literature and ideology, dependent on Althusser and Foucault, assumed that the novel was immersed in a dominant ideology of control and was an agent in transmitting a politics of confinement and domination. *The Novel and the Police* proposed that nineteenth-century fiction was a discourse that did disciplinary work, policed the subjectivities of its readers, and acted as an agent in the management of the social body.

D. A. MILLER'S *THE NOVEL AND THE POLICE* (1988)

Belsey and Miller provided accounts of the ideological immersion of the realist novel in the 1980s, arguing that realism was a part of the rhetoric of the bourgeoisie and its strategies of dominance. Realism became an unappealing subject. But criticism of realism in the late 1970s and 1980s, came also, as Levine acknowledged at the beginning of the extract above, from the epistemological disapproval consequent on post-structuralist ideas of language and meaning,[11] and from deconstructionist critics intolerant of literary texts that appeared to involve a naïve faith in the capacity of language to represent the real. In the light of these political and epistemological difficulties, critical approaches that were hospitable to Victorian fiction in the 1970s and early

THE TURN AGAINST REALISM IN THE 1980s

1980s often valued realist fiction as a composite discourse or one that was eloquent in its silences.

INTEREST IN GOTHIC
An important response to the ideological problems of realism was the investigation of how classic realist texts appropriated forms of non-realist writing. In this critical approach, the moments of non-realism, the interruption of the realist mode, were privileged. Problematic ideologies were thus avoided. Gilbert and Gubar's *The Madwoman in the Attic* (see chapter 3) had established the outline of this approach as valuable for a feminist viewpoint. Chapter 3 of Eve Kosofsky Sedgwick's *The Coherence of Gothic Conventions* (1980), a revised version of her 1976 Yale PhD thesis, investigated 'Immediacy, Doubleness, and the Unspeakable' in Emily Brontë's *Wuthering Heights* and Charlotte Brontë's *Villette*, and was an example of the prioritization of the Gothic as an element of non-realism in Victorian fiction – *Wuthering Heights* was a special focus of this attention (for more on Gothic, see p. 10 above).

INTEREST IN THE NOT-SAID OF REALISM
The other 'politically correct' approach was to emphasize absences in the realist text (this was also a feature of Sedgwick's reading) in order to expose the significant silences in the fiction, to make the lacunae of its narratives speak. Realism was valued for what it did not say. Such readings sometimes took Julia Kristeva's theory of the semiotic, the pre-linguistic *chora* she associated with the feminine, as a useful model (even if challenging other aspects of Kristeva's position). They also used the arguments of the Marxist Pierre Macherey in *Pour une Théorie de la Production Littéraire* (1966) on the significance of the unsaid in the literary and the potential of texts to reveal gaps in ideology. An influential example of this approach was the essay on 'Women's Writing: "Jane Eyre", "Shirley", "Villette", "Aurora Leigh"' by the Marxist Feminist Literature Collective from the 1977 Essex Conference on the Sociology of Literature. The Collective (comprising Cheris Kramer, Cora Kaplan, Helen Taylor, Jean Radford, Jennifer Joseph, Margaret Williamson, Maud Ellmann, Mary Jacobus, Michèle Barrett and Rebecca O'Rourke) proposed that the Kristevan notion of the semiotic, though problematic in its privileging of the female as irrational, was none the less useful in reading the 'explosive and temporarily liberating dissonances'[12] in Victorian women's fiction. The Collective's claim about *Jane Eyre* exemplified their reading of the articulate silences of realism. 'Our reading of *Jane Eyre*', they remarked, 'identifies Charlotte Brontë's interrogation of the dominant ideology of love and marriage; but also suggests the Macherayan "not-said" of the novel — what it is not possible for [Brontë] to "scrutinize and expose," woman as a desiring subject, a sexual object seeking personal fulfilment within the existing structures of class and kinship, i.e. in a patriarchal capitalist society'.[13] What was not said by the realist text was positioned at the centre of reading (for more on the not-said, see p. 319).

The Marxist Feminist Collective had urged avoidance of realism, but not all theoretically inclined critics working with Victorian fiction in the 1980s felt the necessity to approach the realist texts by privileging elements beyond it. Refusing to negotiate with the realist elements of major Victorian novels seemed to some, in a backlash against the early 1980s, to be shutting the door on powerful literary documents and to be disturbing in terms of gender politics. For the feminist Penny Boumelha, in a contribution to a book published in 1988, this critical procedure dangerously silenced female voices and, ironically enough, mimicked the oppressive effect of patriarchy. Overlooking the textures of realism, she argued, was to ignore a key mode of writing that allowed women in the nineteenth century a form of self-expression, a textual space in which to articulate their own experience under patriarchy (for more feminist arguments about fiction and female enfranchisement, see pp. 186–91 below). Rather than listening to the silences of the text, or tracing non-realist discourses, critics, she said, should be returning to the realist material itself. But they should be doing so in a way that was alert to ideological resistance. In her essay 'Realism and the Ends of Feminism', in Susan Sheridan, ed., *Grafts: Feminist Cultural Criticism* (1988), Boumelha feminized Levine's argument with Ioan Williams about the self-consciousness of realism and its awareness of textuality. For women writers, especially George Eliot, Boumehla proposed, this self-awareness indicated a realization that the conventions of realism as a practice of writing corresponded to awareness of the constraining forces impinging continually on female lives. Ideology and form were linked, as Belsey had said, but they were knowingly so. Feminist critics, especially readers of George Eliot, could find in the traces of self-consciousness about the limits of realism, its constraining and limiting conventions, evidence for a feminist recuperation of a mode of Victorian writing that had recently generated such dissatisfaction.

THE FEMINIST RECUPER-ATION OF REALISM IN THE 1980s

Extract from Penny Boumehla, 'Realism and the Ends of Feminism', in Susan Sheridan, ed., *Grafts: Feminist Cultural Criticism* (London: Verso, 1988), 323–9.

[...] Realist texts can be read by and for feminism, not in a flatly mimetic sense but as they enact in both their coherences and their incoherences the struggle between their representation and its own limits and incompletions.

George Eliot has often been cited as a prime example in the accounts of realism I have been discussing, as she is for instance in Belsey's version of the 'classic realism' argument [see above, pp. 123–6], so that if illusionism, controlling truth-voices, unproblematic reproductions of the dominant ideology and wilful suppression of textuality are to be found anywhere, we might not unreasonably expect to find them in her writing. The ways in which Eliot's work is realist – if not 'classically' – are evident enough, and in any event have been widely discussed in criticism of her, though even here, of course, it should be remembered that she also wrote such things as the profoundly non-realist, typological 'half' of *Daniel Deronda*, the story *The Lifted Veil* which draws on the Gothic to show how Latimer's 'visions' of the soul and nature of woman in fact produce their own confirmation in his wife, and other works that do not altogether fill the realist bill. The ways in which Eliot transgresses the boundaries of the 'classic realist' mould also deserve some attention, however. There is, for example, the obviousness of voice and of a narrator's presence in much of her writing. *The Mill on the Floss*, after all, begins by establishing its narrator as immersed in dream and memory; this opening does not initiate what Belsey calls 'a privileged, historic narration which is the source of coherence of the story as a whole'[1] There are, too, those chapters in *Adam Bede* and *The Mill*, often read simply as manifestos of realism, in which the narrative is interrupted with a discussion of the principles on which it is constructed and organised – hardly an illusionist device.

Then again, the epigrams and moral axioms, snatches of verse and apparent extracts from dramas that Eliot wrote as epigraphs to the chapters of some of her novels flagrantly advertise the texuality of the work and its unsettling relation to the putative authority of other texts, as well as suggesting the range of other possible genres and modes in which the work could have been conceived. In the case of *Felix Holt*, this adumbration of alternative discourses and genres reaches beyond the confines of the novel itself into Eliot's political journalism (the article 'Felix Holt's Address to Working Men'). Within that novel, it virtually constitutes itself into a plot: the world of 'the poets' and reading as parable, of tragedy and 'fine stories' associated with the introductory coachman-storyteller and with Mrs Transome is displaced by Esther, 'critic of words' and associate ('affiliate', indeed, in the novel's transposition of literary genealogies into family relationships) of the independent chapel-goers, for whom reading is precisely commentary and dissent. In the space of only about fifteen pages in the novel, Esther discusses and is discussed in relation to ballad heroines, tragic heroes, genteel comedy, the want of romance and the renunciation of utopias. Esther's schooling in realism, in opting for the 'middling lot' of typicality (not the '*via media* of indifference' also evoked in the novel), enacts and argues the novel's case for its own mode. Even the naming of the heroine can be related to this intertextual self-definition: where Charlotte Brontë's *Villette* uses the actress Vashti (and her biblical prototype) to figure the inflammatory but self-dooming spectacle of the woman artist, Eliot's *Felix Holt* counters with its figure of Esther and her biblical prototype.

In the Bible story [2] – I believe it is tactfully customary at this point to add 'you will recall' – Esther succeeds Vashti as wife to Ahasuerus; Vashti is displaced for her refusal to display herself as a spectacle of beauty for his assembled male guests, whereas Esther, orphaned and not beautiful, manages to achieve her ends by continual intercession with her king-husband. The political implications of this story may not be inspiring for feminists, but it, too, has its place in the claim Eliot is staking for realism in the novel's considerations of reading and writing. The point of remarking such elements here is not to insist upon a non-realist or proto-modernist Eliot to stand in the place of the Aunt Sally of classic realism, but to suggest how, even as she stayed largely within the conventions of nineteenth-century realism, Eliot's writing was able to explore its limits, subject its idea of representation to scrutiny and question its practices. That is to say, her practice of realism contains its own elements of self-referentiality even in its claim to mimetic reference.

I want now to go on to use this question of realism as a basis for examining the assumptions implicit in some of the feminist critiques of Eliot's fiction. Eliot has long occupied a privileged, if problematic, place in feminist criticism. The reasons for her pre-eminence are not hard to find; they include her unchallenged place in the great collection of set texts we have come to call the canon, the formidable figure she seems to have been personally, her rare combination of passion and wit, her frequent refusal of the consolations of romance. And yet she has also proved frustrating – even enraging – to some feminists. The reasons for their anger can fairly readily be demonstrated, and some of them conceded without dissent. Eliot displays the injustices and abuses that press upon the lives of her women and then seems to refuse the logic of the insight offered by her own texts, apparently resolving the conflict between romantic, individualist rebellion and the power of community morality all too easily in favour of the latter. She may deplore the restricted lives of her heroines, but she appears to celebrate the morality of martyrdom to which they give rise; Elaine Showalter has commented with as much asperity as aptness that she 'elevates suffering into a female career'.[3] Again, she shows her women to be capable of intellectual and social achievement and aspiration, but offers them no field in which to exercise these abilities, consigning heroines finally for the most part only to death or to marriage. Most offensive of all, for some, is Eliot's refusal to bestow upon her heroines the opportunities that she so fully and joyously seized for herself; for Kate Millett, Eliot 'lived the revolution ... but did not write of it'.[4] The whole tenor of such criticism is summed up in this comment by Jenni Calder: 'Sadly, and it is a radical criticism of George Eliot, she does not commit herself fully to the energies and aspirations she lets loose in these women. Does she not cheat them, and cheat us, ultimately, in allowing them so little?'[5]

This is a serious question and a sad catalogue of complaints, but I doubt whether the critique they frame is in fact a radical one. All of these critiques originate from and exemplify broadly the same kind of criticism, long dominant within English and American feminism at least, that leans heavily upon the presupposed ability of the reader – always, I think, a female reader – to recognise on the basis of her own unproblematised experience the 'authenticity' (or lack of it) in the work under discussion. Evidently, such a naively reflectionist model of realism drastically reduces the scope of texts it can address; that is one reason why Eliot, so closely identified with realism, has figured so largely in this kind of criticism, and it is also the reason why those aspects of her work that escape or question the mimetic have often met with a blank rejection or a puzzled inadequacy of response. But more pertinently for my purposes, this kind of criticism runs into serious theoretical problems even in its address to elements of realism. It tends on the one hand to approach novels for their sociological content – for their depiction of the injustices and abuses suffered by women – but on the other hand it contains a strongly prescriptive strain in its insistence on looking for positive role-models with whom contemporary feminists might expect to identify. The resulting requirement of fantasy heroines in realist textual environments places anachronistic and unanswerable demands upon the possibilities of writing mid-nineteenth-century realism.

The problem is often raised most acutely by fictional endings. Realism, bounded more or less by its project of representing in some typical form the real conditions of social existence, has tended to reduce the options for its female protagonists to either marriage or death. Of course, the virtual interchangeability of the two is itself telling. The kind of feminist readings I have just been discussing (which come from what is, perhaps unfortunately, the strain of feminism from which realist texts have received their most detailed readings) have been apt to see both these forms of closure as not simply representing but reproducing – enforcing, even – the impoverished opportunities that the social order of nineteenth-century Britain afforded actual historical women of the middle class. That is, they have tended to see a final marriage as a cop-out and a final death as a victimisation of the heroine. Yet, at the same time, they work with a moralised version of genre that sees fantasy or romance as unworthy and evasive. A critical double-bind is thus established by which virtually all novels written before the contemporary expansion of both women's opportunities and feminist theory must be judged and found wanting. However, if we look at the endings of realist novels – whether marriage, death, or some other form – in formal and ideological terms rather than these anachronistically mimetic ones, they will often yield more interesting results for feminist criticism than the failure to provide positive role-models or the paucity of social opportunities. The necessity of an ending, after all, is one of the ways in which any fiction, however involuntary, flaunts its textuality. Novels are obliged to end, and therefore to end abruptly, the novel must always have the last word. The endings of the realist text often push to the point of stark visibility the struggle of a self-styled truthful representation to reduce into some form of textual closure those 'truths' of women's desire or aspiration or articulateness that it has itself displayed.

It is in the light, then, of this double concern – to read the work for feminism and to situate it within its generic and historical constraints – that I should like to discuss the endings of some of Eliot's novels. I begin with *The Mill on the Floss*. I am not concerned to establish that Eliot was or was not a feminist (though I do not mean to say that that is a question without interest), but rather to examine the ways in which the novel's focus upon a strong female protagonist troubles its form and brings it up against the limits of its own theoretical project. The novel sets out as a *Bildungsroman*, a form that characteristically concerns itself with the growth of a male protagonist. That this form becomes problematic when it centres upon a girl rapidly becomes easy to see; after all, *Bildung* – culture, education – is the very thing most bitterly denied the novel's heroine. The form of the *Bildungsroman* has built into it the requirement and affirmation of the values of autonomy and self-definition – values by no means always considered appropriate for women. It is an almost generically individualistic fable of identity, whose considerable appeal to Victorian readers depended partly upon its confirmation of the integrity and coherence of the individual over time, and in this it posits character rather than social determination as the motive force of its narrative development. Eliot's project, by contrast, is to show, through the device of compared and contrasted brother and sister, how powerfully forces and expectations not generated within the individual character determine the growth of Tom and Maggie. This central contrast is obviously an effective vehicle for feminist commentary, one that will be taken up again by several of the more polemical women writers of the 1880s and 1890s.

It is Maggie alone, though, who increasingly becomes the protagonist of the novel as the children are progressively separated by education and puberty (*Bildung* and sexuality, the poles of the novel). The violence of the collision between the ideological underpinnings of the form and the range of possibilities for the fictional heroine becomes evident in the ardour of Maggie's espousal of Thomas à Kempis and the renunciation of the self. Of course, this novel of the growth of the individual self is caught in its own trap, and Maggie's self-abnegation must inevitably reveal itself to be an inverted form of the self-affirmation that the *Bildungsroman* demands. Feminine self-suppression and heroic self-affirmation enter into contradiction with one another, and the result has been diagnosed by some character-orientated critics as masochism. But as Maggie grows into adulthood, another problem becomes pressing: within the conventions of realism, the novel can offer Maggie – or the middle-class woman in general – no vocation, no meaningful work to match that of the *gebildete* male protagonist. We are back at the crossroads: marriage or death. It is here that Eliot's refusal of romance comes into play. The paltriness of the temptation provided by Stephen Guest, the unsatisfactory nature of the romantic escapade (Maggie's is a sexual fall only by the rules of community interpretation), enact all over again the restriction of the opportunities available to her. It is sufficient to rule out the possibility of marriage, however, and only death presents itself as a conclusion. It is important, though, that Maggie does not, for example, gently expire from one of those quasi-symbolic brain fevers so apt in this period to strike down heroines with brain enough to become enfevered. Instead, she is at once vindicated and annihilated by the flood which, however well-laid the clues of imagery and rhetoric may be, strikes the reader each time anew as sudden, arbitrary. This ending to the novel has occasioned a great deal of commentary and interpretation, often based on disappointment. It has been seen, by feminists among others, as evasive, abrupt, improbable. The reunion with Tom that the flood effects has likewise been deplored as sentimental, undeserved by him, too transparently a wish-fulfilment of Eliot's longing to overcome the disapproval of her own brother. For some feminist critics, the ending has combined sell-out (reconciliation with the oppressive brother) with victimisation (sacrifice of the woman). But the plot ending is not necessarily the destiny of the text – it may be only its destination. There is more to be said about Maggie's death (as there will be about Dorothea's marriage) than simply that it happens.

And, indeed, quite a lot more has been said. A large and varied range of interpretations of the events of the flood has been offered: in my own and other people's readings, it has figured as (among others) a revenge murder of Tom; a narrator's murder of Maggie; the destruction of the restrictive community; the fulfilment of an incest fantasy; regression to a prepubertal age without sexual difference; the re-emergence of cata-strophic theories of evolution as a series of creations; the reconciliation of male and female elements; anal rage (in this classically Freudian reading, the 'dark masses' floating in the river are, of course, faeces); the projection of Maggie's impulses towards martyrdom and heroism on to the forces of nature; and a moment of sexual release, the 'little death' of orgasm mimicked by the larger death. Any or all of these interpret-ations might be acceptable. But more important, I think, is the sheer excess of the text over such interpretations, the flagrantly fantasised and contrived nature of the ending. It acknowledges and makes unusually visible the formal-cum-ideological impasse that the novel has reached by virtue of its concentration on the development of a woman for whom no meaningful future – no 'end' in its other sense – can be imagined. It breaks out of this impasse only by sweeping the novel out of the realist mode altogether. The irreconcilable contradictions of ideology and form bring the novel hard up against the very limits of its own realism, and the flood that crashed through those barriers submerges the world of history (and of mimetic realism) along with St Ogg's, bringing with it the victory of symbol, legend, fantasy. This, it seems to me, is the most exciting feminist point to be made about *The Mill on the Floss*: the dammed-up energy created by the frustrated ambitions and desires, intellectual and sexual, of the woman is so powerful that it cannot be contained with the forms of mimesis: the repressed and thwarted potential of Maggie conjures into being that destructive, vengeful, triumphant flood. The ending confers upon Maggie those possibilities of heroism that will be withheld from Dorothea and Gwendolen, but there is an ideological price to be paid, as Gillian Beer has argued: 'The subversive vehemence of Maggie's fate both releases from the bonds of social realism, and yet neutralises its own commentary by allowing her, and so us, the plenitude which is nowhere available in her society.'[6] It is the only occasion in these major novels when Eliot will console us with such fantasied plenitude for the narrow, unjust, oppressive world that social realism has to depict. [...]

Notes

1 Catherine Belsey, *Critical Practice* (London: Methuen, 1980), 71–2; see pp. 121–32 above.
2 Esther, i, ii, and v.
3 Elaine Showalter, *A Literature of their Own: British Women Novelists from Brontë to Lessing* (Princeton, NJ: Princeton University Press, 1977), 125. For more on Showalter, see pp. 68–82 above.
4 Kate Millett, *Sexual Politics* (London, 1972), 139.
5 Jenni Calder, *Women and Marriage in Victorian Fiction* (London: Thames and Hudson, 1976), 158.
6 Gillian Beer, *George Eliot* (Brighton: Harvester, 1986), 104.

NEW HISTORICISM AND HISTORICIZING THE REAL

Boumehla's argument reclaimed realism for theoretically informed readers in the late 1980s, and insisted on a more careful reading of the texts than that proposed by Belsey. She offered criticism that was sensitive to self-consciousness, and which resisted seeing the texts of classic realism as the agents of a unitary bourgeois logic. Her understanding of realism's modes of signification related to Peter Garrett's Bakhtinian analysis of the plural meanings of the multi-plot novel discussed on pp. 219–24 below. The debate, however, continued beyond Boumehla, and began to take a distinctive direction in the 1990s. Where post-structuralism and feminism helped define the critical temper of the later 1970s and 1980s, New Historicism emerged to prominence in the 1990s in the Anglo-American academy, and this powerfully influential Foucault-inflected practice of historicization also generated readings of Victorian realism (for an overview of New Historicism, see p. 162). New Historicism's project to describe the discourses flowing through a culture, and to locate the forms of power invested in them, suggested ways of historicizing the real. Rather than debating whether realism was predicated on confidence or doubt, whether it reproduced or critiqued bourgeois ideology, this approach looked closely at historical specificity of representations of the real.

ROTHFIELD'S *VITAL SIGNS* (1992)

Lawrence Rothfield's *Vital Signs: Medical Realism in Nineteenth-century Fiction* (1992) proposed an historically specific way of reading realism in the British and French novel (it also related to the 1990s' interest in Victorian literature and medicine, discussed on pp. 253–7 below). Rothfield argued that too many previous efforts to understand realism had concentrated on the text's relationship with reality as an abstract and objective concept and whether that reality was adequately represented by language. This critical focus had led to a critical *impasse*, he said, which could only be overcome by accepting the fact that the novel consisted of historically determined forms of rhetoric; that, as Bakhtin argued, it 'is woven out of discourses'[14] (for more on the role of

Bakhtin in Victorian fiction, see pp. 212–13). If the novel, Rothfield continued:

> is a texture woven out of discourse, then one ought to be able to describe particular novelistic genres (the realistic novel, the naturalist novel, the sensation novel, the modernist novel, the detective story, and so on) not by their implicit theories of representation – or the impossibility of achieving representation, as is often said of modernist fiction – but by the kinds of discourses, and the relations between discourses, that predominate in each genre. The result of such a description will be to give a more local precision to the 'real' of the realistic novel: a real that can then be aligned to the 'real' offered by the specific discourses that novelists like Balzac, Flaubert, and Eliot adapt in distinctive ways.[15]

Rothfield's study began a process of investigating how nineteenth-century novels deployed particular forms of discourses to represent the real. Where Poovey had seen the idea of the social body influencing the representations of selfhood in Gaskell (see pp. 164–78 below), Rothfield was interested in the role of medical science in shaping the representation of the self, including in Eliot's *Middlemarch*, with its obvious interest in the medical profession. So close, Rothfield argued, was the relationship between the discourse of clinical medicine and realist fiction in the Victorian period, that the changing fortunes of realism could be linked to changes in the medical profession and its transformations of cultural authority: the 'emergence, development, and decline of realism as an authoritative literary praxis can be tied to the vicissitudes of clinical medicine as an ideal profession'.[16]

Rothfield's aspiration to unpack the hierarchy of representations of the real in nineteenth-century notions was developed by other critics in the 1990s. Significant recent works on this theme include Nancy Armstrong's *Fiction in the Age of Photography: The Legacy of British Realism* (1999). Where Rothfield examined the role of science, Armstrong was interested in the growing area of Victorian visuality studies, and specifically the influence of photography in shaping what was known as real. Developing ideas about the role of technology in determining perception from Jonathan Crary's *Techniques of the Observer: On Vision and Modernity in the Nineteenth Century* (1990), Armstrong declared that realist fiction – she was criticized for imprecisely defining what she meant by this – and photography grew together as mutually supporting practices of representation in the Victorian period. She summarized her argument in four propositions:

Proposition 1: By the mid-1850s, fiction was already promising to put readers in touch with the world itself by supplying them with certain kinds of visual information.

NANCY
ARMSTRONG
AND KATE
FLINT

Proposition 2: In doing so, fiction equated seeing with knowing and made visual information the basis for the intelligibility of a verbal narrative.

Proposition 3: In order to be realistic, literary realism referenced a world of objects that either had been or could be photographed.

Proposition 4: Photography in turn offered up portions of this world to be seen by the same group of people whom novelists imagined as their readership.[17]

A further study that involved consideration of the relationship between the visual and discourses of literary realism was Kate Flint's interdisciplinary book on *The Victorians and the Visual Imagination* (2000). Flint aimed to explore the correspondences discussed by Armstrong between seeing and knowing and to problematize them. She was interested in how complex vision was for the Victorians, how it involved a whole matrix of cultural and social practices, and was fraught with contradiction. The project of her book was to reconstruct sight historically and to investigate how the Victorians saw. It continued the contemporary critical interest in ideas about the historical specificity of the real as visualized in the Victorian period.

CONCLUSION   The history of critical readings of the realist mode has been peculiarly rich and peculiarly contentious. The narrative above has, of course, tidied that history into a neat pattern. It has done so partly – as throughout this *Guide* – by overlooking some of the thoughtful and thought-provoking interventions that were individualistic in the past thirty years and were plainly concerned with fresh areas beyond the dominant critical debate (some of these are included in the Further Reading section). But the main lines of that central debate, especially about realism's political identity, are clear. Its history shows with particular clarity the ways in which readers, over the past three decades, with competing assumptions and critical principles, have imagined the Victorian novel in strikingly different ways, particularly its relationship with ideology. The criticism of realism in fiction exposes, with a special force, how the historically situated critic constructs the literary text he or she is investigating at a given moment in the history of the culture, because the investigation of realism has, naturally, involved critics in definitions of the real itself. And therein have been irreducible differences of view.

Chapter Notes

1   See, for instance, Jonathan Crary, *Techniques of the Observer: On Vision and Modernity in the Nineteenth Century* (Cambridge, MA: MIT Press, 1990) and Lindsay Smith, *Victorian Photography, Painting and Poetry: The Enigma of Visibility in Ruskin, Morris and the Pre-Raphaelites* (Cambridge: Cambridge University Press, 1995). An early work was Rachel Bowlby, *Just Looking: Consumer Culture in Deiser, Gissing and Zola* (London: Methuen, 1985).

2 Watt's other important books are: Ian Watt, ed., *The Victorian Novel: Modern Essays in Criticism* (London: Oxford University Press, 1971), and *Myths of Modern Individualism: Faust, Don Quixote, Don Juan, Robinson Crusoe* (Cambridge: Cambridge University Press, 1996).

3 Ian Watt, *The Rise of the Novel: Studies in Defoe, Richardson and Fielding* (Harmondsworth: Penguin, 1972, first pub. 1957), 22.

4 Ibid., 22–3.

5 Ibid., 34.

6 Ioan Williams, *The Realist Novel in England: A Study in Development* (Basingstoke: Macmillan, 1974), x.

7 The best starting-point for considering the post-structuralist response to realism is the extract from Roland Barthes's *The Rustle of Language (Le Bruissement de la Langue*, 1984) reproduced as 'The Reality Effect' in Dennis Walder, ed., *The Realist Novel* (London: Routledge/Open University Press, 1996) (see Further Reading).

8 Astyanax was the son of Hector and Andromache, and therefore the eldest grandson of Priam. He died a baby during the fall of Troy, when the son of Achilles, Neoptolemus, threw him over the wall of Troy.

9 Leo Bersani, *A Future for Astyanax: Character and Desire in Literature* (London: Boyars, 1978, first pub. 1976), 55–6.

10 See Louis Althusser, *Lenin and Philosophy, and Other Essays*, trans. Ben Brewster (London: New Left Books, 1971). This includes 'Letter to André Daspre', Althusser's most important discussion of the relations of art and ideology.

11 For Barthes, see n. 7 above.

12 Marxist Feminist Literature Collective, 'Women's Writing: "Jane Eyre", "Shirley", "Villette", "Aurora Leigh"', in F. Barker, J. Coombes, P. Hulme, C. Mercer, and D. Musselwhite, eds, *1848: The Sociology of Literature: Proceedings of the Essex Conference on the Sociology of Literature July 1977* (Essex: University of Essex, 1978), 188.

13 Ibid., 190

14 Lawrence Rothfield, *Vital Signs: Medical Realism in Nineteenth-century Fiction* (Princeton, NJ: Princeton University Press, 1992), xi.

15 Ibid.

16 Ibid., xiv.

17 Nancy Armstrong, *Fiction in the Age of Photography: The Legacy of British Realism* (Cambridge, MA and London: Harvard University Press, 1999), 7–8.

Further Reading

General studies of realism/Victorian realism:
Erich Auerbach, *Mimesis: The Representation of Reality in Western Literature*, trans. Willard R. Trask (Princeton, NJ: Princeton University Press, 1953): not specifically on Victorian fiction but a classic argument about literary realism. Auerbach discusses

the two dominant styles of realism, the Homeric and the Old Testament, and their determining influence on the representation of reality in European literature.

Roland Barthes: see Dennis Walder (below).

Wayne C. Booth, *The Rhetoric of Fiction* (Chicago and London: Chicago University Press, 1961): another classic, it offers detailed rhetorical analysis of the elements of fiction such as objectivity, telling and showing, and also includes a section on realism, pp. 23–64.

Delia da Sousa Correa, ed., *The Nineteenth-century Novel: Realisms* (London: Routledge, 2000): intended for the Open University, contains specially written essays: part 1 looks at the relationship between literary realism and romance in *Northanger Abbey* (1818), *Jane Eyre* and *Dombey and Son* (1846–8); part 2 considers *Middlemarch*, *Far from the Madding Crowd* (1874) and Zola's *Germinal* (1884–5). Critiques the history of realism from Watt and Leavis onwards (pp. 189–96).

Dennis Walder, ed., *The Realist Novel* (London: Routledge/Open University Press, 1996): includes material by Raymond Williams, Van Ghent, Bakhtin, and Barthes's 'The Reality Effect' from *The Rustle of Language*. Here, in the *locus classicus* of the post-structuralist response to the nineteenth-century discourse of realism, Barthes argues that textual details in a realist text, such as a barometer mentioned in a description in Flaubert's *Madame Bovary*, are there to give the illusion of reality. He suggests that such objects are empty signs, contributing to the modern disintegration of the sign in a regressive way as they occur in 'the name of a referential plenitude'.

Ian Watt, ed., *The Victorian Novel: Modern Essays in Criticism* (London: Oxford University Press, 1971): a selection of essays, including T. S. Eliot on Wilkie Collins and Dickens, Northrop Frye on Dickens, Lukács on Thackeray's *Henry Esmond*, and Tony Tanner on Hardy.

Modern criticism on Victorian fiction and realism:

Robert L. Caserio, *Plot, Story, and the Novel: From Dickens and Poe to the Modern Period* (Princeton, NJ: Princeton University Press, 1979): 'In some of the most prestigious novelistic fiction [including the Victorian] the imitation of actuality becomes opposed to the imitation of acts' and the 'distrust of the imitation of action [. . .] has become a distrust of intelligibility, purposefulness, and morality altogether'.

Simon Dentith, *The Rhetoric of the Real: Studies in Post-Enlightenment Writing from 1790 to the Present* (Hemel Hempstead: Harvester Wheatsheaf, 1990): original study that approaches questions of realism through theory; stresses the rhetorical dimension of all writing but emphasizes also its referential function, arguing that rhetorical success is often dependent on successful reference to the world.

Harry E. Shaw, *Narrating Reality: Austen, Scott, Eliot* (Ithaca and London: Cornell University Press, 1999): includes three chapters on the nature of realism as well as ample discussion of George Eliot and history.

Contrast with Watt and Ermarth:

Lennard J. Davis, *Factual Fictions: The Origins of the English Novel* (New York: Columbia University Press, 1983): proposes another alternative history to the origins of the novel concentrating on the realist discourse. Davis sees the novel arising in the eighteenth century out of journalism and argues that its 'fictionality is a ploy to mask the genuine ideological, reportorial, commentative function of the novel'.

David Trotter, *Cooking with Mud: The Idea of Mess in Nineteenth-century Art and Fiction* (Oxford: Oxford University Press, 2000): scintillating reconsideration of the history of realism by examining the role of mess and disorder as traces of the modern in nineteenth-century art forms.

View of the 'transparency' of Victorian realism by a Modernist critic:

Colin MacCabe, *James Joyce and the Revolution of the Word* (Basingstoke: Macmillan, 1978): says that classic realist texts have a meta-language that claims to be transparent: 'The meta-language within such a text refuses to acknowledge its own status as writing – as marks of material difference distributed through time and space. The text outside the area of inverted commas claims to be the product of no articulation, it claims to be unwritten [...] This relationship between discourses can be taken as the defining feature of the *classic realist text*.' Takes *Middlemarch* as an instance.

Comparison with Levine/Boumehla:

Alison Byerly, *Realism, Representation, and the Arts in Nineteenth-century Literature* (Cambridge: Cambridge University Press, 1997): confronts a significant paradox in the development of literary realism: the novels that present themselves as purveyors and celebrants of direct, ordinary human experience also manifest an obsession with art that threatens to sabotage their realist claims. References to works of art – portraits, caricatures, charades, musical performances – and metaphors compare the novelist's own representation to specific forms of art. 'Insistent reminders of the disjunction between art and life, these artistic references threaten to sabotage the realist claim to unmediated representation.'

J. Jeffrey Franklin, *Serious Play: The Cultural Form of the Nineteenth-century Realist Novel* (Philadelphia: University of Pennsylvania Press, 1999): New Historicist discussion of how play in the realist novel makes visible the boundaries of a dominant discourse that proscribes play as bad. At the most straightforward level, the novels appear to uphold a clear moral discourse, using play to scapegoat activities, social groups and ideologies antithetical to the dominant discourses of the text. But the relationship of realism and ideology is more complex: the realist 'exposes to scrutiny the supposedly critical difference between the privileged figures and the figures of play to which they are juxtaposed. Finance capitalism thus may emerge suddenly as organized gambling on a mass scale.'

Comparison with D. A. Miller:

Barbara Arnett Melchiori, *Terrorism in the Late Victorian Novel* (London: Croom Helm, 1985): considers politically motivated violence in around forty late-Victorian novelists, most of them writers of popular fiction. Emphasizes how the popular novelist gathered material from the press.

Andrew H. Miller, *Novels Behind Glass: Commodity Culture and Victorian Narrative* (Cambridge: Cambridge University Press, 1995): 'among the dominant concerns motivating mid-Victorian novelists was a penetrating anxiety, most graphically displayed in Thackeray's *Vanity Fair*, that their social and moral world was being reduced to a warehouse of goods and commodities, a display window in which people, their actions, and their convictions were exhibited for the economic appetites of others.' Miller thinks that novelists were in an ambiguous position because 'Adopting a moral stance against the commodification of the world, [they] simultaneously understood that literary work itself was increasingly commodified; they were, as a result, required to negotiate between the moral condemnation and their implication in what they opposed.'

A mid-position between Miller/Belsey and Levine:

Michiel Heyns, *Expulsion and the Nineteenth-century Novel: The Scapegoat in English Realist Fiction* (Oxford: Clarendon, 1994): sees a central battle in the Victorian realist novel 'between the need to conform to socially sanctioned values and the urge to defy them; between the generic convention of closure and the barely contained impulse towards disruption'. Concentrates on the scapegoat: 'If we define the scapegoat as that figure that has to bear the burden of guilt of a particular community [...] then, in my model, the narrative itself constitutes a community, generating pressures that eventually expel those characters that disturb the equilibrium which it is the aim of narrative closure to restore.'

Other relevant studies:

Paul Hamilton, *Historicism* (London: Routledge, 1995): includes an evaluation and brief polemical introduction to New Historicism (pp. 150–63). See also pp. 162–3 of the present volume.

Dale Spender, 'Women and Literary History', in Catherine Belsey and Jane Moore, eds, *The Feminist Reader*, 2nd edn (Basingstoke: Macmillan, 1997), 16–25: critiques the gender assumptions of Ian Watt's *The Rise of the Novel*.

5

Social-problem Fiction: Historicism and Feminism

Raymond Williams – Sheila Smith – Patrick Brantlinger – Catherine Gallagher – Mary Poovey – Josephine Guy – Helena Bergmann – Joseph Kestner – Deborah Epstein Nord – Barbara Harman

Victorian social-problem novels have been treated as a group since the work of Louis Cazamian, Arnold Kettle and Raymond Williams. Variously known as *roman-à-thèse*, 'condition of England' fiction, 'industrial fiction', 'social novels' or 'social-problem novels', the category refers to fiction of the early Victorian period that exposed the shortcomings of modern industrial society. Although socially committed, it did not have a unitary political position or advocate, across the genre as a whole, a consistent programme of reform. Conventionally, the precursors and influences of the genre have usually been identified as the fiction of William Godwin, a more general commitment to radical political literature absorbed from Romanticism, and the social criticism of Thomas Carlyle. Harriet Martineau's *Illustrations of Political Economy* (1832–5), designed to communicate to non-professional readers the basics of political economy and Utilitarianism, Charles Dickens's protest against the new Poor Law, *Oliver Twist* (1837–8), and Fanny Trollope's affecting *Michael Armstrong, The Factory Boy* (1840) were early examples of the form. But social-problem fiction really flourished in the 1840s, a decade of particular political unrest that became known as the 'Hungry Forties'. Charlotte Brontë's *Shirley* (1849); Charles Dickens's *The Old Curiosity Shop* (1840–1), *Barnaby Rudge* (1841), *Martin Chuzzlewit* (1843–4), *Dombey and Son* (1846–8) and *David Copperfield* (1849–50); Elizabeth Gaskell's *Mary Barton* (1848); Benjamin Disraeli's *Coningsby* (1844), *Sybil* (1845) and *Tancred* (1847); and Charles Kingsley's *Yeast* (1848) were the principal examples from this decade. Feminists, however, revised this canon, like the canon of Victorian fiction generally, during the 1980s and 1990s, and rethought the history of the genre as I have just described it (see pp. 187–8 below). Although social-problem fiction clustered in the 1840s, novels of social

WHAT IS SOCIAL-PROBLEM FICTION?

criticism continued beyond this decade and the genre is usually thought to have ended with George Eliot's *Felix Holt, the Radical* (1866). The place of social-problem fiction, as literature of contemporary political comment, was taken by utopian writing in the second half of the Victorian period and, in the last years, by New Woman fiction (see p. 10 for an outline of New Woman fiction).

CRITICAL INTEREST IN SOCIAL-PROBLEM FICTION

Social-problem fiction attracted a good deal of scholarly attention from the 1960s onwards. Liberal humanism, as it flourished in the academy in the 1950s and 1960s, avoided contextualization of literature and found no reward in reading fiction that obviously demanded engagement with an extra-literary context. But, in the 1960s and 1970s, social-problem fiction began to gain the attention of those widely opposed to the assumptions of liberal humanism whose interests were explicitly political and radical. Critical interest came especially from cultural materialists and Marxists in these decades and concentrated on identifying the kinds of consciousness and political commitment the novels revealed. Attention was also focused on the moral and intellectual failures of the novelists to grasp the enormity of industrial England's plight and to understand the best ways of improving the lot of its victims. The middle-class stance of the novelists was criticized and their ambivalent regard for the poor regretted.

The main thrust of criticism after this radical work, from the end of the 1970s into the 1980s, was to historicize/contextualize the fiction and to set to one side the political agendas of the previous generation. Patrick Brantlinger approached social-problem fiction without the frame of such politics in the mid-1970s and mapped it against the changes in British reform movements in the first half of Queen Victoria's reign. Subsequently, New Historicism located social-problem fiction in relation to discourses about industrialism and the social body circulating in the culture. The movement critiqued the orientation of 1960s' and 1970s' radical criticism in two important ways: it endeavoured to read the fiction's intervention in Victorian political debates in a more complex way, and it did not see the failures of social-problem fiction to provide solutions to political difficulties as a fault of individual novelists or a function of their middle-class biases. Rather, New Historicism considered that the contradictions and flaws of the novels were a reflection of problems in the whole nexus of discourses on industrialism. Josephine Guy's response to this New Historicist intervention, in 1996, offered another way of contextualizing social-problem fiction by identifying the significance of the individual in the thought-world in which it was written. Guy further developed the modern reader's sense of the historical specificity of social-problem fiction's political critique and also identified grounds for which it should be celebrated rather than criticized.

In addition to these critics of the 1980s and 1990s, who were concerned with historicizing/contextualizing social-problem fiction, there was also a body of feminist critics, discussed in the final section of this chapter. Their main interest was in the gender implications of writing novels that intervened in the public domain of social critique, and their arguments applied widely to Victorian fiction by women. In the 1980s, Joseph Kestner argued that the social-problem novel, specifically, was invented by female writers and enabled their metaphorical enfranchisement. Subsequently, in the 1990s, the broader issue of women's entry into the public world was regarded either as a source of anxiety for the novelists or as admirable resistance to patriarchy (for the inauguration of the idea of patriarchy in feminist criticism, see pp. 66–7 above).

Historicism and the Social-problem Novel

Louis Cazamian's *Le Roman Social en Angleterre, 1830–1850: Dickens, Disraeli, Mrs Gaskell, Kingsley* (1903) set influential terms for the debate about social-problem fiction and his work remained current for generations of writers. Kathleen Tillotson said in *Novels of the Eighteen-forties* (1954) that this was 'still the standard survey of the field'.[1] Indeed, Cazamian saw the period 1830–50 as dominated by a simple antithesis that is still revived in popular arguments: individualism versus idealism (see Poovey, pp. 164–78 below, for a feminist response to this argument). The former was represented by the political economists, the latter involved a desire to bring feeling into political calculation, to make 'sensation and emotion dominate the logical and abstract operations of the mind'.[2] The Victorian novel, Cazamian argued, worked on behalf of the idealists in the struggle against the arid calculations of the economists:

CAZAMIAN'S READING IN 1903

> Literary realism was the best weapon social idealists could have wielded against the attitude of mind they opposed. Utilitarianism and political economy were alike abstract. The idealist reaction was able to castigate individualism for its failure to appreciate the real and concrete; for its substitution of the single faculty of reason for all others; and for its replacement of complex human nature with one single type, economic man. The social novel implanted realism in English thinking. It exposed facts, and selected the most important of these for discussion. Its valuable philosophy of life was experimental and demonstrative: it showed the direct way from experience to principle. And under the writer's guidance the reader took an instructive walk through society which was not offered him by any economist.[3]

The perception of the period as a conflict between individualism and interventionism was, however, over-simplified. Moreover, some thought that, despite the wide reading of the book, Cazamian had transported terms from nineteenth-century French history into the different territory of English history, and the relocation created a mismatch of methodology with material.

THE
SIGNIFICANCE
OF RAYMOND
WILLIAMS

For critics reading social-problem fiction now, the best starting-point is Raymond Williams's work, the other major force in Cambridge literary criticism alongside (and sharply different from) F. R. Leavis (see chapter 2). Raymond Williams (1921–88), a Fellow of Jesus College, Cambridge, then Professor of Drama at the university 1974–83, was the most important English radical critic of his day. His work influenced later generations, including controversial figures in the reshaping of English studies in the academy in the 1970s and 1980s such as the Marxist Terry Eagleton and the advocate of cultural studies, Peter Widdowson.

WILLIAMS'S
'STRUCTURES
OF FEELING'

Raymond Williams developed a Marxist reading of literature, insisting that it was considered in terms of the ideologies of its culture. He was the first major English critic to propose this, and made prominent, in distinction from the New Critics and Leavisites, the study of literary writing in relation to the ideological matrices of its context. He was particularly interested in the ways in which ideology was lived, and developed the concept of the 'structure of feeling' to explain this. The structure of feeling, later absorbed in Louis Althusser's notion of ideology (see Althusser in the Further Reading section), was a mode of perception that was ideologically determined: it was neither thought nor feeling, but an amalgam of both. 'We are talking about characteristic elements of impulse', Williams said, 'restraint and tone; specifically affective elements of consciousness and relationships: not feeling against thought, but thought as felt and feeling as thought: practical consciousness of a present kind, in a living and interrelating communing.'[4]

WILLIAMS'S
CRITICISMS OF
SOCIAL-
PROBLEM
FICTION

Williams discussed the social-problem novel (the 'industrial novel' as he called it) in both his *Culture and Society 1780–1950* (1963) and *The English Novel from Dickens to Lawrence* (1970). In *Culture and Society* he argued that social-problem novels illustrated and helped shape the structure of feeling about industrialism. This comprised a set of ambivalent responses to industrial development and social change. Williams saw the middle-class social-problem novelists as retreating from the difficulties they perceived: 'Recognition of evil was balanced by fear of becoming involved [...] Sympathy was transformed, not into action, but into withdrawal'.[5] He was critical of the novelists for this, for failing to represent the true horrors of industrialization, and for their refusal to suggest solutions to the social turmoil that followed in the wake of the Industrial Revolution. Williams's criticisms in *Culture and Society* were challenged in the 1980s and 1990s. His approach was also judged, as many have pointed out, to be ahistorical: he required the novelists to propose answers to twentieth-century views of nineteenth-century industrialism, and did not consider whether the Victorians would have thought in the same way. He also assumed that it was the explicit task of fiction *to* suggest coherent answers to social problems, that fiction was a form of intervention that should offer clear political solutions.

Williams's chapter, in *The English Novel*, on the novels of 1847 and 1848 also considered structures of feelings. Here, in this major statement of radical English literary criticism, he identified the commonality of purpose in the genre of social-problem fiction, arguing that novels from these years revealed a change in the way men and women thought and felt about politics. They 'mark[ed] above all a new kind consciousness', he said. Williams concentrated on Dickens's *Dombey and Son*, Emily Brontë's *Wuthering Heights*, Thackeray's *Vanity Fair*, Charlotte Brontë's *Jane Eyre*, Gaskell's *Mary Barton*, Disraeli's *Tancred, Town and Country*, and Anne Brontë's *The Tenant of Wildfell Hall*. Central to this new form of consciousness was the idea of the community and its knowability. This was to be a concept that was debated and particularized in the wake of William's work in the 1970s (see Smith, pp. 160–1 below). In the following extract from the 'Introduction' to *The English Novel*, Williams discusses this concern, offering a brief outline of its causes, and suggesting ways in which it was registered in early Victorian social-problem fiction and the nineteenth-century novel in general.

THE KNOWABLE COMMUNITY IN WILLIAMS'S *THE ENGLISH NOVEL* (1970)

Extract from Raymond Williams, *The English Novel* (London: Chatto and Windus, 1970), 9–17.

I KEEP thinking about those twenty months, in 1847 and 1848, in which these novels were published: *Dombey and Son, Wuthering Heights, Vanity Fair, Jane Eyre, Mary Barton, Tancred, Town and Country, The Tenant of Wildfell Hall*.

What was it just then that emerged in England? It was of course no sudden process of just a few months. But we can see, looking back, those months as decisive. The English novel before then had its major achievements; it had Defoe and Fielding, Richardson and Jane Austen and Walter Scott.[1] But now in the 1840s it had a new and major *generation*. For the next eighty years the novel was to be the major form in English literature. And this was unprecedented. What these months seem to mark above all is a new kind of consciousness, and we have to learn to see what this is, and some ways of relating it to the new and unprecedented civilisation in which it took shape.

The changes in society had been long in the making: the Industrial Revolution, the struggle for democracy, the growth of cities and towns. But these also, in the 1840s, reached a point of consciousness which was in its turn decisive. The twelve years from Dickens's first novel to his radically innovating *Dombey and Son* were also the years of the crisis of Chartism.[2] The first industrial civilisation in the history of the world had come to a critical and defining stage. By the end of the 1840s the English were the first predominantly urban people in the long history of human societies. The institutions of an urban culture, from music-halls and popular Sunday newspapers to public parks, museums and libraries, were all decisively established in these years. There was critical legislation on public health and on working-hours in factories. A major economic decision, on free trade and the repeal of the corn laws, had begun a long realignment of politics. In the struggle and disturbance of those years the future, of course, was not known. But the sense of crisis, of major and radical issues and decisions, was both acute and general. It is then not surprising that in just this decade a particular kind of literature – already known and widely read, but still not very highly regarded – should come to take on new life, a newly significant and relevant life. Here, in these hands, a generation of writers, in very different ways, found the common forms that mattered, in response to a new and varied but still common experience.

There were of course immediate and related reasons for the new importance of the novel. Reading of all kinds was increasing. Between the 1820s and 1860 the annual number of new books rose from 580 to over 2,600, and much of the increase was in novels. New methods of binding and printing had brought book-prices down. In the period in which these novels were published there were new cheap libraries: the Parlour and the Railway: not led, of course, by the new generation, but by others: Lytton, Marryat, G. P. R. James. The reading of newspapers and magazines was increasing rapidly, though the major period of expansion was still twenty years ahead. In every way the reading-public was still a minority, and the book-reading public especially so. But serial publication of fiction, in the new family magazines, was significantly expanding the number of readers of novels.[3] Direct market factors were important to writers in more pressing and evident ways.

But this is no simple case, in the end, of demand and supply. Several of the best new writers were involved in the market, and with their eyes wide open to it: Dickens above all. But what was written and what had to be written had many other sources. The crisis of the society and the expansion of reading were themselves related. More and more people felt the need for this kind of knowledge and experience, as customary ways broke down or receded. But beyond even this, as we can see most clearly from the novels themselves, the new pressures and disturbances were not simple moulds out of which new forms came. The men and women who were writing – some at the centre of opinion-forming and the market, some distant and isolated – took from the disturbance of these years another impetus: a crisis of experience, often quite personally felt and endured, which when it emerged in novels was much more than a reaction to existing and acknowledged public features. It was a creative working, a discovery, often alone at the table; a transformation and innovation which composed a generation out of what seemed separate work and experience. It brought in new feelings, people, relationships; rhythms newly known, discovered, articulated; defining the society, rather than merely reflecting it; defining it in novels, which had each its own significant and particular life. It was not the society or its crisis which produced the novels. The society and the novels – our general names for those myriad and related primary activities – came from a pressing and varied experience which was not yet history; which had no new forms, no significant moments, until these were made and given by direct human actions.

What then can we define that emerged from those months: those twenty months in which, looking back, we can see so clearly a particular achievement: a confirmation of a generation; confirmation of a new importance, a new relevance and new forms? From the many possibilities in those varied reading experiences I would choose one bearing as central: the exploration of community: the substance and meaning of community.

From Dickens to Lawrence, over nearly a hundred years, this bearing seems to me decisive. What community is, what it has been, what it might be; how community relates to individuals and relationships; how men and women, directly engaged, see within them or beyond them, for but more often against them, the shape of a society: these related themes are the dominant bearings. For this is a period in which what it means to live in a community is more uncertain, more critical, more disturbing as a question put both to societies and to persons than ever before in history. The underlying experiences of this powerful and transforming urban and industrial civilisation are of rapid and inescapable social change; of a newly visible and conscious history but at the same time, in most actual communities and in most actual lives, of a newly complicated and often newly obscure immediate process. These are not opposite poles: they are the defining characteristics of the change itself. People became more aware of great social and historical changes which altered not only outward forms – institutions and landscapes – but also inward feelings, experiences, self-definitions. These facts of change can be seen lying deep in almost every imagination.[4]

And then of course it was right that the novel should be used to explore and to realise this process, in unprecedented ways. In the great eighteenth-century realists, in the precise social world of Jane Austen and in the historically conscious imagination of Scott, its powers and its possibilities were already evident. But though they drew some of their strength, their starting strength, from their great individual predecessors, these new novelists of a rapidly changing England had to create, from their own resources, forms adequate to the experience at the new and critical stage it had reached.

Two features of this development stand out. The historical novel, as Scott had developed it, has almost run its course – its fashionable course – before this generation began. Dickens used it occasionally; George Eliot went back to it once.[5] But in the main line it had become a separate form: from history as change, eating into human consciousness, to history as spectacle, the spectacular past, as most clearly in Lytton. Each of these possibilities can be seen in Scott: the romantic use of the past to transcend the present had many colourful opportunities in fiction. But the permanent achievement of the romantic imagination, at the point of its deepest engagement with its own time, was not this kind of transcendence. It was the establishment of a position in human experience which was capable of judging – not incidentally but totally – the very society that was forming and changing it. Society from being a framework could be seen now as an agency, even an actor, a character. It could be seen and valued in and through persons: not as a framework in which they were defined; not as an aggregate of known relationships; but as an apparently independent organism, a character and an action like others. Society, now, was not just a code to measure, an institution to control, a standard to define or to change. It was a process that entered lives, to shape or to deform; a process personally known but then again suddenly distant, complex, incomprehensible, overwhelming.

In what had been learned of process in the historical novel, the new novel of social change – of the valuation of change – found its impetus, its initiative, its decisive and eagerly taken opportunity. Thomas Carlyle, who did more than anyone else in his generation to communicate this sense of history – of historical process as moral substance and challenge – came to think that the novel was outdated, that it could be replaced by history. He was of course to be proved wrong, but only by the transformation of the novel in very much the direction of his central argument. It was by becoming history, contemporary history – but a history of substance, of process, of the interaction of public and private life – that one important kind of novel went to the heart of its time. When Balzac, in France, learned from Scott, he went back not to the Middle Ages, at a distance which was bound to be spectacle, but as Scott had done in his best work to the recent and connecting history of Scotland; to the decisive origin of his own epoch: to the years of the French Revolution. He learned in this way, in the search for origins, how to go on to write the continuing history of his time. The new English novelists learned in comparable ways: going back to the decisive origins of their own epoch, in the crises of the Industrial Revolution, of democratic reform and of the movement from country to town: from Charlotte Brontë on the Luddites in *Shirley* to George Eliot on the years before 1832 and on town and country in *Middlemarch* and in *Felix Holt*. It was in this kind of use of the historical imagination, rather than in the fanciful exercises of a *Romola* or a *Tale of Two Cities*, that the real growth took place. And it was in these ways that novelists learned to look, historically, at the crises of their own immediate time: at Chartism, at the industrial struggle, at debt and speculation, at the complicated inheritance of values and of property.

That was one very important line of development, but there is another, even more important, which enters even more deeply into the substance and form of the novel. Most novels are in some sense knowable communities. It is part of a traditional method – an underlying stance and approach – that the novelist offers to show people and their relationships in essentially knowable and communicable ways. Much of the confidence of this method depends on a particular kind of social confidence and experience. In its simplest form this amounts to saying – though at its most confident it did not have to be said – that the knowable and therefore known relationships compose and are part of a wholly known social structure, and that in and through the relationships the persons themselves can be wholly known. Thus from the middle term, of visible and comprehensible relationship, both societies and persons are knowable; indeed certain fundamental propositions about them can even be taken for granted, in terms of a received and mutually applicable social and moral code.

Many factors combined to destroy this confidence, in the process of extraordinary change through which the new novelists were living. One effect of this change has been widely recognised. It has indeed become a dogma – more properly, a half-truth – that persons are only partially knowable in and through relationships; that some part of the personality precedes and survives – is in a way unaffected by – relationships; that in this special sense persons are not knowable, are indeed fundamentally and crucially unknowable. And this is a belief which in itself forces new and very radical experiments in the novel; experiments which have been more active and more exclusive in every subsequent generation.[6]

What is not so often recognised in this well-known effect is that at the other end of the scale a similar process has been evident: an increasing scepticism, disbelief, in the possibility of understanding society; a structurally similar certainty that relationships, knowable relationships, so far from composing a community or a society, are the positive experience that has to be *contrasted* with the ordinarily negative experience of the society as a whole (or of the society as opposed to the local and immediate community). An important split takes place between knowable relationships and an unknown, unknowable, overwhelming society. The full seriousness of this split and of its eventual consequences for the novel can be traced only towards the end of the century. But its pressure is evident from this first period of crisis: Dickens's response to it – a very early and major response – is perhaps the key to understanding him, and especially to understanding his very original and creative use of the novel as a form.

Now we have only to name this particular crisis – the crisis of the knowable community – to see how deeply it is related to the changes through which these novelists were living. We can see its obvious relation to the very rapidly increasing size and scale and complexity of communities: in the growth of towns and especially of cities and of a metropolis; in the increasing division and complexity of labour; in the altered and critical relations between and within social classes. In these simple and general senses, any assumption of a knowable community – a whole community, wholly knowable – becomes harder and harder to sustain. And we have to remember, with this, that there is a direct though very difficult relationship between the knowable community and the knowable person. Wordsworth, in *The Prelude*, had got through to this relationship very early. In the great seventh book – *Residence in London* – he directly related the new phenomenon of the urban crowd – not the occasional but the regular crowd, the new crowd of the metropolitan streets – to problems of self-identity, self-knowledge, self-possession:

> How often in the overflowing Streets,
> Have I gone forward with the Crowd, and said
> Unto myself, the face of every one
> That passes by me is a mystery...
> ...And all the ballast of familiar life,
> The present, and the past; hope, fear; all stays,
> All laws of acting, thinking, speaking man
> Went from me, neither knowing me, nor known.

It is from this critical conjunction – the unknowable crowd and the unknowing and unknown individual – that he created the image of the blind beggar with the label telling his history and his identity:

> It seemed
> To me that in this Label was a type,
> Or emblem, of the utmost that we know
> Both of ourselves and of the universe.

It is a familiar romantic conclusion; but it is important that the insight occurred where it did: in the crowded street of a city. It is a related alienation, of a community and of persons, of the kind which Blake also had seen, with a sharper emphasis on power, in his poem *London*.

The problem of the knowable community, with its deep implications for the novelist, is then clearly a part of the social history of early nineteenth-century England and of the imaginative penetration and recoil which was the creative response. But what is knowable is not only a function of objects – of what is there to be known. It is also a function of subjects, of observers – of what is desired and what needs to be known. A knowable community, that is to say, is a matter of consciousness as well as of evident fact. Indeed it is to just this problem of knowing a community – of finding a position, a position convincingly experienced, from which community can begin to be known – that one of the major phases in the development of the novel must be related. [...]

Notes

1 For Saintsbury's consideration of the Victorian novels' relation to Austen and Scott, see pp. 23–5 above; for Leavis's, pp. 51–64.
2 A working-class reform movement, prominent from the 1830s to 1848, demanding electoral changes. See David Jones, *Chartism and the Chartists* (London: Lane, 1975) and Dorothy Thompson, *The Chartists* (London: Temple Smith, 1984).
3 On serial publication, see pp. 266–84 below.
4 For a New Historicist approach to the idea of community in social-problem fiction, see Mary Poovey's work, pp. 165–78 below.
5 Williams's debt to literary histories (see pp. 21–9 above) is visible here.
6 Compare this view of the unknowable person with Ian Watt's account of the rise of realism, discussed pp. 95–7 above, with its emphasis on the detailed representation of the human personality.

Williams's statement about the knowable community in *The English Novel* was a generalized one. His argument about the period pivoted on loose assertions and bold general statements. His claims that 'people became   WILLIAMS'S GENERALIZA-TIONS aware...' or 'people felt...' did not have ample documentation or evidence, and he selected carefully among the canonical fiction of the years in which he was interested to offer texts to support his argument. Williams did not suggest in any substantial way, moreover, how the wider society of early Victorian writers perceived the issues he described as central to their experience.

SHEILA SMITH'S PARTICULAR-IZATION OF WILLIAMS   The generalized approach prompted efforts to refine and particularize. Of these, the most substantial was Sheila M. Smith's *The Other Nation: The Poor in English Novels of the 1840s and 1850s* (1980). Admitting that Williams was indeed 'somewhat generalized',[6] Smith took his claim that the problem of the knowable community was crucial to the early Victorian novelists and explored the knowableness of the poor in a wide range of early Victorian writing. Like Williams, Smith was interested in the sympathy of the middle-class social-problem novelists to the predicament of the working class: 'Can [...] middle-class novelists', she asked:

> concerned with commenting on the Two Nations [of Rich and Poor] in their society, extend their consciousness to include the life of the Other Nation so that their readers imaginatively experience it? Can they make one Nation 'see' the Other? Can 'truth about' the Other Nation create imaginative truth, the essential reality which commands Lear's reaction to Poor Tom, 'Thou art the thing itself'?[7]

MORE PROBLEMS FOUND IN SOCIAL-PROBLEM FICTION   Smith evoked an ahistorical concept in claiming that there was an 'essential reality', a timeless and immutable human identity, that novelists should recognize. In judging how far the writers realized this universal truth, Smith was, like Williams, evaluative of the attitudes and sympathies of social-problem fiction. Generally, she found the genre unimpressive in its attitude to the lower strata of society. Like other critics of social-problem fiction prior to the mid-1980s (see Craig, Lucas, Howard, and Goode in the Further Reading section, and Kettle, below, p. 162), for Smith, personal and moral failure seemed inscribed in the novelists' achievements because the novelists themselves could not overcome their shock at what they found. The 'most obvious reactions to the Other Nation were horror, disgust, or pity', she said. Disgust or pity, she added, was followed either by withdrawal from the scene of distress or by a gesture of sympathy that had no outcome in political action: scenes of deprivation were 'accompanied by the exhortation to readers to remove the matter for disgust or to share the novelist's pity'.[8] Like Williams, Smith saw the novelists keeping a distance between themselves and the poor. None of their responses was predicated on recognition of the 'essential reality' of the poor's universal humanity, and none was accompanied by suggestions for practical improvement. Worse, novelists ignored developments in the period that, according to Smith, would have ameliorated the condition of the poor. They were, for instance, Smith said, 'completely blind to the importance of Trade Unions in the new society'.[9] Smith assumed that the diagnoses and solutions offered by Victorian fiction – she too believed that it was the task of novels to offer credible solutions to social and political problems – should be similar to those the late twentieth century would offer. She did not allow that structures of thought about political, moral and reform issues in the mid-nineteenth century were different from those in the second half of the twentieth, that different questions were asked, and different moral, spiritual and political agenda influenced the answers.

Patrick Brantlinger's *The Spirit of Reform: British Literature and Politics, 1832–1867* had preceded Smith's study by three years. In some ways, his approach was cognate with Smith's and Williams's. Certainly, Brantlinger resisted the New Criticism's belief in the separation of aesthetic artefact from history, and challenged the literary historians of the early part of the century for thinking only of literary tradition, not of literature's non-linear relationship with complex political history (see pp. 21–9 above for discussion of literary historians). Like Smith, furthermore, he sought to give definiteness and precision to his literary inquiry through detailed examination of non-fictional sources (in a way Raymond Williams had not) in order to relate literature to changes in political beliefs about reform in the public world. But *The Spirit of Reform* was distinct from previous studies in that it was without a radical political agenda of its own and certainly without Williams's theorized concept of the structure of feeling. *The Spirit of Reform* argued that one did not have to be a Marxist to believe literature needed to be read in an historical context for its intentions to be understood.

BRANTLIN-GER'S HISTORICIZA-TION: CONTEXT 1 FOR SOCIAL-PROBLEM FICTION

Brantlinger's interest was in the literature of reform – a wider category than the 'industrial novels' examined in *Culture and Society* – in the middle years of the century. His thesis was the history of a vanishing. Literary writers in the 1830s, he argued, exhibited confidence in their efforts to promote reform. That reform involved 'evangelical and humanitarian protest, the advocacy of limited government intervention to correct social abuses and to refurbish outmoded institutions, and Benthamite and Owenite schemes for improving mankind itself.'[10] In the 1840s, however, ideas about reform changed direction, and it was 'identified less and less with legislation and with bureaucratic social planning than with voluntary humanitarian activity, typified by the Christian Socialism of Maurice, Ludlow, and Kingsley.' Concepts of social reform through politics 'were gradually supplanted by ideas of social progress in spite of politics'.[11] This notion of progress, Brantlinger concluded, defined the temper of the 1850s and 1860s: activist reform that aimed to control industry and working conditions no longer appealed. *The Spirit of Reform*, which was later supplemented by *Rule of Darkness* (1988) with its consideration of imperial politics (discussed on pp. 317–19 below), proposed that the history of 'the spirit of reform in middle-class literature between 1832 and 1867 [...] must be largely a history of its disappearance, as it becomes absorbed either by assumptions of inevitable progress or by theories of progressive evolution'.[12]

NEW HISTORICISM: FURTHER CONTEXTS

Sheila Smith's *The Other Nation* involved problems of historicization. But by the middle of the 1980s, the academy, especially the North American academy, was seeing the emergence of a new approach to historical criticism and a new theorization of the relationship between literary writing and other cultural practices. New Historicism, influenced by Foucault, emphasized the importance of reading literature in its historical context but saw all aspects of the culture as potentially relevant in that context. This was because New Historicists thought cultures involved circulating energies that informed widely dispersed societal practices and artefacts. Thus, the Renaissance account of a trial of a hermaphrodite was as relevant to Shakespeare's drama as Shakespeare's own literary reading because both were shaped by the same determining social energies.

CONTEXT 2: GALLAGHER AND THE DISCOURSE OVER INDUSTRIALISM

New Historicism flourished initially in Renaissance studies, especially with the work of Stephen Greenblatt,[13] but Catherine Gallagher's *The Industrial Reformation of English Fiction: Social Discourse and Narrative Form, 1832–1867* (1985) brought the New Historicist approach to the study of Victorian social-problem fiction. Gallagher, whose *Practicing New Historicism* (2000) was co-authored with Greenblatt, addressed the question of the relationship between literary writing and context to argue that social-problem fiction was penetrated by prominent discourses on industrialization that were circulating through the culture. This 'discourse over industrialism'[14] in the first half of the Victorian period was, of course, distinguishable from actual industrialism; it referred, she said, to every statement, written or spoken, about it. Importantly, Gallagher, whose complex argument resists swift summary, saw the Victorians' discourse over industrialism as riven with contradictions registered and made legible in the social-problem novels.

Gallagher's difficult book offered a way of thinking about the relationship between social-problem fiction and its context that provided a more positive understanding of its contradictions and limitations. It made a break with the radical critics of the 1960s and 1970s. Raymond Williams in *Culture and Society* and Sheila Smith in *The Other Nation* argued that social-problem novelists failed in their sympathy and political proposals. The Marxist critic Arnold Kettle, in his essay on 'The Early Victorian Social-problem Novel' included, in 1958, in Boris Ford's popular *Pelican Guide to English Literature*, had likewise thought in terms of their failure. Kettle criticized Elizabeth Gaskell, for example, as far as her political and social ideas were concerned, as 'a fence-sitter'.[15] She was weak in her political ideas, which did not match up to Kettle's own expectations of appropriate responses. Catherine Gallagher, however, insisted that the intellectual and ideological contradictions visible in the fiction were inscribed in the whole collection of cultural discourses about industrial problems. The novelists did not fail morally or as individual political thinkers but their work and ideas were shaped by discourses that were themselves fractured.

Gallagher's *Industrial Reformation* was a major contribution to the debate about social-problem fiction and its value, but areas of difficulty were found with her New Historicist approach. One question was about what the 'discourse over industrialism' really was: Gallagher's argument did not contain the same level of empirical detail as that of Smith's. And why did she perceive this discourse as central? Her reasons for arguing for it were not amply explained and Mary Poovey later provided another context as more relevant (see pp. 165–78 below). Gallagher, in addition, was not concerned with demonstrating that the key features of the 'discourse over industrialism' were those the Victorians themselves had thought the most pressing. *The Industrial Reformation of English Fiction* was also, finally, open to the charge that it collapsed all kinds of documentary evidence used as sources for the 'discourse over industrialism', with different kinds of authority in the culture, into the over-homogeneous notion of discourse. This all-embracing Foucauldian concept did not allow for discrimination between kinds of knowledge, or for the fact that different forms of knowledge had different statuses in the hierarchies of Victorian culture.

A more modest approach to the question of how social-problem fiction related to its context followed Gallagher's intervention. Kate Flint's collection *The Victorian Novelist: Social Problems and Social Change* (1987) offered the reader a range of documentation from the earlier Victorian period including extracts from government Blue Books, periodical articles, official reports, and pertinent letters to national newspapers that helped augment the reader's own sense of the social-problem novelists' context. Flint did not take issue with Gallagher's methodology but argued against the lingering assumptions of liberal humanism in the academy during the 1980s that literature was separable from context. Her book enabled student readers to reflect on correspondences between fictional representations and non-fictional accounts for themselves. Flint reminded her readers that social-problem fiction did not 'exist in isolation',[16] and she proposed that proper awareness of important elements of context would enable contemporary readers to bring to social-problem novels 'some of the knowledge and opinions with which their original readers [...] would have approached them'.[17] This emphasis on recovering the Victorian reader's sense of the relationship between fictional representation and non-literary forms of evidence escaped the problems of Gallagher's study by enabling individual reflection on contextual filiations.

CONTEXT 3:
MARY POOVEY
AND THE
SOCIAL BODY

A fresh study of the context of social-problem fiction in the 1990s came, however, from another New Historicist. In her collection of essays, *Making a Social Body: British Cultural Formation, 1830–1864* (1995), Mary Poovey provided a new discoursal context in which social-problem fiction could be read. Poovey, who had previously written a pioneering study of the ideological work of gender in the Victorian period,[18] argued for hitherto unconsidered ways of understanding the emergence of mass culture in the nineteenth century and the role of the female in Victorian discussions about the poor. As far as social-problem fiction was concerned, she differed from Catherine Gallagher because her interest was in the novel's complex relationship with the rhetorical formation of the social body, the concept of the population as an aggregate. Poovey thought this concept, widespread throughout early Victorian social discourses, was a rhetorical construction with which social-problem fiction was frequently in negotiation, and she argued that it played a significant role in the formation of British national identity.

In her chapter on Disraeli and Gaskell (an extract of which is reproduced below), Poovey's first concern was with the gendered identity of social-problem fiction. Following a commonplace binary of male/female, reason/emotion, she said that social-problem fiction that aimed to precipitate the reader's emotion about the distressed condition of the English poor was a feminized mode of treatment of a subject customarily treated in the masculinist discourse of politics, statistics and sanitary regulations. This perception of the female identity of social-problem fiction can be compared with Kestner's argument about the gender of the genre discussed below, (pp. 187–8 it can also be compared to Cazamian's view of the idealist role of social-problem fiction in relation to the individualism of the economists, discussed on pp. 151–2 above).

Poovey considered thereafter how Benjamin Disraeli and Elizabeth Gaskell engaged differently with the idea of the social body, and the ways in which they challenged modes of representation that political and social economists thought adequate to contemporary ills. She first analysed (not given in the extract) how Disraeli dismissed the diagnoses of the economists and, through romance, advocated aristocratic paternalism in his fiction. In keeping with the developing interest in masculinities in Victorian studies in the 1990s (see pp. 8–9 above for some discussion of this), Poovey analysed how Disraeli's imaginative engagement with politics involved the suggestion of homoeroticism. Gaskell's *Mary Barton* (1848) is examined next. This was an important novel not only because of its gender implications, Poovey argues, but also for its distinctive, paradoxical handling of the concept of the social body. Gaskell was interested in the representation of what the modern period would call the psychological, but in *Mary Barton*, Poovey says, the realm of the psychological, which would come to be the centre of interest in twentieth-century fiction, was closely linked to the social. Revealing the pressure of the idea of the social body in a prominent example of Gaskell's social-problem fiction, Poovey argues that it was the controlling influence even on the concept of the individual self there.

Extract from Mary Poovey, *Making a Social Body: British Cultural Formation, 1830–1864* (Chicago: University of Chicago Press, 1995), 132–4, 143–53.

When novelists began to address the condition-of-England question in the 1840s, they did so in the context of the success with which political economists and social analysts had established their authority to represent and make decisions about the social domain. According to some contemporaries, however, Carlyle's phrase[1] implied more than the dirt, disease, and debility implied by the word *pauperism*. To the Chartists, for example, the 'condition of England' signaled the political inequality that years of protests had failed to rectify; to trade unionists and Owenite socialists like William Thompson it summoned up the economic inequities that rendered England 'two nations,' in Disraeli's striking phrase; to Christian political economists like Thomas Chalmers, it suggested a state of nearly universal spiritual impoverishment, made worse by the legalization of poor relief and the concomitant decay of inspiriting charity and gratitude.

Despite the fact that political economists and social analysts (who were often called social economists) had successfully established their authority to diagnose contemporary problems, then, neither group had monopolized the right either to specify or to treat the range of woes suggested by Carlyle's phrase. Indeed, each group of 'economists' was divided among itself; followers of Malthus continued to conceptualize society as a body whose maladies could be cured by removing legislative impediments to health, and disciples of Ricardo insisted that society was a machine whose temporary breakdowns could be fixed by additional 'regulators' and 'governors.' Whatever their preferred metaphor, however, and despite competing formulations of the condition-of-England problem, political and social economists *had* generally succeeded in establishing the authority of a mode of analysis for representing these problems. This mode of representation privileged normative abstractions and calculations about aggregates, both of which were (supposedly) derived from empirical observation. The assertion that this mode of representation was authoritative – more than the specific conclusions reached by political or social economists – was the target of novelists like Charles Dickens, Benjamin Disraeli, and Elizabeth Gaskell.[2] According to these writers, the mode of representation epitomized by political economy may have rendered aspects of the social domain visible as never before, but in so doing it also effaced other facets of contemporary life. According to these novelists, paramount among the subjects that political economy obscured were the 'romance' of everyday life and those 'feelings and passions' that animated even the most downtrodden human being.[3]

As an explicit alternative to the abstract aggregations with which political economists appealed to readers' rational judgment, novelists deployed a mode of representation that individualized characters and elaborated feelings in order to engage their readers' sympathy.[4] The implication of this difference in protocols was underscored by another difference, which further distinguished novelistic from political and economic discourse in the 1840s. Largely because of the eighteenth-century disaggregation of moral philosophy into political economy and aesthetics, the ways of knowing epitomized by these discourses had become gendered by the early nineteenth century: the abstract reasoning of political economy was considered a masculine epistemology, while the aesthetic appreciation of concrete particulars and imaginative excursions was considered feminine. This did not mean that all imaginative literature was written by women, of course, or even that political economy was exclusively composed by men. It did mean that men who wrote poetry and novels struggled to acquire the dignity generally attributed to masculine pursuits – whether by asserting, as Percy Shelley did, that poets were the 'unacknowledged legislators of the world' or by taking serious historical events as their subject, as did Sir Walter Scott. It also meant that women who addressed political and economic subjects, like Mary Wollstonecraft and Harriet Martineau, had to contend with the charge that they were 'masculine' or 'unsexed' females.

When novelists entered the condition-of-England debate in the 1840s, then, they were implicitly arguing that a feminized genre that individualized distress and aroused sympathy was more appropriate to the delineation of contemporary problems than were the rationalizing abstractions of a masculine genre like political economy.[5] In this essay I will examine the contributions that two so-called social-problem novelists made to the debate about representation and therefore to the specification of the social domain in this period. Predictably, the precise relationship each novelist established to the emergent social domain was influenced by the author's own position within the field of gendered meanings, which bisected the social – and every other – domain in Victorian England. In Benjamin Disraeli's *Coningsby* (1845), for example, we see Disraeli introduce the condition-of-England debate only to dismiss not only political and social economists' analyses of it, but also the social and economic problems generally associated with this phrase. For Disraeli, the condition of England could only be improved by a political reform that consisted of reestablishing the paternalism of the aristocracy and restoring dignity to the monarch. In order to promote his political program through novelistic conventions, Disraeli dramatized political life as a romance. Because this romance was set in the homosocial worlds of the public schools and the political hustings, however, Disraeli risked mobilizing alongside an imaginative engagement with politics an altogether more dubious identification with homoeroticism. In *Coningsby*, this dangerous homoeroticism emerges as the price one pays for shifting discussions about reform from the social domain, where an appropriative or voyeuristic heteroeroticism obtained, to the political domain, where there could be no heteroeroticism because there were no women.

In Elizabeth Gaskell's *Mary Barton* (1848), by contrast, the social domain lies squarely at the center of narrative attention. In this novel, moreover, the social domain expands to encompass not only politics and economics but also a form of interiority that Freud would specify as the psychological. In Gaskell's account, the feminized mode of representation epitomized by the novel is perfectly appropriate to analyzing domesticity, which is the heart of the social domain, but her depiction of (proto)psychology suggests both that psychological complexity may be an effect of the violation of domesticity by the masculine worlds of work and politics and that the eruption of (what would eventually become) the psychological is ruinous to the feminized discourse of the novel. In *Mary Barton*, then, we see one example of the contribution made by nineteenth-century novelists to the constitution of the psychological. Paradoxically, in Gaskell's account, this most private of all domains turns out to be resolutely social, at the same time that its relationship to the social domain is nothing if not problematic. [. . .]

[. . .] If Disraeli dismisses the social domain as peripheral to his concerns, Elizabeth Gaskell seeks the social body's most intimate recesses and its most private language. And if Disraeli counters the feminization of the novel by larding his work with 'manly conversations' and didactic asides, Gaskell uses the gendered genre to place sexual difference in the foreground as both social symptom and cure. For Gaskell, the crisis of the 'hungry forties' should be addressed not by reforming politics or politicizing the novel, but by using the genre's conventional focus on individual characters to engage readers imaginatively with the problems of the poor. According to Gaskell, the capacious mode of knowing associated with the novel and with women can bridge the gulf between England's 'two nations' by feminizing both masters and workers – that is, by teaching them to identify with each other, as women (and novelists) already do. For Gaskell, the novel is a mode of representation superior to classical political economy because only the former can transport middle-class readers into the homes and minds of the poor.

As we have seen, Disraeli also relies on imaginative identification to promote a program of (political) reform. Whereas Disraeli ultimately directs his reader's attention to public matters, however, Gaskell explores issues that we (like the Victorians) call private. When the secret of the mysteriously arresting portrait turns out to involve a rivalry between men that is political as well as personal, Disraeli serves notice that the primary site of his drama will not be the dark continent of his hero's mind. In *Mary Barton*, by contrast, this dark continent surfaces as the location of a conflict even more formative than contests in the political domain. Along with several other novels published in this decade (*Jane Eyre, Wuthering Heights*, and *Dombey and Son*), *Mary Barton* begins to specify the relationship between the emergent social domain, which was subject to a new form of government administration, and an even less clearly articulated domain, which seemed to require its own administrative apparatus, not to mention a mode of representation suited to its unique dynamics. In *Mary Barton*, the psychological domain does not assume its modern (Freudian) form, however, for Gaskell presents psychological complexity, in the first instance at least, as an effect of the very problems that constitute the social domain.

Most obviously, of course, *Mary Barton* is not a study of individual psychology but an exploration of the 'agony of suffering' endured by the Manchester poor. In this sense, the novel should be read alongside other early attempts to represent the details of working-class life. The affinity between *Mary Barton* and James Phillips Kay's text on Manchester cotton operatives, or even Chadwick's *Sanitary Report*, is clearest in the novel's opening chapters, which contain several graphic descriptions like the following:

> You went down one step even from the foul area into the cellar in which a family of human beings lived. It was very dark inside. The window-panes

many of them were broken and stuffed with rags, which was reason enough for the dusky light that pervaded the place even at mid-day. ... On going into the cellar inhabited by Davenport, the smell was so foetid as almost to knock the two men down. Quickly recovering themselves, as those inured to such things do, they began to penetrate the thick darkness of the place, and to see three or four little children rolling on the damp, nay wet brick floor, through which the stagnant, filthy moisture of the street oozed up; the fireplace was empty and black; the wife sat on her husband's lair, and cried in the dark loneliness. (p. 54)

This passage resembles the descriptions of squalor contained in Chadwick's *Report* both in Gaskell's focus on insanitary details and in her insistence that the house is pervaded – or rather, infiltrated – by the insalubrious environment. The oozing 'moisture' is a sign that, for Gaskell as for Chadwick, the homes of the poor can never be private in the sense that they cannot exclude the literal refuse from the streets. The solution that Gaskell recommends for the condition-of-England problem is not Chadwick's centralized system of government regulation, however, but a liberal application of the sympathy that Kay hoped to incite through education. As the millowner Carson summarizes the novel's 'wish,' it is:

that a perfect understanding, and complete confidence and love, might exist between masters and men; that the truth might be recognised that the interests of one were the interests of all, and, as such, required the consideration and deliberation of all; that hence it was most desirable to have educated workers, capable of judging, not mere machines of ignorant men; and to have them bound to their employers by the ties of respect and affection, not by mere money bargains alone; in short, to acknowledge the Spirit of Christ as the regulating law between both parties. (pp. 375–6)

Mary Barton may resemble the writing of social analysts in the ways I have mentioned, but Gaskell's use of novelistic conventions gives her treatment of these problems a very different emphasis. In the description of John Barton and George Wilson's descent into the Davenport home, for example, Gaskell first solicits her reader's imaginative participation with the pronoun *you*, and then distinguishes between the middle-class reader and the working-class characters by noting that the latter have become inured to the noxious smells that would overwhelm her (and her reader). Gaskell's use of point of view does not encourage scientific detachment or (simply) normative disgust, but forges a sympathetic relationship between the reader and the characters that turns on their shared humanity: some people may have become indifferent to fetid smells, this passage suggests, but noting their coarser senses should make those of us whom smells offend want to improve the conditions that have obliterated delicacy in the poor.

Gaskell's use of novelistic conventions also reinforces her emphasis on domesticity. Like Kay and Chadwick, Gaskell treats domesticity as the heart of the social body. Whereas both Kay and Chadwick use discussions of domesticity to punctuate or support sustained theoretical arguments, however, Gaskell dramatizes the centrality of domesticity both by setting the action of her novel in several working-class homes and by treating the controversial topics of the day – poor relief, factory legislation, Chartist politics – as impediments to the 'plan of living' that every individual must devise (p. 68). Gaskell's novelistic focus on characters' daily lives also leads her to employ simple, domestic images to signify poverty. Whereas Kay and Chadwick calculated poverty through tables of whitewashed buildings and diminished life expectancies, Gaskell captures want through citing an insufficiency of teacups and a meal made solely of raw oatmeal.

Gaskell's emphasis on the narratives of individual lives thus dovetails with her use of mundane details to engage the reader imaginatively in a quest for what all people (theoretically) want: domestic security. So prominent is domesticity in Gaskell's novel that her representation of political events, like the workers' presentation of the People's Charter to Parliament, stresses only the domestic repercussions of the petition's failure, not its political significance. In *Mary Barton*, in fact, this event is not even narrated. Instead, at the moment when John Barton might comment on the political implication of his trip to London, he refuses to speak, and Gaskell offers as an explicit substitute for Barton's political story the narrative of another journey to London – the journey on which Job Leigh learned to care for his daughter's newborn child. Gaskell's treatment of the politically and economically significant subject of imperialism repeats this pattern of displacement. While we discover in passing that Will Wilson has traded in Africa, China, Madeira, and both Americas, his foreign adventures figure most prominently as contributions to the domestic scene to which he returns. Thus, Gaskell registers his trips merely as absences for his aunt Alice, and she immediately domesticates the only exotica Will brings back: his dried flying fish becomes a specimen in Job Leigh's naturalist collection, and his tale about a mermaid is first debunked, then supplanted by a domestic enchantress, as Job's granddaughter Margaret 'enthralls' Will with her lovely singing.

Just as Gaskell's use of novelistic conventions informs her approach to the condition-of-England question, so her attention to domesticity in the context of this debate informs her adaptation of the novel as a genre. As the example of *Coningsby* suggests, the novel was not conceptualized as a precisely defined, rule-governed genre in this (or any other) decade. Although certain features, like a focus on individual characters, the subordination of 'digressions' to closure, and the use of a more-or-less stable point of view had become conventional by this period, individual novels continued to betray the genre's heterogeneous lineage in a variety of ways, including the range of plots that coexisted promiscuously in their pages. *Mary Barton* becomes a domestic novel, for example, which culminates in marriage, by introducing and setting aside a number of competing narratives, any one of which might have governed another contemporary novel. Thus, in the first half of the novel, the presence of Harry Carson holds open the possibility of a sentimental story that focuses on seduction, while Sally Ledbitter threatens to give this narrative a farcical twist; Mary's aunt Esther, with her mysterious appearances and her uncanny resemblance to Mary's mother, threatens a gothic emphasis; John Barton's fall mimics tragedy; and the (momentary) uncertainty over who killed Carson promises a murder mystery. By the end of *Mary Barton*, these competing plots have been absorbed into the marriage plot that focuses on Mary and Jem, but for most of the novel, it is the rivalry between the domestic plot and these other contenders that gives the narrative its momentum.

This contest among plots produces not just narrative conflict but also another effect that decisively distinguishes between *Mary Barton* and contemporary nonfictional treatments of the condition of England. As Gaskell discriminates a normative narrative of domesticity by specifying its similarities to – and differences from – sentimental, gothic, and tragic stories of love, she begins to delineate a domain that does not precisely coincide with the social domain her domestic narrative supposedly illuminates. Many of the characteristics of this emergent psychological domain bear distinct affinities to features of the narrative plots that compete so ostentatiously in *Mary Barton*. As Freud was to describe the psychological domain, its dynamics are characterized by a sublimity that simultaneously baffles representation and insists on being known (like the specters in gothic mysteries); the conflicts of this domain center around sexuality and frustrated, often transgressive desire (like gothic and sentimental conflicts); and its indomitable narcissism rages in vain against an indifferent world (as does a tragic hero). Without suggesting that Elizabeth Gaskell single-handedly created modern psychologized subjectivity, or even that the competing narratives in *Mary Barton* are its only discursive ancestors, I do want to argue that, along with other nineteenth-century novels, *Mary Barton* helped delineate the psychological in a way that facilitated its disaggregation as an autonomous domain, whose operations are governed by a rationality specific to it, not to social relations more generally understood.

Two characters in *Mary Barton* are cursed with (what we would call) psychological complexity: John Barton and his daughter Mary. Because his is the simpler and, in many ways, more revealing case, I will return to John Barton in a moment. In her characterization of Mary, Gaskell begins to construct psychological complexity when she broaches the subject of Mary's feelings for Jem Wilson. Initially, Mary thinks she does not love Jem, largely because, as the narrator tells us, she has become possessed by 'the simple, foolish, unworldly' idea that she is 'as good as engaged' to Harry Carson (pp. 121, 120). Mary has derived this idea not simply from Harry's attention but from the interpretation she has been led to place on his flirtation by reading romances.

At this point in the novel, Gaskell represents Mary's 'contrariness' as a universal condition – that is, as not peculiar to Mary and as amenable to a traditional, theological analytic: 'Such is the contrariness of the human heart, from Eve downwards, that we all, in our old Adam-state, fancy things forbidden sweetest' (p. 121). As the love masked by Mary's 'contrariness' begins to make itself known, we see even more clearly the premodern nature of Gaskell's conceptualization of interiority. In chapter II, when Jem proposes to Mary, Gaskell depicts Mary's emotional response as a process of 'unveiling.' In this scene, Mary's authentic feelings, which Gaskell signifies by the words *heart* and *soul*, seem to lie beneath those delusive impressions that she has internalized from romances. Mary only gradually sees her hidden but genuine love for Jem, through a process that Gaskell initially describes as a conversation between two 'selves':

> It was as if two people were arguing the matter; that mournful, desponding communion between her former self and her present self. Herself, a day, an hour ago; and herself now. For we have every one of us felt how a very few minutes of the months and years called life, will sometimes suffice to place all time past and future in an entirely new light; will make us see the vanity or the criminality of the bye-gone, and so change the aspect of the coming time, that we will look with loathing on the very thing we have most desired. (p. 176)

In Gaskell's representation, the discovery of interior complexity is only momentarily a conflict between two 'selves' that occupy the same mental landscape. After the first sentence of this description, Gaskell shifts her emphasis to time. In so doing, she depicts the interior argument as a transition, a passage from one emotional state to another. In keeping with this depiction, Gaskell represents Mary as acquiring immunity to Harry Carson's attractions as soon as she recognizes the 'passionate secret of her soul' – that she loves Jem: 'In the clear revelation of that past hour, she saw her danger, and turned away, resolutely, and for ever' (p. 177).

It is important to note that, even though it occupies the place of a modern scene of psychic conflict, this description is very unlike Freud's representation of the dynamics of such conflict. In the first place, Mary's self-delusion is not really an *internal* conflict, since the animating force of one of the two 'selves' – the 'unworldly' idea that she loves Harry Carson – originates in and is sustained by influences external to Mary: her reading of romances and the example of her aunt Esther. The extent to which this delusion is separable from Mary is signaled by Gaskell's use of Sally Ledbitter to confront Mary with ever-more-unwelcome, ever-more-overtly-stylized visions of the spectacle Mary once entertained. In the second place, Gaskell's representation of Mary's 'contrariness' is not really a *conflict* between two persistent inclinations. As a transition (from delusion to self-knowledge), Mary's 'unveiling' does not fix her in a dynamic she will forever repeat but frees her from a false impression she temporarily held. The real challenge Mary faces in regard to her feelings for Jem is not resolving psychological ambivalence but finding a socially acceptable way to express her love.

If Gaskell's depiction of Mary's recognition of love is distinctively prepsychological, however, her representation of the conflict that arises when Mary discovers that her father is a murderer more closely resembles our modern notion of psychology. Unlike the earlier confusion over what her true feelings are, the turmoil over her father consists of two sets of feelings, neither of which will go away, and the mutual contradiction of which necessitates a compensatory imaginative gesture from Mary. To accommodate both her love for her father and the dread of him that she now feels, Mary generates two images of John Barton:

> Among the mingled feelings she had revealed in her delirium, ay, mingled even with the most tender expressions of love for her father, was a sort of horror of him; a dread of him as a blood-shedder, which seemed to separate him into two persons, – one, the father who had dandled her on his knee and loved her all her life long; the other, the assassin, the cause of all her trouble and woe. (p. 413)

Mary's response to her father, which would be termed *splitting* in modern psychological discourse, originates in Mary's 'delirium.' This delirium manifests itself most dramatically at Jem's trial when Mary, desperate to tell one truth (that Jem is innocent) without revealing another (that her father is guilty), falls into convulsions (p. 394). The 'madness,' 'hysteria,' or 'delirium' that results effectively blocks Mary's speech. Even if Mary's contradictory feelings about her father are not resolved by her illness, the impermissible half of those feelings is censored by her breakdown.

The dramatic courtroom scene is a repetition of the episode in which Mary experienced in relation to Jem the same conflict she now feels about her father. In chapter 20, fearing that Jem has murdered Harry, Mary is first possessed by the two contradictory thoughts that Jem is guilty and that he is good; then she is overwhelmed by the equally intolerable thought that if Jem is guilty, then she, who has rejected him, is guilty too (p. 285). At this point, Gaskell depicts her as going 'mad,' as afflicted with visions of the gallows while 'pulses career...through her head with wild vehemence' (p. 286). Immediately, however, Mary falls from this agitation into a state of 'strange forgetfulness of the present' that culminates in 'blessed' unconsciousness. The ensuing description is essential to Gaskell's conceptualization of (proto)psychology.

> And then came a strange forgetfulness of the present, in thought of the long-past times; – of those days when she hid her face on her mother's pitying, loving bosom, and heard tender words of comfort...And then Heaven blessed her unaware, and she sank from remembering, to wandering, unconnected thought, and thence to sleep...and she dreamt of the happy times of long ago, and her mother came to her, and kissed her as she lay. (p. 286)

From this dream, Mary wakes to what she momentarily believes to be her mother's voice, as Esther arrives with the paper that ultimately incriminates John Barton.

The fact that memories and then dreams of Mary's mother soothe the interior conflict that Gaskell calls 'madness' suggests that, even in these most modern of all her psychological scenes, Gaskell still does not imagine the psychological as an autonomous domain. In Freud's (reconsidered) conceptualization, the psyche is a domain of originary drives, and the inevitable conflicts among these drives both generate the conditions of not-knowing (the unconscious) and foster an alternative mode of knowledge-production (the symptom). For Gaskell, by contrast, no knowledge is unknown; instead, hysteria and delirium function to block speech – the social communication of knowledge that is intolerable because harmful to the self *and to others.* By the same token, Mary's vision of her mother functions not as a mode of representing something about Mary that she otherwise could not know but as a symbolic consolation for a dilemma she cannot resolve. For Gaskell, then, what would eventually become the psychological domain is social in every sense: its dynamics protect others (not the self), and its conflicts are healed by the mother (not expressed as symptoms).

If we turn for a moment to Gaskell's depiction of John Barton, we can see even more clearly the link Gaskell forges between the social, the economic, the political, *and* the (emergent) psychological domains. Gaskell devotes much less attention to John Barton's interior conflicts than to those of his daughter, and in her most extended treatment of this subject (chapter 15), it is not even clear whether she is suggesting that his 'diseased thoughts' are an expression of internal conflicts or an effect of his political activities, the hunger occasioned by his poverty, or even opium. In some ways, however, this is precisely the point: with increasing emphasis, Gaskell represents John Barton's interior conflicts as originating in the external world. Most obviously captured in the Dives and Lazarus story, conflict – figured most consistently as a 'dark gulf' that reflects some specific injustice – afflicts John Barton from his boyhood and as a consequence of his reading. In the climactic deathbed scene, he describes himself as being 'tore in two' by his struggles to reconcile his sorrow for the suffering around him with the forgiveness the Bible recommends (p. 441). Thus his emotional conflict – the source of his willingness to kill Harry Carson, which is in turn the source of his guilt – is not simply, or even primarily, psychological in a modern sense. Instead, Barton's interior 'deep gulf' replicates the 'deep gulf' that scars social relations, marked, as they are, both by economic inequalities and by the contradiction between the ethical rationality enunciated by the Bible and the economic rationality by which most men understand the acquisition of their daily bread.

I want to make four points about the (proto)psychological domain that begins to surface in *Mary Barton.* First, this domain is unmistakably social. What stands in the place of the modern psychological domain in this novel originates in, functions to protect, and is resolved by some image of social relations. Even though it intermittently resembles Freud's conceptualization of an autonomous psyche, in other words, Gaskell's depiction of interiority is at most a liminal arena, which partakes of inexpressible feelings *as they derive from and respond to* social relationships.

Second, what stands in the place of the psychological in *Mary Barton* is inflicted, *by and large*, on domesticity or its guardians (women) by events in the masculine worlds of work and politics. The turmoil that reduces Mary to convulsions and delirium, after all, originates in the economic and political disputes that set masters against workers, and its immediate cause is the piece of paper that has acquired its deadly meaning by lying around in a public street. Thus, paradoxically, what we now think of as the most personal, the most private, and, often, the most feminized domain – the psychological – appears in this early incarnation as the effect of the violation of domesticity by something else: the work, the politics, and the injustice that disfigure the masculine public sphere. That the psychological is also inflicted on characters by books that are imaginatively engaging only complicates this picture of a feminized sphere that is violated by knowledge of an intolerable world of masculine complexity.

My third point about Gaskell's representation of a (proto)psychological domain follows from this last observation and also takes the form of a paradox. Although Gaskell figures domesticity as the heart of what she and her contemporaries were producing as a *social* domain, the social domain as such recedes from view as she explores that which political and social economy could not depict. As Gaskell begins to develop Mary's interior conflicts in relation to the murder of Harry Carson, not only do the detailed descriptions of working-class domesticity decrease in frequency, but Mary begins to resemble the middle-class heroines of novels like *Clarissa, Evelina,* or *Sense and Sensibility.* In the scenes set in Liverpool in particular, Gaskell emphasizes Mary's frailty, her delicacy, and her modesty. So marked are the indications of Mary's gentility that when the boatman takes her to his house for the night, Mary's virtue is instantly recognizable to her humble hosts – despite the fact that she has appeared in such a compromising situation. By the midpoint of the novel, in fact, Gaskell has all but discounted poverty as a source of meaningful distress, which is now figured as emotional pain. When Mary meets a starving child in the street in chapter 20, her first response is to discredit mere bodily woes: 'Oh, lad, hunger is nothing,' she murmurs, '– nothing!' (p. 284). In this novel, what takes the place of physical suffering is mental distress; and what takes the place of a concern to improve – or administer – the social domain are the two faces of what is primarily a social *emotion*: the sympathy or imaginative engagement that binds the reader to Mary; and the hysteria that curtails her speech.

Finally, as Gaskell adumbrates the dynamics of a domain that, even if not fully psychological in the modern sense, escapes the oversight of government administration, her writing also suggests that the emergence of this domain troubles the narrative conventions with which she gestures toward it. This suggestion appears in the four passages in *Mary Barton* in which the conventional barriers that separate author, narrator, and characters collapse. In the most extended of these passages, which appears in chapter 18, the collapse occurs with the opening of a parenthetical digression.

> Already [Mrs Wilson's] senses had been severely stunned by the full explanation of what was required of her, – of what she had to prove against her son, her Jem, her only child, – which Mary could not doubt the officious Mrs Heming had given; and what if in dreams (that land into which no sympathy nor love can penetrate with another, either to share its bliss or its agony, – that land whose scenes are unspeakable terrors, are hidden mysteries, are priceless treasures to one alone, – that land where alone I may see, while yet I tarry here, the sweet looks of my dear child), – what if, in the horrors of her dreams, her brain should go still more astray, and she should waken crazy with her visions, and the terrible reality that begot them? (p. 259)

Such passages, which differ from the other narrative interpolations in *Mary Barton*, resemble the sympathetic identification that Gaskell advocates as an alternative to government interference in the social domain. So extreme is this identification, however, that Gaskell (or the narrator?) momentarily becomes a character in her novel. Instead of enforcing rules, as any form of administration must do, this identification undermines the conventions necessary to both the reader's trust in the novelist and the fictive nature of the novelistic world. These four passages suggest, then, that imaginative engagement may not be an adequate instrument for administering the social domain. Even more telling, they suggest that the emergent psychological domain both produces and requires new narrative conventions to represent its specific effects.

In this essay, I have argued that novelists' contributions to the debate about the condition of England tended to challenge the modes of representation that political and social economists deemed adequate to contemporary woes. Inevitably, this challenge recast the nature of the problem itself, for as writers like Disraeli and Gaskell abandoned abstractions for the kind of individualizing narratives that were conventional in the novel, they turned from quantifiable features of the urban landscape to the toll that dirt, disease, and debility extracted from the poor. Moreover, because social – and, more specifically, romantic – relationships had become the conventional site of readerly identification by the 1840s, novelists tended to embed stories of individual distress within narratives of affective, often erotic engagement. As a result, practitioners of this most feminized of discourses often linked their hopes for 'improvement' not to specific government policies but to the utopian potential culturally ascribed to love. [...]

Notes

1 Carlyle coined the phrase 'the Condition of England Question' in 1839, partly to describe the Chartist debates but more generally to reflect contemporary debates about the poor and working-class conditions.

2 Mary Poovey echoes an argument first advanced by Louis Cazamian in 1903 (see p. 151 above).

3 Elizabeth Gaskell, *Mary Barton: A Tale of Manchester Life* (Harmondsworth: Penguin, 1985), 37, 457. All future references in text.

4 For a different view on social-problem fiction and sympathy, see Williams (pp. 152–3 above).

5 For other recent views on the gender politics of social-problem fiction, see pp. 186–92 below.

CRITICISMS OF NEW HISTORICISM

Poovey's New Historicist approach was not the only argument about the context of social-problem fiction in the 1990s. Recovering a sense of what was described as the specifically Victorian worldview of the fiction was the intention of Josephine M. Guy's 1996 study *The Victorian Social-problem Novel: The Market, The Individual and Communal Life* that took issue with New Historicist assumptions about circulating energies. In part 1, Guy challenged previous critics for their ahistoricism and for failing to grasp the intellectual/moral context in which the fiction was written. She argued against Gallagher, saying that she had read social-problem fiction with insufficient acknowledgement of nineteenth-century conceptual frames: Guy thought the term 'discourse over industrialism' was too general for the complexity of early Victorian social and political debates. In Foucauldian terms, Guy said that Gallagher had failed to recognize the *epistemes*, the categories of knowledge and ways of thinking, which characterized the early Victorian period. *The Victorian Social-problem Novel* related to Gallagher's book, however, in so far as Guy identified the contradictions and tensions in social-problem fiction as inherent in their context. Both critics proposed that the limitations of the novels were not the result of an individual novelist's failure of understanding or sympathy, but a consequence of the constraints of his or her intellectual environment.

In the extract below, from the second part of this work of intellectual archaeology, Guy discusses one of the features of the early Victorian *episteme* that she sees evident in political economy, Utilitarianism, evolutionary science, and the assumptions of social-problem fiction; in the process, she implicitly critiques Mary Poovey's idea that the social body was the principal discoursal context for social-problem fiction. Guy starts by discussing how far Charles Darwin's ideas of evolutionary development privileged the notion of the individual and took the idea of society to mean an aggregate of individuals. She then connects Darwin's idea with assumptions of political economy and Utilitarianism to show that the concept of society as an accumulation of individuals was embedded in the 'conceptual set' of early Victorian England. This notion is in turn linked to the politics of social-problem fiction in order to reveal that that fiction's assumption that the moral transformation of the individual was the necessary precursor to social change was entirely consistent with a major conceptual set of the early Victorian period.

GUY AND
INDIVIDUAL-
ISM IN THE
VICTORIAN
MIND

Extract from Josephine Guy, *The Victorian Social-problem Novel* (Basingstoke: Macmillan, 1996), 110–16.

[. . .] [S]ustained evidence for the dominance of an individualist conceptual set can be found in the variety of disciplines or areas of thought which it underwrote. In this respect an arresting instance is to be found in what at first sight seems to be an unlikely source, an anecdote about Charles Darwin. The source is unlikely precisely because there is no immediate connection between Darwin's interests and the issues discussed in mid-Victorian fiction. Indeed, with the exception of *Felix Holt*, the social-problem novels all appeared before any of Darwin's writing was published (his first major work, *On the Origin of Species by Means of Natural Selection*, did not appear until 1859). More pointedly, Darwin does not seem to have been at all concerned with either industrialisation or with those problems in contemporary society which mid-nineteenth-century novelists had identified. In a very obvious way, Darwin had much larger concerns than the immediate particularities of contemporary British society: his subject-matter was the origin of life itself, and the materials he drew on were gathered on a five-year trip around the world as a passenger on the *Beagle*. It is, however, the very absence of any obvious topicality or contemporary reference which makes the comparison between his work and the social-problem novels so impressive, for Darwin arrived at his controversial theory of the evolution of species by means of exactly the same conceptual set as that which informed the understanding of society which we find in the social-problem novels: his theory of nature was coterminous with their theory of the social.

On 18 September 1838 Darwin made what historians have come to see as an important jotting in a private notebook:

> Take Europe on an average every species must have the same number killed year with year by hawks, by cold etc. – even one species of hawk decreasing in number must affect instantaneously all the rest. – The final cause of all this wedging, must be to sort out proper structure, and adapt it to changes – to do that for form, which Malthus shows is the final effect (by means however of volition) of this populousness of the energy of man. One may say there is a force like a hundred thousand wedges trying [to] force every kind of adapted structure into the gaps in the economy of nature, or rather forming gaps by thrusting out the weaker ones.[1]

Historians have seen in this entry the first fumbling formulation of Darwin's theory of natural selection, which would not be presented to the general public in anything approaching a finished form for another twenty years. In his *Autobiography*, written in 1876 when he was an old man, Darwin described how he had arrived at this moment of enlightenment:

> Fifteen months after I had begun my systematic enquiry, I happened to read for amusement Malthus on Population, and being well prepared to appreciate the struggle for existence which everywhere goes on, from long-continued observation of the habits of animals and plants, it at once struck me that under these circumstances favourable variations would tend to be preserved, and unfavourable ones to be destroyed. The result of this would be the formation of new species. Here, then, I had at last got a theory by which to work.[2]

Darwin's brief account is a rather modest oversimplification, although one which is perhaps understandable given that he was recalling events which had taken place forty years earlier. What is relevant to my subject is the formative role which Darwin attributes to the work of Malthus and his theory of population growth. There is considerable debate among historians of evolutionary biology about how precisely Darwin's thought developed over the crucial months between July and September 1838 when the outline of a theory of natural selection was first conceived. Some argue that the most important influence was his understanding of the practices of animal-breeders which provided evidence of a process of 'artificial selection' which he later adapted to form the basis of a theory of natural selection. Other historians have taken a broader view, emphasising the continuity between the intellectual paradigms underlying Darwin's thought and those which dominated mid-nineteenth-century intellectual culture in general. So, for example, they see parallels between the theory of natural selection and nineteenth-century accounts of the processes of industrial capitalism. Indeed, Darwin's own repeated reference to Malthus seems to lend support to this argument.

The theory of natural selection was in fact only one aspect of Darwin's thought, although history has judged it to be the most important. In simple terms it describes the mechanism of the processes of evolution. The idea of evolution itself was not Darwin's invention. The notion that the world was neither constant, nor a recent 'on-off' creation, nor in a process of perpetual cycle, had in fact been mooted since the eighteenth century; it was stated most explicitly in J. B. Lamarck's *Philosophie zoologique* (1809) and in a different context in Charles Lyell's *Principles of Geology* (1830–3). Darwin departed from his predecessors in his formulation of a non-teleological and mechanistic explanation of evolutionary change, one which could account for the diversity and apparent harmony of natural life-forms in non-supernatural terms. As I have suggested, his interest in the variety and origins of natural phenomena was first stimulated by his five-year voyage around the Pacific and South America. On his return to England he spent a great deal of time studying and classifying his findings, and it was through this work that he came to the conclusion that the natural world was evolving rather than static. His difficulty, though, was finding an explanation of precisely how evolution worked – how the wonderful variety of life, until then explained in terms of a divine plan or grand 'design' (in which species were fixed), could have come about. The entry in his notebook in September 1838 presents both his solution to this problem and a brief explanation of how he arrived at it – by means of the work of Malthus.

Historians are as divided in their interpretations of Darwin's reading of Malthus as they are about the origins of the theory of natural selection. The basic point of controversy is whether Malthus was merely the catalyst for ideas which Darwin had already been developing, or whether his role was more formative, providing Darwin with a completely new way of thinking which broke dramatically with his thought up to that moment. What is not disputed, though, is that the most important feature of Malthus's work to find a place in

Darwin's theory of natural selection was the proposition that competition took place between individuals and not between social groups. This led Darwin to understand the evolutionary process in terms of what is now called 'population thinking' rather than typology or essentialism. The American biologist Ernst Mayr defines population thinking as a 'viewpoint which emphasizes the uniqueness of every individual in populations of a sexually reproducing species and therefore the real variability of populations'. It is the opposite of typology or essentialism – 'the belief, going back to Plato, that the changing variety of nature can be sorted into a limited number of classes, each of which can be defined by its essence'.[3] The language of these definitions may seem unfamiliar, for the term 'population' is used in evolutionary biology in a specialised sense to refer to a group or community of 'interbreeding individuals, particularly at a given locality'.[4] However, if the term 'society' is substituted for the term 'population', then it becomes easy to see the concepts which Darwin and Malthus had in common and how both shared the individualist conception of the social which dominated early and mid-nineteenth-century intellectual culture. In both cases, contemporary Victorian society and breeding populations are understood atomistically – that is, they are seen as being composed of autonomous individuals. And it is these individuals rather than the group (understood in terms of an abstraction, as social laws, or as a species) which form the basic way of thinking. Two of Darwin's biographers, Adrian Desmond and James Moore, sum up his early formulation of the theory of natural selection as a 'new way of viewing nature [which]...kept faith with the competitive, capitalist, Malthusian dynamics of a poor-law society'.[5]

The theory of natural selection describes the differential survival and reproductive capacities of individual members of a population. This differential in turn is the result of the abundant variation and competition between individuals in every generation. In simple terms, those individuals who are superior are those who are successful in reproduction: indeed, such success is precisely what defines the whole notion of 'superiority'. Significantly, nature itself is not a selecting agent, for nature does not select *for* anything. Like the concept of society invoked by political economy, nature has no agency, nor can it be described as goal-directed. It is only individuals, through their superior physiology – that is, their better adaptation to climate, resistance to disease, or ability to attract mates – who possess agency and goals (to survive and reproduce); and therefore it is *only* individuals upon whom selection acts. Mayr puts it succinctly when he states that in the theory of natural selection 'there is no external selection force';[6] there is also no direction, no teleology, and therefore no 'purpose' to natural selection. It should by now be clear that in all of this there is a marked similarity to the conceptual set underlying political economy and Utilitarianism. Indeed, the terms 'Nature' and 'Society' fit both explanations – so much so that they are virtually interchangeable. So in Darwin's view of nature, as in Malthus's view of human populations, the survival of the individual has nothing to do with the survival or success of the group; rather, the only way a group does survive is through the fitness of the individuals which constitute it. Such a view maps on to the central proposition of political economy – that problems in society can only be resolved by reference to the behaviours of individuals. Also similar to the tenets of political economy is Darwin's characterisation of nature as viciously competitive, rather than (as natural theology had argued) benign and consoling. Moreover, in nature as in society, it is competition which paradoxically produces the apparent harmony and order of the natural world. Darwin's nature was an 'unintended' entity in exactly the manner in which Malthus's or Smith's society was: that is, nature, like society, was not susceptible to any form of human control or intervention. The logic of Darwin's argument is not only that nature embodies the order or regularities of Malthus's or Smith's contemporary society, but also that contemporary society operates as a state of nature.

As I have noted, Darwin's work was not published during the period when most of the social-problem novels were being written, so there is clearly no direct line of influence. However, Darwin was thinking and writing in the late 1830s and 1840s, and despite its radical originality, *On the Origin of Species* nevertheless reveals the typicality of its concerns: that the starting-point of its enquiry was the individual, and that social or natural phenomena could be understood in terms of an aggregation of individual behaviours. [...] [T]he same pattern can be found in any number of areas of mid-nineteenth-century thought, and we should therefore not be surprised to find it also in the social-problem novels, where the theme of individuality takes the form of advocating 'changes of heart' rather than changes in social structures.

In addressing the social disorder increasingly evident in mid-Victorian Britain – the riots in the streets, the conflicts between masters and men at the factory gates, and the appalling suffering from poverty and disease – the primary task of the social-problem novelists was to define a new principle of social cohesion, a new basis for social life. A contemporary reviewer put matters succinctly when he noted that the new kind of fiction was no longer 'content to exhibit society' by 'turning up little social problems illustrative of every-day experiences'. Instead the 'modern' writer was 'boldly invading those realms of politics and economy'.[7] To invade those realms inevitably meant to engage with the descriptions of social life in the areas of thought outlined in this chapter – with Utilitarianism and political economy. [...] [H]owever, the results of the 'invasion', of the attempt to address 'large' issues, have tended to strike modern readers as disappointingly insubstantial. The reasons, though, are not primarily to do with a lack of 'imagination' (and the notion of personal failure which it implies). Nor can it be adequately explained by a simple political prejudice (a tacit desire to retain the status quo). The social-problem novels are 'conservative' in the sense that they do not advocate large-scale structural changes in society, and they exhibit a distrust of collective action, be it Chartist agitation or union activity. But the contradictions and inconsistencies noted in them are not fully explained by such attitudes. After all, a novel may be conservative in its politics, but still be logical, coherent and thematically unified. Furthermore, the proposition that the weaknesses of the works derive from constraints inherent in their narrative devices is also unhelpful. Whether or not a literary form embodies or articulates an intellectual contradiction does not on its own explain why that contradiction should exist (or remain unresolved) in the first instance.

The root source of the novels' limitations can be glimpsed in a much more fundamental paradox: the alternative model of social life which the social-problem novelists offer turns out to share many of the same assumptions (about the nature of the social and the role of the individual) as those of the doctrines which they criticise. As in Utilitarianism and political economy, so in the social-problem novels we find a focus on the individual as the basic unit of analysis. With the exception of Disraeli's work [...], we also find a distrust of politics and the general capacity of socio-political intervention to mould social life. Third, and most significantly, we find a belief in a form of human 'universalism' – that is, the location of the basis of social life in a changeless human nature. These similarities derive from the shared individualist conceptual set. Where the social-problem novelists differ is in their definition of what constitutes human nature. The claim that individuals are selfish egoists is replaced by the assertion that human nature is fundamentally moral and altruistic. For the social-problem novelists it is therefore a moral (as opposed to an economic) agency which holds out the prospect of a more cohesive society. The difficulty in such a position was to explain quite how such a moral agency might work – how *in practice* it could transform social life. Having redefined human nature, the problem was how to understand those elements of social life which political economy and Utilitarianism seemed to explain so fully and so authoritatively. The most important of these elements, because it directly affected conflicts between classes, was the role of the market in determining social relationships. Unfortunately, however, one consequence of opposing morality to political economy as a method of redefining social life was the virtual evacuation of economics as an explanatory category, for the social-problem novelists did not have, and could not conceivably have had, any coherent alternative economic theory. As a result the individualist view of social life which they proposed, one which assumed a fundamentally altruistic human nature, was simply unable to provide the basis for a way of theorising economic activity. More troublingly, their redefined human nature (the basis on which they remodelled social life) was by definition anti-economic; it was defined as 'other' to the profit-seeking agency postulated by political economy. We can glimpse the dimensions of the problem when we recall the willingness of the social-problem novelists (particularly Mrs Gaskell) to acknowledge a link between social unrest and economic circumstances – in, for example, the frequently reiterated references to the connections between trade cycles, unemployment and strikes. This tension between an acknowledgement of the importance of economic circumstances and a conception of social life which seems totally to exclude the economic goes some way to explaining the inconsistencies of the social-problem novels. They derive, I suggest, not so much from the 'refusal' of a theory of social or structural change (that omission is to be expected in the intellectual climate of the mid-nineteenth-century), but from the absence of a 'virtuous' theory of economic activity – one, that is, which was consonant with a belief in a fundamentally moral and altruistic human nature. [. . .] [I]t is precisely an *acknowledgement* of this tension – an awareness that the opposition between altruism and the market might indeed be problematic – which distinguishes the social-problem novelists from one other.

Notes

1   Charles Darwin, quoted in Ernst Mayr, *One Long Argument: Charles Darwin and the Genesis of Modern Evolutionary Thought* (Cambridge, MA, 1993), 84.
2   Ibid., 70.
3   Ibid., 184 and 179.
4   Ibid., 184
5   Adrian Desmond and James Moore, *Darwin* (London, 1991), 275–6.
6   Mayr, *One Long Argument*, 87.
7   Unsigned review, 'A Triad of Novelists', *Fraser's Magazine* 42 (1850), 574.

Feminism and the Social-problem Novel

Feminism's influence on social-problem fiction in the 1980s and 1990s, as in many areas of the study of the Victorian novel, was considerable (for a general overview of feminism and Victorian fiction, see pp. 7–8 above). Moreover, it had consequences well beyond the genre of social-problem fiction: indeed, the material discussed in this section reveals one of the central features of feminist debate about Victorian fiction in the 1990s more broadly. In the 1980s, the most important feminist contribution argued that key facts about social-problem fiction – that it was a genre invented and prolifically explored by women – had been masked by male-centred literary history and a male-dominated canon. Later feminists concentrated on the gender politics represented in the texts, arguing that women's entry into the public domain of politics was transgressive in Victorian culture and novelists were aware of this taint. Most recently, this position has been challenged. Barbara Harman argued in 1998 for recognition of the strategies women used to avoid the contamination associated with entry into the public sphere. Her interest was in scenes represented in the fiction, but had implications for understanding how female authors regarded their own invasion of the public arena.

RECENT WORK ON ELIZABETH GASKELL   Much feminist work on social-problem fiction in the 1980s and 1990s concentrated on a single author: Elizabeth Gaskell. Critical writing in these two decades debated her contribution to social-problem fiction extensively and included Patsy Stoneman's *Elizabeth Gaskell* (1987), Hilary Schor's *Scheherzade in the Marketplace: Elizabeth Gaskell and the Victorian Novel* (1992), Jenny Uglow's large-scale biography *Elizabeth Gaskell: A Habit of Stories* (1993), Kate Flint's brief *Elizabeth Gaskell* (1995), Deirdre d'Albertis's investigation of the oblique strategies employed by Gaskell to consider major public themes including prostitution, industrial conflict, and evolutionary theory, *Dissembling Fictions: Elizabeth Gaskell and the Victorian Social Text* (1997), and Linda K. Hughes's and Michael Lund's study emphasizing Gaskell's intervention in commerce and her handling of the literary marketplace in *Victorian Publishing and Mrs. Gaskell's Work* (1999). (For more on Gaskell, see also Nord and Harman below.)

BERGMANN'S VIEWS ON STRONG FEMALE CHARACTERS   On the subject of the wider feminist interest in social-problem fiction in the 1980s and 1990s, the best place to start is Helena Bergmann's *Between Obedience and Freedom: Woman's Role in the Mid-nineteenth Century Industrial Novel* (1979), a book that marked the beginnings of the modern feminist debate about the genre and the political purposes of Victorian female novelists. Helena Bergmann was interested, as has often been the case in the early stages of a critical movement, in representations: in this instance, the significant political role for female characters in social-problem fiction. Bergmann's criticism, uninflected by theoretical considerations of gender and power, identified positive models and affirmed the political importance of female agency as imagined in the novels. She argued that 'women have an important part in presenting the social message [of social-problem fiction]', and that they typically acted as spokeswomen for a message of social involvement:

> an exhortation to the middle and upper classes to intervene in a situation that demanded immediate action. Basically these novelists put their trust in religion and in the inherent goodness of human beings; what was essential to them was to end the suffering and to prevent outbreaks of violence. Significantly [...], it was the female characters who were used to convey this attitude.[19]

This emphasis on fiction urging social involvement conflicted with Williams's and Smith's readings of the novelists' withdrawal from uncomfortable scenes (see pp. 152–3 above). Bergmann's identification of positive models of female agency in social-problem fiction can also be compared with Sandra Gilbert and Susan Gubar's work discussed in chapter 3, and their perception of strong women subverting patriarchy.

Joseph Kestner's *Protest and Reform: The British Social Narrative by Women 1827–1867* (1985) was not interested in the representation of positive female agency in social-problem fiction but in the way female authors of the genre had been overlooked. Kestner proposed that an important fact had been forgotten: women writers had invented realist problem fiction as a literary mode for pursuing social reform. The modern male-orientated canon had excluded their defining contribution. Kestner's work was an example of feminist canon revision that was a prominent part of Victorian fiction studies in the 1980s and 1990s (see Introduction, pp. 9–11). He argued that modern readers had to recover the lost corpus of female fiction from the 1830s, and showed that social-problem fiction – he used the broader category of 'social narrative' – was a popular field for women. The names of Hannah More, Harriet Martineau, Charlotte Tonna, Frances Trollope, Elizabeth Stone, Geraldine Jewsbury, Eliza Meteyard, Camilla Toulmin, Julia Kavanagh, Fanny Mayne, and Dinah Mulock Craik needed to be 'included along with the more habitually recognized [Maria] Edgeworth, Charlotte Brontë, Elizabeth Gaskell, and George Eliot'.[20] Only when these names were properly acknowledged could a full picture of the extent of female endeavour in social-problem fiction, a genre female from the start, be recognized. Contemporary scholarship has now begun to consider the *oeuvre* of these writers.

KESTNER'S CANON REVISION

Women wrote social-problem narratives in the early years of the Victorian period, Kestner argued, as a way of entering the public world. Fiction writing was a strategy that enabled a form of intervention in the determinedly male arena of politics and gave women an audible voice. It 'allowed women,

although not enfranchised, to participate in the legislative process',[21] satisfying the demand articulated by Florence Nightingale in her autobiographical essay *Cassandra* (1852) that middle-class women be allowed to work usefully. Kestner's argument about women's entry into the public world via fiction related to the work of feminist historians in the 1980s, including Lee Holcombe, Jane Lewis, Martha Vicinus and Judith Walkowitz, emphasizing how women's fields of activity gradually expanded during the nineteenth century: the 'widening sphere', as Vicinus referred to it, of women's lives in the Victorian period.[22]

NORD,
FEMALE
NOVELISTS
AND TRANS-
GRESSION

Kestner's view of the incursions of the female into public spaces was not universally accepted: certainly, it was resisted by Deborah Epstein Nord's well-received study *Walking the Victorian Streets: Women, Representation, and the City* (1995). This book considered representations of the female city stroller in work by Gaskell, Amy Levy, Beatrice Webb and others, and it had an important consequence on the shape of subsequent feminist discussions of social-problem fiction. Nord, a professor at Princeton, was interested in the ways in which the female stroller struggled with the conception of her role as urban spectator and her inevitable and disabling association with sexual transgression and, at the extreme point, prostitution. Nord, conflicting with the historians of the women's sphere in the 1980s and Kestner, was concerned with the constraints on women and the social barriers that hindered their entry into the public world. Her proposition was that women writers on public themes were analogous to streetwalkers and that they were burdened with a fractured sense of self. 'My argument', she said:

> is that the particular urban vision of the female observer, novelist, or investigator derives from her consciousness of transgression and trespassing, from the vexed sexuality her position implies, and from her struggle to escape the status of spectacle and become a spectator. The respectable middle-class woman creating her own city spectacle had to come to terms with woman's place in a well-established literary tradition of urban description as well as with her relationship to the poor women, the female beggars, the factory workers, and the prostitutes she observed on her own tentative rambles. Associated by gender with the very emblems of poverty, disease, and fallenness in urban panoramas created by novelists and social reformers, women writers had to contend with split identifications: they wrote with the cultural (and class) authority of the writer and with the taint of their sex's role in the urban drama.[23]

Nord devoted a whole chapter to Gaskell's social-problem fiction, claiming that Gaskell's experience was coherent with this broader pattern. Gaskell, Nord thought, had entered the public world in her fiction to observe the urban scene in order to reveal its distresses to her middle-class readers, but at a cost. As author and as urban spectator:

Gaskell wanted to have her place as an observer and reformer of the social scene, to fix her urban vision and offer it to her middle-class peers. The impossibility of remaining invisible, however, of claiming the uninhibited status of urban rambler and walking the streets with complete impunity, made exposure a necessary and unavoidable concomitant of spectatorship. Inevitably it was this experience of being jostled or scrutinized by those she wished to observe that gave form to her particular vision of urban life. The moment on the street that appears and reappears in her fiction is a moment of exposure, of engagement with the crowd, of awakened consciousness.[24]

Gaskell's entry into the realm of the public in her social-problem fiction was an act of exposure analogous to walking the Manchester streets, with its risk of misconstruction in sexualized terms.

Nord's view of the streetwalker gave a new dimension to the consideration of social-problem fiction and the nature of female interventions in political debates. Her viewpoint, however, was challenged in the most recent feminist investigation: Barbara Leah Harman's *The Feminine Political Novel in Victorian England* (1998). This was not only about social-problem fiction but considered a broad range of 'feminine political' fiction: none the less, Harman's study was consequential for readers of social-problem fiction because of its argument about female courage and self-assertion and its interrogation of the commonplace notion of separate spheres in the Victorian period. In terms of fictional texts, Harman concentrated on 'Public Restraint and Private Spectacle in [Charlotte Brontë's] *Shirley*' and 'Women's Work in [Gaskell's] *North and South*'. HARMAN, FEMALE NOVELISTS AND TRANS-FORMATION

Harman acknowledged the force of Nord's reading of the female streetwalker, but drew attention to different responses to the act of entry into the public domain. She examined novels in which such entry was not primarily associated with sexual transgression, focusing on 'public women who, though threatened with the taint of exposure, interestingly moved either around, beyond, or through it.'[25] She looked from a positive angle, exploring the courageous efforts of social-problem novelists to resist the cultural stereotyping of public women. Harman summarized her approach to the two examples of social-problem fiction in the following terms:

> In Charlotte Brontë's *Shirley* (1849) – a transitional novel for my purposes – the known risks of exposure cause the heroine to refrain from direct engagement in public affairs and to seek instead indirect access to what Brontë calls 'the struggle for money, and food, and life.' With a keen perception of the risks of female publicity in the late 1840s, Brontë describes a heroine who finds indirect means to effect her charitable designs and who witnesses, even though she cannot directly participate in, the novel's central riot scene. This heroine conserves her unsullied character for intimate, rather than public, expression, but

Brontë interestingly configures intimacy *as display*. In Elizabeth Gaskell's *North and South* (1854–55) Margaret Hale throws herself 'into the mêlée' of an industrial strike in one of the most extraordinary scenes of public exposure in the Victorian novel. Margaret suffers the misconstruction of character that Shirley had feared, but Gaskell transforms Margaret's sense of sexual taint into mature self-acknowledgement; she celebrates, rather than resists, the connection between private and public life, suggesting that the link is powerful and transformative.[26]

Harman problematized the commonplace idea of Victorian gender politics – a binary division between public and private/male and female. Like Susan Meyer's postcolonialist work in the 1990s on Charlotte Brontë's relationship with empire (discussed below pp. 325–9), and Catherine's Judd's consideration of the woman writer's strategic use of pseudonyms to attain authority in the literary marketplace (see pp. 289–302 below), Harman's arguments against the notion of female characters succumbing to the disabling logic of a divisive patriarchy revealed ways in which female writers resisted powerful ideologies. As such, she continued the debate in Victorian fiction studies about the gender politics of the period, and the subversive role of the novel in it. Nothing could have been further away from Lord David Cecil's assumption in the 1930s (discussed on pp. 32–3 above) that literary criticism was, by definition, a conservative occupation.

THE FUTURE OF SOCIAL-PROBLEM FICTION CRITICISM   Criticism of social-problem fiction over the past thirty years has investigated a wide range of claims about how nineteenth-century literature related to history and ideology, from Williams's structures of feeling to the New Historicists' identification of circulating energies. Social-problem fiction was, certainly in the 1960s, at the centre of the debate about the relationship between literature and capitalist ideology; in the 1990s, it was its relation to Victorian gender politics that was central. This area of investigation was not, however, confined exclusively to social-problem novels, and the feminist community's movement away from specific attention to the genre is revealing. Feminism has set a major part of the current agenda in Victorian studies for the examination of fiction's ideological embeddedness, and the other part has been set by postcolonialism. Both have led, in recent years, to a reduction in the significance of social-problem fiction as the principal area of ideological investigation. The publication of Patrick Brantlinger's *Spirit of Reform* on domestic politics (see pp. 161–2 above) – followed eleven years later by *Rule of Darkness* on the empire (see pp. 317–19 below) – is suggestive of the postcolonialist part of this shift in intellectual engagement across the critical community. I am not, however, implying that social-problem fiction will simply be left behind in the next few years. Although treated as a group from the beginning of the twentieth century onwards, it may well be regarded less as a discrete generic category in the early years of the twenty-first. The investigations of feminism and postcolonialism of the ideological vectors of Victorian culture cut across such genres and subgenres. But the history of social-problem fiction has been an important one in the past thirty years, and it will doubtless continue to play, albeit in a modified way, a role in the unfolding narrative of critical analyses of the ideological identity of the Victorian novel.

Chapter Notes

1 Kathleen Tillotson, *Novels of the Eighteen-forties* (Oxford: Clarendon, 1954), 123.

2 Louis Cazamian, *The Social Novel in England 1830–1850: Dickens, Disraeli, Mrs Gaskell, Kingsley*, trans. Martin Fido (London: Routledge and Kegan Paul, 1973, first pub. 1903), 4.

3 Ibid., 5–6.

4 Quoted in Mick Wallis, 'Present Consciousness of a *Practical* Kind: Structure of Feeling and Higher Education Drama', in W. John Morgan and Peter Preston, ed., *Raymond Williams: Politics, Education, Letters* (Basingstoke: Macmillan, 1993), 129.

5 Raymond Williams, *Culture and Society 1780–1950* (London: Chatto and Windus, 1967), 109.

6 Sheila M. Smith, *The Other Nation: The Poor in English Novels of the 1840s and 1850s* (Oxford: Clarendon, 1980), [1].

7 Ibid., 43.

8 Ibid., 203.

9 Ibid., 204.

10 Patrick Brantlinger, *The Spirit of Reform: British Literature and Politics, 1832–1867* (Cambridge, MA: Harvard University Press, 1977), 1.

11 Ibid., 2.

12 Ibid., 7.

13 See, in particular, *Renaissance Self-fashioning: From More to Shakespeare* (Chicago: University of Chicago Press, 1980) and *Shakespearean Negotiations: The Circulation of Social Energy in Renaissance England* (Oxford: Clarendon, 1988).

14 Catherine Gallagher, *The Industrial Reformation of English Fiction: Social Discourse and Narrative Form, 1832–1867* (Chicago: University of Chicago Press, 1985), [xi].

15 Arnold Kettle, 'The Early Victorian Social-problem Novel', in Boris Ford, ed., *The Pelican Guide to English Literature*, vol. 6: *From Dickens to Hardy* (Harmondsworth: Penguin, 1958), 178.

16 Kate Flint, ed., *The Victorian Novelist: Social Problems and Social Change* (London: Croom Helm, 1987), 1.

17 Ibid., 12.

18 See Mary Poovey, *Uneven Developments: The Ideological Work of Gender in Mid-Victorian England* (Chicago: University of Chicago Press, 1988).

19   Helena Bergmann, *Between Obedience and Freedom: Woman's Role in the Mid-Nineteenth Century Industrial Novel* (Göteborg: Acta Universitatis Gothoburgensis, 1979), 15.

20   Joseph Kestner, *Protest and Reform: The British Social Narrative by Women 1827–1867* (London: Methuen, 1985), 16.

21   Ibid., 13.

22   See Lee Holcombe, *Victorian Ladies at Work: Middle-class Working Women in England and Wales 1850–1914* (Hamden, Conn.: Archon, 1973); Jane Lewis, *Women in England, 1870–1950: Sexual Divisions and Social Change* (Brighton: Wheatsheaf, 1984); Martha Vicinus, *A Widening Sphere: Changing Roles of Victorian Women* (Bloomington and London: Indiana University Press, 1980); *Independent Women: Work and Community for Single Women, 1850–1920* (London: Virago, 1985); Jane Walkowitz, *Prostitution and Victorian Society: Women, Class, and the State* (Chicago: University of Chicago Press, 1980); *City of Dreadful Delight: Narratives of Sexual Danger in Late-Victorian London* (Chicago: University of Chicago Press, 1992).

23   Deborah Epstein Nord, *Walking the Victorian Streets: Women, Representation, and the City* (Ithaca and London: Cornell University Press, 1995), 12.

24   Ibid., 177.

25   Barbara Leah Harman, *The Feminine Political Novel in Victorian England* (Charlottesville and London: University Press of Virginia, 1998), 11.

26   Ibid.

Further Reading

Raymond Williams:

Louis Althusser, *Lenin and Philosophy and Other Essays*, trans. from the French by Ben Brewster (London: New Left Books, 1971): includes Althusser's important discussions of the operation of ideology that relates to Williams's 'structures of feeling'.

W. John Morgan and Peter Preston, ed., *Raymond Williams: Politics, Education, Letters* (Basingstoke: Macmillan, 1993): considers the role of adult education in Williams's life and thought and discusses the importance of Williams's formulation of 'two concepts which now occupy a permanent place in cultural studies: "cultural materialism" and "structure of feeling"'.

Igor Webb, *From Custom to Capital: The English Novel and the Industrial Revolution* (Ithaca and London: Cornell University Press, 1981): extends Raymond Williams to argue that 'any novel written between [...] 1780 and the 1850s is necessarily an expression of and a response to the events we have come to call, somewhat narrowly, the Industrial Revolution'; relies heavily on Williams's concept of the structure of feeling.

Social-problem fiction criticism in the 1960 and 1970s:

David Craig, *The Real Foundations: Literature and Social Change* (London: Chatto and Windus, 1973): includes a chapter on 'Fiction and the "Rising Industrial Classes"' based on a reading of Eliot's *Felix Holt*. Argues that there is a tendency in 'our culture' to privilege the moral and idealist over the merely social and practical, and this vitiates the political purchase of much social fiction.

Terry Eagleton, *Myths of Power: a Marxist Study of the Brontës*, 2nd edn (Basingstoke: Macmillan, 1988): Marxist/structuralist argument, first published 1975, that the 'deep structure' of the Brontës' novels reveals the deadlock between ideologies of landed gentry and bourgeoisie. Eagleton later regretted (see Introduction to the second edition) the 'expressionist' Marxism of the study and its refusal to engage with feminism.

David Howard, John Lucas and John Goode, *Tradition and Tolerance in Nineteenth-century Fiction: Critical Essays on Some English and American Novels* (London: Routledge and Kegan Paul, 1966): argues that a range of writers including Cooper, Hawthorne, Dickens, Gaskell and Gissing endeavoured to represent comprehensively complex social change, but ultimately and in various ways failed.

P. J. Keating, *The Working Classes in Victorian Fiction* (London: Routledge and Kegan Paul, 1971): detailed empirical study that discusses representations of urban and working classes in realist fiction including consideration of Gissing, Walter Besant, Kipling and Arthur Morrison.

John Lucas, *Literature and Politics in the Nineteenth Century* (London: Methuen, 1971): includes essays on George Meredith and *Little Dorrit*.

John Lucas, *The Literature of Change: Studies in the Nineteenth-century Provincial Novel* (Sussex: Harvester, 1977): on Gaskell, Hale White and Hardy and their struggle to represent an undivided sense of selfhood in the face of social change; critical of their 'confusions and contradictions' over change.

Rich and poor:

A. Susan Williams, *The Rich Man and the Diseased Poor in Early Victorian Literature* (Basingstoke: Macmillan, 1987): how political treatises, parliamentary reports and social-problem fiction, which 'absorbed the terminology of disease and the theories that were developed to explain its generation', used images and metaphors of disease to describe social ills, the alleged immorality of the poor, and the underlying threat of revolution.

Feminism and political fiction:

Nancy Armstrong, *Desire and Domestic Fiction: A Political History of the Novel* (New York: Oxford University Press, 1987): study examining the growth of the female domestic tradition in the eighteenth and early nineteenth centuries.

Rosemarie Bodenheimer, *The Politics of Story in Victorian Social Fiction* (Ithaca and London: Cornell University Press, 1988): develops Catherine Gallagher's argument (discussed pp. 162–3 above) that the source of the novels' tensions is in the insoluble problems of social theory, and suggests that three major narrative structures emerged in response to them: characters and stories of women, rhetorical appeals to nature, and models of history that transcended politics.

Monica F. Cohen, *Professional Domesticity in the Victorian Novel* (Cambridge: Cambridge University Press, 1998): further develops an aspect of Barbara Harman's argument (discussed pp. 189–90 above) by testing the notion of 'separate spheres', arguing that (female) domesticity was cast in the language of (male) professionalism in the period. Includes discussion of work by Charlotte Brontë, Dickens, Eliot and Gaskell.

Tess Cosslett, *Woman to Woman: Female Friendship in Victorian Fiction* (Brighton: Harvester, 1988): with a chapter on Charlotte Brontë's *Shirley* arguing that it is an exploration of female friendship in which friends discover an asocial position of strength from which to critique the social and cultural oppression of women.

Judith Lowder Newton, *Women, Power, and Subversion: Social Strategies in British Fiction 1778–1860* (London: Methuen, 1981): about 'covert, ambivalent, but also passionate resistances to the ideology of women's sphere' in novels including *Villette* and *The Mill on the Floss*.

Related areas of debate about women's sphere:

Ruth Y. Jenkins, *Reclaiming Myths of Power: Women Writers and the Victorian Spiritual Crisis* (London and Toronto: Associated University Presses, 1995): argues that mid-nineteenth-century religion was dominated by men who were understood as the interpreters of God's word. Women were confined to positions of service and selfless labour: 'As a result, when faced with such restrictive models of behavior, many women experienced spiritual crises: how could they enact what they believed to be God's plan for them when it conflicted directly with clerical and social edicts for female behavior?'

Christine L. Krueger, *The Reader's Repentance: Women Preachers, Women Writers, and Nineteenth-century Social Discourse* (Chicago and London: University of Chicago Press, 1992): reconsiders 'the history of women's social writing in terms of a female preaching tradition' to argue that 'evangelical hermeneutics and the practices which followed, by decentering exegetical authority, encouraged women to bring into public (i.e., male) view – and, specifically, into social discourse – a significant facet of their activities as readers and writers.' In doing so they 'achieved greater political power, "feminizing" social discourse by representing female authority in terms of spiritual gifts, prophesying against their exploitation of women as sinfulness, and calling on their readers to repent of their misogynistic practices'.

Related studies of history/politics/economics and the novel:

Laura C. Berry, *The Child, the State, and the Victorian Novel* (Charlottesville and London: University Press of Virginia, 1999): 'Why is the story of the victimized child told in specific and culturally unique ways in England in the early and middle periods of the nineteenth century? How does that story find its way into such different generic categories at this particular historical moment? [...] What can be learned by interpreting the importance of the child as a widespread social phenomenon in Victorian England, recognizable in literary as well as social discourse?'

Elizabeth Deeds Ermarth, *The English Novel in History 1840–1895* (London: Routledge, 1997): on the use of history in Victorian fiction (including some social-problem novels) and how social issues were variously recuperated, revised and repaired there.

Christopher Harvie, *The Centre of Things: Political Fiction in Britain from Disraeli to the Present* (London: Unwin Hyman, 1991): clear identification of the debates of the political novels of Eliot, Disraeli, Trollope. Historical inquiry more than literary.

Audrey Jaffe, *Scenes of Sympathy: Identity and Representation in Victorian Fiction* (Ithaca and London: Cornell University Press, 2000): emphasizes the idea that the Victorian subject, 'was figured crucially and with increasing emphasis as spectator' to examine how sympathy and spectacle were mutually related in Victorian fiction. Argues that the scene that 'gives shape to and renders visible the meanings of Victorian sympathy involves a spectator's (dread) fantasy of occupying another's social place'.

Barbara Weiss, *The Hell of the English: Bankruptcy and the Victorian Novel* (Lewisburg: Bucknell University Press, 1986): considers novels by Dickens, Charlotte Brontë, Gaskell, Thackeray, Eliot and Trollope, and discusses how the idea of bankruptcy, common in middle-class culture, 'influenced not only the plot, but the language, theme, symbolism, and the structure of the novels in question'.

Critique of New Historicism:

Joseph W. Childers, *Novel Possibilities: Fiction and the Formation of Early Victorian Culture* (Philadelphia: University of Pennsylvania Press, 1995): takes issue with the New Historicists' interest in the language of representation for its constitutive rather than its referential function, and introduces a form of cultural materialism to reconnect the language of fiction back to the reality it tries to describe.

Debate with Nord:

Deborah Parsons, *Streetwalking the Metropolis* (Oxford: Oxford University Press, 2000): about the emergence of Modernism; discusses writers including Amy Levy, Dorothy Richardson, Virginia Woolf, Rosamund Lehmann, Jean Rhys, Janet Flanner, Djuna Barnes, Anais Nin, Elizabeth Bowen and Doris Lessing, highlighting women's changing relationship with the social and psychic spaces of the city.

6

Language and Form

Raymond Chapman – Patricia Ingham – Henry James –
Dorothy Van Ghent – Barbara Hardy – Hillis Miller – Peter
Garrett – the 1990s

Language and the Victorian Novel

The language of the Victorian novel has attracted a small, steady stream of critics over the past thirty years. The 1970s saw interest in stylistic studies, covering the work of many major Victorian novelists. Such criticism, with its common-sense methodology, examined the characteristics of individual novelists' use of language, applying the techniques of descriptive linguistics to identify what was distinctive about a writer's vocabulary and syntax. From the 1970s to the 1990s, there was also a small amount of work on the language of Victorian fiction more generally – not confined to a single author – that adopted a similar stylistic/empirical perspective. Emphasis was placed on the representation of speech, which, in the 1990s, overlapped with the interest of language historians in pronunciation and class. The theoretical developments of the 1970s and 1980s encouraged critics to conceptualize all approaches to Victorian fiction as, by definition, approaches to language. Post-structuralism and deconstruction drew attention to all texts, literary or otherwise, as textures of words alone, so that to read a novel was to recognize it as a form of rhetoric, a particular set of language practices. A recent example of an approach to fiction that developed a post-structuralist perspective on the self-reflexivity of literary language was André Brink's *The Novel: Language and Narrative from Cervantes to Calvino* (1998), which included discussion of Victorian fiction. Brink argued that all fiction, not just that of the twentieth century, was conscious of itself as a texture of language. What 'has so persistently been regarded as the prerogative of the Modernist and Postmodernist novel', he said, '[...], namely an exploitation of the storytelling properties of language, *has in fact been a characteristic of the novel since its inception*'.[1] This argument can be compared to Levine's argument about realism (discussed on pp. 98–120, see also Williams in the Further Reading section). The first half of this chapter, however, is concerned with Victorian fiction and language in a more limited way. Post-structuralist readings of the Victorian novel are discussed throughout the chapters of this book under more specific, topically defined headings (for example, pp. 219–24 and pp. 310–17).

In the highly theorized period of the 1970s and 1980s, those involved with stylistics and descriptive linguistics, and especially those working on realism, were aloof from the high-profile debates in Victorian fiction studies. But efforts were made later to give linguistic approaches to Victorian fiction more theoretical edge. In the 1990s, while descriptive linguistic methods did continue, there was some investment in criticism that brought the insights of Bakhtinian language studies to linguistic approaches, relating particularly to the language of gender and class in the Victorian novel.

Any account of the study of the language of fiction from a linguist's point of view needs to begin by acknowledging general studies of language and the novel. The late Roger Fowler set helpful terms for this in *Linguistics and the Novel* (1977) in which he demonstrated how the terminology and techniques of linguistics could be applied to the larger grammar of the novel. Fowler suggested that the novel's components could be analysed in the same way as those of a single complex sentence could be (for a development of this idea, see Fowler in the Further Reading section). Geoffrey Leech and Michael Short later published *Style in Fiction: A Linguistic Introduction to English Fictional Prose* (1980), providing an accessible account of the verbal fabric of literature generally from a linguistic standpoint. The book considered word choice, rhythm, sentence structure, levels of style, and speech, arguing from a straightforward, *belles-lettristic* critical assumption that detailed analysis of fictional language allowed 'a greater appreciation of what the writer has created'.[2] — GENERAL LINGUISTIC STUDIES OF THE NOVEL

On Victorian fiction specifically, there were studies by linguists from the 1970s onwards of the language practice of individual novelists. These included G. L. Brook's *The Language of Dickens* (1970), J. W. Clark's *The Language and Style of Anthony Trollope* (1975), K. C. Phillipps's *The Language of Thackeray* (1978) and Raymond Chapman's *The Language of Thomas Hardy* (1990). These books were dedicated to precise description of the resources of each novelist's language. Typically, they considered (these categories are taken from Phillipps's study) matters of style, slang, register, syntax, lexis, dialects, and modes of address in the novels of their particular author. They eschewed theorized models of language and literature emerging in the academy in the 1970s and 1980s, and their object was to offer characteristic examples of the vocabulary and syntax of individual authors and to place them in the history of the English language. Additionally, authors saw their role as elucidating language practices now dead or dying.[3] The critical mode was evaluative in — LANGUAGE OF INDIVIDUAL VICTORIAN NOVELISTS its appreciation of style: Phillipps characteristically said of Thackeray that 'one of the novelist's peculiar excellences [is] his fine ear in prose composition [...] a long-breathed impetus in sentence structure, a quiet mastery of the ebb and flow of sentence and paragraph',[4] and this genial manner of evaluation ran through the study. Raymond Chapman's analysis of Thomas Hardy's distinct-ive (and controversial) use of language accepted as a starting-point a principle of evaluation: '[Hardy] was more concerned with theme and approach to literature than with the minutiae of style.'[5] This emphasis linked the descrip-tive linguists' approach in the 1970s and 1980s to earlier schools of criticism, such as those of David Cecil and F. R. Leavis, who prioritized evaluation as a centrepiece of their criticism. Dennis Taylor's *Hardy's Literary Language and Victorian Philology* (1993) was a very different kind of study, setting Hardy's language usage in a widely researched nineteenth-century context of scholarly language study, including discussion surrounding the compilation of the *Oxford English Dictionary.*

CHAPMAN'S
FORMS OF
SPEECH (1994)

Work on the general corpus of Victorian fiction also included critical study not of the whole body of language in the novel but of the more local matter of its representation of speech. In the mid-1990s, this chimed with the interest of language historians in accent and pronunciation in Victorian speech and its policing in primers and pronunciation manuals (see Mugglestone in the Further Reading section). Raymond Chapman's *Forms of Speech in Victorian Fiction* (1994) was the most extensive coverage of the topic of speech, drawing some of its critical approach from Norman Page's earlier *Speech in the English Novel* (1973, second edn, 1988). Chapman developed an interest in the class strata of Victorian society as marked by language discussed in K. C. Phillipps's *Language and Class in Victorian England* (1984). Phillipps, with an over-firm sense of the class boundaries of Victorian England, had illustrated how language usage was a 'principal, precise, pragmatic, and subtle way of defining one's [class] position, or having it defined by others'[6] in the Victorian period (for more on language and class, see Ingham, pp. 200–12 below, and the Further Reading section).

RELATION OF
ARGUMENTS
TO THINKING
ABOUT
REALISM

A noticeable feature of Chapman's *Forms of Speech* was its distance from the arguments about realism discussed in chapter 4. As a descriptive linguist, Chapman did not engage with the theorizations of Victorian literary realism that had preoccupied critics from the 1970s, and he took as a starting-point the assumption that realist fiction aspired to represent the real as accurately as possible. It was against this assumed singleness of purpose that Chapman judged the success of the novels' representation of speech. How real was the dialogue? 'Even in the most realist fiction', he said, 'dialogue has an artificial quality; trying to read a novel which accurately reproduced real conversations would soon be wearisome.'[7] Speech as it was represented in Victorian fiction was measured against 'real' speech, art compared against life, and the underlying assumptions of the realist project were not considered in relation to the arguments of George Levine or Catherine Belsey discussed in chapter 4 (see pp. 98–119, 120–33 above).

Chapman approached the language of speech in Victorian fiction with the purposes of accurate description in mind. As with the early critical stages of feminism or postcolonialism, his interest was in conventions of representation. A typical example of this procedure was his approach to the depiction of non-standard speech in a range of Victorian fiction. Chapman wrote of the codes of Victorian novelists for signifying non-standard spoken English, word usages that indicated in features of spelling or syntax their non-standard identity, even if they were not literal or phonetic transcriptions. A short extract gives a flavour of Chapman's approach to language and class. Although, he remarked, 'individual novelists develop their own special features' for the representation of non-standard English in the period:

> there are certain indicators which are commonly used. The dropped aspirate, together with the hypercorrection of the wrongly inserted aspirate, is the most common, and one of the easiest to represent visually; examples are found almost every time an uneducated character speaks. Trollope's Quintus Slide, showing no other marked speech deviance, is characterised by the misplaced aspirate alone. He is first introduced as 'a young man under thirty, not remarkable for clean linen, and who always talked of the "'Ouse"…though he talked of "'Ouses" and "horgans", he wrote good English with great rapidity (*Phineas Finn* 1869, 26). It is a sign of the new age that standard pronunciation rather than literacy is considered the mark of an educated man; earlier in history the judgement would have been reversed. In a later novel he asks Lady Eustace, 'But 'ow do you know?' [,] asserts his respect for 'the very fountain 'ead of truth', tells Lopez 'you can't 'ide your light under a bushel' and invites him to 'go 'and in 'and with me in the matter' (*The Prime Minister* 50, 51). Gissing has Mrs Goby announce herself as being 'of the 'Olloway Road, wife of Mr C. O. Goby, 'aberdasher' (*New Grub Street* 1891, 21). Thackeray's Arthur Pendennis gives linguistic expression to contemporary social barriers when he says of Fanny, 'She dropped her h's, but she was a dear little girl' (*Pendennis* 1850, 54).
>
> Hypercorrection of the aspirate is particularly common among upper servants and others with pretensions to gentility. Major Pendennis's valet announces 'Lady Hagnes Foker's son' and addresses Pendennis as 'Mr Harthur' (*Pendennis* 11, 20). Fanny Squeers exclaims, 'This is the hend, is it?' and Dickens comments 'who, being excited, aspirated her h's strongly' (*Nicholas Nickleby* 1839, 42). One of Hardy's characters is 'a labouring man known to the world of Welland as Haymoss (the encrusted form of the word Amos, to adopt the phrase of philologists)' (*Two on a Tower* 1882, 1).[8]

Chapman's analysis of nineteenth-century fiction brought to the foreground a variety of linguistic codes. After *Forms of Speech*, however, the study of the language of class in self-writing in the Victorian period complicated the paradigms Chapman used. Regenia Gagnier's *Subjectivities: A History of Self-representation in Britain, 1832–1920* (1991) and Patrick Joyce's *Democratic Subjects: Self and the Social in Nineteenth-century England* (1994), for instance, both employed post-structuralist models of language in their consideration of classed identities.

OTHER DOCUMENTARY WORK ON VICTORIAN LANGUAGE

Other documentary work on nineteenth-century language in the 1990s touched on fiction and provided useful contexts for reading it. Since the Victorian period itself, scholarly attention to language, in the academy, had been concentrated on the medieval period. But the 1990s saw a burst of interest in the formal study of Victorian language. This reminded readers how different Victorian English was from the present day, arguing that its similarities disguised the gulf between the two forms. Richard W. Bailey's *Nineteenth-century English* (1996) was a readable survey that considered transformations of the language during the nineteenth century, consequent on urbanization, technology, travel and new opportunities for communication, concentrating on writing, sounds, vocabulary, slang, grammar and classed voices. The prolific Manfred Görlach's *English in Nineteenth-century England: An Introduction* (1999) outlined the chief features of nineteenth-century language practice, stressing regional and social varieties, spelling and pronunciation, inflection, syntax and lexis, and analysed material from recipes to grammars to literature to university lectures. Susanne Romaine's edition of volume IV of *The Cambridge History of the English Language* (1998), covering the period 1776–1997, was the most technical and specialist of the surveys and had a significant amount of discussion of how novels, especially by Dickens and Eliot, exemplified forms of language usage. Its bibliography (pp. 708–61) is the best starting-point for serious research into the Victorian use of language.

BAKHTIN AND LANGUAGE STUDIES

In the specific area of Victorian fiction studies in the 1990s, effort was made to use a more theorized approach to language study, influenced especially by Bakhtin (for further discussion of the importance of Bakhtin in Victorian novel criticism, see pp. 220–4 of this chapter, and pp. 142–3 above). Accurate linguistic description did not seem enough to Patricia Ingham and her work in the 1990s, which included studies of Charles Dickens and Thomas Hardy, brought tools from contemporary literary/linguistic analysis to the service of feminist arguments about women and the working class, and the politics of their representation in a range of canonical texts. Her linguistic approach – she began her academic career at Oxford University as a medievalist and historian of the language – was not descriptive but influenced by modern notions of language as a site of ideological conflict and contemporary interests in identity politics.

Patricia Ingham's first book on the language of Victorian fiction was about Dickens but it suggested parameters for her subsequent work on the Victorian novel generally. In *Dickens, Women, and Language* (1992), Ingham looked at Dickens's use of stereotypical representations of women in his fiction, such as the fallen woman and the nubile girl, and studied the way in which these types were linguistically marked, how that marking differed from occasion to occasion, and how it developed through his *oeuvre*. In the 'Postscript', she proposed that Dickens's accounts of the real women in his life – Catherine Dickens and Ellen Ternan, chiefly – could also be 'subjected to the same kind of linguistic analysis as preceding chapters have applied to figures in the novels'.[9] Rather than using life to explain art, Ingham, following the post-structuralist's privileging of the textual, argued that there should be no difference in the linguists' approach to textual representations of characters, fictional or real (for more on the language of Dickens, see Sørensen in the Further Reading section).

The *Language of Gender and Class: Transformation in the Victorian Novel* (1996) continued Ingham's investigation of the linguistic signifiers of female characters. She drew on Mikhail Bakhtin's conviction that 'The novel as a whole is a phenomenon multiform in style and variform in speech and voice', and in it 'the investigator is confronted with several heterogeneous stylistic unities often located on different linguistic levels and subject to different stylistic controls.'[10] This sense of the multi-voiced nature of Victorian novels was the guiding idea of her study. She also used the Bakhtinian concept of the 'multi-accentuality' of signs (related, though problematically, in Bakhtin's work, to the idea of the multi-vocality of the novel) as another element of her critical methodology. Multi-accentuality refers to the capacity of a single word to change its 'accent', that is, its ideological connotation, either through time, or in different spaces in society. For instance, in recent history, the term *radical* in social and economic policies, has 'acquired a dominant accent that assigned its favourable connotations to profoundly right-wing extremism. The previous dominant evaluation had ascribed these connotations to pro-foundly egalitarian positions on socio-economic policies. A change has taken place (though another may follow) as the hierarchy of accents shifted.'[11] Multi-accentuality, specifically the accentual shift on a large scale in the key domains of gender and class, enabled Ingham to trace a gradual dissociation, culminating in Hardy's *Jude the Obscure* (1894–5), between ideas of gender (chiefly female) and class (chiefly working and middle) that had previously been linked in earlier nineteenth-century literature and culture.

In the opening discussion of *The Language of Gender and Class*, reproduced below, Ingham set out the two chief signs for women at the beginning of the period, both clearly located in a class category. These, the womanly woman (the Angel in the House) and the fallen woman (the prostitute), were initially confined in middle-class and lower-class contexts respectively (for a feminist approach in the 1970s to the notion of the Angel in the House, see p. 83

INGHAM'S VIEWS ON GENDER AND CLASS

above). But, Ingham argues, their class associations broke down as the century moved on and novelists such as Elizabeth Gaskell and Charlotte Brontë rewrote them. Competing signs for women, alternate fictional descriptors and models, emerged as novelists wrote on the place of women, transacting with the culturally familiar descriptions. Ingham's use of Bakhtinian theory to understand identity politics in the Victorian novel was new in language studies and well received. Its problems lay, despite the freshness of its methodology, in the re-invocation of stereotypes of the culture – the angel/whore binary as the dominant images of women – that had already been widely discussed and rethought. There were also difficulties in her assumptions about the terms 'class' and 'gender' that served as over-homogenized concepts in her study. Finally, *The Language of Gender and Class* could be accused of repackaging an already familiar and challenged argument about Victorian women and gender politics in modern linguistic terms. Ingham's work none the less suggested a methodology for the productive intersection of language and literature in studies of the Victorian novel. Her most recent work, *Invisible Writing and the Victorian Novel: Readings in Language and Ideology* (2000), considered how the 'invisible' mechanisms of language denaturalized and made visible ideological assumptions in the culture.

Extract from Patricia Ingham, *The Language of Gender and Class: Transformation in the Victorian Novel* (London: Routledge, 1996), 20–30.

It is [multi-accentual] change on a large scale that is the focus of my argument. It will deal with those ideological signs in nineteenth-century novelistic discourse which are key terms in the areas of class and gender. They construct the two areas as a single semantic field which holds together a coherent identity for the middle classes, distinguishing them from the socio-economic classes below. In particular, I wish to show how the attempts to reaccent the signs of both the *womanly* woman and the *fallen* woman succeeded in rewriting their significance and what this meant for the treatment of class and gender as a whole.

Built into the general perception of a class – as opposed to a rank-based – society was not merely division but divisiveness. Under capitalism this fact had to be processed so that it could be managed ideologically. One way of achieving this is to characterise the working classes wherever they are represented (in law, social documentation, or art) in terms that justify treating them materially and politically in ways that are different from the treatment of middle and upper classes. And there is a common matrix on which representations of them draw, though by no means uniformly: the working classes are not self-reliant or in a laissez-faire society they might have risen to the top; they are improvident in better times and so make bad times worse; they are too stupid or too unsophisticated to resist the temptation of political agitators who incite them to join trades unions and strikes; and they are not capable of understanding their own long-term interest so far as their employers are concerned. They are also of a strongly animal nature conducive to prostitution, crime and revolutionary impulses.

Holding them down therefore was socially necessary. However, the justification for doing so depended on a construction of the middle class as essentially different in nature. As usual with the coding of cultural values, the principle of the defining 'other' operates to imply illogically that, because the working class are weak, irrational and animal, the middle classes are not. But upon this framework, so crucial to the dominant code, a more positive and powerful image had to be built. This image depended in practice on the contemporary construction of gender in terms of separate spheres and the complementarity of men and women. Ironically what gave imaginative power to the oppressors of the lower orders was the force attributed to the sign of the *womanly woman*, who was represented, shaped, celebrated and offered as an aspirational model in every form of writing from the law and 'non-fictional' documents like conduct books to novels and poetry. She is powerfully present, as a standard for judging by, when inevitably absent from accounts of working-class squalor or promiscuity. And the force of this sign is significant for more than representations of gender alone. As Mary Poovey points out, instead of being articulated upon 'inherited class position in the form of noblesse oblige, virtue was increasingly articulated upon gender in the late eighteenth and early nineteenth centuries... As superintendents of the domestic sphere, [middle-class] women were represented as protecting, and increasingly incarnating virtue' (Poovey, 1989: 10).

Though not uncontested or 'uni-accented', this was the dominant sign for the representation of femininity. Feminine gender was constructed around an elaboration of 'natural' maternal and nurturing instinct into the guardianship at home of morality generally, and sexual purity in particular. Complementary masculinity then fell into place as 'naturally' fit for the marketplace and its struggles: self-interested, aggressive, competitive and with a strong procreative instinct suited to the founding of dynasties. These apparently functional descriptions made available a positive image of the middle classes, differentiating them from and justifying control over the lower. For by uniting himself in marriage to a satisfactory exponent of femininity, a typical exponent of middle-class masculinity could subsume her identity into his, and become possessed of her high-mindedness and purity, along with a domestic haven of comfort. As articulated by the law, the process of marrying changed husband and wife into one person, since 'the very being or legal existence of the woman is suspended during marriage, or at least is incorporated and consolidated into that of the husband' (Manchester, 1980: 368). This now morally excellent man thus became well suited to the duty of restraining the irrational and dangerous working classes.

In conduct books for women where the coding of femininity was reflected, shaped and passed on, there is a bizarre blend of moral injunctions and practical recommendations on household management. These are somehow linked or matched. Fitted into a broad framework laying down the most essential feminine quality as disinterested kindness and selflessness are recommendations as to regularity and judgement in the provision of household linen; advice on supplying food in some variety but in moderate quantity; and on how to keep the all-important domestic hearth. If a man likes stirring the 'glowing embers' himself, his wife should prepare 'a tempting crust for him to break through on his arrival' (Ellis, 1843: 91). Such works are fiercely directive and exhortatory.

In this discourse the ideal middle-class home was (if women came up to scratch) a haven as well as a heaven, managed by an efficient angel whose education had combined a strict formation on Christian principles with a rigorous training in domestic skills:

> the general appearance of his home has much to do with the complacency man naturally feels on returning to it. If his taste is for neatness and order, for the absence of servants, and for perfect quiet, it would be absolute cruelty to allow such a man to find his house in confusion, and to have to call in servants to clear this thing and the other away after his return. (Ellis, 1843: 90)

In this way comfortable and tasteful domesticity becomes the sign for moral excellence, the House for the Angel. It served as a safe expression of physicality and a validation of materialism as virtue.

The supposedly physiologically determined qualities of the Angel were extreme emotional sensitivity, weakness of intellect, unlimited selflessness, and, crucially, a lack of 'animal' passion. Paradoxically these marks of women's inferiority were coded positively as concomitants of moral excellence. Logically, given the essentialist nature of this account, such qualities might be expected to crop up in women of any class, including the lower ones. But also to be accommodated in the scheme of things represented was female sexuality. There was a tacit but universal acceptance of men's fairly ungovernable sexual appetites which were natural enough. Female sexuality, however, was deviant and its natural location was amongst the class which in practice provided the prostitutes in Victorian cities, that 'multitudinous amazonian army the devil keeps in constant field service for his own ends' (Miller, 1859: 5). It is arguable that the containment of female sexuality is a prior cause of the angel figure but I am concerned with the organisation of the semantic field rather than with causal chains.

Clearly, though one task of ideology is to conceal its own illogicalities, not all working-class women could be characterised as sexually 'deviant' just because some of them were. Instead, those who were not became invisible, as is evident from the condition-of-England novels where they are usually peripheral to the class confrontations. Their social invisibility and silence is witnessed by the fact that of the 142 working-class autobiographies listed by Vincent as covering the period 1790 to 1850 only six were by women. His explanation is that women did not lack the necessary skills but lacked the self-confidence to write such accounts; and that their increasing exclusion from 'most forms of working class organisations' cut them off from the training and stimulus for self-expression (Vincent, 1981: 8). Apart from invisibility, two ideological strategies appear. The first is the assumption that middle-class women never 'fall'. An extreme illustration of this is the attack, in Samuel Bracebridge Hemyng's informal documentary account of prostitution, on any claims by the women he meets that they have fallen from a higher social group:

> Loose women generally throw a veil over their early life, and you seldom, if ever, meet with a woman who is not either a reduced governess or a clergyman's daughter; not that there is a word of truth in the allegation – but it is their peculiar whim to say so. (Mayhew, 1861–2: 217)

So sexual deviance, though not universal, is represented as endemic amongst the working classe: 'To be unchaste amongst the lower classes is not always a subject of reproach . . . the depravity of manners . . . begins so very early, that they think it rather a distinction than otherwise to be unprincipled' (Mayhew, 1861–2: 221). As Nead says, writing of signs in nineteenth-century painting,

> The definition of female sexuality across an axis of class made it easier to construct a coherent image of respectable femininity. Beliefs concerning the nature of female sexual desire were extremely fractured, but these differences could be displaced and a consensus could be reached by invoking a generalized notion of female respectability and opposing it to the imagined excess passion and sexual deviancy of the women of the undeserving poor. (Nead, 1988: 7)

Added power is given to the necessary connection between these classes and immorality of all kinds by a second strategy: the symbolism of pollution. Because of its association with venereal disease, prostitution was readily coded as a dangerous contagion which was simultaneously physical and moral. As Judith Walkowitz points out in her historical study of prostitution: 'Pollution became the governing metaphor for the perils of social intercourse between the "Two Nations"; it assumed heightened scatological significance in a society where the poor seemed to be living literally in their own excrement' (Walkowitz, 1980: 4).

The power of the metaphor is displayed in the description of the prostitute, Martha Endell, in Dickens's *David Copperfield*, when she stands contemplating suicide on the bank of the Thames. Her subsequent comparison of herself to the river turns the narrator's description of it into an image for her. Like the wrecks of machinery that surround it, she represents human debris 'vainly trying to hide itself'. She is the vessel that transmits human pollution as the river does. She stands for a corruption that is merely enacted by the physical plague of disease and goes beyond it:

> Slimy gaps and causeways, winding among old wooden piles, with a sickly substance clinging to the latter, like green hair, and the rags of last year's handbills offering rewards for drowned men . . . led down through the ooze and slush to the ebb tide. There was a story that one of the pits dug for the dead in the time of the Great Plague was hereabout; and a blighting influence seemed to have proceeded from it over the whole place. Or else it looked as if it had gradually decomposed into that nightmare condition, out of the overflowings of the polluted stream. (ch. 47)

To the narrator she is 'a part of the refuse' the river had cast out and left to 'corruption and decay'. It is hard to distinguish here between emotional, physical and moral blight. The *fallen woman* is thus a linguistic coding as important as the Angel/House trope in the interlocking of class and gender. In the dominant discourse of the period she signifies the inescapable corruption of the working classes, which must be contained at any cost.

Even hard-headed official reports on the vile living conditions of workers in cities 'reinforce' the connection between class and vice. Chadwick (1842), for instance, quotes a Poor Law official's description of a family of eleven who live in only two rooms:

> The man, his wife, and four children, sometimes five, slept in one of the rooms, and in one bed ... The other part of the family slept in one bed in the keeping-room, that is, the room in which their cooking, washing, and eating were performed. How could it be otherwise with this family than that they should be sunk into a most deplorable state of *degradation* and *depravity*? (Flinn, 1965: 190; my emphases)

Facts thus seem to 'support' a significant contrast between the well-ordered and well-equipped middle-class home, cultivating peace, love and morality, and inhuman living conditions spawning sexuality, promiscuity and crime. For crime, like vice, is seen as natural to the lower orders: both environmentally determined and innate, a familiar confusion in the Victorian novel. As Lucia Zedner has shown in *Women, Crime and Custody in Victorian England* (1991: 27–33), the gravity of female criminality in particular was usually seen to involve what were called 'crimes of morality' and was measured by the failure of working-class women to live up to the middle-class model.

My account indicates how the signs for middle-class femininity/domesticity and for the fallen woman hold together a coding of society in which the working classes are represented as irrational, immoral and in need of restraint. At the same time the middle classes are their natural masters, possessed of the qualities necessary and proper to control them. This dominant discourse was more fluid than my simplification so far makes clear. It was, as has been said, challenged, contested and eventually reworked. Undoing such an ideological web was not an easy process. What rendered it most potent were the powerful images evoked in a communal language and across a wide range of media. However, as has been made clear, each use of the fallen-woman image in the early Victorian period is not a replica of every other use but an individual variation on it. This can be seen in the variety found in a writer whose fallen women are often regarded as identical stereotypes: Dickens's use of the trope includes variants as different as Nancy in *Oliver Twist*, Martha Endell as well as (less obtrusively) the respectable Rosa Dartle in *David Copperfield*, and the independent and forceful Miss Wade in *Little Dorrit*. The individual variants, expressive of the multi-accentual nature of signs, represent a site for possible change in novelistic language. When a whole semantic area such as class or gender is at issue, the process of change is slow and difficult. It *can* be attempted at a discursive level, as when Hardy tried to rewrite the image of the 'pure woman' by adding that phrase as a subtitle to a novel concerning Tess Durbeyfield, whose fornication, adultery and crime of murder marked her as outrageously 'impure' in conventional terms. The rewriting had to work at a symbolic level within the text if it was to work at all: a sign cannot be defused or drained of power merely by a verbal contradiction asserting that it does not mean what it usually means. A trivial example will illustrate this. The current health warning mandatory on cigarette advertisements fails to break down the arbitrary connection long made, by the use of verbal and visual images, between cigarette-smoking and sophistication. The link creating that meaning is arbitrary but has become strong – so strong that skilful users of the advertising code have now shrewdly managed to perpetuate it by creating ironic images of purely visual sophistication above the health warning. These sustain the connection previously made by pictures of elegant or 'sophisticated' individuals smoking cigarettes.

Similarly it is at the level of symbolism and rhetoric that ideological codings of a more extensive kind can begin to break down. For this reason the chapters that follow [in *The Language of Gender and Class*] will focus mainly, though not exclusively, on the fictional treatment of the two (central) signs relating to middle-class femininity and to fallen women already discussed. It is apparently in narratives that the process of dismantling images that help to hold together ideology can be seen to begin. This happens, of course, alongside a non-fictional debate, in which novels are an intervention. Some of that debate [...] includes the writings of Carlyle, J. S. Mill, political economists, social reformers and others. The narrative form which initiates this shift in the representation of gender is a vehicle for many contradictory voices. I therefore intend to discuss extensively only works which appear to develop markedly this change in the coding of class and gender. For a wide variety of novelists in the period from the 1830s to the 1850s address the looming problem of the industrialised working classes. The most well known of these are: Harriet Martineau's *Manchester Strike* (a fable-like novella published in 1832); Frances Trollope's *Michael Armstrong, the Factory Boy* (1840); Benjamin Disraeli's *Sybil, or the Two Nations* (1845); Elizabeth Gaskell's *Mary Barton* (1848); Charlotte Brontë's *Shirley* (1849); Charles Kingsley's *Alton Locke, Tailor and Poet* (1850); Charles Dickens's *Hard Times* (1854); and Elizabeth Gaskell's *North and South* (1855).

As already stated, non-fictional and fictional writings (as well as visual signs) in any period share a common range of signs with established though fluid meanings. The advantage that novels have over other kinds of writings is that they place signs within a narrative which, like the syntactic frame of a sentence, attempts to determine and control meaning. Plots, like signs, make statements. They do not simply answer the question 'What happened next?' Their main function is to show 'what it all means', how these events add up, even if they add up to meaninglessness. They are part of the method of re-accenting signs. Walkowitz demonstrates, for instance, that several contradictory narratives were constructed from the Whitechapel murders of prostitutes by 'Jack the Ripper' in the 1880s. These stories were 'expressive of important cultural and social divisions within Victorian society' and were shaped by 'the alternative perspectives of feminists, libertarians, of the Whitechapel poor' or 'people in positions of power' (Walkowitz, 1992: 225–6). So my discussion of the chosen novels will always take place within this broad framework of signs within plots or narrative syntax.

In each of these occur central confrontational events which act as signs for class division. The confrontation could be of various kinds. It could involve direct cruelty from a member of one class to another: the brutal overseer Joseph Parsons and the factory owner Elgood Sharpton who victimise pauper apprentices in Frances Trollope's *Michael Armstrong*; or the Poor Law guardians maltreating the Green family and the cruel Mr Z tyrannising the factory where Helen Fleetwood dies in Charlotte Elizabeth's novel of that name (1839–41). Though these sympathetic accounts of working-class suffering are fortified by details drawn directly from reports in government Blue Books, they lack narrative specificity. Historical verisimilitude does not prevent them from merging with traditional tales of brutality, myths of cruel ogres and innocents.

More explanatory significance is latent in alternative confrontational plots which accommodate the fact that class-based society is built out of groups with conflicting interests. Such narratives are typified by workers' riots resulting in attacks on middle- or upper-class property. The have-nots trying to become haves are seen in the assault on Mowbray Castle in *Sybil*, the machine-breaking attempts in *Shirley* and the riots in *Alton Locke*. All these focus the economic issue more clearly than the cruelty novels. But the event which can be most forcefully expressive of an economically and socially divided society is the strike, where the property attacked is the machine for wealth-making, the factory itself, that crucial ideological figure. The strike could simplistically spell out the cause of class hostility, the 'gradation of ranks and inequality of fortunes' which Dickens's *bête noire*, J. R. McCulloch, saw as 'the essence of society' (Ford and Monod, 1966: 322). The potential meaning of the strike, however, encompasses the clash of economic interests; a testing of the power of capital and labour; a questioning of the rights of combination; and a measuring of the threat of violence and disorder inherent in the way society is structured.

What the first three novels[1] to be discussed share at a general level is a common narrative syntax. The dynamic of each is an attempt to negotiate an apparently intractable problem: class hostility created by the emiseration of the working classes. They draw on a wide range of linguistic discourses both to construct the problem and to handle the negotiation. To shape the problem into a narrative is to control its meaning. Martineau, for instance, a strict authoritarian, deploys the languages of political economy and of Utilitarianism to represent strikes as causes of distress, not symptoms. Disraeli draws on the descriptions found in Blue Books or official reports on housing, hours of labour, the truck system, to characterise the condition of a second nation to which the first nation could in an ideal world play the role of all-powerful and benign father. But surprisingly the language which could most neatly, in ideological terms, 'resolve' the problem of a divided England was that of the romantic novel in which divided middle-class lovers are finally united.[2]

Such narratives are fuelled by the desire of a middle-class 'master' for the sexual and romantic satisfaction as well as the domestic comfort and prospect of heirs that the middle-class woman represented. The plot's reversal hinges on the resolution of the disharmony between the two. The struggle for this feminine object of male desire displaces the conflict between class and class onto that between the sexes. The process is helped by a compassionate sympathy felt by the true woman for individual workers. The expression of such sympathy is ideologically safe because it is part of her natural mothering role and has no wide implications in the factory, where she has no place. Once accepted by a suitable woman like this as a proper master and father in the home, the 'hero' becomes a proper master in the workplace through a token action of disinterested kindness towards his workers. Harmony at a domestic level is thus transposed onto the class level. Romantic novels can apparently 'demonstrate' that an anomic society, in which accepted social standards and values are lacking, really has moral cohesion.

Their narrative syntax provides a pattern of struggle becoming harmony which strongly reinforces the use of the language of gender to contain the class issue in the first half of the nineteenth century. Hence my concentration on 'romantic' novels. What I wish to argue is that, in the first three novels to be discussed at length, the dominant significance of the House/Angel and Whore/Disorder signs begins to break down. In this breakdown the gender of the narrating voice proves crucial. As Walkowitz points out: 'That individuals do not fully author their texts does not falsify Marx's insight that men (and women) make their own history, albeit under circumstances they do not produce or fully control' (Walkowitz, 1992: 9). This involves historians, as Spiegel says, in explaining cultural constructs in terms of a 'historically-situated authorial consciousness' (Spiegel, 1990: 62). Similarly it involves critics of nineteenth-century novels in considering the gender of the speaking voice historically constituted as feminine or masculine. Certainly the gender of the narrator, if 'feminine', was usually prominent for contemporary reviewers. 'Femininity' had as corollary social class: to be a *lady*, not a female, was to be middle-class.

The result of a 'feminine' perspective is that, as Lynda Nead says of feminist visual art, 'the image itself is seen as part of a process that constructs possible viewing positions for its audience' (Nead, 1992: 61). In the early nineteenth century there was an accepted range of such positions. But there was also the possibility that the individual circumstances of a novelist might shift her from these in various ways. The relevance of this to the novels under discussion is that the first three to be discussed are virtually contemporaneous but two are written by women and one by a man. And close reading reveals that Brontë and Gaskell each perceive and re-present domesticity and the Angel/House sign in a subversive way, whereas Dickens has an unstable perception of the Whore/Disorder sign. Their individual uses of novelistic language are shaped by these facts, as the idiolect (personal language) of each works to reacent the communal system of signs. These individual perceptions have the consequence of releasing the representation of gender from its task of neutralising class conflict, and of allowing new accounts of femininity to emerge. [...]

Notes

1   Ingham concentrates first on Charlotte Brontë's *Shirley*, Gaskell's *North and South*, and Dickens's *Hard Times*. In the second half of the book, after looking at changes in the representation of class in the century, she considers Eliot's *Felix Holt*, Gissing's *The Unclassed*, and Hardy's *Jude the Obscure*.
2   For more on Disraeli and gender, see Poovey (pp. 164–7 above).

References

Ellis, S. S. (1843) *The Women of England: Their Relative Duties, Domestic Influence and Social Obligations* (London: Fisher).

Flinn, M. W. (ed.) (1965) *Edwin Chadwick: Report on the Sanitary Condition of the Labouring Population of Great Britain* (Edinburgh: Edinburgh University Press).

Ford, G. and Monod, S. (eds) (1966) *Charles Dickens, 'Hard Times'* (New York: Norton).

Manchester, A. H. (1980) *A Modern Legal History of England and Wales 1750–1950* (London: Butterworth).

Mayhew, H. (1861) *London Labour and the London Poor: A Cyclopaedia of the Condition and Earnings of Those That Will Work, Those That Cannot Work, and Those That Will Not Work* (London: Griffin, Bohn).

Miller, J. (1859) *Prostitution Considered in Relation to its Cause and Cure* (Edinburgh: Sutherland and Know/London: Simpkin Marshall).

Nead, L. (1988) *Myths of Sexuality: Representations of Women in Victorian Fiction* (Oxford: Blackwell).

Nead, L. (1992) *The Female Nude: Art, Obscenity and Sexuality* (London and New York: Routledge).

Poovey, M. (1989) *Uneven Developments: The Ideological Work of Gender in Mid-Victorian England* (London: Virago).

Spiegel, G. M. (1990) 'History, Historicism, and the Social Logic of the Text in the Middle Ages', *Speculum*, 65: 59–86.

Vincent, D. (1981) *Bread, Knowledge and Freedom: A Study of Nineteenth-century Working Class Autobiography* (London: Europa).

Walkowitz, J. (1980) *Prostitution and Victorian Society: Women, Class and the State* (Cambridge: Cambridge University Press).

Walkowitz, J. (1992) *City of Dreadful Delight: Narratives of Sexual Danger in Late-Victorian London* (London: Virago).

Zedner, L. (1991) *Women, Crime, and Custody in Victorian England* (Oxford: Clarendon).

BAKHTIN AND LITERATURE STUDIES Ingham's use of Bakhtin to provide theoretical paradigms for the analysis of Victorian fiction was by no means the only such appropriation in the recent history of criticism of the nineteenth-century novel. Mikhail Bakhtin has played a major role in recent critical approaches to language, form and the nature of realism in the Victorian novel. He has been popular for obvious reasons as a major twentieth-century theorist of the novel as a genre, whose ideas are much to do with the political but do not presuppose a single political affiliation. He is 'very fashionable',[12] wrote Jeremy Hawthorn in 1992, and he may prove more than that. The clarity and accessibility of Bakhtin's thought has certainly aided this widespread acceptance, and the range of political readings possible in Bakhtinian analysis has also helped extend his appeal for critics of nineteenth-century fiction: Bakhtin, after all, allows political readings of literature without inscribing a definite political position for the reader. Perhaps also, at a more local level, his idea of the novel registering multi-vocality and a continuous struggle for dominance by particular ideologies has appealed because it mirrors not only the condition of modern political society generally but the condition of English studies in the Anglo-American academy particularly, and provides a way of modelling and containing it.

Form and the Victorian Novel

Some of the most visible criticism of the Victorian novel that deployed Bakhtin's ideas as a theoretical basis in the 1980s related to discussions of form. Bakhtinian approaches to this subject, and analyses of the multi-plot nature of much Victorian fiction need, however, to be set in the larger narrative of thinking about the Victorian novel's characteristic and challenging formal properties.

Henry James issued a key statement about the form of mid-Victorian fiction at the beginning of the twentieth century, and the matter raised was central to the wider debate. Subsequent critics returned to it frequently. The publication of all of James's fiction in a revised collection began in 1907, and the author provided new prefaces for this. The 1907 'Preface' to *The Tragic Muse* (1890) was a critical statement of interest to all readers of Victorian fiction. James reflected on the principles of his own approach to form in comparison with the long, multi-layered and random 'monsters', as he called them, of other European novels, including Thackeray's *The Newcomes* (1853–4). Thackeray's novel served, or has been taken to serve, as a representative example of other mid-Victorian multi-plot novels in James's argument:

HENRY JAMES ON MONSTER NOVELS

> The more I turn my pieces over, at any rate, the more I now see I must have found in them [. . .] my fear of too ample a canvas quite dropped. [. . .] A story was a story, a picture a picture, and I had a mortal horror of two stories, two pictures, in one. The reason of this was the clearest – my subject was immediately, under that disadvantage, so cheated of its indispensable centre as to become no more use for expressing a main intention than a wheel without a hub is of use for moving a cart. It was a fact, apparently, that one *had* on occasion seen two pictures in one; were there not for instance certain sublime Tintorettos at Venice, a measureless Crucifixion in especial,[13] which showed without loss of authority half a dozen actions separately taking place? Yes, that might be, but there had surely been nevertheless a mighty pictorial fusion, so that the virtue of composition had somehow thereby come all mysteriously to its own. Of course the affair would be simple enough if composition could be kept out of the question; yet by what art or process, what bars and bolts, what unmuzzled dogs

and pointed guns, perform that feat? I had to know myself utterly inapt for any such valour and recognize that, to make it possible, sundry things should have begun for me much further back than I had felt them even in their dawn. A picture without composition slights its most precious chance for beauty, and is moreover not composed at all unless the painter knows *how* that principle of health and safety, working as an absolutely premeditated art, has prevailed. There may in its absence be life, incontestably, as [Thackeray's] *The Newcomes* has life, as [Dumas *père's*] *Les Trois Mousquetaires* [1844–5], as Tolstoi's *Peace and War* [1863–9], have it; but what do such large loose baggy monsters, with their queer elements of the accidental and the arbitrary, artistically *mean*? We have heard it maintained, we well remember, that such things are 'superior to art'; but we understand least of all what *that* may mean, and we look in vain for the artist, the divine explanatory genius, who will come to our aid and tell us. There is life and life, and as waste is only life sacrificed and thereby prevented from 'counting', I delight in a deep-breathing economy and an organic form. My business was accordingly to 'go in' for complete pictorial fusion, some such common interest between my first two notions as would, in spite of their birth under quite different stars, do them no violence at all.[14]

James privileged the organic novel with a streamlined economical plot that was harmonious in its formal coherence, a 'pictorial fusion', eschewing the loose, random, accidental, ragged multi-plot design of many nineteenth-century novels that did not satisfactorily resolve their structural elements into coherent aesthetic unity.

VAN GHENT'S REACTION AND EMPHASIS ON UNITY

This matter of the coherence of Victorian fiction prompted a vigorous debate. A basic question presented itself: did fiction *need* to be the streamlined narrative that James preferred in order to be a coherent whole, or could unity of elements be found in the ample, multi-plot textures of the 'large loose baggy monsters' themselves? Was unity possible in complex, multi-layered structures? Dorothy Van Ghent, writing from the perspective of New Criticism in her *The English Novel: Form and Function* (1953), proposed, following the New Criticism's emphasis on the way in which great literature resolved its elements into coherent wholes, that Victorian monster novels were in fact remarkable for their structural harmony, their underlying and pleasurable unity. Van Ghent's book took a range of novels from different periods, including the Victorian – Charles Dickens's *Great Expectations*, W. M. Thackeray's *Vanity Fair*, Emily Brontë's *Wuthering Heights*, George Eliot's *Adam Bede*, George Meredith's *The Egoist*, Thomas Hardy's *Tess of the d'Urbervilles*, and Henry James's own *Portrait of a Lady* – and exposed the structures of interrelationship between elements of these texts, held together by dominant ideas, that worked to secure unity and satisfying harmony. For her, coherence in a work of fiction was a sign of its greatness, and she concluded, with a phrase resonating with the language of F. R. Leavis, that such richly satisfyingly novels extend 'our lives in amplitude and variousness' (for more on Leavis, see chapter 2). The brief 'Introduction' to *The English Novel*, reproduced here, articulated her central assumptions with clarity.

Extract from Dorothy Van Ghent, *The English Novel: Form and Function* (New York: Harper and Row, 1961, orig. pub. 1953), 3–7.

The subject matter of novels is human relationships in which are shown the directions of men's souls. This is the subject matter also of drama and of the great histories. Let us make a few distinctions among these kinds of writing that have the same subject matter. The distinctions are fairly obvious, but for the sake of common points of reference and common consent it is helpful to get the obvious expressed.

Drama is subject to the conventions of the stage; people are conceived as if they were to be seen and heard in person, under the physical restrictions of tangible space and time. The novel is free of these conventions, although it has others. It can use all sorts of discursive methods that the drama cannot use. But it employs dramatic method most liberally, for it represents human beings *as if* in tangible space and time, that is, 'scenically' placed and related. Both the novel and the drama are history in a certain sense: they tell of how people lived or live, their manners, what they held important, how they went about getting what they got, their conflicts, their errors, their heroism. Since some novels look very much like 'real' history, like a factual social record, we need to be rather careful in defining the characterizing differences between novels and history.

Like a science, or like mathematics, but unlike history, the novel proceeds by hypothesis. It says, implicitly, 'Given such and such conditions, then such and such would take place.' The hypothesis on which a novel is built is the abstract aspect of its form. It takes from life the conditions for its hypothesis; that is, it starts from the empirical data that are the 'given' data of sentient experience. But it selects and organizes them in a way that suggests a purely creative issue – a series of hypothetical events not 'given' at all but cogent as cause and effect from the initial selection.

Being a hypothetical structure, the novel is able to give a leverage to the empirically known and push it into the dimension of the unknown, the possible. Its value lies less in confirming and interpreting the known than in forcing us to the supposition that *something else might be the case*. It is for this reason that the novel is a source of insight. [...]

Human experience is organized in patterns that are in movement, patterns that some philosophers call 'events' – emphasizing the temporal or moving aspect of them – and that some psychologists call 'fields of perception,' or Gestalten – emphasizing the content of them, as if the content were momentarily static. Inhering in the patterns are sensuous traits (temperature, light, color, texture, sound, and so on); inhering in them also are multitudes of traits of memory, emotion, and thought. We tend to think of events in experience as bodiless, because they slide into each other as stones and trees do not. But held quiet by the mind they are seen to have bodies – to have individual form and function. Fiction tries to isolate the principle of coherence in events, the active principle that holds together all the multitude of particular traits that an event has, and the more extensive principle that makes one event slide into another in human lives. Reflected by the mind, the principle that makes the traits in an event cohere, and the principle that controls the relationship between events, are what we call 'ideas.'

Philosophy and the sciences use certain abstractive languages for the expression of ideas; and, because of the association of ideas with abstractive language, the reader who turns to the novel from other disciplines may not be willing immediately to recognize the novel's ability to express ideas; for he may feel that the novel's reliance on imagery – imagery of speech sounds and physical groupings and all the other kinds of imagery that make for the novel's necessary 'embodiment' of its subject – incapacitates this medium for the expression of valuable ideas. Or he may have the impulse to locate the ideas in a novel only in those passages where the language is that of abstract conceptualism – passages in which, it is possible, the novel's ideas may show at their poorest, or in which the author may even clumsily and blindly falsify the ideas actually inherent in his work. The novel is able to express the most profound ideas, but, because of the nature of this medium, these will lie implicitly in the conjunction of the events that are bodied forth. The ideas in a novel are largely for the reader's inference, his inference of the principles by which the happenings in the book are related to each other.

A novel itself is one complex pattern, or Gestalt, made up of component ones. In it inhere such a vast number of traits, all organized in subordinate systems that function under the governance of a single meaningful structure, that the nearest similitude for a novel is a 'world.' This is a useful similitude because it reflects the rich multiplicity of the novel's elements and, at the same time, the unity of the novel as a self-defining body. The novel's planetary orbit lies through different minds and different generations of minds, each exerting its special pushes and pulls upon the novel's substance, each interpreting it according to the different spiritual constitution of each. How are we to judge a novel? How are we to evaluate it among other novels? Its strenuous orbit through different minds and generations, each observing it and understanding it with some measure of difference, would seem to deny it any final value status for the reader who approaches it with an awakened critical instinct and a desire for objectively valid judgment.

The sound novel, like a sound world, has to hang together as one thing. It has to have integral structure. Part of our evaluative judgment is based on its ability to hang together *for us*. And like a world, a novel has individual character; it has, peculiar to itself, its own tensions, physiognomy, and atmosphere. Part of our judgment is based on the concreteness, distinctness, and richness of that character. Finally, we judge a novel also by the cogency and illuminative quality of the view of life that it affords, the idea embodied in its cosmology. Our only adequate preparation for judging a novel evaluatively is through the analytical testing of its unity, of its characterizing qualities, and of its meaningfulness – its ability to make us more aware of the meaning of our lives. All these tests test the value of the novel only *for us*, and value for us is all the value that matters. But if the particular novel has been integral and characterful and meaningful for other individuals and other generations as well, however different its appearance to them, the book automatically extends our lives in amplitude and variousness.

What lay at the heart of good fiction in Van Ghent's perception was a set of ideas: the novel articulated hypotheses and these gave to the fiction the basis of its coherence. Her notion of the novel dealing with ideas could not have been further from George Saintsbury's declaration in 1887 (discussed in chapter 1, p. 22) that the novel 'has nothing to do with any beliefs, with any convictions, with any thoughts in the strict sense, except as mere garnishings'.[15] There can be few who disagree now with Van Ghent because they accept Saintsbury's view of the intellectual content of Victorian fiction, but Barbara Hardy had a different objection to her approach to form. Doubting Van Ghent's privileging of unity, Hardy staked out a mid-point between James and Van Ghent in her reply to *The English Novel* called *The Appropriate Form* (1964). Here, she queried New Critical views on harmony, declaring that over-emphasizing unity undervalued the possibilities for liberty and range given to the novelist by a more multifarious structure. The multi-plot

BARBARA
HARDY'S
REACTION:
THE
ADVANTAGES
OF FLUIDITY
IN FORM

novel conferred a 'richness and freedom', she said, and it was an error to sideline this diversity. 'We insist', she argued, returning to James's provocative phrase, 'that the large loose baggy monster has unity, has symbolic concentration, has patterns of imagery and a thematic construction of character, and in the result the baggy monster is processed by our New Criticism into something strikingly like the original Jamesian streamlined beast'.[16] Hardy endeavoured to resist the temptation of reducing diversity to an over-emphasized unity:

> I have tried to show that there is after all some sense in calling novels like *Middlemarch* and *Anna Karenina* large and loose, but that this largeness and looseness has a special advantage, allowing the novelist to report truthfully and fully the quality of the individual moment, the loose end, the doubt and contradiction and mutability. James was wrong to call such novels 'fluid puddings' but we might do worse than keep his adjective while rejecting his noun.[17]

Hardy rejected the New Critical emphasis on unity in preference for a greater sensitivity to the possibilities of complex structures that contained multiple elements. She celebrated diversity over unity. But her rhetoric suggested the key problematic of her reading because, when she insisted on the fluidity of the multi-plot novel, she recuperated the approach she was elsewhere rejecting. Her metaphor retained the idea of unity, of the organic fusion of elements into a whole, albeit a freer and, in James's words, looser one. Peter Garrett, via deconstruction, challenged both Hardy's position and Van Ghent's in 1980 in favour of a more radical view of fictional complexity (see pp. 219–24 below).

HILLIS MILLER AND FORM WITHOUT GOD   Hardy's perspective extended the debate, and for a while the argument about the form of Victorian fiction oscillated between the three points I have described: other critics of Victorian fiction initially found it difficult to move in a new direction outside this pattern (see the Further Reading section). J. Hillis Miller, for instance, in *The Form of Victorian Fiction* (1968), returned to a position similar to Van Ghent's, at least in terms of the unity debate, when he declared that:

> A Victorian novel is, finally, a structure in which the elements (characters, scenes, images) are not detachable pieces, each with a given nature and meaning, each adding its part to the meaning of the whole. Every element draws its meaning from the others, so that the novel must be described as a self-generating and self-sustained system, like the society it mirrors.[18]

At one level, this was a familiar argument. At another, Hillis Miller was distinctive in proposing a theological explanation for the form of the Victorian novel. He saw Victorian fiction offering a version of the social only possible in a world without God. In the Victorian novel, he said, 'the individual human heart generates the game of society and establishes its rules. Society rests on human feeling and human will. It is created by the interplay of one mind and heart with another.'[19] Such fiction was structured around the representation of overlapping consciousnesses, comprising a texture of 'intersubjectivities',[20] which placed the human in the foreground. This was a result of God's disappearance from the belief systems of the culture. The Victorian novel offered a fictional replacement, a consoling formal unity, for a world devoid of God. This view was fresh, but in regarding the novel as a system, Hillis Miller was connecting with Van Ghent's reading. As with other approaches to form, Hillis Miller's use of the term 'Victorian fiction' was a source of difficulty. It was Kathleen Tillotson in *The Novels of the Eighteen-forties* who declared in 1954 that the category of 'Victorian novel' was no longer a useful one. One does not have to go that far to see that Hillis Miller's homogenizing term 'Victorian novel' generated difficulty through lack of specificity in the discussion of form (see also Introduction, p. 2 above).

Deconstruction in the 1970s and 1980s, with its belief in the fractured and divided nature of texts, provided the single largest opponent to the argument about the unity of the multi-plot novel, as it did somewhat indiscriminately to arguments about the unity of any literary production or any effort to explain language utterances as coherent. The organicist beliefs of the New Criticism were thoroughly ruptured by the rising prominence of deconstruction in English studies, whether the subject was Victorian fiction, metaphysical poetry, Shakespeare's plays or Romantic period verse. There were also ideological objections to the idea of the unity apparently achieved by realist fiction: for a Marxist critique of this, see Catherine Belsey's work discussed on pp. 120–33 above, which had a major influence on the reading of the coherence of realist fiction in the 1980s.

DECON-STRUCTION AND INCO-HERENCE

As far as deconstruction and the criticism of Victorian fiction were concerned, the period of theory's dominance did see important work on the form of the nineteenth-century novel that did not involve either embattled restatements of the New Critical position or simply generalist applications of deconstructive principles that revealed as flawed any notion of unity inhering in the text, approaches that lost in the process a meaningful sense of the specificity of the Victorian realist mode. Peter K. Garrett's work on the multi-plot novel, *The Victorian Multiplot Novel: Studies in Dialogical Form* (1980), was an instance of this judicious use of the implications of deconstruction. It was a critical reading that resisted the organicism of the New Critics, the hesitant mid-way position of Barbara Hardy, and the generalized deconstructive assumption of the impossibility of coherence in any text. Instead, Garrett identified what he saw as the particular formal properties of multi-plot

GARRETT'S DECON-STRUCTION-IST VIEWS OF MULTI-PLOT FICTION

Victorian novels, and explained how their multiple elements and inconsistencies worked by insisting on the novel's capacity to mean different things at
once.

Mikhail Bakhtin's notion of the dialogic provided Garrett with the basis of
his critical methodology for reading the complex, interleaved quality of
Victorian multi-plot fiction. Garrett extrapolated a general theory of form,
serviceable for a range of Victorian fiction, from Bakhtin's conception of the
'plurality of independent and unmerged voices and consciousnesses'[21] apparent in the novels of Dostoevsky (see Baktin's *Problems of Dostoevsky's Poetics*).[22]
He offered a new way of reading the instability of the multi-plot novel that
was distinct from previous positions because it affirmed the multi-plot novel
as constitutively indeterminate. No approach that emphasized merely unity or
restated James's view of incoherence would do, for the ideal critical route into
Victorian fiction allowed for both: 'The form of these novels is neither single-
nor multiple-focus', he said, 'and it is the interaction and tension between
these structural principles which produces some of their most important and
distinctive effects. No single model can accommodate texts in which different,
incompatible principles of coherence are in play.'[23]

This idea is visible here in his brief account of Emily Brontë's *Wuthering
Heights*. The extract begins with Garrett's argument about the relationship
between his own practice of reading the indeterminacies of Victorian fiction
and deconstruction's general argument about the ultimate incoherence of all
forms of writing.

Extract from Peter Garrett, *The Victorian Multiplot Novel: Studies in Dialogical Form* (New Haven, Conn.: Yale University Press, 1980), 16–21.

By identifying the double logic of single and multiple focus as the
common and distinctive structural problematic of the major Victorian
multiplot novels, we can develop analyses that recognize not only the
qualities they share but also the individual qualities of each novel and
novelist. When we encounter the split in *Bleak House* between the wide-
ranging authorial narrative and the narrower focus of Esther's first-
person narrative, or the shift in *Middlemarch* from the first ten chapters
focused on Dorothea to a multiple narrative in which her story becomes
only one among several, we are encountering significantly different
forms of a common dialogical tension that require different interpret-

ations.[1] To work out those interpretations we cannot simply rely on broad generic patterns like comedy and romance or satire and apologue; we must pay close attention to the specific features of each novel's form, following the dialogue of competing coherences through the alternations of its narrative voices and perspectives, the shifts and splits, twists and intersections of its lines of development.

That kind of attention to form also distinguishes the readings I am proposing from more abstract deconstructive interpretations. By considering dialogical form as an unstable tension between determinate patterns and focusing on concrete fictional elements, we can explore the problems of meaning each novel develops without turning them into illustrations of universal philosophical themes. The work of Derrida and other post-structuralists has made it easier to extricate multiplot novels from the restrictions of monological assumptions, but we shall not be making the most of this opportunity if we only use it to rediscover and deconstruct the pervasive system of Western metaphysics in every text we read. Instead, we need to recognize how the processes of narrative perform their own constructions and deconstructions, how the interplay of centering and decentering impulses at work in Dickens' mystery plots or Thackeray's shifting authorial stances, in George Eliot's networks of thematic analogies or the uncertain status of Trollope's protagonists produces very different meanings and effects. Clearly these novelists are not as insistent or as radical in their transgressions and transformations of traditional modes of writing as the avant-garde writers favored by theorists like Kristeva, but it is precisely that difference, that apparent deference to established modes that gives them their special interest. In them we encounter the problems and possibilities developed more explicitly in modern writing but encounter them within the traditional system of representation, a system whose grounds of meaning, such as the stability of personal identity, the intelligibility of cause and effect, the authority of the authorial voice, are both exploited and subverted. My readings of these novels will attempt to do justice to their mixed mode by working within the familiar categories of character, plot, and theme, but they will also attempt to show some – and necessarily only some – of the ways in which their double logic composes and decomposes those elements to produce effects of remarkable and irreducible complexity.

As a preliminary example of some of the effects produced by dialogical form, let us briefly consider *Wuthering Heights*. It is neither large nor loose and seems monstrous mainly as a 'sport' (as F. R. Leavis calls it), unrelated to other Victorian fiction. Yet in the way it plays double-against single-focus narrative and holds both patterns open to alternative interpretations it closely resembles several other longer novels of the period, while its formal compression permits a more concise analysis. As a single-focus narrative it appears to center in the figure of Heathcliff, who is certainly the most important character and whose career runs from the beginning to the end of the novel. But this pattern is disrupted by several discontinuities: time-shifts which reverse the order of cause and effect, gaps such as Heathcliff's three-year absence and radical transformation between chapters 9 and 10, and the shift of emphasis in which he is progressively displaced by the second Catherine and Hareton. In the course of this displacement he assumes the role of opponent and blocking figure between the young lovers which Hindley played between himself and Catherine, a shift from 'hero' to 'villain' which indicates a sharp reversal of perspective. For all the appearance and importance of a single focus, the novel eventually requires us to recognize a dual pattern. As William Empson observes, '*Wuthering Heights* is a good case of double plot in the novel . . . telling the same story twice with the two possible endings.'* This pattern of repetition and difference involves not only parallels between characters but a detailed counterpoint of events, such as the first Catherine being 'captured' in the Grange (7) and the second in the Heights (27). The movement of doubling is also at work in the repetition and recombination of names, the doubling and merging of identities (Catherine declares, 'I am Heathcliff' [9]; he calls her his 'life' and 'soul' [16]), and in the doubled narration of Lockwood and Nelly, whose obvious biases and limitations require us to redouble their accounts with alternative interpretations; it assumes the most inclusive thematic form in the opposition between the worlds of the Heights and the Grange, or between the energy of natural or supernatural forces and the restraints of civilized order and reason.

These thematic oppositions have often been discussed in commentaries on the novel and need not be pursued here. My main concern is with the possibilities of interpretation produced by the interaction of single and dual focus, linear progression and binary alternation. Like the decrepit house adjoining the Gimmerton chapel, its 'two rooms threatening speedily to determine into one' (3), the double narrative can be construed as two phases merging into a single, continuous history, organized by a precise chronology. But the actual narrative order, with

---

* *Some Versions of Pastoral* (1935; rpt. Norfolk, Conn.: New Directions, 1960), 84. Empson's study of double plots in Elizabethan drama is less preoccupied than most with establishing unity, and his conception of 'double irony' involves conflicts of meaning similar to those produced by what I call dialogical form.

its initial departure from chronology (Lockwood begins very near the 'end') and subsequent shifts backward and forward, makes the two plots unfold concurrently. As reconstructed sequence, *Wuthering Heights* traces a cycle of disruption and renewal, a tragic metaphysical love story followed, complemented, and reversed by a comic counterplot in which less extreme versions of the original tormented lovers converge to restore civility. This is the version presented by Lockwood and Nelly, with its final note of peaceful resolution.

But against this closed, linear pattern, in which conflict is resolved by the elimination of Catherine and Heathcliff, we can set another, suggested by the belief of 'the country folks' that they still walk the moors, in which they and their violent, visionary world remain as a perpetual alternative, coexisting with the more normal, conventional world of the second generation as the two plots coexist. This tension between structural principles is expressed within the novel in Heathcliff's and Catherine's struggles to break out of an irreversible linear sequence and (re)gain their private eternity, and in those moments, like Lockwood's dream, when the past or another world breaks into the present. It is likewise expressed in the many readings of the novel which attempt to assert one extreme of its polarized values against the other, to privilege one plot and subordinate the other, or to encompass their opposition in some sort of dualism. Both the dramatic conflicts and the conflicting possibilities of interpretation arise from the novel's dialogical form.

The dual logic of *Wuthering Heights* cannot be mastered by critical concepts of center, hierarchy, and totality, by either choosing one interpretation or imposing a fixed order on alternative interpretations, by any strategy that attempts to enclose and stabilize the text's production of meaning. This instability is quite clearly not the result of formal 'looseness.' The devices of analogical and causal connection, metaphoric and metonymic links between the novel's double plots (devices which are always, and always differently at work in every multiple narrative, however large or loose) produce a high degree of formal coherence, but they are all subject to the play of shifting perspectives, a movement of continual substitution which exceeds and resists any monological formulation. We can observe this movement even in the final lines of *Wuthering Heights*, as Lockwood wonders 'how anyone could ever imagine unquiet slumbers, for the sleepers in that quiet earth.' His words declare the end of the narrative's movement, the end of all its stormy conflicts in a mood of permanent calm, yet they also ironically invite us to remedy his deficient imagination, to conceive what he cannot, and so to begin again the substitution of perspectives.*

To consider *Wuthering Heights* and other Victorian multiplot novels as dialogical forms requires us to follow the movement in which meaning is continually produced and effaced. To read them in this way is not to claim mastery of their complexity or to unmask their latent contradictions but to continue the process of setting one perspective against another in which the novels themselves are already engaged, a process which the conventions neither of narrative nor of critical argument can ever bring to more than a provisional conclusion.

Note

1 See Catherine Belsey's account of classic realism (pp. 121–32 above) for a different reading of the split narrative of *Bleak House*.

KEEN AND NARRATIVE ANNEXES Peter Garrett's argument provided a challenging approach to the question of the form of Victorian fiction in the early 1980s, right in the heart of the deconstructionist period, and it continues to be well regarded. Recently, Suzanne Keen added a further dimension to the study of the multiple layers of signification in Victorian fiction and that fiction's capacity to embrace conflicting elements in her *Victorian Renovations of the Novel: Narrative Annexes and the Boundaries of Representation* (1998). Here, Keen discussed how 'narrative annexes' allowed for unexpected elements to be included in the novel's plot, extending the inclusiveness, multiplicity and range of meaning in the fiction. Such annexes permitted 'unexpected characters, impermissible subjects, and plot-altering events to appear, in a bounded way, in fictional worlds that might be expected to exclude them. Like other Victorian renovations, narrative annexes may appear to disfigure the structure they alter, but they at the same time reveal Victorian novelists' creative responses to the

---

* The unresolvable instability of *Wuthering Heights* can also be seen by comparing it with its monological sibling, *Jane Eyre*, where we find a powerfully centripetal organization around a single focus (characters and events gain significance only as they contribute to Jane's development), reinforced by the protagonist's own, thoroughly reliable narration. Conflicts of self-assertion and submission, of the forces of passion or desire with those of repression or renunciation, are expressed not as dialogical tensions but as a dialectical progression in the alternating stages of Gateshead and Lowood, Thornfield and Moor House, which arrives at a final, stable synthesis in the union of Jane and Rochester at Ferndean. Any reading of *Jane Eyre* that seeks to dismantle this synthesis will have to work against the logic of its form, not by following it as we have followed the double logic of *Wuthering Heights*.

capacities and limitations of their form.'[24] Keen considered chiefly Charlotte Brontë, Dickens, Disraeli, Hardy, Kingsley and Trollope.

But, even in the heart of the 1980s, the decade of deconstruction, other approaches to form were being developed independent of Garrett's paradigms (sometimes this independence generated problems). These readings, covering a wide range of scholarly work, are discussed under other headings in this book. Most notably, the historical determination of the formal properties of fiction was privileged in the 1980s and 1990s as critics explored its cultural embeddedness. What were chiefly examined in the 1980s were the connections between fictional narrative and modern empirical science, including correspondences between the plots of the novel and the evolutionary plots of Darwin's *Origin of Species* (1859). This criticism is discussed in chapter 7 (see pp. 230–52), and it gave a fresh perspective to the understanding of organic form that has now become a commonplace. Spurred by the growing discipline of the History of the Book, or by Marxist models of economic determinants, the 1970s and 1980s also saw studies of fictional form's relation to the material conditions of production. Materialist approaches are discussed in chapter 8 (see pp. 265–85). These likewise had lasting consequences on understanding the Victorian novelists' use of multi-plot form. In the mid-1990s, postcolonialism offered the most controversial reading of form since Belsey's critique of the ideology of realism in 1980 (see pp. 121–32 below). Postcolonialists developed ideas about the embeddedness of Victorian fiction inherited from the 1980s, but concentrated on imperial ideology. Rejecting Bakhtinian readings of the polyvocality of fiction, they considered how the Victorian novel was formally determined by and reproduced an ideology of empire in its silencing of marginalized voices, seeing the coherence of fiction narrated by single voices as predicated on an exclusion that mirrored oppressive politics. This understanding of form, the newest ideological critique of the unity of Victorian fiction, did not take Garrett's views into account and represented, at one level, a return to earlier, much-challenged assumptions about the wholeness of the Victorian novel. This postcolonial approach is considered in chapter 9 (see pp. 321–3). Other approaches to form in the 1990s, and to the related area of narratology, are given in the Further Reading section.

Approaches to form in the 1980s and 1990s

Chapter Notes

1 André Brink, *The Novel: Language and Narrative from Cervantes to Calvino* (Basingstoke: Macmillan, 1998), 6–7 (italic in original).
2 Geoffrey Leech and Michael Short, *Style in Fiction: A Linguistic Introduction to English Fictional Prose* (London: Longman, 1980), 2.

3   Cf. K. C. Phillipps's statement that there is 'much in the language these great authors used which now calls for comment, and even elucidation', *The Language of Thackeray* (London: Deutsch, 1978), 7.

4   Ibid., 35.

5   Raymond Chapman, *The Language of Thomas Hardy* (Basingstoke: Macmillan, 1990), 36. For another study of Hardy's language from a more historicized point of view, see Dennis Taylor, *Hardy's Literary Language and Victorian Philology* (Oxford: Clarendon, 1993).

6   K. C. Phillipps, *Language and Class in Victorian England* (Oxford: Blackwell in association with Deutsch, 1984), 3.

7   Raymond Chapman, *Forms of Speech in Victorian Fiction* (London: Longman, 1994), 1.

8   Ibid., 18–19.

9   Patricia Ingham, *Dickens, Women, and Language* (Toronto Buffalo: University of Toronto Press, 1992), 144.

10   Quoted in Patricia Ingham, *The Language of Gender and Class: Transformation in the Victorian Novel* (London: Routledge, 1996), 30.

11   Ibid., 20.

12   Jeremy Hawthorn, *Studying the Novel: An Introduction*, 2nd edn (London: Arnold, 1992), 143.

13   James refers to the Tintoretto paintings in the Scuola di San Rocco in Venice, and particularly to the *Crucifixion*, a work that Ruskin described in the third volume of *The Stones of Venice* (1853) as 'beyond all analysis, and above all praise', *The Library Edition of the Complete Works of John Ruskin*, eds E. T. Cook and Alexander Wedderburn, 39 vols (London: Allen, 1903–12), xi. 428. Ruskin had brought these pictures to national attention, and used them to exemplify particular aspects of his own aesthetic principles. James was choosing a picture that had already served in a major aesthetic argument to express his own views on a different aesthetic question.

14   Henry James, 'Preface' to *The Tragic Muse*, in Roger Gard, ed., *Henry James: The Critical Muse: Selected Literary Criticism* (Harmondsworth: Penguin, 1987), 514–16 (italic in original). For a useful study of James's work as a critic, see Vivien Jones, *James the Critic* (London: Macmillan, 1984).

15   John Charles Olmsted, ed., *A Victorian Art of Fiction: Essays on the Novel in British Periodicals* 1870–1900 (New York: Garland, 1979), iii. 397.

16   Barbara Hardy, *The Appropriate Form* (London: Athlone, 1964, corrected 1971), 7.

17   Ibid., 8.

18   J. Hillis Miller, *The Form of Victorian Fiction* (Notre Dame, Indiana: University of Indiana Press, 1968), 30.

19   Ibid., 140.

20   See ibid., 1–27.

21   Peter K. Garrett, *The Victorian Multiplot Novel: Studies in Dialogical Form* (New Haven, Conn. and London: Yale University Press, 1980), 9.

22   See Mikhail Bakhtin, *Problems of Dostoevsky's Poetics*, ed. and trans. Caryl Emerson, with an introduction by Wayne C. Booth (Manchester: Manchester University Press, 1984).

23   Garrett, *The Victorian Multiplot Novel*, 8.

24   Suzanne Keen, *Victorian Renovations of the Novel: Narrative Annexes and the Boundaries of Representation* (Cambridge: Cambridge University Press, 1998), 1.

Further Reading

Form and narratology:

Gillian Beer, 'Origins and Oblivion in Victorian Narrative', in Ruth Bernard Yeazell, ed., *Sex, Politics, and Science in the Nineteenth-century Novel* (Baltimore: Johns Hopkins University Press, 1985), 63–87: suggestive argument about the relation between form and Victorian evolutionary science. Beer writes that the form of the multi-plot novel 'makes it difficult for the reader to remember all that passes by' and explores how this connected with fears of remoteness and forgetting in Victorian fiction.

Leon Edel, *The Prefaces of Henry James* (Paris: Jouve, 1931): 'An attempt to give an exposition of Henry James's theories and methods in fiction as contained in the prefaces which he wrote for the definitive edition of his novels and tales'.

Michal Peled Ginsburg, *Economies of Change: Form and Transformation in the Nineteenth-century Novel* (Standford, CA: Stanford University Press, 1996): takes issue with structuralist efforts to find narrative paradigms behind multiply different literary forms, and argues for 'a reading that foregrounds the specificity of each narrative project'. Emphasizes transformation, and says that 'by dealing with certain cultural issues through the manipulation of formal possibilities, an author produces new articulations – produces a specific configuration that is not entirely determined by context'.

Ian Gregor, 'Reading a Story: Sequence, Pace, and Recollection', in Ian Gregor, ed., *Reading the Victorian Novel: Detail into Form* (London: Vision, 1980), 92–110: on the reader's experience of form and how it determines particular kinds of reading.

Percy Lubbock, *The Craft of Fiction* (London: Cape, [1921]): consideration of novel form from a Jamesian point of view.

Carol Hanbery MacKay, *Soliloquy in Nineteenth-century Fiction* (Basingstoke: Macmillan, 1987): considers two models of soliloquy in the nineteenth century: the 'self-debate model' and the 'regret to resolution' pattern, particularly evident in Thackeray. Sees the soliloquy as a particularly Victorian way of dramatizing conflicts between opposites, and a form that exploits the 'imagery of isolation [...] to energize that self out of the inaction of indecision, regret, or despair'.

D. A. Miller, *Narrative and its Discontents: Problems of Closure in the Traditional Novel* (Princeton, NJ: Princeton University Press, 1981): considers George Eliot in a discussion about how novels endeavour to narrate things that are not susceptible to narrative, and the tension this generates. For more on Miller, see p. 133 above.

Edwin Muir, *The Structure of the Novel* (London: L. and V. Woolf, 1928): written in response to Modernist experimentations with novel form, and including much discussion of Victorian novels, divides prose fiction into character novels, dramatic novels, and the chronicle, and argues for the prestige of the form. The 'plot of the novel is as necessarily poetic or aesthetic as that of any other kind of imaginative creation'.

Knud Sørensen, *Charles Dickens: Linguistic Innovator* (Aarhus: Arkona, 1985).

Michael Wheeler, *The Art of Allusion in Victorian Fiction* (London: Macmillan, 1979): important argument about the use of allusion, to Biblical and literary texts, as a formal property of Victorian fiction, and its role in making the novel cohere. Wheeler extends Van Ghent's assumptions about the wholeness of the novel form (see above pp. 214–17), arguing that there is an 'accumulative effect of allusion' in Victorian novels. 'Sets of allusions to a single adopted text can provide the analogical matrix which shapes part of the novel [. . . and] allusions to a wide range of adopted texts can contribute to an adoptive text's central symbolism.'

Jeffrey Williams, *Theory and the Novel: Narrative Reflexivity in the British Tradition* (Cambridge: Cambridge University Press, 1998): related to Brink's work (above p. 196), this discussed self-consciousness in narrative, concentrating on 'moments in which the act of narrative itself is depicted and then thematized or called into question'; includes consideration of James's *The Turn of the Screw* and Emily Brontë's *Wuthering Heights*.

Austin M. Wright, *The Formal Principle in the Novel* (Ithaca and London: Cornell University Press, 1982): 'My aim is to test the claim of formal unity to importance – to centrality – in the novel's art.' Especially interested in plot unity: includes discussion of Henry James.

Language:

Tony Crowley, ed., *Proper English?: Readings in Language, History and Cultural Identity* (London: Routledge, 1991): anthologizing texts from 1690 to the present day, the book aims to show the myriad ways in which language and political history are interlinked. All the texts are concerned with the question of 'proper English'.

Roger Fowler, *Linguistic Criticism*, 2nd edn (Oxford: Oxford University Press, 1996): extends in clear language the application of linguistic principles to the reading of all literary genres.

David Lodge, *Language of Fiction: Essays in Criticism and Verbal Analysis of the English Novel* (London: Routledge and Kegan Paul/New York: Columbia University Press, 1966): part II is a critique of stylistics as an approach to fiction that owes much to Leavis (see chapter 2). Lodge argues that 'The language of the novel [. . .] will be most satisfactorily and completely sounded by the methods, not of linguistics or stylistics (though these disciplines can make valuable contributions), but of literary criticism, which seeks to define the meaning and value of literary artefacts by relating subjective response and objective text.'

Lynda Mugglestone, *'Talking Proper': The Rise of Accent as Social Symbol* (Oxford: Clarendon, 1997): on the association between qualities of speech and class in the nineteenth century: much use of fiction as examples.

Roy Pascal, *The Dual Voice: Free Indirect Speech and its Functioning in the Nineteenth-century European Novel* (Manchester: Manchester University Press, 1977): considers Victorian fiction, pp. 67–97.

Katie Wales, *A Dictionary of Stylistics*, 2nd edn (Harlow: Longman, 2001): useful single-authored book from 'a-verse' to 'zeugma' and including discussion of theoretical movements in literary criticism and their contribution to stylistic studies.

7

Science and the Victorian Novel

Leo Henkins – Tess Cosslett – Gillian Beer – George Levine –
Helen Small – Sally Shuttleworth – Peter Logan – the 1990s

Literary critics now recognize literature and science, once thought to be two separate and oppositional activities, as fruitfully interrelated cultural practices. The study of their relations has, accordingly, in the past few decades, developed into a major intellectual concern across the terrain of contemporary English literary criticism. Victorian fiction and its relationship with science is no exception and work in this area includes some of the most significant and frequently cited critical texts of recent years. With major books completed in the 1980s and 1990s, essays, books, and university theses continue to push the boundaries of this field in the twenty-first century. Such criticism has changed the way in which the Victorian period's ordering of knowledge is comprehended; it has had a profound influence on an understanding of organic form in Victorian fiction, and on perceptions of the relationship between cultural practices in the nineteenth century (for other discussions of form and unity, see pp. 213–25 above). Increasing in its profile in twentieth-century studies, the study of science and the novel constitutes the most prominent aspect of contextual studies currently explored in Victorian fiction.

EARLY
APPROACHES
TO THE FIELD
The broad outline of this critical history is as follows. Early works on literature and science in the Victorian period concentrated, with one exception, on poetry. This corpus of writing allowed the topic of literature and science to gain some prominence in the academy and prepared for its take-off as a major area of critical investigation in the 1980s. These early approaches focused on how literature borrowed and gave emotional substance to concepts or language taken from science. The first important interpretative works on Victorian fiction in the early 1980s followed from this and thought likewise of the way in which fiction responded to or borrowed from science. They implicitly or explicitly gave cultural priority to science in its relationship with literary discourse. This methodology was challenged in the mid-1980s by critics who thought that works of science and literature should be read

more as equivalent discourses, and, as Gillian Beer insisted, alongside each other. Conceptualization of the ways in which science and literature worked together, and an argument that they were discourses of equivalent status, articulating and helping produce the culture from which they emerged, also characterized this period. Concentration in the 1980s was on evolutionary biology and Charles Darwin in particular, while the 1990s saw a shift into other areas of nineteenth-century science, with a particular emphasis on mind sciences, and a growing fascination with pathologies, physical or mental. There was also continued debate about critical methodology, though less dramatically than previously.

Lionel Stevenson's 1932 book, *Darwin Among the Poets* (originally his doctoral thesis at the University of California), was an early instance of literary scholarship examining interconnections between science and Victorian literature, though his focus was on poetry. His work was the first stage in the gradual build-up of interest in Victorian literature and science that eventually blossomed in the 1980s. Stevenson urged readers to remember that 'The irruption of science is probably the most interesting phenomenon in nineteenth-century literature',[1] and he showed how Tennyson, Browning, Meredith and Thomas Hardy made use of scientific language and ideas in their poetry. His interest was in how these poets borrowed concepts and metaphors from the language of science; it was a study that saw science and literature as two different activities in the period but which recognized that there was some one-way borrowing, during which 'hard' images taken from science were transformed into the affective language of poetry. William Wordsworth, in the 1802 'Preface' to *Lyrical Ballads*, had declared that this was exactly what science needed in order to become of serious human interest, a 'dear and genuine inmate of the household of man',[2] and a suitable subject for poetry. Later critics saw Stevenson's Wordsworthian understanding of the relationship between the two cultural practices as limited. But the broad concept of the relation of literary writing to scientific ideas none the less made *Darwin Among the Poets* an innovative study, and a propadaeutic one. A related book was J. Warren Beach's *The Concept of Nature in Nineteenth-century English Poetry* (1936), which pursued an argument about the inevitable disappearance of nature poetry as a consequence of evolutionary science's influence on how nature was perceived.

STEVENSON'S *DARWIN AMONG THE POETS* (1932)

The New Criticism downplayed the significance of context in reading texts, seeing literary works as set apart, as verbal artefacts sufficient in themselves. This dependence on the text without recognition of the shaping power of history meant that the scientific context of nineteenth-century writing was ignored in those areas of scholarship dominated by New Critical procedures. None the less, the New Criticism was not exclusive in the middle years of the century, and work was done in this area, though it was chiefly, like Stevenson's and Beach's, on poetry. Alfred Tennyson, for obvious reasons as a poet explicitly interested in the significance and problems of science, was a frequent subject.[3] Douglas Bush in *Science and English Poetry: A Historical Sketch, 1590–1950* (1950), and Georg Roppen in *Evolution and Poetic Belief: A Study in Some Victorian and Modern Writers* (1956), focused more or less exclusively on poetry, though Roppen glanced at fiction by Thomas Hardy and Samuel Butler. Roppen was interested in how writers' beliefs about religion, metaphysics and morals related to, or were expressed in terms of, scientific ideas in the nineteenth century. Again, his concern was with the question of how and what literature borrowed for its own purposes from science.

HENKIN'S *DARWINISM IN THE ENGLISH NOVEL* (1940)   The only significant exception as a work on fiction during this period was Leo Henkin's *Darwinism in the English Novel, 1860–1910* (1940). Henkin, looking for direct commentary on science in fiction, divided his study into two sections. In the first part, he considered the influence of Darwin on religious beliefs and examined the literature of faith and doubt that reflected this. 'Evolution in science meant revolution in religion', he said, and the 'literature which chose to reflect to these earnest Victorians spiritual doubts by which untold thousands were beset, and a spiritual conflict in which blast and counter-blast sounded in earshot of all, was bound to appeal with all the force of the intimately personal and intimately familiar.' In the second section, he examined the popular scientific romances of the second half of the century, arguing that 'the Victorian passion for science and practical information guaranteed a constant demand for popular literature in the form of the evolutionary novel. "To the world of the 1880's the story of life, of the origin and branching out of species, of the making of continents, was still the most inspiring of the new romances." The Victorian generations that had formed the Mechanics Institutes, the Mutual Improvement Societies, the Athenaeums, and Philosophical Institutions were able to stomach meaty dishes; but the tasty stew of mixed science and romance purveyed by the novel proved especially palatable.'[4] Henkin analysed literary responses to Darwin of a clearly thematic kind, and was specially interested in satire. He covered a wide range of major and minor fiction, seeking out all explicit comments about modern science in his two sections.

As historicism asserted itself in areas of the academy in the 1970s, the study of the relationship of Victorian novels to science grew in importance. While it established itself across the international field of Victorian studies, the question of the nature of this relationship came to be the major feature of the methodological debate. In relating literature to science, critics in the 1980s accepted the existence of relationships between the two, but *how* did literature and science correspond? Stevenson thought in terms of borrowing, but was this an adequate paradigm? What model of literature's place in the

culture, and science's, could prove more satisfactory for reading the correspondences between science and the novel, between the discourse of empirical
science and that of imaginative prose fiction (or of any literary practice)? The
history of work on science and the novel in nineteenth-century studies in the
1980s saw influential answers to these questions.

Important work in the 1980s on the relation of science to fiction in the
nineteenth century began with Tess Cosslett's *The 'Scientific Movement' and
Victorian Literature* (1982).[5] This started life as a doctoral thesis on the poetry
of George Meredith.[6] Much new work on Victorian science and literature, in
fact, was done originally in the context of historicist doctorates. This indicates
the extent of the empirical material that had to be recovered by intense
archival activity before new arguments could be offered about the interplay
of science and literature. Cosslett's book, covering both poetry and fiction,
was dedicated to dissolving the idea that science and literature were two
markedly different and conflicting activities in the Victorian period. Cosslett,
who later edited the Cambridge University Press anthology on *Science and
Religion in the Nineteenth Century* (1984), referred to U. C. Knoepflmacher's
statement in the introduction to his co-edited collection *Nature and the
Victorian Imagination* (1977) that 'the imagination of the scientist and the
artist never coalesced'[7] in the Victorian period. This she repudiated by
demonstrating strong points of interrelationship. But the relationships were
not merely the borrowings from science that concerned Stevenson. Cosslett
insisted that literature transacted with science in the period, but also that
science was concerned with aspects of human experience associated with the
literary. It was not a cold, materialistic activity as some of its Victorian critics
believed, but one concerned with 'our sense for conduct and beauty, and
touched with emotion'.[8] Science in the nineteenth century was preoccupied
with values, and, as such, it intersected with the terrain of literature.

Cosslett saw science and literature as pursuing similar questions. But in
practice her critical methodology presupposed the priority of science. She was
interested in writers' responses to scientific ideas first and foremost, and
literature was reactive to science in her model. She showed some of the
'ways in which the values and the world view of the prevailing scientific
culture were [...] implicitly assimilated into a wide range of literature',[9] and
literature was seen as taking science on board, absorbing it (or at times
resisting it). Specifically, Cosslett saw science relating to a number of key
'values' that were reflected in literature: these comprised 'truth', 'law', 'kinship
with nature', 'organic interrelation' and 'scientific imagination'. She discussed
ways in which two novelists, Thomas Hardy and George Eliot, registered or
resisted these ideas. On Hardy, she looked at his dramatization of the
'uncomfortable gap between the two ways Victorian sciences related man to

COSSLETT'S
WORK ON
OVERLAPS OF
SCIENCE AND
LITERATURE

Nature – conscious, intelligent observation, and evolutionary kinship to the most primitive, unconscious forms of life',[10] concluding that he eventually assimilated the findings of evolutionary science into his pessimistic world view. Cosslett's book was important in revising the traditional map of knowledges in Victorian culture, showing for the first time evidence of a rich overlap between contemporary science and the domain of fiction.

Another useful overview that charted correspondences of ideas between science and literature followed in the form of J. A. V. Chapple's *Science and Literature in the Nineteenth Century* (1986). Peter Morton's *The Vital Science: Biology and the Literary Imagination 1860–1900* (1984) came two years after Cosslett and was more focused. It narrowed the field of investigation to a more specific area: a life science and Darwin. Morton's view of the way literature connected with science was cognate with Stevenson's notion of literature transforming 'hard' scientific information into aesthetically pleasing and imaginatively contoured material. Morton believed that novelists 'searched among the data of the life sciences and found material peculiarly susceptible to imaginative transformation'.[11]

BEER ON
DARWIN AND
FICTION
Morton's focus on Darwin prepared the ground for the most significant work of the early 1980s: Gillian Beer's book, which studied the influence of Darwin's *Origin of Species* (1859) on the form and intellectual project of fiction by Eliot and Hardy, *Darwin's Plots: Evolutionary Narrative in Darwin, George Eliot and Nineteenth-century Fiction* (1983, second edition, 2000). This was one of the most significant critical books on Victorian fiction to appear in the 1980s: in England, it made the relations between science and the Victorian novel a major academic subject, just as it made Gillian Beer's name. Beer continued Cosslett's argument against the division of science and literature into two conflicting enterprises in the nineteenth century and deepened it. She was interested in novelists who read the new scientific works, in a culture where serious science was more accessible to non-scientific readers than in ours, and in the way in which Darwinian ideas and narrative forms migrated during that reading, understood or misunderstood, into literary work. She argued that Darwin struggled to articulate his ideas in language that was accessible, using familiar terms and metaphors to articulate unfamiliar concepts and such familiar language assisted in the prolific expansion of Darwinian concepts in the culture.

Beer considered how the superfluity of Darwin's ideas about history, growth, calamity, metaphor, analogy, comedy, tragedy, and the position of the human in the natural world corresponded to fiction at the level of structure, ideas and language. She concentrated on George Eliot and Thomas Hardy, looking for correspondences that were the product of the migration of unruly metaphors and concepts between evolutionary science and the novel. In a later essay on Darwin and late Victorian fiction entitled

'Origins and Oblivion in Victorian Narrative' (1986), Beer explained the methodology of her essay. Her words served as a description of her book as well. She said:

> My project does not use the metaphor of 'background,' with literature as the foreground and all other writing as a system of clues that will give access to literary experience. Rather, I [...] examine creative narratives such as those of the geologist Sir Charles Lyell, Darwin, or the philologist Max Muller, and Winwood Reade, *alongside* Victorian works of fiction.[12]

This practice of positioning scientific writing beside fiction and exposing coincidences and commonalities implied, though Beer did not develop the idea, an equivalence between the discourses of science and literature that was made explicit in the work of George Levine.

Beer's book highlighted the way in which evolutionary science related to the form of Victorian fiction. The major debate about form prior to the 1980s (as discussed on pp. 213–25) was the question of unity. Beer argued that interrelations of theme and plot in George Eliot's work were part of its shared exchange with Darwin's concept of the web of affinities, the interlinking relations of the organic world that were a source of wonder to the Victorians. The organicism explored by Eliot was thus identified as culturally specific. Beer's approach challenged Catherine Belsey's reading of organic form as an expression of bourgeois ideology (see pp. 121–32) and provided a way of approaching the complex plots of Victorian fiction and their relation to biological science that has now become widely accepted.

The extract below, from the third section of the book, provides an example of the kind of criticism Beer pursued in *Darwin's Plots*. Here, she maps correspondences between George Eliot's *Middlemarch* (1871–2) and ideas from Darwin and other mid-period scientists including Eliot's partner, George Henry Lewes, revealing common ground, shared ideas, and the community of language between writers.

Extract from Gillian Beer, *Darwin's Plots: Evolutionary Narrative in Darwin, George Eliot and Nineteenth-century Fiction* (London: Routledge and Kegan Paul, 1983), 149–56.

George Eliot was often taken to task by contemporary reviewers for the persistent scientific allusions in her works. Henry James, indeed, complained that '*Middlemarch* is too often an echo of Messrs. Darwin and Huxley.'[1] And R. H. Hutton objected to her use of the word 'dynamic' in the opening sentences of *Daniel Deronda* as being pedantically over-scientific: 'Was she beautiful or not beautiful? and what was the secret of form or expression which gave the dynamic quality to her glance?'[2] The surprise that any modern reader is likely to feel at Hutton's particular objection should alert us to the degree to which language that has now lost its scientific bearing still bore a freight of controversy and assertion for George Eliot and her first readers. If, in the light of James's remark, one turns to the Prelude to *Middlemarch* words that may now read as flat generality renew their powers of controversy.[3] The concluding paragraph asserts ironically the problems of treating the social lot of women:

> if there were one level of feminine incompetence as strict as the ability to count three and no more, the social lot of women might be treated with scientific certitude. Meanwhile the indefiniteness remains, and the limits of variation are really much wider than any one would imagine from the sameness of women's coiffure and the favourite love-stories in prose and verse. (1;1:2–3)

To take up only one of several possible words from that passage: 'variation'. 'The limits of variation' are part of the controversy about species and about how far it is possible to describe species through their characteristics. They are part also of that argument about whether resemblances of appearance and use could count as 'real affinities' or as 'analogical or adaptive resemblances' – resemblances brought about, that is, by a common response to the pressures of environment. Although the example that Darwin uses is remote from George Eliot's, the argument follows the same course: 'The resemblance, in the shape of the body and in the fin-like anterior limbs, between the dugong, which is a pachydermatous animal, and the whale, and between both these mammals and fishes, is analogical.'[4] Response to environment can make very diverse creatures look and behave alike: 'the limits of variation are really much wider than any one would imagine from the sameness of women's coiffure.'

Within each species, in Darwin's argument, *variation* is the key to evolutionary development. Diversification, not truth to type, is the creative principle, as he emphasises throughout the first chapter of *The Origin of Species* whose title is 'Variation Under Domestication'. George Eliot takes the word 'variation', in which so much current controversy is moving and applies it to 'the social lot of women':

'variation under domestication' is for them a difficult endeavour. So her use of the phrase 'limits of variation' is a polemical signal which harbinges much for the 'domestic epic' she is about to present.

Some of her critics appreciated this weighting of words with the fullest concerns of the time – those concerns in which emotion and intellect are not kept apart but most completely imply each other. Colvin commented in these terms on her use of medical knowledge and imagery in *Middlemarch*,[5] and Edward Dowden, in particular, seized upon the implications for language of the turmoil of scientific ideas and hypotheses current in the period:

> She has actually employed in a work of fiction such words as 'dynamic' and 'natural selection', at which the critic picks up his delicate ears and shies. ...Language, the instrument of literary art, is an instrument of ever-extending range, and the truest pedantry, in an age when the air is saturated with scientific thought, would be to reject those accessions to language which are the special gain of the time. Insensibility to the contemporary movement in science is itself essentially unliterary.... The cultured imagination is affected by it, as the imagination of Spenser's time was affected by his use of the neo-classical mythology of the Renaissance.[6]

The comparison with Spenser is particularly just and telling. The acquired cultural language of science, like that of neo-classical allusion, offers a controlled range of imaginative consequences shared by writer and first readers. It offers an imaginative shift in the valency of words, new spaces for experience to occupy in language, confirmation of some kinds of vocabulary, increased prowess of punning, in which diverse senses are held in equipoise within the surveillance of consciousness. These effects register a moment when a particular discourse has reached its fullest range. It can then suggest new bearings for experiences which had earlier seemed quite separate from each other. At such moments of transposition emotion can find its full extent in language.

One can find specific sources in scientific writing of the time for certain famous passages in *Middlemarch*: for example the imaginative reach of Lydgate's scientific exploration:

> But these kinds of inspiration Lydgate regarded as rather vulgar and vinous compared with the imagination that reveals subtle actions inaccessible by any sort of lens, but tracked in that outer darkness through long pathways of necessary sequence by the inward light which is the last refinement of Energy, capable of bathing even the ethereal atoms in its ideally illuminated space. (1:16:249)

G. H. Lewes quotes the following passage from John Tyndall in *Problems of Life and Mind*:

> Indeed the domain of the senses in Nature is almost infinitely small in comparison with the vast region accessible to thought which lies beyond them. From a few observations of a comet when it comes within the range of his telescope, an astronomer can calculate its path in regions which no telescope can reach; and in like manner, by means of data furnished in the narrow world of the senses, we can make ourselves at home in other and wider worlds, which can be traversed by the intellect alone.[7]

The complex of ideas (intellect outgoing instruments, heat and energy as images of the productive and transforming powers, the vastness and plurality of the words beyond the reach of unaided sense) is shared by the two writers.

Like Tyndall, George Eliot emphasises the congruity between all the various processes of the imagination: the novelist's and the scientist's enterprise is fired by the same prescience, the same willingness to explore the significance even of that which can be registered neither by instruments nor by the unaided senses; the same willingness to use and to outgo evidence. At the end of his Rede lecture, Tyndall remarks that

> It is thought by some that natural science has a deadening influence on the imagination...But the experience of the last hour must, I think, have convinced you, that the study of natural sciences goes hand in hand with the culture of the imagination. Throughout the greater part of this discourse we have been sustained by this faculty. We have been picturing atoms and molecules and vibrations and waves which eye has never seen nor ear heard, and which can only be discerned by the exercise of imagination.[8]

The imagery of transcendence, of the invisible world, is one which George Eliot shares. The microscope and the telescope, by making realisable the plurality of worlds, scales, and existences beyond the reach of our particular sense organisation were a powerful antidote to that form of positivism which refused to acknowledge possibilities beyond the present and apparent world. They were permitting factors in that particular strain of Romantic materialism – a sense of the clustering mystery of a material universe – which is dominant in both the scientific writing and the literature of the period. Far from eschewing mystification, the extension of possibility through scientific instruments and scientific hypothesis-making actually gave at this time a fresh authority to the speculative and even to the fictive. Projects cannot rest in the present – they rely upon extension and futurity.

Perhaps better known as an example of George Eliot's 'scientific' discourse is the close parallel between her famous passage on the limits of sensibility in chapter 20 and T. H. Huxley's essay 'The Physical Basis of Life,' published in *The Fortnightly Review*, February 1869, which illustrates the dullness of human senses in this way:

> the wonderful noonday silence of a tropical forest is, after all, due only to the dullness of our hearing; and could our ears catch the murmur of those tiny Maelstroms, as they whirl in the innumerable myriads of living cells which constitute each tree, we should be stunned, as with the roar of a great city.[9]

In *Middlemarch* we read:

> That element of tragedy which lies in the very fact of frequency, has not yet wrought itself into the coarse emotion of mankind; and perhaps our frames could hardly bear much of it. If we had a keen vision and feeling of all ordinary human life, it would be like hearing the grass grow and the squirrel's heart beat, and we should die of that roar which lies on the other side of silence. (1.20:297–8)

In that same essay, 'The Physical Basis of Life', Huxley draws attention to the religious panic experienced by many in the face of material explanations, and compares it to Max Müller's explanation of 'solar myth'.

> The consciousness of this great truth weighs like a nightmare, I believe, upon many of the best minds of these days. They watch what they conceive to be the progress of materialism, in such fear and powerless anger as a savage feels, when, during an eclipse, the great shadow creeps over the face of the sun. The advancing tide of matter threatens to drown their souls; the tightening grasp of law impedes their freedom; they are alarmed lest man's moral nature be debased by the increase of his wisdom.[10]

He claims that far from demeaning the world, scientific materialism *extends* the range of connectedness within the natural order, even while it inhibits 'spirit and spontaneity'.

To come closer to home (and to destabilise the question of priority) consider this passage from G. H. Lewes's series of articles for the *Fortnightly Review* in 1868 on 'Mr. Darwin's Hypotheses':

> Let us for a moment glance at the resemblances and diversities observable in all organisms. All have a *common basis*, all being constructed out of the same fundamental elements: carbon, hydrogen, nitrogen and oxygen... Beside this community of *Substance* we must now place a community of *History*.[11]

Lewes's argument draws upon the work particularly of Claude Bernard, which has succeeded that of Bichat (Lydgate's mentor):

> That great Frenchman first carried out the conception that living bodies, fundamentally considered, are not associations or organs which can be understood by studying them first apart, and then as it were federally; but must be regarded as consisting of certain primary webs or tissues, out of which the various organs – brain, heart, lungs, and so on – are compacted... This great seer did not go beyond the consideration of the tissues as ultimate facts in the living organism, marking the limit of anatomical analysis; but it was open to another mind to say, have not these structures some common basis from which they have all started, as your sarsnet, gauze, net, satin and velvet from the raw cocoon? (*Middlemarch* 1:15:223–4)

The phrase *common basis*, which Lewes italicises, is used again for the *Middlemarch* passage in a very similar context and in the light of Lewes's analysis of the several 'organogens', we understand more precisely why Lydgate's question 'What was the primitive tissue?' does not put the problem 'quite in the way required by the awaiting answer'.

There is not one 'primitive tissue', just as there is not one 'key to all mythologies'. Lewes diverged from Darwin's history on one major point: the idea of the single progenitor. He postulated instead that 'the earth at the dawn of Life was like a vast germinal membrane, every diversified point producing its own vital form'. This emphasis upon plurality, rather than upon singleness, is crucial to the developing argument of *Middlemarch* which, with all its overtly taxonomic ordering, has as its particular deep counter-enterprise the establishment of individual diversity beneath ascribed typologies: 'the favourite love-stories in prose and verse'.

Middlemarch is a work that draws attention to its own organisation; the naming of the individual books emphasises categorisation ('Waiting for Death', 'Two Temptations', 'Three Love Problems'). But the process of reading leads into divergence and variability. Even while we are observing how closely human beings conform in the taxonomy of event we learn how differently they feel and think. For Dorothea and Casaubon waiting for death means something very different from what it means for Mary Garth and Featherstone. The *relations* are different. The distances between people are different. Lydgate, here at one with the project of the book, 'longed to demonstrate the more intimate relations of living structure' (1:15:225). In this double emphasis on conformity and variability George Eliot intensifies older literary organisations by means of recent scientific theory. In Darwinian theory, variability is the creative principle, but the type makes it possible for us to track common ancestry and common kinship. It makes it possible also for us to assess the degree to which common environment bends creatures unlike each other to look alike.

In the Victorian period the Romantic search for the 'One Life' had been set back in time and become a search for origins. In *Middlemarch* 'relations' and 'origins' are set in a particular historical sequence: 'Beside this community of Substance we must now place a community of History'. In George Eliot's later novels we have an imagination permeated by scientific ideas and speculations, an imagination which can achieve what Wordsworth looked towards in the second Preface to the *Lyrical Ballads*. Incarnation summarises all that is most difficult for her and rewarding to her as a novelist. As Dowden implies George Eliot both registered and extended the imaginative and emotional implications that current scientific discovery and practice carried for her culture. She draws on the 'vital influence of the period' so that she responds to shared anxieties, moves within shared controversies, and creates a reader alert equally to the scientific potential of everyday language and to the everyday potential of scientific terminology: as in that word 'dynamic' or as in the almost obliterated scientific reference implicit in Dowden's own phrase 'vital influence'. This communality and novelty of system and of enquiry is essential to her project.

In indicating specific parallels and sources which draw on the writing of scientists, it is important to emphasise that this is not a matter simply of discrete passages which struck her attention (though clearly some did that). Rather, it is an engagement with the controversies and enquiries of which those texts are themselves a part. Within all these controversies two precepts are persistently presented, criticised, celebrated: 'The power of nature is the power of motion', and 'Evolution is the universal process.' The two principles are understood as inter-extensive. The universality of both laws and their preoccupation not with replication but with change are seen as mutually confirmatory. Both laws carry within them many of the properties expressed particularly by narrative: extension of time: sequence; shifting relations; complex movement from one phase to another. The two laws diverge in one important way – movement does not necessarily imply transformation or change. Evolution does. In *Middlemarch* the historical aspect of both laws is expressed: individuals are trapped in the determined pace of successive historical moments. Particularly in *Daniel Deronda* George Eliot springs the argument of the book on the contradiction between untransformed extension and irreversible change and development.

In the preface to *Roderick Hudson*, published in the same year as *Daniel Deronda* (1876) Henry James recognised the problems for the artist because 'Really, universally, relations stop nowhere' but he interpreted his duty as being not to reproduce this process but, 'by a geometry of his own', to interfere with it and find a satisfying means of enclosing 'the continuity of things' which is 'the whole matter with him'.

> Really, universally, relations stop nowhere, and the exquisite problem of the artist is eternally but to draw, by a geometry of his own, the circle within which they shall happily appear to do so. He is in the perpetual predicament that the continuity of things is the whole matter with him.

Even in James's vocabulary there is an underlying assumption that it is the scientific level which represents enduring actuality: 'really, universally'. The artist must create by means of a counter-fictior, which will contain that which is truly not to be contained. Through the geometric image of the circle or the round framing eye of microscope or telescope, a readable focus is achieved and enquiry can be both initiated and brought to a conclusion.

In *Middlemarch* George Eliot distinguished her enterprise from that of 'the great historian' Fielding with his 'copious remarks and digressions'.

> We belated historians must not linger after his example ... I at least have so much to do in unravelling certain human lots, and seeing how they were woven and interwoven, that all the light I can command must be concentrated on this particular web, and not dispersed over that tempting range of relevancies called the universe. (I:15:214)

The problems of a system of thought which promises 'no vestiges of a beginning ... no prospect of an end,' in the geologist Hutton's phrase, are being borne in on writers from the mid-nineteenth century on. In *The Mill on the Floss* George Eliot wrote in 1861: 'In natural science, I have understood, there is nothing petty to the mind that has a large vision of relations, as to which every single object suggests a vast sum of conditions. It is surely the same with the observation of human life.'[12] In the late novels however this infinite implication or infinite extension is perceived as at once alluring and yet artistically and existentially threatening. [...]

Notes

1   Henry James, in *Galaxy*, 15 (1873): 424–8.
2   R. H. Hutton, *Spectator*, 49 (1876): 1131–3.
3   All references to *Middlemarch* are to the Cabinet Edition, London, 1878.
4   Charles Darwin, *On the Origin of Species* (London: Murray, 1859), 410.
5   Sidney Colvin, *Fortnightly Review*, n.s. 13 (1873): 142–7.
6   Edward Dowden, *Contemporary Review*, 29 (1877): 348–69.
7   G. H. Lewes, *Problems of Life and Mind* (London, 1874): 261.
8   John Tyndall, *On Radiation* (London, 1865): 60–1.
9   T. H. Huxley, 'The Basis of Physical Life', *Fortnightly Review*, n.s. 5 (1869): 132.
10   Ibid., 143.
11   G. H. Lewes, 'Mr. Darwin's Hypotheses', *Fortnightly Review*, n.s. 4 (1868) 494.
12   *Mill on the Floss*, ed. G. Haight (Oxford, 1980): 238.

Beer's work in *Darwin's Plots* continues to be the most frequently cited study of science and the nineteenth-century novel. But it has not remained uninterrogated. In the first instance, Beer's privileging of Darwin and *On the Origin of Species*, excluded detailed study of other scientists in the period. It left a map of Victorian natural philosophy that seemed dominated by the life sciences and a single towering figure. Other scholars moved further into the plurality of sciences of the period, both heterodox and orthodox (and the early to mid-Victorian era was a time when such divisions were unstable).[13] Beer herself later regretted the exclusion of *Darwin's* other works, saying in the 'Preface' to the second edition that she should have considered *The Descent of Man* (1871) more extensively. She also said that she would have included, if writing the book now, 'the insights offered by [...] recent race and gender analysis'.[14] Furthermore, Beer emphasized the shared ground between science and literature, but her text left the periodic impression that science and literature were more or less the same thing. In breaking down the historical perception of the two cultural practices as separate, she sometimes went too far in the other direction and did not always discriminate between the discourses of empirical science and those of literature, nor preserve a sense of what was different, resistant and specific in each. In addition, although Beer's style was appealingly lucid, her mode was descriptive: some readers found it difficult to argue with her as her descriptions were self-evidently justified, but conceptual issues that arose from specific instances of correspondences were more difficult to discern.

Beer declared in her title that she was referring to 'nineteenth-century fiction', but her book looked only at two literary writers and gave the largest portion of its attention to the most scientifically literature of all mid-Victorian

SCIENCE AND LITERATURE READ ALONGSIDE EACH OTHER

novelists – George Eliot. Eliot was a prominent subject in other studies of science and the novel in the early 1980s, such as Tess Cosslett's *The 'Scientific Movement' and Victorian Literature* and Sally Shuttleworth's *George Eliot and Nineteenth-century Science: The Make-believe of a Beginning* (1984). In this, Shuttleworth argued that evolutionary science and the problematization of organic theory in psychology were important contexts in which Eliot's work was written and by which it was shaped. 'The traditional ideal of organic social harmony presented in *Adam Bede*', Shuttleworth wrote, comparing Eliot's first novel with her last:

> is reflected in the psychological theory, and in the unified, cyclical narrative structure of the work. *Daniel Deronda*, by contrast, portrays both a society and characters riven by contradiction, while the unified structure of the earlier work is supplanted by a more open and fragmented narrative form which disrupts both spatial and temporal continuity.

This change, Shuttleworth said, 'can be correlated with transformations in contemporary scientific theories of the organic' which saw a shift from continuity and unity to an acceptance of disruption and discontinuity.[15] Shuttleworth grounded the novels firmly in the psychological debate, but was less interested in literature's resistance to, or transformation of, science: science almost served in *George Eliot and Nineteenth-century Science* to 'account' for the fiction as its determining factor. Other writers examined further aspects of Eliot's scientific thinking in the 1980s: T. R. Wright, for instance, explored Eliot's interests in sociology and the positivism of Auguste Comte in *The Religion of Humanity: The Impact of Comtean Positivism on Victorian Britain* (1986).[16]

LEVINE'S STUDY OF NOVELISTS WHO DID NOT READ SCIENCE

George Eliot was naturally susceptible to contextual studies of literature and science. But could scholars interested in the relation of literature and science go beyond her and consider novelists who did not read science so extensively? This question was pertinent to George Levine in the mid-1980s, whose work on realism was discussed in chapter 4 (see pp. 98–119). Levine read *Darwin's Plots* in proof while researching at Cambridge University and it intersected with his own interests. His response came a few years later in *Darwin and the Novelists: Patterns of Science in Victorian Fiction* (1988), a book that was concerned with writers who were not as scientifically literate as George Eliot, novelists 'who probably did not know any science first hand, who could have been "influenced" by Darwin only indirectly'.[17] Such indirect influence was possible, Levine said, because scientific ideas were widely available in the Victorian period in journals, newspapers and popular lectures: Darwinian ideas were easily picked up second hand. This view of the mobility of evolutionary concepts in the period allowed Levine to consider the evolutionary elements in work from a wide range of novelists whose expertise in science was considerably less than Eliot's. Even the work of the 'unscientific Trollope', he said provocatively, related to evolutionary ideas to a great extent: indeed, Levine made him 'my central example of Darwinian novelist [*sic*]'.[18] Relevant to this argument was Trollope's uniformitarianism, his belief in 'the English traditions of precedent and convention that [...] leave no space for abrupt violations of the social or natural order',[19] which Levine saw fitting with a Darwinian emphasis on continuity unbroken by catastrophe.

Levine's book theorized more explicitly than Shuttleworth's or Beer's how science and literature were culturally related. Beer and Shuttleworth provided accounts of how specific relationships worked, but Levine took a step backwards from textual analysis to propose a model of the relationship itself. In 1987, he edited a collection entitled *One Culture: Essays in Science and Literature*, and this title indicated the assumptions behind *Darwin and the Novelists*: science and literature were equal discourses and the former assumed no priority in the culture. 'Science', Levine said in *Darwin and the Novelists*:

> as I discuss it here, is a shared cultural discourse, 'a cultural formation,' as Michel Serres believes, 'equivalent to any other.' Although it certainly has been privileged, both in Victorian times and in some quarters even in our own, as an activity somehow exempt from the scepticism to which almost all other cultural discourse is subject, it works with the culture and responds to its exigencies. Internalist histories of science are surely necessary, but they go only part way in elucidating how science develops and, in particular, what sort of interplay between scientific and nonscientific discourses characterise their mutual development. Katherine Hayles seems to me exactly right when she argues that '*both* literature and science are cultural products, at once expressing and helping to form the cultural matrix from which they emerge.'[20]

This was a more explicit theorization than previously of the relationship between the two cultural activities. Levine's paradigm – which was not, clearly, original to him – remains powerful. It was, however, critiqued significantly in the 1990s. No one now wants to return to the idea of science and literature as two entirely separate cultural practices, but scholars in the 1990s recovered a greater sense than suggested by Levine's one-culture model of their generic and cultural specificity.

The following extract from Levine's work gives an outline of the themes pursued in his book, and a summary of the scientific concepts, issues and motifs he saw connecting with prose fiction, and registered in a range of Victorian novels. The correspondences of these ideas between the literary and the scientific indicated for Levine the *one culture* that existed (and exists) in a community, and the discoursal interrelations of both science and literature.

Extract from George Levine, *Darwin and the Novelists: Patterns of Science in Victorian Fiction* (Chicago: University of Chicago Press, 1991, first pub. 1988), 13–20.

[...] What I am after is a sort of gestalt [shape or structure] of the Darwinian imagination, a gestalt detectable in novels as well as in science; and no simple list of 'Darwinian' ideas will quite suffice to evoke it. Nevertheless, the Darwinian gestalt includes several clearly identifiable ideas, whose presence might be recognized anywhere, and certain fundamental attitudes toward science and toward the study of life that, if not exclusively Darwinian, were essential to Darwin's project. These ideas recur throughout the arguments of [*Darwin and the Novelists*], and it will be useful here briefly to intimate what they are, how they work within Darwin's argument, and how they manifest themselves in the fiction.

The human subject. Part of the Darwinian enterprise was to create a theory that would be recognized as 'scientific' within already acceptable terms for science, which Darwin had found most attractively formulated in John Herschel's *Preliminary Discourse on the Study of Natural Philosophy* (1830). What made Darwin's work problematic both for lay and scientific culture at the time was the attempt to apply scientific procedures appropriate to stars and chemicals to biological phenomena, and particularly to the 'human': 'Precisely because he was extending science into an area that his contemporaries thought unsuitable,' writes Peter Bowler, 'he was determined to minimize the risk of being criticized on grounds of inadequate methodology.'[1] That is, the very attempt to be scientifically conservative was a radical act, and this doubleness is characteristic of the Darwinian imagination, and is implicit in even the most conservative nineteenth-century narrative. The patient, ostensibly detached registration of human character and behavior is an aspect of the Darwinian ethos central to the experience of the Victorian novel; it is part of a movement describing a new place for man in nature and tends to imply an ultimately material explanation for human behavior. As is evident in George Eliot's self-conscious commitment to the 'natural history' of agrarian life, it is potentially disruptive of established social and moral categories. Although we take for granted the strategies of representation within a third-person realist novel, there is nothing inevitable about those strategies. The classics of eighteenth-century fiction, for example, *Robinson Crusoe, Pamela, Tristram Shandy,* or even *Tom Jones,* all take a different view of the human experiences they describe. Even the third-person stance of the narrator of *Tom Jones* is deeply personalized, and the voice at its most solemn is not that of a scientist but of a moralist. Within Victorian fiction, novels that seem to resist the conventions of 'realism' – like *Wuthering Heights* – reject also that stance of third-person detachment through which the Victorian novelist seeks the authority of science in the recording of human life.[2]

Observation. The authority of science and its extension from natural phenomena to human was both a condition of Darwin's enterprise, and its consequence. The Baconian shift from traditional authority to the authority of experience (qualified by the self-conscious purgation of the idols that distort experience) was almost official dogma in the early nineteenth century, not least for Darwin himself. While recent study of Darwin makes clear that he was anything but a true Baconian in practice – 'his entire scientific accomplishment must be attributed not to the collection of facts, but to the development of theory'[3] – Darwin expressly insisted on the accumulation of facts, most notoriously in his *Autobiography.* His work, with its sometimes disingenuous style of patient and plodding detail, helped foster the illusion that the power of science, and hence its authority, lay in its self-denying surrender to observed fact.

Only the establishment of an authority alternative to religious tradition made it rhetorically possible to extend the rule of science to the human. And that authority was a rigorously defined 'experience' to be achieved through disinterested observation and experiment. Observation is the power that opens up the fact and subdues it into knowledge, and the disinterested observer is the true scientist. In nineteenth-century realist narrative not only is observation the primary source of the materials of the story, but the observer and the act of observation become increasingly the focus as much as the means of attention. The omniscient author convention – with its apparently unself-conscious directness of representation – does not inevitably treat the novelist's and narrator's activity of observation as unproblematic, and even when it seems to, it raises the problems of observation by filling narratives with unreliable spectators. It has become a commonplace of modern thought that the capacity to know is a form of power, as is evident in Fanny's story in *Mansfield Park* and in figures like Dickens's Jaggers and Tulkinghorn. The trick, as Darwin's own self-effacing strategies attest, is to avoid the exposure and thus the vulnerability that the act of observing normally if ironically entails. The peculiar Darwinian wrinkle in the scientific preoccupation with observation is that the observer becomes vulnerable, particularly because – as Darwin extends the rule of science from inorganic to organic phenomena – the observer also becomes the observed.

Uniformitarianism. I have already discussed briefly some aspects of this idea in its crossover from science to fiction. Novels as much as geology depended on the apparent plausibility conferred by the idea that all events can be explained causally, and by causes now in operation, and that extremes are to be regarded as the consequence of the gradual accumulation of the ordinary. Lyell's[4] uniformitarianism was meant as a sanction for secular scientific explanation against biblical authority. In its purest form, Darwinism broke from Lyell's essentially antihistorical position and implied development but without teleology.[5] The central tradition of Victorian realism – as we can see it in such different writers as Eliot and Trollope – adopts that form, although the pressure of teleological thinking can be detected in that tradition, just as it can in Darwin's own writing. Dickens tended to find thoroughgoing gradualism inadequate and often implied through his narratives the possibility of causes outside the secular. His complex relation to this idea is an important register of the culture's ambivalence about Darwinism and about the extension of scientific study to human history; and it suggests some of the limitations and contradictions within the realist project.

The scientifically conservative affirmations of authority implicit in these first three ideas were essential to Darwinism in part because his theory itself implied radical disruptions of epistemological, religious, and moral traditions. Again, it is not that Darwin's theory introduced such notions for the first time – far from it; nor is it that the disruption of tradition always worked against social, political, even religious stability. It was easy to *use* Darwinism to serve a multiplicity of antithetical purposes. But for the lay public, as well as for many scientists, Darwinism could be deeply threatening, and if [. . .] the lay model for understanding the natural and human world before Darwinism was natural theology, in any of its various forms, then Darwinism could indeed be seen as a radical dislocater of the culture's understanding of nature and of the self. It is certainly the case that most science before Darwin – Lyell's even in its resistance to biblical authority was no exception – could have been assimilated to natural theology. And in England, far more than on the continent, science and religion were allies (if sometimes nervously), many of the best known scientists themselves clergy. But the accumulated secular emphases of Darwin entailed other forms of compromise if religion were to avoid hostility to science.

Change and history. Obviously, the theme of change did not need Darwin to invent it. But in his world *everything* is always or potentially changing, and nothing can be understood without its history. Species, which had been conceived as permanent, transform into other species or are extinguished. The earth and all of its local ecological conditions are shifting. Traditionally, the more things change, the less 'real' – that is, ideal – they are, the more corrupt and corrupting. But in submitting all things to time, Darwin challenged the ideals of a permanent substratum of nature and of permanent categories of thought. Categories become fictions, historical and conventional constructions, mere stopgaps subject to the empirical. In realist narrative change and development become both subject and moral necessity, and they tend to be as well a condition of plausibility; character can only be understood fully if its history is known because character, as George Eliot wrote, is not 'cut in marble,' and it is intricately embedded in 'plot.' Moreover, closure is perceived as artificial and inadequate because it implies an end to history and is incapable of resolving the problems raised by the narrative. Conventional comic marriages are subjected to ironies of time and are often explicitly treated, as by Thackeray, as mere conveniences that allow books to end. The alternative tradition, as in a novel like *Jane Eyre* or in some of Dickens, provides closure and appropriate resolution to what has preceded. Here again, the most obvious and 'natural' aspects of fiction turn out to belong to a particular historical formation, and one that operates with great force theoretically and substantively in Darwin's theory.

Blurring of boundaries. The continuum of time is, in Darwin's world, an aspect of the continuum of life itself and of all other sharply defined categories. The boundaries between species and varieties blur, and the further Darwin carries his investigations the more this is the case. All living things in Darwin's world are quite literally related, and, as he will say in a variety of ways, graduate into each other. Isolated perfection is impossible, and science and fiction both concern themselves with mixed conditions. Fiction's emphasis on the ordinary and the everyday, its aversion to traditional forms of heroism and to earlier traditions of character 'types,' all reflect the tendency obvious in Darwin's world to deny permanent identities or sharply defined categories – even of good and evil. Note how rarely in Trollope or, more programatically, in Eliot, genuinely evil characters appear. Typical stories are of decline or of development; the case in Dickens, of course, is quite different. Character tends increasingly to be a condition of time and circumstance rather than of 'nature.' In Dickens, the tension between these two ways of imagining is reflected in his attempts to move in his later novels from characters whose natures are fixed to characters who, like Pip, appear to develop. Change, in Dickens's world, nevertheless tends to be radical and 'catastrophic,' rather than gradual; like Dombey, rather than like Pip.

Connections – ecological and genealogical. Darwin's world is, as the famous last extended metaphor of the *Origin* puts it, a 'tangled bank.' All living things are related in intricate and often subtle patterns of inheritance, cousinship, mutual dependence. Adaptation of organism to environment is not, as in natural theology, a consequence of a divine fiat, but a result of history – of organic and environmental changes. To discuss the life and nature of any organism requires discussion of the many others with whom it struggles, on whom it depends, in seemingly endless chains of connection. Victorian realist narratives equally entail complex and intricately inwoven stories of many figures so that it is often difficult to determine which characters are the true protagonists, which the subordinate ones. The Victorian multiplot novel is a fictional manifestation of the attitudes implicit in the metaphor of entanglement in Darwin. Such entanglement is an aspect of the gradualism discussed earlier and reflects a distrust of abrupt intrusions from outside the system such as one might find in 'metaphysical' fictions like, *Jane Eyre* or *Wuthering Heights*, whose narratives are also sharply focused on a small, defined set of characters.

Abundance. The ecological vision is connected with a view of a world bursting with life, always threatening overpopulation. In Darwin's world survival ultimately depends on variation and diversification, multiplicity of life and of kinds, some of which, from the vast and continuing waste and competition, will survive. Absence of diversity means vulnerability to change, and change is similarly a condition of life. The overpopulated worlds of the Victorian novel, those 'large, loose baggy monsters,' as James called them, are narrative equivalents of Darwin's 'endless forms, most beautiful, most wonderful.'[6] Like Darwin's theory itself, they reflect the Victorian taste for excess in ornamentation, the Victorian sense of a newly crowded and complicated life in which there were new opportunities for variety in possessions, art, relationships.

Denial of design and teleology. The Darwinian narrative unfolds 'naturally,' that is, without external intrusion. It is, as it were, self-propelled, unfolding according to laws of nature with no initiating intention and no ultimate objective. Adaptation, a key element in Darwinian as in natural-theological thought, seemed to imply design and intention, but Darwin had to show that it was merely 'natural.' His rejection of the natural-theological assumption of teleology fundamentally undercut the basis of most Western narrative. In the realist novel itself, certain conventional elements continue, willy-nilly, to imply teleology, but the movement is very clearly away from 'plot'; and the Trollopean determination to focus on characters and to let the plot emerge from their encounters is a characteristically Darwinian way to deal with narrative and change. The characters, like Darwinian organisms, learn to adapt to their environments. The explanation of that adaptation is not metaphysical but 'natural,' and the emphasis on psychology is a means to explanation. In character-oriented narrative, the events appear 'natural'; they grow from the posited conditions of the fictional world and do not seem to be imposed by the author. This Jamesian ideal was implicit in the realistic narratives James often criticized, and it disguised well the romance or mythic elements that Northrop Frye suggests are the ultimate source of all literary narrative. The growing nineteenth-century dissatisfactions with closure – the most marked and inevitable feature of 'plotting' – are further reflections of this Darwinian movement away from teleology and, as I have suggested, toward a new kind of emphasis on continuing change.

Mystery and order. In the multitudinous and entangled Darwinian world, order is not usually detectable on the surface, but the apparent disorder of nature is explicable to the keen observer in terms of general laws that can be inferred from phenomena. Similarly, the world of the realistic novel tends to be explanatory and analytic, showing that behavior is psychologically explicable and that events are 'probable,' that is, consistent with what might be regarded as empirical law, even if not strictly logical. Darwin's science aspired to the regularity of physics and astronomy, but in its biological preoccupation with individual differences could not achieve that. Nevertheless, Darwin demonstrates the regularity and comprehensibility of phenomena without reducing them to the strict form of logic and mathematics. On the contrary, 'metaphysical' fiction, corresponding to the modes of natural theology, tends to be very strictly and rationally ordered. (The symmetries of *Wuthering Heights* are perhaps the most obvious example.)[7] But no rational explanation can account for the order. Some force beyond nature is required. Full evidence for Darwin's theory is not immediately available, but the mysteries can be filled in by induction and extrapolation from the observable. In realistic fiction, similarly, mystery is merely a temporary gap in knowledge (despised by Trollope), but in metaphysical fiction, as in natural theology, mystery is the effect of a spiritual and inexplicable intrusion or initiation from outside of nature.

Chance. Darwin abjured chance but required it for his argument. Minute chance transformations are the source of all variations (Darwin could not explain the mechanism although he ventured a distinctly unsuccessful theory of 'gemmules' later in his career), which are the first steps in speciation. Realism is programatically antagonistic to chance, but like Darwin almost inevitably must use it to resolve its narrative problems. The complications of chance in Darwin's theory and in narrative will require extensive discussion (and speculation), but it is important to note that like Darwinian theory, realism tends to depend on the smallest of events and on psychological minutiae for its stories and for change within those stories. Moreover, chance encounters seem like intrusions from another mode when they occur in realistic narratives. By contrast, in 'metaphysical' fiction chance and coincidence play important roles, though almost invariably they seem not an intrusion from another mode but evidence of design and meaning in the world.

To some extent, all that follows in this book will expand this list and explain in some detail the complexities hidden in it. [...]

Notes

1 Peter Bowler, *Evolution: The History of an Idea* (Berkeley, Calif., 1984), 160.
2 Levine's fuller views on realism are detailed on pp. 98–119 above.
3 Michael Ghiselin, *The Triumph of the Darwinian Mind* (Chicago, 1984 edn), 4.
4 Charles Lyell (1797–1875), geologist, proposed the great antiquity of the world (in distinction from accounts in Genesis).
5 Teleology = view that developments are due to the purpose or design that is served by them.
6 Charles Darwin, *On the Origin of Species by Means of Natural Selection; or, The Preservation of Favoured Races in the Struggle for Life*, ed. J. W. Burrow (Harmondsworth, 1959).
7 For a view of the discontinuities of *Wuthering Heights*, see pp. 221–4 above.

DICKENS AND SCIENCE

One of the novelists who had significantly failed to appear in critical arguments before Levine's was Charles Dickens. Dickens's interests lay outside the domain of evolutionary science, and his reading in the life sciences was, compared with Eliot's, nugatory. Levine, concerned with novelists who had read little or no science, none the less thought evolutionary science *was* a relevant context for Dickens because, he argued, there was a potent Darwinian sense of the complexity of organic relationships in Dickens's fiction. He was 'the great novelist of entanglement, finding in the mysteries of the urban landscape those very connections of interdependence and genealogy that characterise Darwin's tangled bank'.[21] Levine argued that the formal characteristics of Dickens's multi-plot novels could, like Eliot's, be related to the scientific environment. He also revealed how other scientific concepts were relevant for Dickens, especially ideas of entropy and the laws of thermo-dynamics. Anxieties about the death of the sun and the irreversible decay of the earth's useful energies were attractive to his imagination, said Levine, especially in *Little Dorrit*, with its world of 'entropic decline'.[22] Prior to Levine, other scholars had looked beyond mainstream evolutionary theory for germane scientific contexts for Dickens's novels, including Fred Kaplan. Kaplan's *Dickens and Mesmerism: The Hidden Springs of Fiction* (1975) considered the role of mesmerism (or animal magnetism as it was also known) in Dickens's life and work, proposing that the novelist found in this highly popular but, for many, quack science, 'a terminology and a series of related images through which to express his major perceptions'.[23] Other discussions of Dickens's relationship to scientific practices include Helen Small's work on *Great Expectations*, discussed below.

After Levine's book, scholars working in the now major field of science and literature struck out in new directions. The privileging of Darwin came under scrutiny. Critics working in the 1990s looked at the term 'science' and reminded us of its blandness as an over-generalized category for the multifarious activities in lecture theatres, laboratories, universities, industries, and hospital wards in the nineteenth century. Walter Pater said in *Plato and Platonism* (1893) that modern thought was multiple, kaleidoscopic in its variety: the present, he said, is 'a time so rich and various in special apprehensions of truth'.[24] This certainly applied to the development of the sciences. Biology, increasingly attentive to evolutionary modes of thinking, developed from the mid-century onwards besides mathematics, medicine, the mind sciences and especially psychology, engineering, physics and chemistry. Branches of empirical inquiry organized and professionalized themselves into the categories with which we are familiar today. Literary scholars in the 1990s, acknowledging this diversity of empirical investigation, were interested in particular in the mind sciences, most obviously overlapping with the psychological territory of the Victorian novel, and with forms of mental or physical pathology.

Pathology surfaced as a subject in the critical community in the last decade of the twentieth century with two important texts. Miriam Bailin's work on *The Sickroom in Victorian Fiction: The Art of Being Ill* (1994) gave the general issue of sickness in Victorian novels critical prominence. Bailin was interested in the symbolic meaning of the sickroom and scene of illness, discussing the narrative effects and the cultural implications of the sickroom scene, employed as a 'cure for self and narrative incoherence'[25] in Victorian fiction. Athena Vrettos's *Somatic Fictions: Imagining Illness in Victorian Culture* (1995), following a year later, was a wide-reaching study that examined the discourses of illness throughout the period, with a feminist dimension. Vrettos brought novels by Charlotte Brontë, Elizabeth Gaskell, George Eliot, Henry James, Louisa M. Alcott, Harriet Beecher Stowe, George Meredith, Bram Stoker and

1990s'
INTEREST IN
PATHOLOGY
AND MIND
SCIENCES

H. Rider Haggard into the context of diverse discussions of illness in the period, in order to consider how sickness, especially psychosomatic illness, was invested with cultural meaning.

HELEN SMALL
AND LOVE'S
MADNESS

Helen Small took the study of pathology into a more specific area: madness. *Love's Madness: Medicine, the Novel, and Female Insanity 1800–1865* (1996) investigated the relationship between a particular literary convention – the love-mad woman – in fiction from 1800 to 1865 and developments in medicine and the treatment of mental disease. Her study thus connected with the writing of Sandra Gilbert and Susan Gubar, and Elaine Showalter, discussed in chapter 3. But Small's approach was more historicized and did not include a frame of radical feminism. She argued that the languages for describing love's madness in fiction and medicine were closely related to the rhetoric of sentimentality at the beginning of the nineteenth century. But, as

SMALL'S
CRITIQUE OF
THE 'ONE-
CULTURE'
MODEL

the period moved on, the discourses diverged partly because medicine dramatically reorganized and professionalized its practices for the study of mental disorders and partly as a result of a decline in the cultural place of sensibility: 'The attack on sensibility helped change a climate in which medicine and fiction had [once] shared much the same language and the same assumptions.' The result of these forces was, in the middle of the nineteenth century, that there was no longer a mutually supporting language between medicine and the novel for the depiction of love's madness. Small's study, which included discussion of popular sensation fiction, Charlotte Brontë's *Jane Eyre*, Wilkie Collins's *The Woman in White*, and Charles Dickens's *Great Expectations*, was interested in what it meant to speak of the relationship between literature and science and their common ground in the Victorian period. But, she argued, in the fields of fiction and medical ideas about the insane, the relationship was one of growing separation. *Love's Madness* thus comprised the first significant critique of Levine's idea of one culture.

SALLY
SHUTTLE-
WORTH ON
PSYCHOLOGY

Other work on the mind and its pathologies in the 1990s included Sally Shuttleworth's. After her investigation of Eliot and organicism in *George Eliot and Nineteenth-century Science* (1984), Shuttleworth considered the development of psychology as a clinical practice in the Victorian period. Parts of Shuttleworth's preliminary work were published in her contribution to Levine's *One Culture* as an essay on '"The Surveillance of a Sleepless Eye": The Constitution of Neurosis in *Villette*',[26] but its final form came with *Charlotte Brontë and Victorian Psychology* (1996). Shuttleworth worked against a view of the Brontë sisters as solitary and isolated writers, whose fictions sprang from peculiarly gifted but lonely imaginations, and who were separated, in seclusion in Haworth Parsonage, from dominant intellectual debates, including scientific ones. She insisted on the embeddedness of their fiction, especially Charlotte's, in contemporary ideas about psychology, phrenology and modern economics, arguing that the sisters were familiar with these topics through lectures on the local Haworth circuit, press articles and trial accounts, and even from advertisements for medical remedies. Shuttleworth, deploying Foucauldian methods, read Charlotte Brontë's fiction as both assimilating and challenging prevalent notions of selfhood and identity found in these contemporary discussions, and at all times relating to the 'language and preoccupations of mid-nineteenth-century social, psychological and economic thought'.[27]

Charlotte Brontë and Victorian Psychology revealed the early Victorian debates about female hysteria, the unconscious, and psychological drives that provided the context for Sigmund Freud. It unsettled the notion of Freud as a supreme originating authority whose ideas about the human personality had come from a vacuum. The indebtedness of Freudian psychoanalysis to a Victorian context, and the role of fiction in that context, was the theme of Carolyn Dever's study, *Death and the Mother from Dickens to Freud: Victorian Fiction and the Anxiety of Origins* (1998). Levine's argument about one culture had, of course, involved acceptance of the idea that science was shaped by the non-scientific, and Dever explored the implications of this by showing how prior fictional narratives of psychological development informed Freudian psychoanalysis. She argued that narratives about mothers, incapacitated, abandoning or dead in the Victorian novel, constructed maternal loss as a prerequisite for the representation of domestic life. This fictional paradigm helped shape Freud's assumptions about the necessities of metaphorically killing off the mother figure as a crucial part of a child's development into a properly functioning adult. Dever's focus on fiction included novels by Dickens, Wilkie Collins, George Eliot, and Virginia Woolf's *To the Lighthouse*. Her study was a significant investigation in the traffic of ideas moving the other way from those examined by scholars previously: the influence of literature on science.[28]

Peter Melville Logan considered territory discussed by Small in *Nerves and Narratives: A Cultural History of Hysteria in Nineteenth-century British Prose* (1997). He was mostly interested in Romantic period prose and its reaction to a new body that had appeared in Britain in the late eighteenth century. Logan's work was part of a widespread interest in the late 1980s and early 1990s in the body as a site of ideological inscription. That new eighteenth-century body was 'one marked by its susceptibility to hysteria and a host of related nervous conditions, variously called hypochondria, spleen, vapours, lowness of spirits, melancholia, bile, excess sensibility, or, simply, nerves'.[29] Part 3 concerned Victorian bodies, and examined developments that affected the earlier eighteenth-century idea and the cultural status of the hysteric. 'The nervous body' in the Victorian period, Logan said:

> was a paradigm that the middle class used to explain itself to itself and to differentiate itself from other classes. With the rise of the new urban working class, that self-definition underwent a change, and we can see that shift by

LOGAN ON HYSTERIA, WOOD ON NEUROLOGY

looking at the new discourse of public health, which arose as the medical science of the working-class body. In this new genre of middle-class discourse, the working class became the inheritor of the problem of an excessive environmental determinism. In comparison, the middle-class body appeared to be relatively healthy.[30]

Discussion was based around *Middlemarch* (for more on medicine and *Middlemarch*, see pp. 142–3).

The interest in mind sciences and/or pathologies in the 1990s continued into the new millennium. It was developed, though not in the context of Freudian analysis, by Jane Wood's study of Victorian fiction and neurology, *Passion and Pathology in Victorian Fiction* (2001). In its consideration of ideas about how fiction and a branch of medical science related, this added a further layer to Small's querying of the one-culture model by insisting on the discoursal specificity of fiction and neurology as they developed in the century. Wood's approach did not assume 'that beliefs and attitudes simply passed between [science and fiction] in a mutually confirming continuity'. Rather, she was interested in seeing where literature and science generated fiction that itself became the subject of consideration. 'One of the purposes of this book', she said, 'is to examine the ambivalences and the points of contention which were not just by-products – the inevitable fallout – of the exchange of ideas but were consciously addressed by medical writers and novelists alike.'[31] Wood, unpacking the implications of the relationship between fictional representations and discourses of mental pathology, including ideas of masculinity in the mid-period, considered novels by Harriet Martineau, Charlotte Brontë, George Eliot, examples of New Woman writing, George Gissing, and Thomas Hardy (for more on masculinity and the novel, see pp. 8–9).

Other books looking at related areas of fiction and illness/the body included Lucy Bending's interdisciplinary study, also interested in the body, *The Representation of Bodily Pain in Late Nineteenth-century English Culture* (2000). Bending argued that Victorian novels were awash with suffering. She explored late-Victorian discussions of fire-walking, tattooing, and flogging, to show the ways in which the experience of pain and its representation was affected by class, gender, race and notions of criminality.

EUGENICS AND THE NOVEL

An interest in Charles Darwin in the 1980s modified into a focus on mind sciences and pathologies in the 1990s that is still visible in work today. But more areas of scientific activity included beneath the umbrella term 'Victorian science' are now being considered. In the past few years, the late nineteenth-century science of eugenics, inspired by the implications of Darwin's *The Descent of Man* (1871), also began to be a subject of literary critical analysis. Work on this includes William Greenslade's *Degeneration, Culture and the Novel 1880–1940* (1994) and Angelique Richardson's forthcoming *The Eugen-*

ization of Love: Darwin, Galton and Late Nineteenth-century Fictions of Heredity and Eugenics. Richardson's preliminary ideas for this study have appeared in '"Some Science underlies all Art": The Dramatization of Sexual Selection and Racial Biology in Thomas Hardy's *A Pair of Blue Eyes* and *The Well-Beloved*' in the *Journal of Victorian Culture*, 3(2) (1998) and 'The Eugenization of Love: Sarah Grand and the Morality of Genealogy' in *Victorian Studies*, 42 (1999–2000).

The study of Victorian literature and law may gain in status over the next few years (see pp. 6–7 for a discussion of this). But work on fiction and science shows no sign of having reached a conclusion. Interdisciplinary criticism is a major feature of literary studies in the Anglo-American academy – indeed, some continue to demand that literary studies transforms itself into cultural studies to become interdisciplinary by definition – but cross-pollination between work in science and Victorian fiction has been a particular area of interdisciplinary significance for three decades. Collectively, it has made an indelible impression on the way in which the Victorian novel is read.

Chapter Notes

1 Lionel Stevenson, *Darwin Among the Poets* (Chicago: University of Chicago Press, 1932), 1.
2 *Wordsworth and Coleridge: Lyrical Ballads 1798*, ed. W. J. B. Owen, 2nd edn (Oxford: Oxford University Press, 1969), 168.
3 Tennyson's interest in science had been of interest to critics for many years. See N. and W. L. Lockyer, *Tennyson as a Student and Poet of Nature* (London: Macmillan, 1910).
4 Leo J. Henkin, *Darwinism in the English Novel 1860–1910: The Impact of Evolution on Victorian Fiction* (New York: Russell and Russell, 1963, first published 1940), 10.
5 Cosslett's title alluded to Edward Dowden's 1877 essay called 'The Scientific Movement and Literature'.
6 A. T. Cosslett, 'The Relation of Scientific Thought and Poetry, in the Poems of George Meredith', Oxford University D. Phil 1978.
7 Quoted in Tess Cosslett, *The 'Scientific Movement' and Victorian Literature* (Sussex: Harvester, 1982), 2.
8 Ibid.
9 Ibid., 3.
10 Ibid., 152.
11 Peter Morton, *The Vital Science: Biology and the Literary Imagination 1860–1900* (1984), 6.
12 Gillian Beer, 'Origins and Oblivion in Victorian Narrative' in Ruth Bernard Yeazell, ed., *Sex, Politics, and Science in the Nineteenth-century Novel: Selected*

Papers from the English Institute, 1983–84 (Baltimore and London: Johns Hopkins University Press, 1986), 65.

13   For a discussion of the shifting nature of such boundaries in the life sciences, see Alison Winter, 'The Construction of Orthodoxies and Heterodoxies in the Early Victorian Life Sciences,' in Bernard Lightman, ed., *Victorian Science in Context* (Chicago: University of Chicago Press, 1997), 24–50.

14   Gillian Beer, 'Preface' to the second edition of *Darwin's Plots* (Cambridge: Cambridge University Press, 2000), xxiv.

15   Sally Shuttleworth, *George Eliot and Nineteenth-century Science: The Make-believe of a Beginning* (Cambridge: Cambridge: Cambridge University Press, 1984), xii.

16   For another science investigated in relation to Eliot, see Jonathan Smith, 'The "Wonderful Geological Story": Uniformitarianism and *The Mill on the Floss*', *Papers on Language and Literature: A Journal for Scholars and Critics of Language and Literature*, 27 (1991), 430–52.

17   George Levine, *Darwin and the Novelists: Patterns of Science in Victorian Fiction* (Cambridge, MA: Harvard University Press, 1988), 3.

18   Ibid., [177].

19   Ibid.

20   Ibid., 3.

21   Ibid., 119.

22   Ibid., 165.

23   Fred Kaplan, *Dickens and Mesmerism: The Hidden Springs of Fiction* (Princeton, NJ: Princeton University Press, 1975), 240.

24   Walter Pater, *Plato and Platonism: A Series of Lectures*, 2nd edn (London: Macmillan, 1898), 156.

25   Miriam Bailin, *The Sickroom in Victorian Fiction: The Art of Being Ill* (Cambridge: Cambridge University Press, 1994), 1.

26   Sally Shuttleworth, '"The Surveillance of a Sleepless Eye": The Constitution of Neurosis in *Vilette*', in George Levine with Andrew Rausch, ed., *One Culture: Essays in Science and Literature* (Wisconsin: University of Wisconsin Press, 1987), 313–35.

27   Sally Shuttleworth, *Charlotte Brontë and Victorian Psychology* (Cambridge: Cambridge University Press, 1996), 2.

28   Catherine Tingle's doctorate at the University of Leeds, 'Symptomatic Writings: Prefigurations of Freudian Theories and Models of the Mind in the Fiction of Sheridan Le Fanu, Wilkie Collins, and George Eliot', unpublished PhD thesis (Leeds University, 2000), extended and developed the territory suggested by Dever's argument.

29   Peter Melville Logan, *Nerves and Narratives: A Cultural History of Hysteria in Nineteenth-century British Prose* (Los Angeles: University of California Press, 1997), 1.

30   Ibid., 4.

31   Jane Wood, *Passion and Pathology in Victorian Fiction* (Oxford: Oxford University Press, 2001), 1–2.

Further Reading

Gillian Beer, *Open Fields: Science in Cultural Encounter* (Oxford: Clarendon, 1996): wide-ranging selection of essays including Victorian science; especially good on Hopkins and on entropy.

Peter Allan Dale, *In Pursuit of a Scientific Culture: Science, Art, and Society in the Victorian Age* (Madison: University of Wisconsin Press, c. 1989).

Walter Gratzer, *The Longman Literary Companion to Science* (Harlow: Longman, 1989): general reader's anthology of extracts from literature about science.

Kelly Hurley, *The Gothic Body: Sexuality, Materialism, and Degeneration at the Fin de Siècle* (Cambridge: Cambridge University Press, 1996): see p. 10.

Catherine Judd, *Bedside Seductions: Nursing and the Victorian Imagination, 1830–1880* (Basingstoke: Macmillan, 1998): 'From the early to the mid-nineteenth century, the nurse develops as a category for perceptions about gender and class, consolidating for Victorian writers fundamental political and social anxieties – especially concerns over class conflict, public health, the Woman Question, female heroics, and the construction of middle-class sexuality. The overdetermined fascination nursing images generate points to the nurse's importance as a paradigm for imaginary resolutions to ideological problems faced by the mid-Victorians.'

Robert J. G. Lange, *Gender Identity and Madness in the Nineteenth-century Novel* (Lampeter: Mellen, 1998): psychobiological study with a simplified view of Victorian gender politics but useful bibliography. Argues that 'the language used by many nineteenth-century novelists to discuss and demonstrate gender issues was couched in a vocabulary of insanity, since no other vocabulary seemed adequate to reflect the conflict and turmoil manifest in these personal issues'.

George Levine, ed., *Realism and Representation: Essays on the Problem of Realism in Relation to Science, Literature, and Culture* (Madison/London: University of Wisconsin Press, 1993).

Laura Otis, *Membranes: Metaphors of Invasion in Nineteenth-century Literature, Science, and Politics* (Baltimore: Johns Hopkins University Press, 1999): examines how the image of the biological cell became one of the dominant metaphors of the period. At the heart of this account is the rise of a fundamental assumption about human identity: the idea that selfhood requires boundaries showing where the individual ends and the rest of the world begins.

James Paradis and Thomas Postlewait, *Victorian Science and Victorian Values: Literary Perspectives* (New Brunswick: Rutgers University Press, 1981): includes essays on 'Dickens and Victorian Dream Theory' (Catherine Bernard) and 'The Language of Science and Psychology in George Eliot's *Daniel Deronda*' (Sally Shuttleworth).

Rick Rylance, *Victorian Psychology and British Culture, 1850–1880* (Oxford: Oxford University Press, 2000): more psychological than literary, a discussion of the work of Alexander Bain, Herbert Spencer, George Henry Lewes, and the development of psychology, but does include discussion of George Eliot.

Elinor Shaffer, ed., *Comparative Criticism 13: Special Issue – Literature and Science* (Cambridge: Cambridge University Press, 1991)

Elinor Shaffer, *The Third Culture: Literature and Science* (New York: de Gruyter, 1998): omits serious consideration of the Victorian period, but there is some discussion of the general relations between literature and science, including Gillian Beer's consideration of the role of 'nature' in scientific arguments.

Sally Shuttleworth and Jenny Bourne Taylor, ed., *Embodied Selves: An Anthology of Psychological Texts, 1830–1890* (Oxford: Clarendon, 1998): areas covered include: phrenology and mesmerism; theories of dreams, memory, and the unconscious; female and male sexuality; insanity and nervous disorders; theories of degeneration. Texts are chosen from a variety of scientific, medical, and cultural sources to illustrate the social range of psychological debates.

Jonathan Smith, *Fact and Feeling: Baconian Science and the Nineteenth-century Literary Imagination* (Madison: University of Wisconsin Press, 1994): 'This study begins [...] with the assumption that science is a form of cultural discourse: like literature or history or music or art or religion, it both shapes and is shaped by the culture of which it is a part [...] "Science" and "literature" are not cultural monoliths but diverse and always changing, like the culture itself.'

Megan Perigoe Stitt, *Metaphors of Change in the Language of Nineteenth-century Fiction: Scott, Gaskell, and Kingsley* (Oxford: Clarendon, 1998): bafflingly dense at times and mostly about language change, but considers geology in the nineteenth century, arguing that 'narratives of change on the earth's surface – the texts of geology – were spilling through the presses at a time when narrative, in fiction, was becoming more explicitly a medium for noting (and commenting on) changes in speech and writing.'

Chris Wiesenthal, *Figuring Madness in Nineteenth-century Fiction* (Basingstoke: Macmillan, 1997): mixes nineteenth-century medical theory and contemporary psychoanalytic semiotics (Lacan and Shoshana Felman) in order to uncover the significance of how madness was represented in English and American fiction. Includes discussion of Trollope's *He Knew He Was Right*, James's *The Turn of the Screw* and Collins's *Heart and Science*.

More on Freud and Victorian culture:

Catherine Robson, *Men in Wonderland: The Lost Girlhood of the Victorian* (Princeton, NJ: Princeton University Press, 2001): examines how Victorian literary men imagined themselves in terms of girlishness, challenging Freud's model of male development.

Jenny Bourne Taylor, 'Obscure Recesses: Locating the Victorian Unconscious', in J. B. Bullen, ed., *Writing and Victorianism* (London: Longman, 1997), 137–79.

8

The History of the Book

*John Butt and Kathleen Tillotson – Richard Altick – John
Sutherland – N. N. Feltes – Gaye Tuchman – Simon Eliot –
Kate Flint – Garrett Stewart – Catherine Judd*

The History of the Book is rapidly expanding as an area of English studies in universities and colleges. Cambridge University Press's seven projected volumes, *A History of the Book in Britain* (1999–) neatly symbolizes its increasing status in the contemporary academy; the *The Book History Reader* (2001) from Routledge, edited by David Finkelstein and Alistair McCleery from the Scottish Centre for the Book, gives an indication of its growing presence as a university course. But the 'History of the Book' is no single subject: it covers a wide range of academic inquiry, extending far beyond its earliest manifestation as 'Bibliography' and the old 'Book History'. The modern History of the Book includes work on manuscript description, library history, the library-as-culture-institution, the 'sociology of the text',[1] studies of the circulation and transmission of printed and manuscript texts, studies of readers, hypertexts, electronic media, and publishing history, while also including the older practice of descriptive bibliography exemplified by the *Soho Bibliography* series. It is a plural activity involving scholars with diverse interests, as well as competing methodologies and ideological positions. As the History of the Book has grown in prestige in recent years across the range of English studies, there has certainly been no shortage of energy from scholars working on the fiction of the nineteenth century: in publishing history, the study of reading practices, book circulation, the conditions of authorship, and the implications of the growth of mass culture. Methodological diversity has been the rule here too.

Such diversity has been a problem for some. John O. Jordan and Robert L. Patten noted in their useful survey of nineteenth-century History of the Book studies, *Literature in the Marketplace: Nineteenth-century British Publishing and Reading Practices* (1995), how contested and contradictory many approaches to the subject currently were. The History of the Book had extended its presence in literary studies and cultural history, they remarked, but they agreed with John Sutherland that, unfortunately, it still 'lack[ed] binding theoretical coherence',[2] and reluctantly accepted Robert Darnton's view that it was best characterized as 'interdisciplinarity run riot'.[3] Jordan and Patten concluded, however, by reminding their readers that the modern discipline of the History of the Book was only in its infancy, and its methodology was in a crucial period of growth: it was, they said, 'still in its formative phase'.[4] This diversity in History of the Book studies – which is apparent even from my brief chapter here – need not be perceived, however, as a function of immaturity or as a serious problem for the integrity of the subject. As with postcolonialism in the contemporary academy, lively debates about the nature of the critical enterprise can be energizing and essential in sharpening the intellectual identities of the project (see p. 307 below). This chapter indicates key examples of some of the most important work on Victorian fiction, with its range of methodologies and interests, from the 1970s to the present.

OUTLINE OF THE CHAPTER   Readers of Victorian fiction can still profit from a number of studies from the 1950s, and I note these first. I then consider the beginnings of the modern History of the Book studies in the 1970s and discuss the emphasis on Victorian modes of production and forms of fiction, and the influence of publishing/ distribution practices on the way in which novels were written. In the 1980s, guided by the theoretical agenda of Marxism and feminism, critics considered how material conditions not merely influenced but determined the content of the Victorian novel, and how the mechanisms of distribution and publication affected women novelists differently from men. In the 1990s, influenced by the academy's post-structuralist acknowledgement of the role of the reader in creating meaning, there was a shift from studying modes of production to modes of consumption: work on readers was prominent during this decade. Feminist revisionist scholarship also influenced the History of the Book, and the last extract given in this chapter overturns an assumption about the use of male pseudonyms in the period to reveal women novelists as strategically deft in playing the power games of the Victorian literary marketplace. It is a striking example of the intellectual eclecticism of modern History of the Book studies.

BIBLIOGRAPH-ICAL WORK OF RELEVANCE TO VICTORIAN FICTION   Before its ascendancy in the academy, much work had been completed in areas now covered by the umbrella term 'the History of the Book'. The initial positivist methodology had, however, given it a greater sense of unity. The ground covered was (the old) book history (the empiricist study of the book as material object), publishing history, and descriptive bibliography. In the field of the Victorian novel, a classic in this last category was Michael Sadleir's *XIX Century Fiction: A Bibliographical Record Based on his own Collection* (1951). Many important empirical, archival studies of the history of nineteenth-century publishing houses that had produced major and minor Victorian novelists appeared before the end of the Second World War, including Arthur Waugh's

A Hundred Years of Publishing: Being the Story of Chapman and Hall Ltd (1930) and Charles Morgan's *The House of Macmillan (1843–1943)* (1943). These enabled readers of Victorian fiction to understand the commercial pressures on novelists, the kinds of audiences novelists aimed at, and the power of the publisher to shape the fiction. For modern readers, however, influenced by the agenda of late twentieth-century identity politics, the ideological and gender assumptions of these works are now in need of revision.

Descriptive, scholarly bibliography continues in the twenty-first century to play a role in facilitating research and enabling informed reading of Victorian fiction. The major undertakings of the past three decades, bringing bibliography to the service of literary critics, include Walter E. Houghton's *The Wellesley Index to Victorian Periodicals, 1824–1900* (1966–89, now available electronically). This five-volume work enables readers to identify what articles were published in a single edition of a periodical, allowing them to see what non-fictional articles appeared at the same time as instalments of serialized fiction in the Victorian period, enabling precise forms of intellectual contextualization. Another recent work of empirical bibliography relevant to readers of Victorian fiction is the third edition of volume 4 of the *Cambridge Bibliography of English Literature 1800–1900* (2000), edited by Joanne Shattock, with its indispensable listings of authors and publications providing a good picture of the range of Victorian fiction.

Other studies from earlier generations of scholars remain important. The 1950s and 1960s saw two works, one on Dickens, and one on Victorian reading patterns, that continue to be influential. Where it had been a commonplace in the criticism of Renaissance drama to insist that the material conditions with which the playwright worked were taken into account when reading the plays, John Butt and Kathleen Tillotson were the first Victorianists to give sustained attention to the material conditions of Victorian authorship. Butt and Tillotson's *Dickens at Work* (1963) provided an account – drawing extensively on manuscripts, working notes, and number plans for the novels – of how Charles Dickens organized his writing of fiction for serialized publication and how this affected meaning. Their book recovered Dickens as a periodical writer, stressing that he was able to engage more intimately with his audience through serial publication, and examining the constraints this imposed on form. In privileging the role of material conditions in the production of fiction, Butt and Tillotson defined the subject that constituted the main area of investigation in the 1970s.[5] Their consultation of manuscripts and other pre-publication texts also led to observations about the developing nature of Dickens's intentions. Writing about *Little Dorrit* (1855–7), Butt and Tillotson noted that Dickens's original plans were for a book called 'Nobody's Fault' which represented the '"one idea and design" of social criticism of which "society, the Circumlocution Office and Mr. Gowan" [were] "three parts"'.[6] Little Dorrit herself 'was not at

BUTT AND
TILLOTSON
AND THE
MATERIAL
CONDITIONS
OF
AUTHORSHIP

first intended to be so important a character', but, 'in manuscript, proofs, and letters we can trace the way she grew in importance',[7] until she became the eponymous heroine. Amy Dorrit's importance increased as Dickens rethought the direction of the work and moved from hard-edged social critique to greater hopefulness: switching the title to *Little Dorrit* confirmed this shift, and the novel's new 'optimism about humanity'.[8] *Dickens at Work* offered many such empirically derived arguments.

ALTICK AND
THE READER   The second study that remains well read is Richard D. Altick's *The English Common Reader: Social History of the Mass Reading Public 1800–1900* (1957). If Butt and Tillotson anticipated the agenda of the 1970s, Altick presciently anticipated the focus on reading and the reception of texts in the 1990s. Altick's study, a 'preliminary map of [a] vast territory',[9] detailed the conditions of publication, transmission of texts, and the book trade in the nineteenth century, in an effort to map the growth and nature of 'common' readership and to find out how texts were read by non-professional readers. Altick's empirical methodology used a seam of factual data, presented in readable form, and *The English Common Reader* was one of the books – others included Lucien Febvre and Henri-Jean Martin, *The Coming of the Book: The Impact of the Book 1450– 1800* (1958, trans. 1976), John Sutherland's *Victorian Novelists and Publishers* (1976), and Elizabeth Eisenstein's *The Printing Press as an Agent for Change* (1979) – that laid the foundations for the History of the Book's emergence in the academy in the 1980s. More recently, Jonathan Rose[10] reconsidered Altick's achievement. He noted that one of his fundamental questions, 'How do texts change the minds and lives of common (i.e., nonprofessional) readers?'[11] had not yet been answered in Victorian studies. Rose pointed out that, thanks to the work of David Vincent and others,[12] there was now more material available than Altick could have known to answer this question. This was because the number of working-class autobiographies now in the public domain – such as those discussed in Vincent's *Bread, Knowledge and Freedom: A Study of Nineteenth-century Working Class Autobiography* (1981) – had grown substantially. These provided evidence of the common reader's response to texts, literary and non-literary, and made a history of audiences more of a possibility. In general terms, none the less, the question of how texts affect readers, what the reading process involves in terms of a book's influence, remains an intriguing uncertainty in literary studies.

Butt and Tillotson were interested in Dickens as a serial writer, and the study of the forms of Victorian fiction came to dominate the 1970s as part of an overall interest in modes of production. The most important book was John Sutherland's *Victorian Novelists and Publishers* (1976), a work that offered with clarity a survey of the conditions of publication and distribution of nineteenth-century middle-class fictional prose with an emphasis on form. Sutherland's book, as has been said, was a foundational text in the emergence of the History of the Book as a discipline. Where Butt and Tillotson explored the relationship between Dickens's writing and the serial market, Sutherland, now Lord Northcliffe Professor of English Literature at University College London, examined the whole of the period in his investigation of how different canonical writers and publishers used the three-volume novel format, and the ways in which novelists and publishers endeavoured to break away from its constraining place in the literary culture. Sutherland's interest was in the literary marketplace and the economical imperatives that heavily influenced the publishing of fiction. His methodology was not Marxist but, none the less, the force of economics on the shape of cultural forms fascinated him.

The three-volume ('three-decker') format of the novel was the dominant one for the publication of nineteenth-century fiction. It imposed, as Sutherland argued in the first chapter of his book, part of which is reproduced below, distinctive requirements of form and plot organization, and many novelists regarded it as a tyranny. Unpopular with writers, it was also unpopular with many readers because of its expense. The historian of the book, Simon Eliot, wrote in 2000 that Victorian fiction publishing is best understood in terms of strategies to escape the crushing dominance of the three-volume form: 'The publishing history of the novel for most of the nineteenth century is', he said, '[...] the history of how publishers, librarians, and readers adapted to, or got around, [its] price.'[13] Sutherland had already made this point. He detailed four different ways in which publishers, librarians and novelists endeavoured to circumvent the price of the three-decker and escape its constraints on form. First, he considered the revival of serial publication in monthly numbers. Secondly, he looked at the circulating libraries' provision of volumes at a lower cost than that involved in individual purchase. The third feature was the cheap reissue of collected editions, and the last, related to the first, was the use of fiction-carrying journals to publish serialized fiction, a development that dramatically increased the number of readers of middle-class fiction.

Sutherland argued for recognition of how different modes of circulation influenced the form and content of Victorian fiction. He noted in particular the power of Charles Edward Mudie (1818–90) and his circulating library to determine the moral tone of middle-class fiction, making a link between a financial imperative (the need to escape the inhibiting expense of the three-decker), the censoring of middle-class fiction, and the modern reader's ideas about the moral tone of the era (for more on Mudie's library, see Guinevere L. Griest's *Mudie's Circulating Library and the Victorian Novel* (1970), which emphasized the aesthetic consequences of the three-volume format on Eliot, Trollope and Reade). Sutherland's account of Victorian publishing practices remains the best starting-point for understanding the material conditions of the publication and circulation of Victorian fiction, and why this matters for readers.

THE THREE-VOLUME NOVEL AND ITS PROBLEMS

Extract from John Sutherland, *Victorian Novelists and Publishers* (London: Athlone Press, 1976), 20–40.

[…] It is a paradox of the Victorian publishing world, […] that while it retained the three-volume novel as the foundation stone of its production, it was constantly trying to find ways around the barrier which the high price erected. The desired effect was not to undermine the three-decker, but to underpin it, creating an interdependence of expensive and cheaper forms serving an ever expanding and fiction-hungry market. One could go only so far with the 6s reprint; if this followed too hard on the three-volume issue it competed and upset the publishing apple cart. Something new was needed to supplement the traditional multi-volume novel. In the period from the forties to the sixties four major breaches were made in the established system which opened an enlarged supply of fresh, quality fiction to literate, but not necessarily wealthy classes of the population. These were: part publication, the 'Leviathan' circulating library, the prompt collective reissue and magazine serialisation.

The first of these innovations occurred in 1836 when Dickens, together with Chapman and Hall, revived the serial publication of fiction in shilling monthly numbers, with immense success. The part issue of fiction had a venerable history, going back at least 200 years but the better novelists, following Scott, had tended to avoid it in the 1820s and 30s. For some time before *Pickwick*, however, there had been experimental stirrings with new, or nearly new novels in numbers, such as the 1836 issue of Lytton's *Pilgrims of the Rhine* from Saunders and Otley in 2s 6d parts. (The work was a travel book whose interest lies in a number of digressive tales; this was one of the original conceptions of *Pickwick*, as declared in the advertisement of 26 March 1836.) And for a year or so before that Colburn had been running his 'Colburn's Modern Novelists' series which offered novels in weekly 1s. parts. (Numbers 1–6, for example, made up Lytton's *Pelham*.)

Dickens's serial differed from its predecessors in one simple and all important feature. Whereas Colburn took a novel published originally in volumes and broke it down into 1s. parts Chapman and Hall had *Pickwick* designed from the first as 1s. parts with a view to subsequent consolidation in volumes. The reader had the fiction, as the phrase went, 'warm from the brain' and usually before any critical judgement could be imposed on it, giving the work a singular freshness. The process by which this mode of serialisation was arrived at seems to have been largely accidental but, once it caught on, *Pickwick* established 1s. monthly numbers as a pre-eminent form of Victorian publishing. By it as many as 40,000 subscribers were provided with a 300,000-word, well printed, large paged, illustrated, original novel at £1, in easy payments. Dickens brought out all but two of his full length works in this way, Thackeray four of his six, Ainsworth, Lever, Trollope and (in modified form) George Eliot a number of theirs. All in all serialisation in monthly parts accounts for a rich slice of our canonised Victorian fiction.

Rich in every sense. Monthly serials, one should emphasise, were a way of producing novels as sumptuous as the three-decker, but at a more affordable price. Illustration, which was a luxury the multi-volume novel did not normally offer, was of an expensively high standard. Dickens illustrated by Phiz, Trollope by Millais or Thackeray by Thackeray were at least equivalent to Smollett illustrated by Rowlandson or Sterne by Hogarth. And in the forties and fifties reproductive processes were costly – roughly £120 of the £400 total monthly expense of a 30,000 issue (but in the sixties illustration costs were cut by one-third with new technology – interestingly this coincides with decline of the monthly number novel).[1] Nor is it true to say that the novel in numbers catered for 'a new naive public...the shopkeeper and the working man'.[2] The semi-literate public had its own presses, churning out penny serials before, during and after *Pickwick*'s success. Admittedly Chapman and Hall and Bradbury and Evans borrowed some of the techniques of the slum publishers but they refined them for an essentially middle-class readership. (The same line was pursued, even more profitably, by Cassell's.) In itself the novel in monthly numbers remained an article for the discriminating, literate and fairly affluent for whom it was that beloved Victorian thing, 'a cheap luxury'.

The value of the monthly serial was not just that it lowered the price of expensive novels. It also raised the reward for authors. 'No novel would be worth £10,000 to a publisher by any author,' declared Trollope magisterially to a correspondent who had mentioned that magic number, 'no house could afford to give such a sum.'[3] In the normal course of publishing this economic commonsense held true enough. But serialisation broke the rules. It was certainly worth Chapman and Hall's while to give Dickens £10,000 for *Our Mutual Friend* and for Smith to offer the same amount for *Romola*. Serialisation rendered the old ceiling payments irrelevant. Not all novelists got higher wages but the fact that any novelist might attain to fabulously high rewards changed the whole notion of the profession. Writing of Dickens in 1858 Cordy Jeaffreson made the point that his huge individual earnings had raised the art of writing novels generally: 'With us every calling, however mean in itself, becomes honourable by custom, if it can be shown to be lucrative by experience, for the simple reason that the enterprizing of the best ranks of society join it.'[4] By dying a rich man (unlike Scott) and leaving an estate of £93,000 Dickens had helped make fiction writing as professionally respectable as the law, medicine or the civil service. No longer was authorship a 'beggarly profession', nor did the aspiring writer have to console himself with the famously incommensurate rewards of literary history; £10 for *Paradise Lost*, £60 for *The Vicar of Wakefield*. It is probable that Dickens's gross fortune, which was made largely from monthly serials, did more to raise the profession than any number of Thackerayan or Carlylean lectures on 'The Dignity of Literature', or 'The Hero as Man of Letters'.

Although Dickens himself continued to make money from the monthly serial up to the time of his death in 1870, it declined as a form in the late fifties and sixties. The probable reason was that it had been overtaken by the increasing efficiency and cheapness of reproduction which made feasible even better bargains for the consumer. Comparing some costs for *Dombey and Son* (1846) and *Our Mutual Friend* (1865) one can see how the industry had advanced in a purely technical sense (Table 1).

In the sixties there were richer pickings to be had from the magazine which capitalised on the cheaper machine processes (especially for illustration); the *Cornhill* for 1s could offer *two* fiction serials by big

Table 1 Costs for *Dombey and Son* (1846) and *Our Mutual Friend* (1865) compared

	Dombey and Son (3rd number)			Our Mutual Friend (3rd number)		
Printed	32,000			30,000		
Composing	£5	15s	6d	£4	10s	0d
Corrections	5	5	0	3	4	0
Stereotyping	4	0	0	2	8	0
Working (64 rms at 7s 9d)	24	0	0	(60 rms at 6s 6d) 19	10	0
Pressing at 2s	6	8	0	(at 1s 6d) 4	10	0
Paper (64 rms at 32s)	102	8	0	(60 rms at 25s 6d) 76	10	0
Illustration work	118	0	0	79	9	9
Advertiser	67	5	0	64	10	0
Stitching (23s 6d per 1,000)				(16s 0d per 1,000)		
Total costs	£416	18s	2d	£217	15s	9d

names, illustrations and a wealth of supplementary material. This and the heavy production costs of monthly numbers (even a modest serial could cost £5,000) account for their being used only by a relatively few best-selling authors over a relatively short period. Nonetheless the monthly serial in shilling numbers probably did more than anything else to open up a mass market for fiction.

Serialisation by no means threatened the three-decker in which the majority of lesser novelists continued to appear. The *Publisher's Circular* listed six times as many in 1887 (184) as in 1837 (31). A prime factor in its survival, and increased prosperity, in the mid-century period was the dramatic growth in the circulating library business. In the 1840s and 50s Mudie's library in particular expanded to control a major section of the metropolitan market and a sizeable portion of that in the country and overseas. At his zenith, in the 1860s, he earned up to £40,000 a year in subscriptions. His biggest selling point was cheapness: for an annual fee of only a guinea (a fraction of what early rivals charged) the customer was entitled to the loan of a volume which could be exchanged as often as he cared. Proportionately more lavish subscriptions were available and it was calculated that using Mudie's facilities a year's reading for half-a-dozen members of a family could be had for two to three guineas, equivalent to £200 worth of new books bought in the shops. But it was the talismanic one guinea, one volume, one year offer which remained Mudie's trademark throughout his century of trading.

As he grew from Southampton Row to New Oxford Street and across the country Mudie rationalised not just the library system but many aspects of production as well. Before his Select Library established itself novels were delivered in quires and sold in an undignified scramble by the dealers who could bind them first in the ugly, grey boards which one still finds on some old copies. Mudie bound books himself and soon encouraged publishers to follow his example. At the same time the order and supply of novels was regularised. Mudie entered into treaty with the major houses for subscription rates and pre-publication orders. (Of the 3,864 novels Bentley sold by subscription in 1864, 1,962 were bought by Mudie.) This helped set up orderly sequences of manufacture and delivery. There were no price wars in new fiction while Mudie's dominated the scene. In this process of centralising, cheapening and expanding service Mudie may be seen as literature's Rowland Hill.[5]

Other forms of rationalisation followed. It was no accident that the two greatest entrepreneurs of fiction in mid-Victorian England, Mudie and W. H. Smith[6] set themselves to impose middle-class decencies on the English novel, 'purifying the sources of amusement and information' as Smith's biographer puts it in an image that links railway reading and contemporary sanitary reform.[7] Mudie read likely novels himself and, as his brochure discriminated with subtle accentuation, his library contained 'the best New Works' but 'the *best* Works of Fiction are also freely admitted'.

Mudie, another Scottish founder, had fundamentalist religious views. He had begun providing books for the new population of London University students and intellectuals around Bloomsbury and it is conceivable that he might just as well have gone on to become a great bookseller like Blackwell or James Thin.[8] Arguably he might have been happier than he was satisfying the age's insatiable demand for novels; but on the other hand his natural censoriousness was good business in his chosen line. Mudie prospered partly because the West-Central area of London was becoming more bourgeois. There had been circulating libraries plying there when Mudie 'could scarcely have reached the dignity of long clothes'.[9] But the aristocracy and gentry moved further westward and the old genteel libraries did not adapt to the new clientele. Mudie did adapt. It was the new middle classes who must have taken out most of his subscriptions and they were principally reading groups of mixed ability and mixed age; the family circle had replaced the 'reader on a sofa'. Mudie had a 'Juvenile Department' larger than many of his predecessors' total stocks. If he truckled to Mrs Grundy he was repaid by the little Grundys' custom.[10]

It is undeniable, however, that Mudie's influence was frequently a trespass on artistic freedom. The severe moral tone of his judgement is evident in a crusty little note he sent Bentley in 1876:

> dear Mr Bentley
>   Readers and Critics differ in opinion as to the 'New Godiva' – My own personal opinion is that the too suggestive title is the worst thing about it.
>   I do not intend to withdraw the book entirely from circulation, but I must ask you to be so good as to take back 50 of the 75 copies I have still uncut.[11]

Publishers doubtless needed few such touches of the whip to know who was in the driving seat and what were his ways. 'Mr Mudie', *The Saturday Review* observed in 1860, 'is in a position to make himself the dictator of literature.'[12] He was not entirely disinclined to assume that power. In ten years his annual acquisition of volumes rose, as his advertisements tell us, from 5,000 to 120,000; this must have made him the largest single purchaser of novels in the world. And as his business grew he would occasionally interfere directly with the novelist (by a ban as on Reade's *Cream* or by withholding a work from general circulation as with Meredith's *Ordeal of Richard Feverel*).

'Novels of objectionable character or inferior ability are almost invariably excluded' his advertisements declared – 'almost' is an interesting concession. Occasionally he was accused outright of refusing a book on moral or religious grounds but the indirect pressure of his 'petticoated mind'[13] on publishers and thereby on authors was both more pervasive and in its way more irresistible than a clear exclusion. The source of his power may be estimated from the sales figures of Trollope's *Barchester Towers* in its first three-volume edition, 1857:

> 750 printed and advertised at a cost of £266 15s 1d
> 6 author's free copies
> 26 presented
> 200 sold to Mudie, 25 as 24, at 13s 6d Receipts £129 12s 0d
> 126 sold to trade, 25 as 24, at 21s Receipts £127 1s 0d
> Amount short of expenses £10 2s 1d[14]

On the basis of these figures Longman's felt justified in going on with a highly remunerative cheap, one-volume edition in Spring 1858, another in June 1859 and yet another in June 1860, making some 4,000 cheap copies in all. More importantly for Trollope this success with *Barchester Towers* got his career as a novelist off the ground. Yet it is obvious that the Mudie sale was the pivot of commercial success. Without these 200 cleared off (even at the near giveaway price of 13s 6d, giving only half-a-crown's profit at most) the project would have been a dead loss. At June 1860 123 copies of the first edition remained on hand; without Mudie's purchase there would have been half the impression still in the warehouse after three years. No publisher could have gone forward on those figures.

The notoriously straight-laced, hymn-writing Mudie could not, therefore, be offended and his crotchets were elevated to precautionary rules of the trade. When he read the manuscript of *Barchester Towers* Longman's adviser insisted on its being extensively purged of its 'vulgarity' and 'exaggeration.'[15] (It would be nice, Michael Sadleir muses, to read the 'uncensored' *Barchester Towers*.) One example of the kind of alteration required is on record; 'fat stomach' had to be changed to 'deep chest'. It is a prime instance of what came to be called 'Mudie-itis'.

Like most of the great breakthroughs in the nineteenth-century fiction market Mudie's triumph was the outcome not of cautious whittling down of costs but of slashing them dramatically, so short circuiting the gap that existed between high book prices and low income. Yet unlike, for example, Bentley's stab at reducing the three-decker's price to 24s in the late 1830s, it was achieved not by cheapening the product but by exploiting the expendability of fiction once it is read. One reason that fiction tends to gravitate towards the cheapest form of publishing is that in most cases it is read once only, and then quickly. In America this economic logic led to books of incredible cheapness, designed to be thrown away after use. In Britain it was not the book which was cheapened but the reading of it.

To the public Mudie was a benefactor. For less than the price of a new novel one had English fiction at one's disposal. For publishers, on the other hand, Mudie was a harsh opponent, beating them down on bulk orders and sometimes withholding payment until dunned.[16] He was also capable of sharp practice; in October 1852 he bought 430 copies of Thackeray's *Esmond* at the library discount price (probably around 18s). In February he was selling off surplus copies of the novel – after they had had the run of his shelves – for 15s, in direct competition with Smith's second edition of the novel at 31s 6d. If he had a publisher in his hand Mudie squeezed relentlessly. Shilling by shilling he pushed down what the book producer could expect for his product. In September 1850 Bentley's wrote proposing a standing order arrangement by which Mudie would have any three-volume novel for £1 (25 for 24). Eight years later the publisher was glad to get 13s 6d for the same kind of novels. In this way Mudie undoubtedly helped create the uncomfortably Hobbesian world of bookselling between the introduction of 'free trade in books' in 1852 and its regulation in 1899 with the net book system.

It was not mere cussedness or ruthlessness that made Mudie deal so competitively with the publishers. Although he made his money from novels every new three-decker he took posed a financial problem. Hence we find him negotiating and renegotiating, often on single titles. The nature of his problem is clear if we look at his advertised list. It was made up of established favourites and classics (mostly in one-volume editions) and new multi-volume novels. Assuming that an average subscriber took out the three-guinea, eight-volume option and changed his books every fortnight this would mean that a volume in Mudie's stock earned less than 6d on every loan (before deductions for carriage, warehousing and overhead costs). Bearing this in mind, consider a typical novel, *The Ladies of Bever Hollow*, by Miss Manning, brought out by Bentley in two volumes at 12s in June 1858. On July 16 Mudie took 1,000 copies of this novel at just over half price, 6s 6d. In November Bentley, having cleared his expensive edition, brought out a 5s one-volume reprint. (Mudie would often try to enjoin publishers not to bring out cheap editions of novels he had taken in bulk, for a year; such requests were, as the trade was not slow to point out, unenforceable.)

The cheap version of *The Ladies of Bever Hollow* would to a large extent syphon off the immediate popularity of the novel. Either subscribers would buy it at the cheap price or it would have lost the aura of being the latest thing. Now there was little chance that at 6d a journey the two thousand volumes of *Bever Hollow* could have earned what Mudie paid for them, plus service costs, in three months. Admittedly there was a substantial rebate in selling off surplus copies at a reduced price to lesser libraries and in his sales department. But in the main *Bever Hollow* and other new fiction of its kind, must have been regarded as loss leaders to attract and keep subscribers. His real money must have come from the one-volume veterans of his shelves or those few multi-volume copies he kept in stock after a novel lost its bloom.

Mudie's was particularly strong on fiction (although after 1860 he always put it at the end of his catalogue). Of the million-or-so volumes he bought between 1853 and 1862 half were novels. In 1858 his stock stood thus:

History and Biography	56,472 volumes	} slow turnover
Travel and Adventure	25,552	
Fiction	87,780	} fast turnover[17]
Miscellaneous	46,450	

Since he worked on a subscriber-volume allowance it suited Mudie to build his system round the redundancy of the three-decker, which meant that his expensive, fast turnover fiction went that much further. Looking over his catalogues one perceives a distinct trend towards more multi-volume fiction between 1850 and 1870. Rather than restock with one-volume reprints Mudie tended rather to keep back a proportion of his original three- or double-deckers. Thus in 1857 Lytton had twenty titles listed in the Mudie catalogue of which five are multi-volume works; in 1871 he had twenty-one titles of which eighteen are multi-volume. It was, one imagines, partly by this means that Mudie contrived to show such an increase in his stock in the early 1860s.

It also suited Mudie to keep the price of novels sky-high for those who, unlike himself, did not enjoy a 60 per cent discount. This would include not only the private buyer but the small libraries whom he was driving to the wall. Thirty-one shillings and six pence on the open market gave a scarcity value to his stock and a glamorous overvaluation in the public eye. To acquire fiction cheaply whilst keeping intact its luxurious reputation was good business.

All this served to reinforce the expensive, multi-volume form long after one would have expected it to disappear. With the help of the libraries English fiction thus had the security which came from assured high prices and concurrent wide circulation. It was obviously an artificial situation. For one thing it meant that novelists had to write in what many of them felt was an unnaturally long format. But it is probable that the artificial maintenance of the thousand-page novel in this way made for greater as well as bigger fiction. In the weaker artist it encouraged diffuseness, bulking and padding (Miss Manning, for example, was prevailed on by Bentley to add two chapters to *Bever Hollow* to give each volume a respectable girth); but for the novelist trying to do something great in fiction it allowed that 'epische Breite'[18] which seems inextricably tied in with physical massiveness. A curtailed *Mill on the Floss* or *Esmond* is unthinkable. The three-decker was thus an ordeal and at the same time an opportunity for the novelist, Charles Reade, in a letter, expresses its possibilities and burdens eloquently: 'I am a writer. I *cannot scribble*. A 3 vol Novel is a great prose Epic. I hope never to write another...'[19]

The third, and in some ways the most significant innovation, was the cheap reissue in 'collective editions' of the works of authors who had achieved classic status in their lifetimes; notably Dickens and Bulwer Lytton, though Lever, Eliot, Disraeli and Ainsworth were subjected to the same honorific treatment. These collectives were the nearest the Victorian publishing world came to issuing good fiction, at minimal prices, while it was still seasonally fresh.

Although they were not synonymous with novels for railway reading a main precondition of the collective reissues was the railway 'mania' of 1846. By their very nature Victorian rail-travellers were an up-market, literate class with money and leisure. The thousands of miles of rail-line laid in the mid 1840s meant that journeys were now long enough to take up the reading of a novel. And the franchise awarded to W. H. Smith,[20] who insisted on certain standards in the fiction he purveyed, gave the better novelists a foothold in this new market. A selective chronology will give some idea of the suddenness with which price levels fell in the novel-publishing boom that swept along with the railway boom:

1831 Bentley and Colburn's 'Standard Novels' selling at 6s.
July 1844 Smith, Elder begin a collective of G. P. R. James at 8s per volume.
1845 Saunders and Otley complete their collective of Lytton at 6s per volume.

1846 Simms [and] M'Intyre introduce the 'Parlour Novelist' at 2s and 2s 6d per volume.

March 1846 Longman's bring out their collective of Mrs Bray's novels at 6s per volume.

February 1847 Simms and M'Intyre announce that their 'Parlour Library' will bring out new works of fiction 'of the highest character' at 1s and 1s 6d per volume.

March 1847 Chapman and Hall announce their 'Cheap' edition of the novels of Dickens selling at $1\frac{1}{2}$ d a part and (on average) 3s 6d the entire novel.

Autumn 1847 Bentley issues a 'New Edition' of the 'Standard Novels' (109 titles) at 5s per volume.

October 1847 Chapman and Hall announce their cheap edition of Lytton's novels on the same pattern as Dickens's, earlier in the year.

November 1848 Routledge's 'Railway Library' begins with a collective of Fenimore Cooper's novels at 1s per volume.

1849 Bentley drops the 'Standard Novels' to 2s 6d and 3s 6d.

November 1849 Chapman and Hall begin a collective of Ainsworth's novels at 1s and 1s 6d.

1849 Simms [and] M'Intyre purchase all G. P. R. James's copyrights for issue at 1s and 1s 6d.

1852–3 Bentley's 'Standard Novels' are supplemented by his 'Shilling Series' and Bentley's 'Railway Library' at 1s.

April 1853 Bryce brings out a collective of Disraeli's novels at 1s 6d.

1854 Routledge purchases all Lytton's copyrights to be brought out in the 'Railway Library' at 1s 6d and upwards.

The most daring in conception and admirable in quality of these ventures were, probably, Chapman and Hall's cheap editions of Dickens and Lytton in 1847. The scheme worked by fixing rock bottom prices and going for the widest possible sales. The format for the issue of these novels was, in fact, taken from the world of popular journalism; specifically Sharpe's weekly *London Magazine* which was started up in October 1845, offered sixteen double columned pages and sold for a $1\frac{1}{2}$d a week or 7d monthly. (It advertised itself, unironically, as 'the cheapest of cheap journals' a tag which gives one some notion of the respectability of the adjective 'cheap' at this time.) With Chapman and Hall's 'Cheap Edition' *Martin Chuzzlewit* (a book less than three years old in March 1847) would cost a subscriber 4s in thirty-two weekly $1\frac{1}{2}$d parts. *Oliver Twist* on the same terms would cost 2s 6d. The novels could also be had in monthly 7d parts or bound up as volumes after issue was complete.

These were tiny sums and great conveniences compared with fiction in the orthodox three-volume form.

Success with these collective editions required a shrewd knowledge of the market, a big name on the title page and a long haul for profits. Both prices and the books themselves were fractionalised to their smallest tolerance. Huge figures were involved. In 1847, for example, Chapman and Hall printed 2,290,000 'parts' of Dickens's novels. The profit from this output produced around £1,000 a year for the interested parties, which was relatively small considering the capital investment on the one side and the literary investment on the other. Its overriding value, however, was its durability and what it was doing for the better class of the reading public. Charles Lever, who was dealing with Chapman and Hall at the time, rightly saw the 'Cheap Edition' as 'the greatest trial of cheapness ever made in bookselling'. But, as he pointed out, 'it has shown that the profits . . . cannot be reckoned on till after a considerable lapse of time. When an author's popularity has lasted long enough to be more than a passing taste and to stand the test of a new generation of readers – then, and only then can successive editions be regarded as profitable.'[21]

In other words it was necessary to have a public educated in the discriminating reading of novels. The general application of critical standards in the evaluation of fiction had become something more than a belletristic exercise. As part of the general uplift that occurred about this period one witnesses the emergence of reliable reviewers, publishers' readers and a public capable of judgement based on sound critical reasoning. This presented a new and stimulating challenge to the author. 'The public', Reade told his publisher in 1852, 'is more intelligent than it was . . . I am ready for them.'[22]

What the collective editions demonstrated most tellingly was the hitherto unplumbed depth of the fiction market. The cheap edition of *Oliver Twist* had to compete with the novel's original magazine publication (1837–9), Bentley's first book edition in 1838 together with several reprintings, Chapman and Hall's three-volume edition of 1841, Bradbury and Evans's issue in ten numbers (January-October 1846) and their one-volume edition of 1846. There was, in addition, a whole gallery of plagiarisms and pirated copies. Almost every publishing finger had been in this pie, and, unlike pies, books do not disappear once they are consumed. Yet it was still worthwhile to bring out the biggest ever issue in 1850.

Ostensibly the collective editions were democratic. Lytton's declaration in Chapman and Hall's advertisements of October 1847 indicates the general feeling that publisher and author were breaking upon a new, uncolonised territory:

> May these works, then, thus cheaply equipped for a wider and more popular mission than they have hitherto fulfilled, find favour in those hours when the shop is closed, when the flocks are penned, and the loom has released its prisoners; – may they be read by those who, like myself, are workmen.

But one suspects that the cheap collective edition found a richer market in professional people like the young Anthony Trollope. Trollope had been educated at Harrow, clearly had a literary bent yet was earning only about £100 a year in the early 1840s – about enough to buy a three-volume novel a week and a loaf of bread a day. However was someone in his position to get the best contemporary novels which were now the vehicle for the best contemporary writers? Book clubs tended to favour improving literature; Mudie's worked best for family groups; new novels were for the rich and monthly serials only offered half an hour's ration of reading every month, poor fare for a diet trained on three-deckers.

Chapman and Hall went in for the cheap reissue methodically in the 1840s and after, doing it for Lytton, Dickens, Ainsworth and Lever – but especially Dickens and all while the authors were in their prime. At one point they were handling simultaneously the 'Library', the 'People's', the 'Cheap', and the 'Charles Dickens' editions for Dickens, as well as his new fiction (after 1859). In the 1850s the system was brought to its highest pitch of success by Routledge's with their 'Railway Library'. By backing the market's insatiability Routledge was to make a fortune through acquiring copyrights which more orthodox publishers thought worn out. His most famous coup was the ten-year purchase of nineteen of Lytton's copyrights for £20,000, which he started to exercise in 1854 with thirty-five separate volumes, including a twenty-volume 'complete' Lytton for £3 11s 6d. The risk was considerable and three years later the traditional publishing world was gloating over the fact that he was still ten thousand pounds out of pocket. But using fiction's new outlets, Smith's bookstands, Routledge saturated the market with his Railway Library editions of these 'FIRST CLASS WORKS' eventually proving, in Lytton's case at least, that it was impossible to exhaust a good book by a good author. At first not even Lytton himself (who was not a modest man) believed that Routledge could make money from the agreement: 'he pays high for a leading article in order to set up a periodical',[23] he told John Blackwood. But Lytton's copyrights were not, finally, the expensive gilt on the Railway Library; they returned the publisher's investment, and more. In 1857 W. H. Smith reported Lytton as 'heading the list' of popular reading fare, a position that novelist held for twenty years. Take one title, *Pelham*, which had been first published in 1828 and was in and out of print between then and Routledge's purchase in 1853. With its new owner this somewhat moth-eaten novel sold 46,000 in five years in its 1s 6d Railway Edition. The 2s Railway Library Edition of 1859 sold 35,750 copies in 34 years. In various more or less expensive forms the work continued to sell consistently for Lytton's lifetime. When he died in 1873 (Routledge commemorated the event with a 3s 6d edition) this still extremely popular 'Adventures of a Gentleman' of 1828 must have had the flavour of an antiquity.

Basically the collective reissue worked by turning a prime disadvantage of the writing profession in the practising author's favour. The disadvantage was that, as one writer complained, 'we suffer... from the competition of great writers who have passed beyond the necessity of earning their bread'.[24] In 1832, for example, Bentley bought five of Jane Austen's copyrights for the paltry sum of £210. For forty years these novels ran in the Standard Novels at a few shillings. In a market which was dominated by limited money supply for fiction there is no doubt that Jane Austen was taking work from contemporary writers with whom she shared Bentley's list.

In the superheated conditions of the midcentury an author could achieve early in his lifetime the classic status previously accorded only after death. Dickens was keenly aware of this, and waxed fulsome on the prehumous nature of the venture in the launching advertisement for the first series:

> It had been intended that this CHEAP EDITION, now announced, should not be undertaken until the books were much older, or the Author was dead... To become, in his new guise, a permanent inmate of many English homes, where, in his old shape he was only known as a guest, or hardly known at all; to be well thumbed and soiled in a plain suit that will be read a great deal by children, and grown people, at the fireside and on the journey; to be hoarded on the humble shelf where there are few books, and to lie about in libraries like any familiar piece of household stuff that is easy of replacement: and to see and feel this – not to die first, or grow old and passionless, must obviously be among the hopes of a living author, venturing on such an enterprise.[25]

Certainly in their own day Lytton and Dickens's work was, all of it, continuously on display before the public. Some idea of the scale of production (and the relative popularity of the novels) may be gathered from the printing figures for the 'Charles Dickens' edition, the last collective that the novelist saw through the press (Table 2). (Royal

Table 2 Printing figures for the 'Charles Dickens' edition

	HT	PP	MC	DS	NN	GE	DC	OT	OCS	CB	BH	LD	BR	UT	TTC	SB	AN	OMF
1867		50	30	30	25		25	25	25	25	22	22	25					
1868	18	13	5				5	5							22	25	20	
1868					5	22	5	5	5					15				20
1869		5	5	5	5		5		5	5	5			5				5
1869			5	5	5		5	5	5	5		5	5					
1870	5	8															5	5
Totals	23	76	45	40	40	22	45	40	40	35	27	27	30	20	22	25	25	30

Grand Total: 612,000

Units are in thousands printed. HT = Hard Times, PP = Pickwick Papers, MC = Martin Chuzzlewit, DS = Dombey and Son, NN = Nicholas Nickleby, GE = Great Expectations, DC = David Copperfield, OT = Oliver Twist, OCS = Old Curiosity Shop, CB = Christmas Books, BH = Bleak House, LD = Little Dorrit, BR = Barnaby Rudge, UT = Uncommercial Traveller, TTC = Tale of Two Cities, SB = Sketches by Boz, AN = American Notes, OMF = Our Mutual Friend.

16mo, illustrated, it sold at 3s and 3s 6d, the eighteen-volume set costing £2 18s plain, £3 10s fancy.)

One effect of this kind of collective issue was to keep all of Dickens simultaneously before the public. Almost four-fifths of the volumes printed by Chapman and Hall in this edition were works written before 1850. In this way Dickens had a kind of total and continual existence for the readers of his age.

At first many novelists were inclined to be suspicious of 'cheap rascals'[26] like Routledge, or Chapman. It was Dickens who had the keenest business mind of all his colleagues who took up the collective edition and profited most from it. Dickens also made the most of the fourth of the innovations in the practice of fiction selling. This occurred in the late fifties and early sixties when he, Bradbury and Evans, Smith, Macmillan's, Bentley and others established magazines and weeklies with circulations of up to 100,000 copies and more as vehicles for top grade fiction. In essence this was a new lease of life for serialisation and did for it what monthly numbers had done in the forties and mid fifties. Thackeray's later novels came out in this form as did many of George Eliot's, Wilkie Collin's, Reade's, Trollope's, Mrs Gaskell's and Hardy's.

The development of these fiction-carrying journals was part of the logic of the increasing growth and power of a nucleus of very large firms. The peculiar organisation of English fiction publishing meant a necessarily heavy expenditure on advertising. Publishing is anomalous in this respect since it is the manufacturer rather than the retailer who bears the cost of enticing the purchaser. When firms became rich enough it was practicable to have their own house journal (according to some authorities it was essential) so as to give the house's products adequate exposure. These journals were ideal for selling fiction as well, and at costs even lower than monthly numbers could achieve. The *Cornhill*, for example, offered two serials by name novelists every month, and a wealth of other matter.

It is likely that the fiction-carrying journal did not merely offer an alternative mode of purchase, it actually enlarged the gross size of the reading public by taking in a whole new sector of customers. Charles Reade, a professionally thoughtful novelist, made this point in 1856 on the subject of serialising a story in the *London Journal*:

> It is I am aware the general opinion that a story published in a penny journal is exhausted – I do not think so. I am a great believer in *rascally* bad type – I believe there is a public that only reads what comes in a readable form. I may

be wrong – we shall see: if I am right the London journal will do little more than advertise my story to Public No. 2.[27]

Events would seem to bear out Reade's belief that magazine and journal serialisation created second markets rather than redeploying old ones. George Eliot at the same period was reluctant to run *Mill on the Floss* through *Blackwood's Magazine* for fear that it would 'sweep away perhaps 20,000 – nay, 40,000 – readers who would otherwise demand copies of the complete work from the libraries'.[28] In the same spirit she withdrew a promised serial from *Harper's* in 1861. The truth was that readers were swept up rather than away. After *Great Expectations* had run through *All the Year Round*, the biggest selling of the quality fiction carriers, Mudie was still prepared to take 1,400 three-volume copies and Chapman and Hall cleared their 3,750 three-decker version of *Great Expectations* with no trouble whatsoever, the work going through five editions in a year.

In the period we are dealing with, every major house eventually acquired its own journal and used it as a vehicle for top quality fiction. These journals after the initial and considerable expense of founding them, earned revenue for the publisher, displayed his wares and enabled him to test the market to see how a novel 'pulled' with the public. The advantages even went so far as to outweigh the occasional unprofitability of the venture from a purely book-keeping point of view. Tinsley cheerfully sustained a loss on his *Tinsleys' Magazine* observing: 'what cheaper advertisement can I have for twenty five pounds a month? It advertises my name and publications and it keeps my authors together.'[29] There was, in fact, a fearful increase in the expense of advertising between the mid fifties and sixties. It cost Bradbury and Evans around £200 to advertise the early numbers of *Little Dorrit* in 1855. Chapman and Hall spent £1,000 in pre-publication advertisement of *Our Mutual Friend* ten years later (among their expenses were 1,000,000 bills). Since the unit cost had been brought down by only about a penny on the production of a shilling number (from 3d to 2d) this meant that advertising was beginning to bite sharply into profits.

From every point of view, then, the magazine was a rational investment and fiction carrying journals prospered for thirty years or so. To some they seemed the securest of all literary institutions. In April 1861 the *Publishers' Circular* speculated about 1960 when the *Cornhill* premises would have expanded to take over Wimbledon Common. But in fact things were no more stable in the publishing world than they had ever been. Novels in volumes were given a new impetus by the price reductions of the 1890s and the journals became less clients of publishing houses and more independent bodies in their own right and then went on to a new phase of existence in which fiction was to play a less important part.

High prices, multiple outlets, wide sales and abundant creative genius combined to make 1850–80 one of the richest periods that fiction has known. The variety of channels by which the great novelist might reach his public can be seen from the following list of George Eliot's novels, together with the ways in which they first presented themselves:

1857	*Scenes of Clerical Life*. Magazine serial (*Blackwood's*, 2s 6d)	
1859	*Adam Bede*. Three volumes (31s 6d)	
1860	*Mill on the Floss*. Three volumes (31s 6d)	
1862–3	*Romola*. Magazine serial (*Cornhill*, 1s)	
1866	*Felix Holt*. Three volumes (31s 6d)	
1871–2	*Middlemarch*. Bimonthly numbers (8 × 5s)	
1876	*Daniel Deronda*. Monthly numbers (8 × 5s)	
1878–85	Cabinet Edition. 24 vols. Collective reissue.	

Part-issue, library editions (which is what the three-deckers were in essence), bookstall editions (which is what the collective reissues were in essence) and magazine serialisation had one feature in common. They could each bypass the bookshop. This bypass was a valuable, perhaps even a necessary, facility after 1851. 'From what I hear', Blackwood's London manager wrote to his chief in October of that year, 'it seems not unlikely that we are on the eve of a revolution in trade prices.'[30] It had been a decade of revolutions and publishing did not escape. Free trade in books became the rule after 1852 when Lord Campbell's judgement abolished retail price maintenance by publishers' pact as 'indefensible and contrary to the freedom which ought to prevail in commercial transactions'. The unbridled competition which resulted led to the elimination or degradation of many bookselling retailers. Outside London, Alexander Macmillan claimed in 1868, 'the trade has become so profitless that it is generally the appendage to a toyshop, or a Berlin wool warehouse.'[31] The innovations we have examined created an arterial system by which new, or nearly new, fiction might still reach a mass, countrywide readership. They supported the novel until the 1890s brought in the net book, the reduction of the price of novels on first publication to 6s and a market vastly expanded and enhanced by the literacy acts of the previous twenty years.

Notes

1   Figures derived from the accounts Dickens's publishers rendered the novelist, now in the Forster collection.

2   See Q. D. Leavis, *Fiction and the Reading Public* (London, 1932), 151–7.

3   *The Letters of Anthony Trollope*, ed. B. A. Booth (Oxford, 1951), 269.

4   J. C. Jeaffreson, *Novels and Novelists* (London, 1858), ii. 313.

5   Sir Rowland Hill (1795–1879) invented the modern postal system (payment by weight, sender pays) which, from 1840, improved Britain's postal service.

6   Henry Walton Smith founded the stores in 1792; in 1846 the company changed its name to W. H. Smith (his son). In 1851 W. H. Smith secured the rights to sell books and newspapers at railway stations, a hugely profitable business.

7   See H. Maxwell, *Life and Times of the Rt. Hon. W. H. Smith* (London, 1893), i. ch. 2. Free enterprise at railway stations in the early 1840s sucked in a large number of French novels (whose copyrights were unprotected and could be more cheaply produced). The dubious tone of these works helped Smith to his franchise (see note 6).

8   James Thin (1824–1915), distinguished bookseller in Edinburgh.

9   E. Marston, *After Work* (London and New York, 1904), 43.

10 Mrs Grundy is an imaginary person, proverbially referred to as a personification of the tyranny of social opinion in matters of conventional propriety.

11 Bentley Papers, University of Illinois [Illinois], Mudie to Bentley, 11 March 1876.

12 *Saturday Review*, 3 November 1860, 550.

13 George Meredith's phrase. See Stewart Marsh Ellis, *George Meredith* (London, 1919), 103.

14 Trollope papers, Bodleian Library, Oxford, MS Don. c. 9–10*.

15 See A. Trollope, *An Autobiography*, ed. F. Page (Oxford, 1950), 103–4, and M. Sadleir, *Trollope: A Commentary* (London, 1927), 174.

16 To dun is to make repeated and persistent demands on, to importune; especially for money due (*OED*).

17 See G. Griest, *Mudie's Circulating Library* (Bloomington, Ind., 1970), 38, for an indication of how much Mudie's stock increased over the next few years.

18 *Letters of George Eliot*, ed. G. S. Haight (Oxford, 1954–5), iii. 317. For a devastating analysis of the authorial and publishing inflationary tricks, see C. E. and E. S. Lauterbach, 'The Nineteenth-century Three-volume Novel', *The Papers of the Bibliographical Society of America*, 51 (1957), 263–302.

19 Huntingdon Library, California, letter from Reade to J. T. Fields, 1855.

20 See note 6.

21 Pierpont Morgan Library [PML], Lever to Spencer, 10 May 1847.

22 Illinois, Reade to Bentley, 1852?

23 Blackwood's papers, National Library of Scotland [Blackwood], 4102, Lytton to J. Blackwood, 15 October 1853.

24 A. J. Church, 'Authors and Publishers', *Nineteenth Century* (May 1907), 895.

25 Taken from the advertisement in the *Atheneum*, March 1847.

26   PML, Lever to Spencer, 9 October 1847.
27   Illinois, Reade to Bentley, 'Tuesday', 1856. Reade, as usual, was even more courageous than any of his novel-writing colleagues. The *London Journal* had a somewhat sensational reputation.
28   See F. D. Tredrey, *The House of Blackwood* (Edinburgh, 1954), 117.
29   E. Downey, *Twenty Years Ago* (London, 1905), 246–7.
30   Blackwood, 4094, Langford to J. Blackwood, 29 October 1851.
31   Quoted in R. D. Altick, *The Common Reader* (Chicago, 1957), 305.

Sutherland's study went on to analyse case histories: Thackeray's *Henry Esmond*, Kingsley's *Westward Ho!*, and novels by Trollope, Charles Lever, and Harrison Ainsworth. Sutherland then considered Dickens's activities as a publisher, the marketing of Eliot's *Middlemarch*, and Thomas Hardy's handling of publication at the beginning of his career as a novelist. The book was welcomed, and Sutherland's insistence that there was 'no Victorian novel [...] which was not materially influenced by the publishing system' (p. 6) is now a truism. None the less, he had only begun to scratch the surface in accounting for the production and circulation of Victorian fiction. Indeed, when Sutherland looked back in the middle of the 1990s to his earlier work, in a book that gathered together a number of his essays on the same area, *Victorian Fiction: Writers, Publishers, Readers* (1995), he regretted the continued absence of ready knowledge about the conditions from which Victorian fiction emerged: 'Despite fifty years of intense, academically-sponsored research into the form, we still make do with only the sketchiest sense of the infrastructure of Victorian fiction – how the bulk of it was produced; who originated, reproduced, distributed and consumed the product.'[14]

Although studies of the production of the Victorian novel may not have gone in the direction Sutherland wanted, fiction and History of the Book studies did none the less develop in distinctive directions, critiquing his assumptions or extending his methodology in three principal ways. His ideas in 1976 about the determining power of economics on the shape of fiction, the role of gender in the marketplace, and the status of non-middle-class, uncanonical literature in histories of Victorian fiction, have each been re-examined.

FELTES AND MARXIST READINGS OF PRODUCTION AND AUTHORSHIP   N. N. Feltes, in his *Modes of Production of Victorian Novels* (1989), agreed with Sutherland's argument that economic conditions mattered for the form and content of Victorian fiction. But, as a Marxist, he saw the material conditions as determining the novel's plots. Feltes's argued, with the Marxian belief that the economic base determined the superstructure, that major works of Victorian fiction were oblique statements about the economic and material conditions of Victorian publishing and the place of the author in the literary marketplace. *Modes of Production* proposed materialist readings of a range of nineteenth and early twentieth-century fiction – Dickens's *Pickwick Papers*, Thackeray's *Henry Esmond*, Eliot's *Middlemarch*, Hardy's *Tess of the d'Urbervilles*, and E. M. Forster's *Howards End* – claiming that their narratives were all effects of their conditions of production. Feltes's reading of *Middlemarch* was characteristic. He argued that the pressures Eliot experienced as a woman writer entering the cut and thrust of the literary marketplace determined the novel's plot. *Middlemarch* reflected her 'woman's material need',[15] he said (meaning the means of life and literary status), as she tried to make her literary labour commercially and culturally successful. Feltes saw *Middlemarch* influenced by the mid-Victorian emphasis on professionalism as a category of labour, and the 'ideological exclusion of women from professions';[16] he proposed that this permeated the novel and that its main plot features were reflexes of it. Characters in the narrative enacted a version of Eliot's own contest for professional status. Feltes read the figure of the doctor, Tertius Lydgate, for instance (a man struggling to introduce new forms of medical practice into provincial society), as an effect of Eliot's own position as an author struggling for professional position. He saw her 'portrayal of Lydgate's attempt to earn a livelihood as a determinate ideological effect of the willed insertion of her woman's professional project into a profession of authorship which constructs women as amateurs'.[17] Multifarious features of *Middlemarch* were linked to a consistent argument about the political nature of the writing as Feltes revealed how far it was a novel about the struggle to become a professional female writer in a competitive, capitalist and male marketplace (for more on female strategies in the male marketplace, see pp. 289–302 below).

Feltes's reading of Eliot involved the role of gender in the mid-Victorian literary market. But another dispute with John Sutherland's methodology in the 1980s placed gender in the foreground, and rethought the implications of his map of Victorian publishing from a feminist perspective. Sutherland, whose subsequent work included a critical biography of the late Victorian and Edwardian uncanonical novelist Mrs Humphry Ward,[18] concentrated on male writers in *Victorian Novelists and Publishers*. Feminism in the 1980s asked questions about what happened to those who were women. Gaye Tuchman and the late Nina E. Fortin's lively study *Edging Women Out: Victorian Novelists, Publishers, and Social Change* (1989) now needs to be read alongside Sutherland's book because it provides an alternative feminist history/herstory, documenting the decline in status of female writers and the corresponding rise in the cultural prestige of the novel evidenced partly in the increased acceptance by publishing houses of fiction by men. Elaine Showalter, championing the recovery of lost female voices in the period (see pp. 71–82 above), provided the impetus for this alternative history in a general intellectual sense and also more literally because it was she who suggested that Tuchman

FEMINIST REVISION OF SUTHERLAND'S PUBLISHING HISTORY

consider the testimony of the Macmillan archives, central to the argument about female exclusion in *Edging Women Out*.

Tuchman, developing Feltes's interest in nineteenth-century professionalization and its gender implications, investigated the place of women novelists in systems of publishing in the Victorian period. She mapped the conditions of female authorship in the formal organizations of the modes of production, especially Macmillan's, tracing what she saw as a major transition in the period: 'Before 1840 the British cultural elite', she said, 'accorded little prestige to the writing of novels, and most English novelists were women. By the turn of the twentieth century "men of letters" acclaimed novels as a form of great literature, and most critically successful novelists were men.'[19] Tuchman plotted a narrative in which the rise of the novel as a prestigious literary genre in bourgeois culture involved an increasingly exclusionary affirmation of male cultural labour over female. The outline of Tuchman's narrative was questionable (she was not a literary critic) not least because the position of the novel at the end of the century, as I discussed on pp. 18–20 above, was more fraught and uncertain than she allowed. Tuchman argued for a tripartite history of women's relationship with a major publishing house that was reminiscent of Showalter's triple division of nineteenth-century and early twentieth-century women's writing (see pp. 71–82). Tuchman's narrative was not, like Showalter's, one of female progress, but showed the gradual exclusion of the ordinary female novelist as the novel grew in status as a male form of writing:

> We term the first stage, from 1840–1879, *the period of invasion*. Most novelists were probably women, but men began to value the novel as a cultural form. During the period of invasion, women submitted appreciably more novels to Macmillan than men did, and women's fiction was more likely to be accepted than men's.
>
> We call the years 1880–1899 *the period of redefinition*, when men of letters, including critics, actively redefined the nature of a good novel and great author. They preferred a new form of realism that they associated with 'manly' literature – that is, great literature. During the period of redefinition, men submitted more novels to Macmillan than women did, but women and men were equally likely to have their fiction accepted.
>
> The years 1901–1917 are *the period of institutionalisation*, when men's hold on the novel, particularly the high-culture novel, coalesced. The Macmillan Archives indicate that in these years men submitted less fiction than women but enjoyed a higher rate of acceptance.[20]

Tuchman used this model to provide an historical frame in which to read the history of the non-professional female novelist. With the classic feminist revision of the Marxist perspective, her book claimed that gender politics not economics was the defining feature of the Victorian literary marketplace.

Sutherland's interest in 1976 was in the canonical writers of the period. This involved an emphasis on male writers. It also involved an emphasis on the literary productions of and for the middle class. Class and fiction proved the third area of scholarly activity after the publication of *Victorian Novelists and Publishers*.[21] The increasing interest in Victorian studies in the academy of the 1980s and 1990s in working-class reading and writing in all genres[22] and in popular fiction in particular is noted in the Introduction (see pp. 10–11) and Historians of the Book also registered this emphasis. The simplest way of making clear this shift is to compare Sutherland's 1976 account with Simon Eliot's essay on 'The Business of Victorian Publishing' (2001). The comparison reveals how far class is now a factor in History of the Book studies. Eliot's argument followed Sutherland's study in so far as it was organized into an account of the prestige and problem of the three-volume novel and the strategies adopted by publishers and novelists to get round it. But it was different in its use of material about working-class culture. Eliot, whose publications include the monograph *Some Patterns and Trends in British Publishing, 1800–1919* (1994), was interested in increasing literacy in the period and the fictional forms that prospered in popular culture as a consequence.

Eliot argued that if we stay only with middle-class writing we have a distorted picture of Victorian reading and an impoverished sense of the literary culture in which the great novelists wrote. We also have a mistaken sense of what literary popularity meant. He noted the emergence of a new working-class form of fiction in the 1830s and 1840s: a lengthy prose fiction serialized in one-penny or two-penny weekly parts. This form grew side by side with the rising fame of Charles Dickens, though it has been lost in today's understanding of Victorian literature. Eliot said we need to be discriminating in describing literary fame: Dickens's sales, for instance, approximating to the legendary in middle-class culture, cannot 'begin to compare with the sales of genuine working-class texts. *Dombey and Son* (1846–48) sold on average about 32,000 copies of each monthly issue. Dickens's most successful novel, *The Old Curiosity Shop* (1840–41), was selling about 100,000 a month by the end of its run. But, in contrast, as early as 1828 a broadside [a single, long sheet usually giving an account of some sensational or horrific event], "Confession and Execution of William Corder," sold an estimated 1,166,000 copies.'[23] The forms of literature in high culture and popular culture were simultaneously treated in Eliot's survey, changing the readers' sense of the range of Victorian fiction and the nature of literary fame (for more on Dickens and popular culture, see p. 11).

Work on the production, marketing and circulation of Victorian fiction dominated the 1970s and 1980s. In the 1990s, work focused on consumption, one of the areas Sutherland declared in 1995 was hardly documented. Altick's attention had been on this question, but it was the development in the academy

WORKING-CLASS FICTION RECOVERED

1990s' EMPHASIS ON THE READER

of reader-response theory, and a more general Barthesian emphasis on the role of the reader in constructing meaning, that encouraged study of the readers of Victorian novels. Feminism, with its interest in the influence of culture and history on selves, with the identity and responses of individual subjectivities, also played a role. Kate Flint's feminist work on reading and gender, which has focused on the woman as a reader of fiction, was the most important contribution in the 1990s to studies of Victorian reading practices. Flint, whose work on social-problem fiction is discussed on p. 163 and on realism on p. 144, single-handedly brought to prominence the idea of the woman reader in the nineteenth century, her expectations and responses, as well as the ways in which she was imagined and her activities policed.[24] Flint's *The Woman Reader 1837–1914* (1993) provided an account of a range of reading-related issues, examining advice manuals, visual and literary representations of reading, and records of actual readers' responses, concluding that a woman's reading in the Victorian period allowed her space both for escape from the social and for the assertion of self: it 'provided the means not only,' she said, '[. . .] for the Victorian woman to abnegate the self, to withdraw into the passivity [induced] by the opiate of fiction. Far more excitingly, it allowed her to assert her sense of selfhood, and to know that she was not alone in doing so.'[25] A related fiction-specific argument was advanced in Flint's essay 'The Victorian Novel and its Readers' (2001).[26] Flint's feminist approach to reading was joined by Garrett Stewart's witty, revisionary study *Dear Reader: The Conscripted Audience in Nineteenth-century British Fiction* (1996), a book that examined how Victorian novels addressed specific kinds of readers and determined their responses for them. Stewart investigated the implications for literary theory of taking into account a readership that was narrated rather than merely implied. He discussed how the audience was conscripted, written with, and figured in the texts themselves, and what the consequences of this were for understanding the operation of ideology in Victorian fiction.

The operation of gender ideologies in the Victorian period is still often imagined in overly straightforward or even clichéd terms. The influence of Elaine Showalter and Gilbert and Gubar (discussed in chapter 3) remains considerable and still persuades many critics to see the period simply in terms of crudely enacted 'patriarchal' oppression, of male power and female repression. Such a clear-cut model has been greatly problematized in modern gender studies, but it still persists and appears regularly in many, sometimes high-profile, accounts of the Victorian period. Of the range of questionable generalizations made about gender and writing in the nineteenth century, the idea that the woman writer's adoption of a male pseudonym was a sign of the oppressive nature of Victorian patriarchy is still a familiar example. Showalter, with her firm views on Victorian sexual roles, discussed its apparent significance for gender politics in *A Literature of their Own* (see p. 72 above). I end

FLINT AND THE WOMAN READER

GENDER AND THE MARKETPLACE

this chapter with a significant piece of recent feminist revisionist scholarship that contested Showalter's view and problematized conventional readings of Victorian gender politics more generally. Under the mantle of the History of the Book, it rethought a tenacious commonplace with force.

The methodologies of the History of the Book are diverse, ranging from the highly theorized to the securely empirical: within this heterogeneity, Catherine A. Judd's essay on 'Male Pseudonyms and Female Authority in Victorian England' (1995) was an example of eclecticism in a single article, an instance of feminist revisionism with its roots in empirical History of the Book scholarship joined with a Foucauldian concern about the operation and subversion of dominant power structures in the nineteenth century. Revisionary feminism in the 1990s has changed the way we think about the relationship between female-authored texts and dominant ideologies because it has emphasized the strength of women in resisting hegemonic ideologies and restrictive forms of power. Feminism of the 1990s affirmed the courage and resourcefulness of female novelists writing social-problem fiction, seeing their entry into the public world as bold rather than as a source of problems (see pp. 189–90 above); in postcolonial criticism, feminists similarly emphasized, in the same decade, how female writers critiqued rather than reproduced ideologies of empire (see pp. 325–30 below). Catherine Judd's work, overthrowing the most familiar of modern commonplaces about gender, authorial status and Victorian fiction, was part of this feminist movement. Her essay examined how female novelists exerted themselves in the combative literary marketplace of Victorian Britain, manipulating myths of authorship by using the male pseudonym to their own professional advantage.

Extract from Catherine A. Judd, 'Male Pseudonyms and Female Authority in Victorian England', in John O. Jordan and Robert L. Patten, eds, *Literature in the Marketplace: Nineteenth-century British Publishing and Reading Practices* (Cambridge: Cambridge University Press, 1995), 250–68.

It has become a critical commonplace to assert that the use of male pseudonyms by Victorian women writers, especially domestic novelists, illustrates the repression and victimization of the female writer. Male pseudonyms, so the argument goes, bespeak the struggle of women writers for authority and acceptance. By shrouding the 'disability' of femininity, male pseudonyms offered a way for women to overcome the prejudices of the marketplace. Patricia Lorimer Lundberg, for example, asserts that 'female writers, especially those nineteenth-century novelists struggling to write in a patriarchal society, often have taken male pseudonyms to disguise their identities.'[1] In specifying 'especial-ly...nineteenth-century novelists' as needing to hide behind a male pseudonym, Lundberg's assertion dodges the question of why femininity would disable domestic novelists more than it would women writing in other genres.

In fact, the pervasive notion that many Victorian women writers published under a masculine *nominis umbra* [name without a substance = pseudonym] skews our understanding of the nineteenth-century literary marketplace, for most of these women writers did not use pseudonyms. Furthermore, of the small number who did hide their identities, the majority used female pseudonyms or published anonym-ously. Basing her analysis of patterns and trends in mid-Victorian pub-lishing on her study of the Macmillan archives, Gaye Tuchman, for example, determines that 'pseudonymous submissions in general were rare' during the mid-nineteenth century. She concludes that women writers were no more inclined to use pseudonyms than were their mas-culine counterparts, and that both male and female authors were far more likely to adopt a pseudonym from their own gender than to cross over. Surprisingly, of the writers who published under *noms de plume* [pen names], men apparently were more likely than women to use a cross-gendered pseudonym. Tuchman writes that 'solid data seem to support the assumption that many male writers masqueraded as women in the novel's heyday...in the 1860s and 1870s men submitting fiction were more likely to assume a female name than women were to use either a male or a neuter name.'[2]

The discrepancy between the historical record of women writers' publication trends in the nineteenth century and modern perceptions of those patterns indicates the existence of a cluster of mythic images surrounding the Victorian woman writer – especially the Victorian domestic novelist. This cluster has three major components. The first stems from a belief in the gender bias of the marketplace – that is, that the male pseudonym was a necessary mask due to the prejudices and exclusions of the literary marketplace. This reading results in a concep-tion of the woman writer caught in a heroic struggle against male prejudice and exclusion. The second component derives from the notion of the domestic novelist as at once family protector and family martyr – that is, she shields her name both to protect her family honor and to protect herself from the wrath of her disapproving family. The third explanation of the need for the male pseudonym stems from twentieth-century readings which claim that the male pseudonym is a mark of the androgyny of the female domestic novelist and a symptom of her need to feel somehow masculinized before she could pick up the 'phallic' pen. As we shall see, these readings of the male pseudonym were born and promoted during the nineteenth century by women writers themselves.

In reexamining the myth of the origins of the male pseudonym, I am not trying to diminish or deny the very severe legal, social, medical, political, educational, or vocational discrimination suffered by women in the nineteenth century. Nor am I trying to reinforce another fiction – that of the open and equitable marketplace. The inclusions and exclusions of the literary marketplace are vexed and complex topics, and there is little doubt that women writers experienced prejudice in the largely masculine world of publishing. There were inequities in rates of pay and no doubt many women writers were rejected for publication, or had their publications reviewed unfairly, based solely on their gender. One reads with exasperation, for example, Robert Southey's famous letter discouraging the young Charlotte Brontë, a letter that simultaneously acknowledges her unusual literary talents and dissuades her from attempting to become a professional writer because 'literature cannot be the business of a woman's life, and it ought not to be.'[3] Nonetheless, it was during the nineteenth century that the female voice gained authority and dissemination, more than in any previous century. Tuchman argues that the 'edging out' of women occurred toward the end of the nineteenth century when men began to regain the literary marketplace after a brief field victory by their female rivals.[4]

For mid-Victorian women writers, publishing under a male pseudonym was a choice – it was not forced or deemed necessary solely by the publishing climate – and it was a choice that few writers made. None heless, the enormous amount of emphasis given to the infrequent phenomenon of the male pseudonym is not misplaced, for the masculine *nom de plume* does have great import despite its rarity. Sandra Gilbert and Susan Gubar write that 'certainly, as we all now recognize, by the mid-nineteenth century the male pseudonym was quite specifically a mask behind which the female writer could hide her disreputable femininity.'[5] As we shall see, the male pseudonym was quite patently a mask, but the 'disreputability' resided in the mask itself. Conversely, the feminine self that the pseudonym veiled was believed to be at once domestic, heroic, creative, sacred, and martyred. Thus the 'veiling' of the female writer's identity by a male pseudonym, exceptional as it was, helped a certain group of Victorian women writers establish important claims of possessing a moral and social authority within the context of the ideological separation of the public and the domestic realms and the Romantic notions of creativity and genius that separation supported. For the remainder of this essay, I will examine the origins and the use of the male pseudonym by its most significant employers – Charlotte Brontë and Mary Ann Evans.

There is an element of happenstance in the fact that the four most canonical nineteenth-century female novelists – Jane Austen, Charlotte Brontë, Emily Brontë, and Mary Ann Evans – published under pseudonyms, and that three of these writers used a masculine or a masculinized name (Jane Austen's 'A Lady' was the pseudonym used most frequently in both the eighteenth and nineteenth centuries by women writers).[6] Yet, as we shall see, Evans and the Brontës decided to use male pseudonyms for reasons other than general difficulties in finding a publisher or a fear of being unjustly attacked by critics or dismissed by the reading public because of their gender.

In her 1850 preface to *Wuthering Heights* and *Agnes Grey*, Charlotte Brontë gives a detailed account of the reasons behind her decision to use a male pseudonym. She writes that adopting a masculinized pseudonym was an unsophisticated decision based on a 'vague impression.'[7] However, Brontë's apprehensions did not stem from the fear that her gender would thwart her quest for a publisher. Rather, she worried that her work would be dismissed as typically 'feminine' writing. The Brontë sisters perceived themselves to be mavericks, but not because they were breaking into a male-dominated field. On the contrary, they wanted to distance themselves from the large group of women who were then writing domestic fiction: 'we veiled our own names...because – without at the time suspecting that our mode of writing and thinking was not what is called "feminine"...we noticed how critics sometimes use for their chastisement the weapon of personality, and for their reward, a flattery, which is not true praise.'[8] In a letter written only a few years after Brontë's preface to *Jane Eyre*, Evans gives further evidence of a commonly held belief in the proliferation of women writers and the sense of an ease, approaching laxity, with which their works were published and critically evaluated. Here she wonders 'how women have the courage to write and publishers the spirit to buy at a high price the false and feeble representations of life and character that most feminine novels give.'[9]

The fear expressed by Charlotte Brontë and Mary Ann Evans of being judged as women writers does not indicate their apprehension of being silenced as women in the marketplace but rather their dread of being judged by a 'class standard.' Ironically, this standard was believed to grant excessive license to female writing, and it was this critical permissiveness that Brontë and Evans claimed to loathe more than uncharitable appraisal. In 1868, for example, Emily Davies wrote: 'That the greatest of female novelists [that is, Charlotte Brontë and Mary Ann Evans] should have taken the precaution to assume a masculine nom de plume for the express purpose of securing their work against being measured by a class standard, is significant of the feeling entertained by women.'[10]

Yet these statements seem to be in direct conflict with the abundance of gender-based attacks then appearing in many English periodicals. It helps to clarify this conflict by recognizing the context of nineteenth-century England's misogynistic critical legacy. With the exception of a few serious literary critics (including, of course, Evans herself and George Henry Lewes), the art of Victorian literary criticism consisted largely of partisan puffery or attacks based on the politics of the writer, his or her publisher, and the journal reviewing the work. From this viewpoint, femininity became one more weapon in the arsenal of biased literary criticism. Furthermore, male authors were not exempt from this critical vituperation – recall, for example, Shelley's assertion in his preface to 'Adonais' that Keats was murdered by John Wilson Croker's harsh review of *Endymion*. In 1857, Mary Ann Evans wrote to Sara Sophia Hennell:

> Don't let your soul be moved by newspaper criticisms. If you knew well what sort of books the Spectator praises ... you would not care about its blame. It is only as a question of sale that such notices are at all important, and even in that light, they can't stop the sale of a book that really lays hold of the readers' minds. One person who has admired and enjoyed tells another, and by and bye Athenaeum, Spectator and Co. are forgotten. On the other hand, no dithyrambs ... can make a bad book successful.[11]

Evans herself made it a rule never to read reviews of her own fiction: 'I have found this abstinence necessary to preserve me from that discouragement as an artist which ill-judged praise, no less than ill-judged blame, tends to produce in me.'[12]

Indeed, this issue of 'ill-judged praise' being given to women writers seemed to trouble Evans more than did 'ill-judged blame.' In 'Silly Novels by Lady Novelists,' for example, Evans wrote that 'we are aware that the ladies at whom our criticism is pointed are accustomed to be told, in the choicest phraseology of puffery,' that their novels are brilliant, well drawn, fascinating, and lofty.[13] Evans claimed that this puffery was especially evident in reviews of inept women writers. She felt that talented women writers kindled far less critical enthusiasm: 'when a woman's talent is at zero, journalistic approbation is at the boiling pitch; when she attains mediocrity, it is already at no more than summer heat; and if ever she reaches excellence, critical enthusiasm drops to the freezing point. Harriet Martineau, Currer Bell, and Mrs Gaskell have been treated as cavalierly as if they had been men.'[14] Thus, rather than the expected denunciation of the biased condemnation of women writers by the press, Evans instead begged journalists to 'abstain from any exceptional indulgence towards the productions of literary women' so that women writers would be forced to write toward the same higher standards applied to their male counterparts.[15]

Accompanying the explanations of gender bias as a motivation for the use of male pseudonyms by Victorian women writers in general, those critics who have focused specifically on the personal situations of the Brontës and Evans have often concluded that the male pseudonym served as a strong shield of privacy for these writers, all of whom had extraordinary personal lives that would not bear the public scrutiny that comes with fame. Although Charlotte Brontë, Evans, and their biographers laid claim to their urgent needs for privacy, these accounts overlook the fact that they had made the decision to become public women, and to become a popular writer in England during the mid-nineteenth century was to renounce all claims to anonymity, as the examples of Scott, Dickens, or any number of celebrated writers would have shown. Charlotte Brontë and Evans were professional writers, and as professionals they had (or sought to obtain in the case of Charlotte Brontë) a real sense of the literary marketplace. This awareness of a professional identity held true especially for Evans, who became a novelist only after years of work as a translator, critic, and editor in London. As professional writers, both Brontë and Evans had some awareness of the significance of putting their names in the marketplace, and to believe that any sort of pseudonym would long protect an illustrious writer's identity from the curiosity of the press and the reading public would be an ingenuous hope at best. Jane Austen, for example, who was not even very popular during her lifetime compared with writers such as Walter Scott and Maria Edgeworth, gave up any attempts to conceal her identity very early in her career and desired instead to profit from her fame:

> the Secret has spread so far as to be scarcely the Shadow of a secret now – & that I beleive [*sic*] whenever the 3d [volume] appears, I shall not even attempt to tell Lies about it. – I shall rather try to make all the Money than all the Mystery I can of it. – People shall pay for their knowledge if I can make them.[16]

The cult of authorship and the commodification of the signature had been growing throughout the nineteenth century, the two key examples of the marketability of the personal name in literature being Walter Scott and Charles Dickens. No doubt both Brontë and Evans learned lessons in authorial commodification from these two celebrated examples, both male, one using pseudonyms and the other publishing under his given name after briskly dropping his original pseudonym of 'Boz.' Mary Poovey writes that 'the commercial marketing of books by linking a writer's name to a unique and recognizable image' was one of the 'critical components' in the advent of the expansion of the mass-marketing of the book trade, and that this unique image of the writer, the writer as celebrity, was 'often an "autobiographical" image derived from the writer's work.'[17] In Charles Rowcroft's 1844 novel *The Man Without a Profession*, an experienced London journalist, Mr Seedy, gives a young novelist advice about the publishing industry:

> the sale of a work depends not on the merits of the book, but on the personal reputation of the author...so that an author must write several works...before his name becomes popular. Then, when his name is up, he may for some time sell anything that is not positively and glaringly bad...When the name of an author is well up, he can obtain easily a thousand pounds and upwards for a new work.[18]

Evans's business acumen is well known, and her letters exhibit a sophisticated awareness of the commodification of the name described by Mr Seedy. In 1877 Evans wrote to her future sister-in-law Mary Finlay Cross that 'I read your touching story aloud yesterday...Your Brother wrote to me that you had doubts about giving your name. My faith is that signature is right, in the absence of weighty special reasons against it.'[19] Several years earlier, in 1862, she wrote far more vehemently to her close friend Sara Sophia Hennell after Hennell wondered if Eliot had written a recently published anonymous piece:

> I am NOT the author of the Chronicles of Carlingford. They are written by Mrs Oliphant...A little reflection might, one would think, suggest that when a *name* is precisely the highest-priced thing in literature, any one who has a name will not, except when there is some strong motive for mystification, throw away the advantages of that name. I wrote anonymously while I was an unknown author, but I shall never, I believe, write anonymously again.[20]

The irony that this name she justified so ardently is a pseudonym does not seem to have occurred to Evans – by this time, the pseudonym had become the mainstay of her sense of a public self. Yet as crucial as 'George Eliot' was to Mary Ann Evans's life, the pseudonym was not meant to usurp or replace the woman who had existed for close to forty years before she had invented her public persona.[21]

Rather than displace her personal name with her pseudonym, Evans rarely referred to herself in private life as 'George Eliot.' Indeed, her earliest letters to her publisher, John Blackwood, were signed 'George Eliot,' but once she revealed her identity she signed the rest of her professional correspondence as 'M. E. Lewes.' To friends, family, and fans she continued to be known as 'Marianne Evans Lewes,' or by one of the nicknames generated among her intimate acquaintances (Pollian, Polly, Clematis, Mother, Madonna, and Mutter were among the most common at different periods in her life).[22] In one of the very few personal letters that she signed with her pseudonym (in this case simply 'G.E.'), Evans added an insistent postscript: 'my *name* is Marian Evans *Lewes*.'[23]

None the less, the Brontë sisters' and Evans's professional identities were inexorably bound up with their male pseudonyms. They never published under their own names even though their identities were well known within several years of their debuts as novelists. Thus the division between the Brontë sisters' and Evans's professional and per-sonal life seems not only emphatic, but gendered as well. With the adoption of male pseudonyms, the Brontës' and Evans's writing and public persona appear to derive from a 'masculine' sphere or a masculine aspect of their characters. Gilbert and Gubar give this reading to the Brontës' and to Evans's use of the pseudonym – that they were uncom-fortable being women writers, that writing was an exclusively male enterprise, and that the male pseudonyms bespoke both an attempt at acceptance and a need to feel somehow masculinized before they could legitimately pick up the phallic pen: 'the most rebellious of [Behn's and Cavendish's] nineteenth-century descendants attempted to solve the literary problem of being female by presenting themselves as *male*. In effect, [Evans and the Brontës] protested not that they were "as good as" men but that, as writers, they *were* men.'[24]

Yet, as with George Sand, Evans's and the Brontës' audiences did not think of them as men; rather, they perceived them to be women almost from the beginning of their careers. *Jane Eyre*, for example, was seen as a revolutionary book in terms of the history of the British novel precisely because it articulated the passions and desire of a specifically feminine experience. In examining the question of why Charlotte and Emily Brontë 'should occupy a place of such prominence in the British cultural consciousness,' Nancy Armstrong believes that this centrality derives from their skill at 'formulating universal forms of subjectivity' and con-

verting history into desire.[25] Raymond Williams states that with Charlotte and Emily Brontë there came 'an emphasis on intense feeling,
a commitment to what we must directly call passion, that is in itself
very new in the English novel.'[26] Thus, what seemed so exhilarating
or threatening to many readers in the late 1840s was *Jane Eyre*'s giving
voice to a previously unarticulated realm of feminine desire, and it
was this voice that seemed to open the door for the establishment of
a new kind of female authority. In 1855, Margaret Oliphant wrote
that 'suddenly, without warning, *Jane Eyre* stole upon the the scene,
and the most alarming revolution of modern times has followed th[is]
invasion.'[27]

Ironically, rather than averting or dissipating this authority, the male
pseudonym actually served to enhance feminine domestic authority and
reinforce the split between the public and private realms. In 1853,
Elizabeth Gaskell characterized Brontë's life as being 'divided into
two parallel currents – her life as Currer Bell, the author; her life as
Charlotte Brontë, the woman,' thus underscoring the way that the male
pseudonym helped to create a distinct and emphatic division between
Brontë's professional and domestic selves.[28] As a mechanism for literary
production this division functioned in the following way: Charlotte
Brontë the artist was seen to conceal herself in a feminine, domestic,
and hidden space, thereby invoking the Romantic image of creativity as
an idiopathic and clandestine enterprise. By presenting her public self as
both masculine and a known fiction, this division between the public
and the domestic, the masculine and the feminine, also becomes aligned
with a division between false and authentic selves. Since it was in this
private, feminized, creative realm that the masculine public self was
invented and then brought forth for public display and consumption,
women writers who used male pseudonyms implied that the private
space was the realm of origination that took precedence over the public
and the masculine. Therefore the 'artificial' male identity served to
shelter the woman writer's 'real' (feminine and domestic) self from the
corrupt public realm.[29]

As with Brontë, Evans's use of a male pseudonym became not a
pathway to androgyny but a means of protecting and emphasizing
what the ideology of Romantic literary production identified as her
specifically feminine creativity. In her 1856 essay 'Silly Novels by Lady
Novelists,' Evans touches on her belief in a creativity accessible only
though female genius, a belief that was more fully articulated by Lewes in
his 1852 essay on female novelists. Lewes argues that great literature
depicts 'universal truths' of 'the forms and orders of human life,' hence
the 'universality and immortality of Homer, Shakspeare [*sic*], Cervantes,

Moliere.' For Lewes, literature is 'essentially the expression of experience and emotion – of what we have seen, felt, and thought.' Yet the 'universal and immortal' authors Lewes lists are all men, and he raises the question: 'What does the literature of women mean?' In answering this query, Lewes claims that 'while it is impossible for men to express life otherwise than they know it – and they can only know it profoundly according to their own experience – the advent of female literature promises woman's view of life, woman's experience: in other words, a new element.' Lewes believes that this new element derives from women's special knowledge of the human heart. Using rigid notions of sexual difference, he asserts that the 'Masculine mind is characterized by a predominance of the intellect, and the Feminine by the predominance of the emotions':

> Woman, by her greater affectionateness, her greater range and depth of emotional experience, is well fitted to give expression to the emotional facts of life... To write as men write, is the aim and besetting sin of women; to write as women, is the real office they have to perform... To imitate is to abdicate. We are in no need of more male writers; we are in need of genuine female experience. The prejudices, notions, passions, and conventionalisms of men are amply illustrated; let us have the same fulness [*sic*] with respect to women.[30]

According to Lewes's logic in 'The Lady Novelists,' the greatest literature tells universal truths about human emotions; women are more emotional than men and are more able to depict those emotions. Consequently, women are more privy to universal truths and are thus more likely to write great literature. Lewes argues that this has not happened quite yet because most women writers are busy trying to imitate men, but the few who have tapped into the emotional truths of humanity (Maria Edgeworth, Jane Austen, George Sand, Currer Bell, and Elizabeth Gaskell) are the pioneers of a profoundly emotional literary voice – a voice that is at once universal and feminine.

Thus Evans's and the Brontës' use of the male pseudonym is not a usurpation of the patronym, rather it is a creative appropriation of the possibilities inscribed in the nineteenth-century myth of subjectivity's division into distinct public and private realms. Gilbert and Gubar, for example, contend that this pseudonymic self functions as 'a name of power, the mark of a private christening into a second self, a rebirth into linguistic primacy,' but I would maintain that for these novelists the power was seen to rest with the private self.[31] Like the Brontës, Evans employed the pseudonym as a fictional creation and a detachable identity, locating the source of power – the 'real' self who was responsible for the creation of the pseudonymic self – in the private, domestic self, a self sheltered from the contamination of the marketplace in part through the pseudonym itself.

The conflict between the didactic or messianic aspirations of Victorian writers and the commercial aspects of publishing and marketing was profound during the mid-nineteenth century. George Meredith conveys a sense of this uneasiness in *Rhoda Fleming*: 'You can buy any amount for a penny, now-a-days – poetry up in a corner, stories, tales o'temptation.'[32] In *Lucretia*, Francis Edward Paget expresses this fear even more harshly: 'Most of the worst sensational novels are republished, vile type and vile paper combining to secure for the dissemination of still viler sentiments a very low price.'[33] Mary Poovey writes of the confusion felt by male writers during the mid-nineteenth century over their place in society, the status of their profession, and their ancestry of not only medieval court scribes and Renaissance intellectuals but also 'early and mid-eighteenth-century hacks who sold ideas by the word and fought off competitors for every scrap of work.'[34] Brontë and Evans, I would argue, found a partial solution to the conflict that all Victorian writers felt over their profession by exploiting the potentially crippling oppositions of Romantic ideology, by splitting the self into the public, male writer and the private, female genius.

In her essay on Aphra Behn, Catherine Gallagher makes an argument similar to the one that I am making here when she writes of Behn's construction of an innocent self that existed above the exchange of writing:

> authorship for the marketplace and self-hood are here dissevered, for the author that can be inferred from the work is merely a 'way of writing' dictated by the Age, an alienable thing below the true self... Aphra Behn constructs the effect of an authentic female self on the basis of the very need to sell her constructed, authorial self. By making her authorial self an emanation of the marketplace, then, she saves this putative authentic self from contamination.[35]

Yet, as Gallagher notes, Behn's tainted professional identity was construed as 'woman writer as prostitute,' not as a male as with Brontë and Evans. By the nineteenth century, the 'woman writer as whore' had transmuted into the 'woman writer as man.'

Behn may have aimed for a sense of purity and decorum existing in the realm of her 'true self,' while her marketable self was a whore, but for both Evans and Charlotte Brontë, the 'true self' was a complex construction of domestic angel and messianic leader, martyred daughter and sibyl. Furthermore, all of these 'private' selves were understood to be specifically feminine, the domestic self obviously so, but even the oracular teller of universal truths was believed to speak with a woman's voice. Thus the domestic self and the self of genius worked in tandem to create what Lewes and Evans had defined as 'great' literature – the domestic self gave women writers the emotional authority that derived especially from domestic martyrdom. The self-sacrificial experiences of the mother, wife, daughter, and sister were then recreated in the crucible of literary genius – a hidden, ultraprivate self that transformed the everyday emotional events of women into 'universal truths.'

What, then, of the commodified, marketable author – the public self? This was the self that was most tainted and ephemeral: a self who writes, as Evans puts it, 'drivel for dishonest money.'[36] The commercial self, interested in profit and bargaining and business deals, certainly would dilute a writer's claims of possessing a disinterested, universal voice marked with the stamp of Romantic genius. Thus in order to separate fully the public from the private self, the public self becomes a masculine mask – a mask that shields the private, feminine self from the tarnish of the marketplace.

Notes

1   Patricia Lorimer Lundberg, 'George Eliot: Mary Ann Evans's Subversive Tool in *Middlemarch?*', *Studies in the Novel*, 18(3) (1986), 270.
2   Gaye Tuchman with Nina E. Fortin, *Edging Women Out: Victorian Novelists, Publishers, and Social Change* (New Haven: Yale University Press, 1989), 53. Some female pseudonyms used by male writers include [...] Margaret Nicholson (Percy Bysshe Shelley), Theresa MacWhorter (William Makepeace Thackeray), Ellen Alice (Col. Thomas Bangs Thorpe), Sappho of Toulouse (Clarence Isaure), Clara Gazul (Prosper Mérimée), Fiona Macleod (William Sharp), and Mrs Horace Manners (Algernon Swinburne).
3   Robert Southey to Charlotte Brontë, March 1837, quoted in T. J. Wise and J. A. Symington, eds, *The Brontës: Their Lives, Friendships, and Correspondence*, 4 vols (Oxford: Oxford University Press, 1931–8), 154–6.
4   For a fascinating reading of the competitions of the nineteenth-century British literary marketplace that takes class (but, uncharacteristically, not gender) into account, see Mary Poovey, *Uneven Developments: The Ideological Work of Gender* (Chicago: University of Chicago Press, 1987), 101–16.
5   Sandra Gilbert and Susan Gubar, 'Ceremonies of the Alphabet: Female Grandmatologies and the Female Authorgraph', in Domna C. Stanton, ed., *The Female Autograph* (New York: New York Literary Forum, 1984), 28.
6   I have settled on 'Mary Ann Evans' because this was the name she was using when she translated Strauss's *Leben Jesu* and is thus her first professional name.

7   The full quotation is: 'we had a vague impression that authoresses are liable to be looked on with prejudice.' Quoted in Elizabeth Gaskell, *The Life of Charlotte Brontë*, ed. Alan Shelston (New York: Penguin, 1975), 286.

8   Ibid., 285–6.

9   George Eliot, *The Yale Edition of the George Eliot Letters*, ed. Gordon S. Haight, 9 vols (New Haven, Conn., Yale University Press, 1978), iii. 86.

10   Quoted in ibid., viii. 429, n.9.

11   Ibid., ii. 305.

12   Ibid., vi. 378.

13   George Eliot, 'Silly Novels by Lady Novelists', *The Westminster and Foreign Quarterly Review* 6 (2) (October 1854), 460.

14   Ibid.

15   Ibid.

16   Quoted in Mary Poovey, *The Proper Lady and the Woman Writer: Ideology as Style in the Works of Mary Wollstonecraft, Mary Shelley, and Jane Austen* (Chicago: University of Chicago Press, 1984), 211.

17   Poovey, *Uneven Developments*, 108.

18   Charles Rowcroft, *The Man Without a Profession*, 3 vols; 1844, vol. 3, 157, 160; quoted in Myron F. Brightfield, *Victorian England in its Novels (1840–1870)*, 4 vols (Los Angeles: University of California Library, 1968), i. 157.

19   Eliot, *Letters*, v. 171.

20   Ibid., iv. 25.

21   Ibid., ii. 91.

22   Please refer to note 6.

23   Eliot, *Letters*, iii. 217 (her emphasis).

24   Gilbert and Gubar, 'Ceremonies of the Alphabet', 65.

25   Nancy Armstrong, *Desire and Domestic Fiction: A Political History of the Novel* (Oxford: Oxford University Press, 1987), 186.

26   Raymond Williams, *The English Novel from Dickens to Lawrence* (London: Hogarth Press, 1984), 60.

27   Quoted in Sandra Gilbert and Susan Gubar, *The Madwoman in the Attic: The Woman Writer and the Nineteenth-century Imagination* (New Haven, Conn.: Yale University Press, 1979), 337.

28   Gaskell, *The Life of Charlote Brontë*, 334.

29   Evans, too, wrote about Brontë as a person with multiple selves; Eliot, *Letters*, ii. 91.

30   George Henry Lewes, 'Lady Novelists', *Westminster Review*, 2 (1852), 130, 131, 132.

31   Gilbert and Gubar, 'Ceremonies of the Alphabet', 29.

32   George Meredith, *Rhoda Fleming* (London: Tinsley, 1865), 73.

33   Francis Edward Paget, *Lucretia or, The Heroine of the Nineteenth Century: A Correspondence Sensational and Sentimental* (London: 1868), 302.

34   Poovey, *Uneven Developments*, 103.

35   Catherine Gallagher, 'Who was that Masked Woman?: The Prostitute and the Playwright in the Comedies of Aphra Behn', *Women's Studies*, 15 (1) (1988), 30.

36   George Eliot, *George Eliot's Life as Related in her Letters and Journals*, arranged and edited by her husband, J. W. Cross, 3 vols (Edinburgh: William Blackwood & Sons, 1885), ii. 262.

Chapter Notes

1   This term was coined by the late D. F. McKenzie to describe the extended range of knowledges that are necessary for comprehending the history of a book as a material production. See D. F. McKenzie, *Bibliography and the Sociology of Texts* (London: British Library, [1986]) and Further Reading.

2   John Sutherland quoted in John O. Jordan and Robert L. Pattern, *Literature in the Marketplace: Nineteenth-Century British Publishing and Reading Practices* (Cambridge: Cambridge University Press, 1995), 1.

3   Robert Darnton quoted in ibid., 1.

4   Jordan and Pattern, *Literature in the Marketplace*, 2.

5   The most recent extended work on Dickens and his publishers is Robert L. Patten, *Charles Dickens and his Publishers* (Oxford: Clarendon, 1978). For previous work on Dickens's readers, see George H. Ford, *Dickens and his Readers: Aspects of Novel Criticism since 1836* (Cincinnati: Princeton University Press, 1955). Ford asks such questions as 'What kinds of English readers have read Dickens's novels [in the nineteenth century]? What aspects have they enjoyed or failed to enjoy? What were they expecting from prose fiction?' (vii).

6   John Butt and Kathleen Tillotson, *Dickens at Work* (London: Methuen, 1963), 230, quoting from Dickens's letters.

7   Ibid., 231.

8   Ibid., 230.

9   Richard D. Altick, *The English Common Reader: Social History of the Mass Reading Public 1800–1900* (Chicago: University of Chicago Press, [1957]), 9.

10   See Jonathan Rose, 'Rereading the English Common Reader: A Preface to a History of Audience', *Journal of the History of Ideas*, 53 (1992), 47–70.

11   Ibid., 48.

12   See David Vincent, *Bread, Knowledge and Freedom: A Study of Nineteenth-century Working Class Autobiography* (London: Europa, 1981); John Burnett, David Vincent and David Mayall, eds., *The Autobiography of the Working Class: An Annotated, Critical Bibliography*, 3 vols (Brighton: Harvester, 1984–9). Working-class autobiographical writing and the formation of class identities have been the subject of Regenia Gagnier's *Subjectivities: A History of Self-representation in Britain, 1832–1920* (Oxford: Oxford University Press, 1991) and Patrick Joyce, *Democratic Subjects: The Self and the Social in Nineteenth-century England* (Cambridge: Cambridge University Press, 1994).

13   Simon Eliot, 'The Business of Victorian Publishing', in Deirdre David, ed., *The Cambridge Companion to the Victorian Novel* (Cambridge: Cambridge University Press, 2001), 38.

14 John Sutherland, *Victorian Fiction: Writers, Publishers, Readers* (Basingstoke: Macmillan, 1995), 151.

15 N. N. Feltes, *Modes of Production of Victorian Novels* (Chicago: Chicago University Press, 1989), 38.

16 Ibid., 49.

17 Ibid., 50.

18 See John Sutherland, *Mrs Humphry Ward: Eminent Victorian, Pre-eminent Edwardian* (Oxford: Clarendon, 1990).

19 Gaye Tuchman with Nina E. Fortin, *Edging Women Out: Victorian Novelists, Publishers, and Social Change* (London: Routledge, 1989), 1.

20 Ibid., 7–8 (italic in original).

21 Sutherland in his later study of Victorian publishing says that critics will need to go beyond the 'classic canon', though he sees this, in evaluative terms, very much as a move downwards and his descriptions of those outside the canon are strongly pejorative: 'Beneath these 878 [very successful and relatively successful Victorian novelists] is a still invisible sub-stratum (of several thousands) composed, one suspects, of failures, rank amateurs, third rate hacks and utter nonentities. Some future literary archaeological tool will have to be devised to investigate these lower reaches'; Sutherland, *Victorian Fiction*, 164.

22 See, for instance, the texts cited in note 12 and the recent work of Brian Maidment on various genres, e.g., B. E. Maidment, ed., *The Poorhouse Fugitives: Self-taught Poets and Poetry in Victorian Britain* (2nd edn, Manchester: Carcanet, 1992); *Reading Popular Prints, 1790–1870* (Manchester: Manchester University Press, 1996); and 'Re-arranging the Year: The Almanac, the Day Book and the Year Book as Popular Literary Forms, 1789–1860', in Juliet John and Alice Jenkins, eds, *Rethinking Victorian Culture* (Basingstoke: Macmillan, 2000), 93–113.

23 Eliot, 'The Business of Victorian Publishing', 42.

24 See also Kate Flint, 'Reading Uncommonly: Virginia Woolf and the Practice of Reading', *Yearbook of English Studies*, 26 (1996), 187–98; and Flint, 'Women, Men, and the Reading of *Vanity Fair*', in James Raven, Helen Small, and Naomi Tadmor, eds, *The Practice and Representation of Reading in England* (Cambridge: Cambridge University Press, 1996), 246–62.

25 Kate Flint, *The Woman Reader 1837–1914* (Oxford: Clarendon, 1993), 330.

26 In Kate Flint, 'The Victorian Novel and its Readers', in Deidre David, ed., *The Cambridge Companion to the Victorian Novel* (Cambridge: Cambridge University Press, 2001), 17–36.

Further Reading

On Victorian publishing and fiction:

Allan C. Dooley, *Author and Printer in Victorian England* (Charlottesville and London: University Press of Virginia, 1992): argues that 'several technical advances employed by Victorian printers significantly influenced the texts of classic works of

English literature as we read them today'. Reveals the fluid nature of the Victorian novel as text, and the many opportunities printing gave for corrections. Argues that Victorian novelists 'seldom aimed in revising to change a work from what it had been before; they habitually honored themselves as they had been when they wrote a work, and tended to tidy their texts, not renovate them, for each successive reprint. In this the Victorians were unlike both the romantic predecessors and their modernist descendants, who in several notorious cases reworked their texts so completely as to create separate versions of works. Yet the consistency and continuity of the Victorians' attention to their texts does not mean that the last corrected impression of the final edition revised by the author is automatically the literary scholar's text of choice. For the same technology that created a sequence of opportunities for authors to revise, thus increasing for both Victorian authors and later scholars the importance of reprints, also imposed limits on the nature and extent of authorial revision.'

Lee Erickson, *The Economy of Literary Form: English Literature and the Industrialization of Publishing, 1800–1850* (Baltimore: Johns Hopkins University Press, 1996): mostly on poetry but some discussion of the transformations of novel publishing and efforts to sell fiction widely and cheaply.

N. N. Feltes, *Literary Capital and the Late Victorian Novel* (Wisconsin: University of Wisconsin Press, 1993): concept rather than empirically driven, this difficult book was the first to concentrate on the publishing business at the end of the century in an attempt 'to bring marxist [*sic*] structuralist theory to bear on the empirical records of late Victorian novel production'. Looks at how empirical facts about the late-Victorian publishing scene were 'symptomatic of determinate historical processes'.

Linda K. Hughes and Michael Lund, *The Victorian Serial* (Charlottesville: University Press of Virginia, 1991).

Michael Lund, 'Novels, Writers, and Readers in 1850', *Victorian Periodicals Review*, 17 (1984), 15–28: reader-response theory explored in a consideration of Dickens's and Thackeray's construction of the professional man of letters and the constraints this professionalism imposed.

Peter L. Shillingsburg, *Pegasus in Harness: Victorian Publishing and W. M. Thackeray* (Charlottesville and London: University Press of Virginia, 1992): patient documentation of bibliographical data about the publication of Thackeray's major works, revealing the illusory nature of the idea of a 'first edition', and the multiple variances of a single novel in its publishing history.

Michael Twyman, *Printing 1770–1970: An Illustrated History of its Development and Uses in England* (London: Eyre and Spottiswoode, 1970; repr. London: British Library in assoc. with Reading University Press, 1998): standard work on the technological changes in printing.

Deborah Wynne, *The Sensation Novel and the Victorian Family Magazine* (Basingstoke: Palgrave, 2001): analyses the thematic relationships between sensation novels and the magazines in which they were serialized. Concentrates on Wilkie Collins, Mary Braddon, Charles Dickens, Ellen Wood, and Charles Reade, as well as *All The Year Round*, *The Cornhill*, and *Once a Week*.

Bibliography:
D. F. McKenzie, *Bibliography and the Sociology of Texts* (London: British Library, 1987 [Panizzi Lectures 1985]): key text in transforming the direction of bibliography, which was concerned with the history of books independent of their meaning, into the modern History of the Book. McKenzie argues that 'bibliography is the discipline that studies texts as recorded forms, and the processes of their transmission, including their production and reception [...]. For any history of the book which excluded study of the social, economic and political motivations of publishing, the reasons why texts were written and read as they were, why they were rewritten and redesigned, or allowed to die, would degenerate into a feebly degressive [*sic*] book list and never rise to a readable history.'
William Proctor Williams and Craig S. Abbott, *An Introduction to Bibliographical and Textual Studies* (New York: Modern Language Association, 1999): covers analytical bibliography, descriptive bibliography, the text, textual criticism, editorial procedure, textual notation.

Working-class reading:
Jonathan Rose, *The Intellectual Life of the British Working Classes* (New Haven, Conn./London: Yale University Press, 2001): published too late to be discussed in the main text, this is Rose's major response to the question of readers considered on p. 264 above. Documents working-class reading patterns in great detail.

Reviewing:
Nicola Diane Thompson, *Reviewing Sex: Gender and the Reception of Victorian Novels* (Basingstoke: Macmillan, 1996): on the gender politics of fiction reviewing.

9

Postcolonial Readings

Edward Said – G. C. Spivak – Patrick Brantlinger – Daniel Bivona – Suvendrini Perera – Jenny Sharpe – Thomas Richards – Firdous Azim – Deirdre David – Susan Meyer

RANGE AND DIVERSITY OF POSTCOLONI-ALISM The field of literary study that has begun to flourish most recently in the academy is that now called 'postcolonialism'. It is a branch of the discipline with a rapidly increasing number of undergraduate courses in higher education and an already substantial corpus of critical and theoretical texts. Opening their collection of essays on *Postcolonial Criticism* (1997), Bart Moore-Gilbert, Gareth Stanton and Willy Maley were able to remark that 'Postcolonialism is one of the most fruitful and rapidly expanding fields in current academic study',[1] and its expansion continues. The range of postcolonialism is not, as this statement implies, confined to literary study. John McLeod's recent introductory survey, *Beginning Postcolonialism* (2000), was marketed by its publishers as useful for 'anyone studying English, History, Philosophy and Theory', but theologians, historians of art, those involved in cultural studies and in modern languages have also seen a surge of interest in postcolonialism, and this is not an exhaustive list. Postcolonialism's central interest is, like Marxism, feminism, and queer theory, in voices traditionally marginalized by conventional literary criticism, voices that, in actual life, are subjected to oppressive practices of power. For the postcolonialist, cultural difference is the key focus, and postcolonialist literary critics are concerned with the textual politics of ethnicity, discourses of race and otherness, the foreign, and the experience and representation of the colonized and the once-colonized. In bringing cultural difference to the foreground in its consideration of the political, postcolonialism made the most significant contribution to the development of identity politics in literary criticism in the 1990s.

John McLeod, in the body of his accessible introductory text, observed that the diversity of the postcolonial enterprise in the academy, as it stretched across disciplinary barriers, is at times problematic for literary critics as it has 'helped create "postcolonial theory" almost as a separate discipline [...] sometimes at the expense of criticism of postcolonial literature'.[2] There are other issues of debate in this emerging field: the growth and breadth of appeal of postcolonialism has not equated to agreement about scope, methodology or politics. Even more than with the History of the Book, with an ancestry that is longer than postcolonialism, the methodologies and critical/theoretical assumptions at work in the postcolonial enterprise are diverse and, in places, sharply contested. It is a highly politicized area and its sites of conflict are more than ordinarily contentious. Moore-Gilbert, Stanton and Maley labelled it an 'oppositional activity'.[3] They meant partly that it stands in opposition to certain forms of political oppression, but also, in the wider sense, that its practitioners are often in disagreement.

That disagreement can be energizing. Postcolonialism draws attention to its own continual methodological debate, often to celebrate it as productive, believing that out of dispute frequently comes a more refined sense of the nature of the critical enterprise. A few features of the main debates current among postcolonialists, an indication of some of the lines of division and disagreement, are visible in the relatively slim body of postcolonial work on the Victorian novel. Much critical work under the banner of postcolonialism has, naturally enough, been focused, where it has concentrated on literary texts, on the contemporary literature of postcolonial cultures. But the Victorian period, the age of particularly active British colonization, and later of empire, has none the less drawn some attention. Over the past two decades a small but significant corpus of work on Victorian fiction has emerged. This, clearly, is an area that will develop.[4]

CENTRAL INTERESTS OF POST-COLONIALISM

The main lines of argument about the Victorian novel are as follows. The first postcolonial studies of Victorian fiction in the 1980s concentrated on the representation of empire, race and Otherness, and the explicit expression of imperial/colonial ideology[5] in Victorian literature. Subsequently, attention turned towards covert expressions of and oblique relationships between fictional narratives and imperial themes. The emphasis was on significant silences, the unspoken, and the hinted, and what these revealed about ideas of empire in the culture. Generally speaking, the thrust of these approaches was to analyse how Victorian fiction was embedded in imperial ideology and how it helped sustain it. Even the form of the Victorian novel was discussed, in the early 1990s, as connected with the imperialist's relationship with the colonized. Feminism intervened prominently in the postcolonialist debate in the 1990s, however, to examine the role of women in the transmission of imperial ideology. A distinctive element of this feminist/postcolonial debate was the examination of how Victorian fiction had a more contradictory relationship with imperial ideology and, in places, contested it. Here, the accent of critical interpretation fell not on fiction's complicity with imperial ideology, nor on its function as its transmitter and naturalizer, but on how the novel could be read as a complex space in which ideology was both transmitted and queried, produced and challenged.

EARLY VIEWS OF VICTORIAN FICTION AND EMPIRE   This modern corpus has its own genealogy. There is a critical literature on the fiction of empire in the nineteenth century written well before the establishment of postcolonialism in the academy. Early criticism was, of course, distinct from the postcolonialism inspired by Foucault in that it did not consider the politics of textual representation and was not interested in critiquing how fictional discourse correlated with (or resisted) expressions of imperial power. Susanne Howe's brief *Novels of Empire* (1949) was an early example, though she was chiefly interested in later fiction. Other early texts included Jeffrey Meyers's *Fiction and the Colonial Experience* (1973), discussing Kipling, Conrad and Forster among others, and Martin Green's *Dreams of Adventure, Deeds of Empire* (1979), referred to below (see p. 317). Hugh Ridley's *Images of Imperial Rule*, though published in 1983, really belonged in the earlier tradition of writing. His methodology was independent of the implications of theory and did not negotiate with the emerging field of cultural studies. Ridley surveyed French, German and English literature that was buoyant about imperial conquests, that 'describ[ed] and prais[ed] the achievements of the colonial expansion of the late nineteenth century'.[6] He was uninterested in critiquing the politics behind this.

Ignoring the colonized, the effect of colonial expansion on the native peoples, Ridley's book expressed a critical position that was challenged by postcolonialism. Ridley argued that literature about empire and the colonies revealed almost nothing about native cultures: 'I treat colonial literature as an exclusively European phenomenon with next to nothing worthwhile to say about other races and cultures. No more than anti-Semitic literature can be used as a handbook to Jewish culture should colonial literature be treated as a source-book on the Third World.'[7] This was a problematic comparison to say the least. But Ridley's notion of the insignificance of the unrepresented was overthrown in postcolonial criticism. What was not said, who was not represented, not allowed to speak, and who or what was marginalized from the centre of the discourse became questions of key concern for postcolonialists, as they have been in different ways for feminists, Marxists and queer theorists.

SAID'S ORIENTALISM (1978) AND ITS CONSEQUENCES FOR FICTION   Edward Said's *Orientalism* (1978) is often taken as the founding work of the academy discipline of postcolonialism, though, certainly, critiques of the colonial enterprise had been articulated in critical texts earlier, not least by Ngugi wa Thiong'o[8] (see also Young's *Postcolonialism: An Historical Introduction* (2001) in the Further Reading section). Positioning Said at this point of origin is not without difficulties. But *Orientalism* did give the first significant, high-profile and theorized expression to the idea that literary artefacts from the nineteenth century were legible in terms of their implications for, and embeddedness in, imperial/colonial politics. Said moved from the study of representations of empire to consider the operation of power in those representations and this was a major event in the production of the field of postcolonial studies. Said's central claim utilized Foucault's notion of discourse and applied it to 'Orientalism', the Western practice of imagining, studying, cataloguing and writing about the East, which reached its apogee at the end of the nineteenth century. Orientalism, Said said, had to be considered not as an innocent academic discipline but 'as a Western style for dominating, restructuring, and having authority over the Orient'. 'My contention', he continued, 'is that without examining Orientalism as a discourse one cannot possibly understand the enormously systematic discipline by which European culture was able to manage – and even produce – the Orient politically, sociologically, militarily, ideologically, scientifically, and imaginatively during the post-Enlightenment period.'[9] In Said's work, Orientalism was understood as a discourse of imperial power through which Europe articulated authority over the East, and, by setting itself against this imagined Orient, honed its own sense of identity.

Said had little specific to say about Victorian fiction, though he made glancing comments about European and North American literary writers including Flaubert, Twain, Proust, Fitzgerald, Ruskin, Browning and Carlyle. But the overall thrust of his study, and his view of the interplay between writing and imperial ideology, was suggestive. It indicated that Victorian literature could be read as a site multiply inscribed by ideologies of empire. This has been the guiding assumption of postcolonial criticism of Victorian fiction ever since.

The first major text on the subject of Victorian fiction and ideologies of empire was Patrick Brantlinger's *Rule of Darkness: British Literature and Imperialism, 1830–1914* (1988). But prior to Brantlinger's study, and therefore before substantial work had been done on Victorian classic fiction and its relation to imperial ideology, came an essay that still reverberates in postcolonial studies and which needs to be discussed first. Gayatri Chakravorty Spivak's 'Three Women's Texts and a Critique of Imperialism', which appeared in *Critical Inquiry* (1985), raised uncomfortable questions for feminism and emergent postcolonialism in the Anglo-American academy, inaugurating a debate about the relationship between the Western feminist subject and imperialism that produced significant results in the 1990s (see Sharpe and David, below, pp. 320, 323–4). Also, Spivak offered a reading of a Victorian novel that helped set in motion assumptions for subsequent postcolonial readings of nineteenth-century fiction about fiction's complicity with ideology that continue to be debated.

SPIVAK AND THE EMBEDDEDNESS OF FICTION IN COLONIAL IDEOLOGY

Spivak, drawing on Derridean procedures (for instance, reading texts against the grain of their empirical logic),[10] aimed to critique the assumptions about ethnicity in what she framed monolithically as Western feminism. Her primary objective was not to contribute to the study of Victorian fiction. But the first text of her inquiry was Charlotte Brontë's *Jane Eyre* – subsequently to become a novel of special interest for postcolonial critics – and her views had considerable significance for the postcolonial analysis of Victorian fictional prose. Spivak argued, in the extract reproduced below, that Brontë's text offered a narrative of the triumph of a unified female subject who was a figure that anticipated demands of contemporary Western feminism for independence and self-fulfilment (compare this argument with my discussion of Gilbert and Gubar's *The Madwoman in the Attic* on pp. 82–91 above). Spivak saw the emergence of this figure in *Jane Eyre*, however, and the novel's narrative of Jane's progress towards fulfilment, as dependent on the destruction of the colonial subject, Bertha Mason, Rochester's mad Creole-descended wife. The western feminist subject was established, according to Spivak's reading of *Jane Eyre*, via the erasure of the Other, the colonial woman, the non-western subject.

Extract from Gayatri Chakravorty Spivak, 'Three Women's Texts and a Critique of Imperialism', *Critical Inquiry*, 12 (1) (1985), 243–9.

It should not be possible to read nineteenth-century British literature without remembering that imperialism, understood as England's social mission, was a crucial part of the cultural representation of England to the English. The role of literature in the production of cultural representation should not be ignored. These two obvious 'facts' continue to be disregarded in the reading of nineteenth-century British literature. This itself attests to the continuing success of the imperialist project, displaced and dispersed into more modern forms.

If these 'facts' were remembered, not only in the study of British literature but in the study of the literatures of the European colonizing cultures of the great age of imperialism, we would produce a narrative, in literary history, of the 'worlding' of what is now called 'the Third World.' To consider the Third World as distant cultures, exploited but with rich intact literary heritages waiting to be recovered, interpreted, and curricularized in English translation fosters the emergence of 'the Third World' as a signifier that allows us to forget that 'worlding,' even as it expands the empire of the literary discipline.

It seems particularly unfortunate when the emergent perspective of feminist criticism reproduces the axioms of imperialism. A basically isolationist admiration for the literature of the female subject in Europe and Anglo-America establishes the high feminist norm. It is supported and operated by an information-retrieval approach to 'Third World' literature which often employs a deliberately 'nontheoretical' methodology with self-conscious rectitude.

In this essay, I will attempt to examine the operation of the 'worlding' of what is today 'the Third World' by what has become a cult text of feminism: *Jane Eyre*. I plot the novel's reach and grasp, and locate its structural motors. [...]

I need hardly mention that the object of my investigation is the printed book, not its 'author.' To make such a distinction is, of course, to ignore the lessons of deconstruction. A deconstructive critical approach would loosen the binding of the book, undo the opposition between verbal text and the biography of the named subject 'Charlotte Brontë,' and see the two as each other's 'scene of writing.' In such a reading, the life that writes itself as 'my life' is as much a production in psychosocial space (other names can be found) as the book that is written by the holder of that named life – a book that is then consigned to what *is* most often recognized as genuinely 'social': the world of publication and distribution. To touch Brontë's 'life' in such a way, however, would be too risky here. We must rather strategically take shelter in an essentialism which, not wishing to lose the important advantages won by US mainstream feminism, will continue to honor the suspect binary oppositions – book and author, individual and history – and start with an assurance of the following sort: my readings here do not seek to undermine the excellence of the individual artist. If even minimally successful, the readings will incite a degree of rage against the imperialist narrativization of history, that it should produce so abject a script for her. I provide these assurances to allow myself some room to situate feminist individualism in its historical determination rather than simply to canonize it as feminism as such.

Sympathetic US feminists have remarked that I do not do justice to Jane Eyre's subjectivity. A word of explanation is perhaps in order. The broad strokes of my presuppositions are that what is at stake, for feminist individualism in the age of imperialism, is precisely the making of human beings, the constitution and 'interpellation' of the subject not only as individual but as 'individualist.' This stake is represented on two registers: childbearing and soul making. The first is domestic-society-through-sexual-reproduction cathected as 'companionate love'; the second is the imperialist project cathected as civil-society-through-social-mission. As the female individualist, not-quite/not-male, articulates herself in shifting relationship to what is at stake, the 'native female' as such (*within* discourse, *as* a signifier) is excluded from any share in this emerging norm. If we read this account from an isolationist perspective in a 'metropolitan' context, we see nothing there but the psychobiography of the militant female subject. In a reading such as mine, in contrast, the effort is to wrench oneself away from the mesmerizing focus of the 'subject-constitution' of the female individualist.

To develop further the notion that my stance need not be an accusing one, I will refer to a passage from Roberto Fernández Retamar's 'Caliban.'[1] José Enrique Rodó had argued in 1900 that the model for the Latin American intellectual in relationship to Europe could be Shakespeare's Ariel. In 1971 Retamar, denying the possibility of an identifiable 'Latin American Culture,' recast the model as Caliban. Not surprisingly, this powerful exchange still excludes any specific consideration of the civilizations of the Maya, the Aztecs, the Incas, or the smaller nations of what is now called Latin America. Let us note carefully that, at this stage of my argument, this 'conversation' between Europe and Latin America (without a specific consideration of the political economy of the 'worlding' of the 'native') provides a sufficient thematic description of our attempt to confront the ethnocentric and reverse-ethnocentric benevolent double bind (that is, considering the 'native' as object for enthusiastic information-retrieval and thus denying its own 'worlding') that I sketched in my opening paragraphs.

In a moving passage in 'Caliban,' Retamar locates both Caliban and Ariel in the postcolonial intellectual:

> There is no real Ariel–Caliban polarity: both are slaves in the hands of Prospero, the foreign magician. But Caliban is the rude and unconquerable master of the island, while Ariel, a creature of the air, although also a child of the isle, is the intellectual.

> The deformed Caliban – enslaved, robbed of his island, and taught the language by Prospero – rebukes him thus: 'You taught me language, and my profit on't / Is, I know how to curse.' ('C,' pp. 28, 11)

As we attempt to unlearn our so-called privilege as Ariel and 'seek from [a certain] Caliban the honor of a place in his rebellious and glorious ranks,' we do not ask that our students and colleagues should emulate us but that they should attend to us ('C,' p. 72). If, however, we are driven by a nostalgia for lost origins, we too run the risk of effacing the 'native' and stepping forth as 'the real Caliban,' of forgetting that he is a name in a play, an inaccessible blankness circumscribed by an interpretable text. The stagings of Caliban work alongside the narrativization of history: claiming to *be* Caliban legitimizes the very individualism that we must persistently attempt to undermine from within.

Elizabeth Fox-Genovese, in an article on history and women's history, shows us how to define the historical moment of feminism in the West in terms of female access to individualism.[2] The battle for female individualism plays itself out within the larger theater of the establishment of meritocratic individualism, indexed in the aesthetic field by the ideology of 'the creative imagination.' Fox-Genovese's presupposition will guide us into the beautifully orchestrated opening of *Jane Eyre*.

It is a scene of the marginalization and privatization of the protagonist: 'There was no possibility of taking a walk that day... Out-door exercise was now out of the question. I was glad of it,' Brontë writes (*JE*, p. 9). The movement continues as Jane breaks the rules of the appropriate topography of withdrawal. The family at the center withdraws into the sanctioned architectural space of the withdrawing room or drawing room; Jane inserts herself – 'I slipped in' – into the margin – 'A small breakfast-room *adjoined* the drawing room' (*JE*, p. 9; my emphasis).

The manipulation of the domestic inscription of space within the upwardly mobilizing currents of the eighteenth-and nineteenth-century bourgeoisie in England and France is well known. It seems fitting that the place to which Jane withdraws is not only not the withdrawing room but also not the dining room, the sanctioned place of family meals. Nor is it the library, the appropriate place for reading. The breakfast room 'contained a book-case' (*JE*, p. 9). As Rudolph Ackerman wrote in his *Repository* (1823), one of the many manuals of taste in circulation in nineteenth-century England, these low bookcases and stands were designed to 'contain all the books that may be desired for a sitting-room without reference to the library.'[3] Even in this already triply off-center place, 'having drawn the red moreen curtain nearly close, I [Jane] was shrined in double retirement' (*JE*, pp. 9–10).

Here in Jane's self-marginalized uniqueness, the reader becomes her accomplice: the reader and Jane are united – both are reading. Yet Jane still preserves her odd privilege, for she continues never quite doing the proper thing in its proper place. She cares little for reading what is *meant* to be read: the 'letter-press.' *She* reads the pictures. The power of this singular hermeneutics is precisely that it can make the outside inside. 'At intervals, while turning over the leaves of my book, I studied the aspect of that winter afternoon.' Under 'the clear panes of glass,' the rain no longer penetrates, 'the drear November day' is rather a one-dimensional 'aspect' to be 'studied,' not decoded like the 'letter-press' but, like pictures, deciphered by the unique creative imagination of the marginal individualist (*JE*, p. 10).

Before following the track of this unique imagination, let us consider the suggestion that the progress of *Jane Eyre* can be charted through a sequential arrangement of the family/counter-family dyad. In the novel, we encounter, first, the Reeds as the legal family and Jane, the late Mr Reed's sister's daughter, as the representative of a near incestuous counter-family; second, the Brocklehursts, who run the school Jane is sent to, as the legal family and Jane, Miss Temple, and Helen Burns as a counter-family that falls short because it is only a community of women; third, Rochester and the mad Mrs Rochester as the legal family and Jane and Rochester as the illicit counter-family. Other items may be added to the thematic chain in this sequence: Rochester and Céline Varens as structurally functional counter-family; Rochester and Blanche Ingram as dissimulation of legality – and so on. It is during this sequence that Jane is moved from the counter-family to the family-in-law. In the next sequence, it is Jane who restores full family status to the as-yet-incomplete community of siblings, the Riverses. The final sequence of the book is a *community of families*, with Jane, Rochester, and their children at the center.

In terms of the narrative energy of the novel, how is Jane moved from the place of the counter-family to the family-in-law? It is the active ideology of imperialism that provides the discursive field.

(My working definition of 'discursive field' must assume the existence of discrete 'systems of signs' at hand in the socius, each based on a specific axiomatics. I am identifying these systems as discursive fields. 'Imperialism as social mission' generates the possibility of one such axiomatics. How the individual artist taps the discursive field at hand with a sure touch, if not with transhistorical clairvoyance, in order to make the narrative structure move I hope to demonstrate through the following example. It is crucial that we extend our analysis of this example beyond the minimal diagnosis of 'racism.')

Let us consider the figure of Bertha Mason, a figure produced by the axiomatics of imperialism. Through Bertha Mason, the white Jamaican Creole, Brontë renders the human/animal frontier as acceptably indeterminate, so that a good greater than the letter of the Law can be broached. Here is the celebrated passage, given in the voice of Jane:

> In the deep shade, at the further end of the room, a figure ran backwards and forwards. What it was, whether beast or human being, one could not ... tell: it grovelled, seemingly, on all fours; it snatched and growled like some strange wild animal: but it was covered with clothing, and a quantity of dark, grizzled hair, wild as a mane, hid its head and face. (*JE*, p. 295)

In a matching passage, given in the voice of Rochester speaking *to* Jane, Brontë presents the imperative for a shift beyond the Law as divine injunction rather than human motive. In the terms of my essay, we might say that this is the register not of mere marriage or sexual reproduction but of Europe and its not-yet-human Other, of soul making. The field of imperial conquest is here inscribed as Hell:

> 'One night I had been awakened by her yells ... it was a fiery West Indian night ...
> ' "This life," said I at last, "is hell! – this is the air – those are the sounds of the bottomless pit! *I have a right* to deliver myself from it if I can ... Let me break away, and go home to God!" ...
> 'A wind fresh from Europe blew over the ocean and rushed through the open casement: the storm broke, streamed, thundered, blazed, and the air grew pure.... It was true Wisdom that consoled me in that hour, and showed me the right path....
> 'The sweet wind from Europe was still whispering in the refreshed leaves, and the Atlantic was thundering in glorious liberty....
> ' "Go," said Hope, "and live again in Europe.... You have done all that God and Humanity require of you." ' (*JE*, pp. 310–11; my emphasis)

It is the unquestioned ideology of imperialist axiomatics, then, that conditions Jane's move from the counter-family set to the set of the family-in-law. Marxist critics such as Terry Eagleton have seen this only in terms of the ambiguous *class* position of the governess.[4] Sandra Gilbert and Susan Gubar, on the other hand, have seen Bertha Mason only in psychological terms, as Jane's dark double.[5]

I will not enter the critical debates that offer themselves here. Instead, I will develop the suggestion that nineteenth-century feminist individualism could conceive of a 'greater' project than access to the closed circle of the nuclear family. This is the project of soul making beyond 'mere' sexual reproduction. Here the native 'subject' is not almost an animal but rather the object of what might be termed the terrorism of the categorical imperative.

I am using 'Kant' in this essay as a metonym for the most flexible ethical moment in the European eighteenth century. Kant words the categorical imperative, conceived as the universal moral law given by pure reason, in this way: 'In all creation every thing one chooses and over which one has any power, may be used *merely as means*; man alone, and with him every rational creature, is an *end in himself*.' It is thus a moving displacement of Christian ethics from religion to philosophy. As Kant writes: 'With this agrees very well the possibility of such a command as: *Love God above everything, and thy neighbor as thyself.* For as a command it requires respect for a law which *commands love* and does not leave it to our own arbitrary choice to make this our principle.'[6]

The 'categorical' in Kant cannot be adequately represented in determinately grounded action. The dangerous transformative power of philosophy, however, is that its formal subtlety can be travestied in the service of the state. Such a travesty in the case of the categorical imperative can justify the imperialist project by producing the following formula: *make* the heathen into a human so that he can be treated as an end in himself. This project is presented as a sort of tangent in *Jane Eyre*, a tangent that escapes the closed circle of the *narrative* conclusion. The tangent narrative is the story of St John Rivers, who is granted the important task of concluding the *text*.

At the novel's end, the *allegorical* language of Christian psychobiography – rather than the textually constituted and seemingly *private* grammar of the creative imagination which we noted in the novel's opening – marks the inaccessibility of the imperialist project as such to the nascent 'feminist' scenario. The concluding passage of *Jane Eyre* places St John Rivers within the fold of *Pilgrim's Progress*. Eagleton pays no attention to this but accepts the novel's ideological lexicon, which establishes St John Rivers' heroism by identifying a life in Calcutta with an unquestioning choice of death. Gilbert and Gubar, by calling *Jane Eyre* 'Plain Jane's progress,' see the novel as simply replacing the male protagonist with the female. They do not notice the distance between sexual reproduction and soul making, both actualized by the unquestioned idiom of imperialist presuppositions evident in the last part of *Jane Eyre*:

> Firm, faithful, and devoted, full of energy, and zeal, and truth, [St John Rivers] labours for his race.... His is the sternness of the warrior Greatheart, who guards his pilgrim convoy from the onslaught of Apollyon.... His is the ambition of the high master-spirit[s]... who stand without fault before the throne of God; who share the last mighty victories of the Lamb; who are called, and chosen, and faithful. (*JE*, p. 455)

Earlier in the novel, St John Rivers himself justifies the project: 'My vocation? My great work?... My hopes of being numbered in the band who have merged all ambitions in the glorious one of bettering their race – of carrying knowledge into the realms of ignorance – of substituting peace for war – freedom for bondage – religion for superstition – the hope of heaven for the fear of hell?' (*JE*, p. 376). Imperialism and its territorial and subject-constituting project are a violent deconstruction of these oppositions. [...]

Notes

1 See R. F. Retamar, 'Caliban: Notes Towards a Discussion of Culture in our America', *Massachusetts Review*, 15 (1974), 7–72. Hereafter 'C' in text.
2 E. Fox-Genovese, 'Placing Women's History in History', *New Left Review*, 133 (1982), 5–29.
3 R. Ackerman, *The Repository of Arts, Literature, Commerce, Manufactures, Fashions, and Politics* (London, 1823), 310.
4 In T. Eagleton, *Myths of Power: A Marxist Study of the Brontës* (London, 1975).
5 In *The Madwoman in the Attic*, see pp. 82–91 above.
6 I. Kant, *Critique of Practical Reason* (Chicago, 1952), 328, 326.

Patrick Brantlinger's *The Spirit of Reform: British Literature and Politics 1832–1867* (1977) (discussed on pp. 161–2 above) located fiction in the matrix of British politics, but it was domestic politics that interested him. He said little about the expanding empire, the politics of colonial administration, the pressure placed on internal governments by the increasingly complicated and volatile international scene. This, as Brantlinger admitted himself, was misleading. His *Rule of Darkness: British Literature and Imperialism, 1830–1914* (1988), three years after Spivak's intervention, was offered as a 'sequel'[11] that covered this omitted territory. Brantlinger's thesis, at one level, was simple: 'Imperialism', he said, 'understood as an evolving but pervasive set of attitudes and ideas toward the rest of the world, influenced all aspects of Victorian and Edwardian culture.'[12] It was a claim that massively expanded Said's argument about cultural artefacts' relation to Orientalism. Brantlinger also imagined the nature of that influence in relatively straightforward terms, and his argument was related to Spivak's reading of *Jane Eyre* in so far as he saw fiction as implicated in colonialist politics. Additionally, he saw literature as one of the ways in which colonial ideology was produced and circulated.

BRANTLINGER'S *RULE OF DARKNESS* (1988) AND EXPLICIT ENGAGEMENTS WITH EMPIRE

Brantlinger investigated how colonial/imperial ideology was registered in the textures of Victorian fiction (and other literary forms), regardless of the views of the authors about domestic politics. Moreover, he was not confined to a single genre. Martin Green, arguing that 'Adventure [...] is the energizing myth of empire'[13] in his *Dreams of Adventure, Deeds of Empire* (1979), investigated three hundred years of adventure fiction and its connection with ideas and ideals of empire. It was this form of generic limitation that Brantlinger loosened. 'Imperialism', he said, 'influenced not only the tradition of the adventure tale but the tradition of "serious" domestic realism as well. Adventure and domesticity, romance and realism, are the seemingly opposite poles of a single system of discourse, the literary equivalents of imperial domination abroad and liberal reform at home.'[14]

Brantlinger, concerned with explicit representations of empire and imperial themes, reminded his readers that empire was not an invisible presence in Victorian literature, but merely an overlooked one. In chapter 1 he provided an overview of the politics of empire in the century, while in chapter 2 he looked at the seaman's tales of Frederick Marryat; chapter 3 was on Thackeray and *The Newcomes* (1853–5), and chapter 4 considered the theme of emigration and transportation in Dickens, Reade, and Bulwer-Lytton. Literary treatments of the Near East from Byron to Sir Richard Burton's *Pilgrimage to Al-Medinah and Mecca* (1855) were examined in chapter 5; explorers' narratives and the myth of the dark continent in chapter 6. Representations of the Indian 'Mutiny', the links between occultism and imperialism in late Victorian and Edwardian England, and the novels of Joseph Conrad formed the topics of the last three chapters.

The reading of Thackeray in *Rule of Darkness* provides a discrete example of the kind of connections between literature and colonial ideology that Brantlinger explored. As Brantlinger was concentrating on writers who wrote explicitly about colonial possessions, William Makepeace Thackeray was ideal. Not only was he born in Calcutta in 1811, and lived there before being sent to school in England at the age of 6, his novels featured India significantly. Brantlinger read Thackeray's *Pendennis* (1848–50) and *The Newcomes* for what they said about his native country, finding them expressive of colonial ideologies and racist politics, visible most in the negative construction of India and Indians:

> The plots of both *Pendennis* and *The Newcomes* are series of more or less successful maneuvers to keep the central characters uncontaminated by lower, peripheral social realms. In both novels, immorality, crime, and disease emanate in part from India, the farthest periphery. In *Pendennis* the criminal element, represented most fully by the Colonel Altamont, is European, though with Indian and colonial links. In *The Newcomes*, the chief villain is Rummun Loll, who bears ultimate blame for both the fortune and the misfortune of the British protagonists, father and son. (Indeed, the fortune the Colonel makes from the bank is a kind of misfortune, as is its loss.) On to Rummun Loll's unsavoury character Thackeray projects all his own resentment for the loss of his Indian-based fortune in 1833. The Bengali tycoon serves as a scapegoat for any lingering guilt Thackeray and his readers may have that the British do not really belong in India – that they conquered an empire there by unlawful force, and by force they have been extracting fortunes from that empire ever since. Thackeray's treatment of the Bengali businessman offers an especially clear instance of blaming the victim, a racist pattern that underwrites all imperialist ideology.[15]

Brantlinger, thirteen years after *Rule of Darkness*, stated in more concise terms his views about the whole of the Victorian novel's connivance with offensive ideology in 'Race and the Victorian Novel' in the *Cambridge Companion to the*

Victorian Novel (2001). Here, he argued, qualified only briefly by reference to Susan Meyer's work, discussed below, that 'most Victorian novels' were implicated in racist representations, presenting racially marked outsiders as 'either comic stereotypes or figures of monstrosity meant to repel rather than to evoke sympathy'.[16]

Reading the embeddedness of nineteenth-century fiction in ideologies of empire, or exposing more directly levels of complicity, continued to be powerful strategies for other critics after *Rule of Darkness* in the 1990s. But, in distinction from Brantlinger's interest in the explicit, other writers at the beginning of the decade considered ways in which imperial ideology was detectable in the silences and gaps of textual representation or was obliquely represented through allegory. Daniel Bivona, in *Desire and Contradiction: Imperial Visions and Domestic Debates in Victorian Literature* (1990), extended Said's Foucauldian views on Orientalism to consider imperialism as the hidden heart of Britishness, the 'unconscious' of nineteenth-century English identity. Its presence was secret but pervasive; it was 'lurking under the surface of a variety of discourses'.[17] In literature, Bivona argued, it was detectable in a multiplicity of forms including apparently unrelated fictional texts such as Lewis Carroll's *Alice's Adventures in Wonderland* (1865) and Thomas Hardy's *Jude the Obscure* (1894–5). *Jude*, Bivona argued, was a 'parable of the exercise of the imperial power to exclude translated into the terms of social class'.[18]

Suvendrini Perera, in *Reaches of Empire: The English Novel from Edgeworth to Dickens* (1991), a book that gained a wide circulation, developed ideas absorbed from Foucault and Edward Said, together with notions of ideological disclosure suggested by Pierre Macherey. Like Brantlinger and Bivona, Perera proposed that the Victorian novel was implicated in ideologies of empire and helped in its transmission and naturalization: 'Empire', she said, 'is not simply expressed or reflected in the novel; in the period I discuss, it is [...] processed and naturalized by it'.[19] Like Bivona, Perera analysed the not said or the half-said in Victorian fiction. However, because she was interested not only in fiction's complicity with ideology but in how it registered anxieties about the imperial project, she also looked, distinctively, at the way in which novels were secretly inscribed by cultural concerns about colonized subjects and the threats posed by the foreign. She argued that fiction obliquely registered an increasingly urgent set of fears about engulfment, feminization and violence associated with the colonies. Victorian fiction's nervous engagement with the 'suggestive hidden presence'[20] of empire, she said, reached a climax in Dickens's unfinished novel *The Mystery of Edwin Drood* (1870). This text, which has also attracted a lot of attention from postcolonialists, silently brought anxieties of empire into a rural English setting, turning 'many of the tensions of empire' into 'sexual and economic tensions [...in] an ancient English cathedral town'.[21]

BIVONA AND THE HIDDEN PRESENCE OF EMPIRE

PERERA AND IMPERIAL ANXIETIES

SHARPE AND
FICTION'S
COLLUSION
WITH
IDEOLOGY

Jenny Sharpe's *Allegories of Empire: The Figure of Woman in the Colonial Text* (1993) continued to focus attention on Victorian texts and their relationship with imperial ideology. She also introduced a prominent feminist dimension that related to Spivak's ideas about the development of the feminist subject as dependent on the erasure of the colonial Other. Sharpe's interest was partly, like Spivak's, in contemporary feminism and she used feminist theories of rape and sexual difference to argue that present-day notions of female agency were implicated in an imperial past. Sharpe's claim involved consideration of nineteenth-century fiction, however, and her proposition here was that fiction revealed how the figure of the woman was instrumental in shifting a colonial system of meaning from self-interest and moral superiority to self-sacrifice and racial superiority. She returned to Charlotte Brontë's *Jane Eyre* to read it, again, as a narrative propagating a racist politics of British supremacy. Sharpe maintained that Brontë's novel cleared a space for a new model of female selfhood, enabling 'a new female subjectivity[:] the domestic individual', by imaging its heroine as ethically and racially above the foreigner: it 'ground[ed] "women's mission" in the moral and racial superiority of the colonialist as civilizer'.[22] Affirming the suggestion made by Spivak, Sharpe said that *Jane Eyre* represented the emergence of the feminist individualist as dependent on the silencing of the foreign.

RICHARDS
AND THE
IMPERIAL
ARCHIVE

Another significant book published in 1993, this time unconnected with gender, considered late Victorian fiction and its relationship with cultural efforts to control the empire through information. Thomas Richards's *The Imperial Archive: Knowledge and the Fantasy of Empire* (1993) argued that the novel – he concentrated on Kipling, Wells and Stoker – was indebted to British imperial practices because it was fascinated by the acquisition of knowledge about the empire. The gathering of information was, Richards argued, the most prominent way in which British administrators after the mid-1860s could deal with the far-flung reaches of their colonial possessions: they could not actually govern foreign lands as they were too distant, but through maps and surveys, censuses, and statistics, they created the illusion of governance. Britain thus made sense of an empire that existed in the first place textually and, to an extent, was literally a fiction (for a different view of the role of the British colonial administrator, see Bivona's *British Imperial Literature* (1998) in the Further Reading section). Richards considered four late-Victorian and early twentieth-century fictional texts in which knowledge acted as 'much more than a convenient surrogate for power', but was its cutting edge: in these novels, the 'pursuit of knowledge is the vanguard, not the rearguard, of the pursuit of power'.[23] Richards considered how, in Stoker's *Dracula* (1897), 'a monster is defeated by mastery of the means of information', while in Kipling's *Kim* (1901), the India Survey, a geographical bureau, 'defeats a Russian plot to extend influence in the Indian subcontinent'.[24] Richard's interest in how these novels presented a body of information as an expression of power generated a particularly fresh reading of how late-Victorian fiction expressed an imperial impulse.

Understanding the way in which Victorian fiction was inscribed by imperial ideology took a new direction in Firdous Azim's consideration of fictional form in 1993. Susanne Howe, in her early *Novels of Empire* (1949), had implied that there was a correspondence between the growing boundaries of the British Empire and the growth of the nineteenth-century novel as a form.[25] This hint was chased up by a number of writers – Perera discussed it – but it was given its most ample analysis in Azim's *The Colonial Rise of the Novel* (1993). I referred, in chapter 6 and 7, to the critical interest in cultural and ideological embeddedness among writers on novel form in the 1980s and 1990s. Discussion of the connections between Darwinian narrative and the form of mid-Victorian fictional narrative was a prominent example of the former (see pp. 230–52 above); Catherine Belsey's argument about the bourgeois ideology of coherence in classic realism was a significant example of the latter (see pp. 121–32 above). But in 1993 the embeddedness of the novel's form in ideologies of empire was outlined, as Azim, augmenting Howe's observation, argued that critics should acknowledge the political significance of the authoritative, silencing, narrating voice of the novel as related to colonial expansion and the rise of imperialist authority. Azim suggested that there was a parallel between the assumptions and narrative procedures of the classic Victorian novel and the practices of colonial domination: both were built on a principle of exclusion and the marginalization of non-central voices.

AZIM AND THE IMPERIAL FORM OF FICTION

Extract from Firdous Azim, *The Colonial Rise of the Novel* (London: Routledge, 1993), 29–31.

The imperialist heritage of the novel can be traced to the moment of its birth, and is visible in its themes, as well as in the problematic nature of its status as 'literature'. The novel is placed in a position of difficulty – it oscillates between a factual and fictional world, it reproduces, while subverting, the tenets of capitalism, it has a long history which places it somewhere on the fringes of respectable writing. Its uneasy positioning is echoed in the history of its reception and criticism.

Feminism's stress on the novel initially took the notion of unified subjectivity unquestioningly. That moment had been prompted by a desire to formulate a history of women's writing, through which a community of women could be defined. The impossibility of that notion is brought into focus when the historical and social processes guiding and controlling novel production and the access of women to this sphere of writing are analysed. The formation of a list of texts leading to the formation of a nation/community is belied, as the differentiated arena in which texts are produced and disseminated is analysed.

Feminism's journey through the annals of the English novel is especially interesting and significant as it records an effort to find an *other* voice in this genre of writing. This voice had been identified as women's voice, which had been marginalised and dominated within a system of patriarchal bourgeois ideology. But differences in the positioning of women (earliest brought out in Françoise Basch's *Relative Creatures*, 1974) made it impossible to hold on to this voice as central and as centrally determining of all women's realities. In this early feminist historicising of the novel, Charlotte Brontë's writings occupied a central position. In that work (Showalter, Moers, Millett, Gubar and Gilbert)[1] the writing of the Brontës provided a popular point of departure, and the lives and works of the Brontë sisters were read as representing many of the problems associated with women. Charlotte Brontë wrote 'about' women: her books are seen to be female-centred, to embody a protest against and to present a critique of the feminine situation. The first break with this was the recognition of the Gothic as part of the tradition of women's writing, resulting in a diversion from realism to concentrate on the fantasy elements in the text.[2] Even within this, Charlotte Brontë's works remain central, representing, as they do, a blend of, or oscillation between, realist and fantasy forms.

However, this easy celebration of women's voices in the novel overlooked crucial factors in the history of the origins of the novel. Gayatri Spivak, commenting on *Jane Eyre*, writes that nineteenth-century British literature cannot be read 'without remembering that imperialism, understood as England's social mission, was a crucial part of the cultural representation of England to the English'.[3] The birth of the novel coincided with the European colonial project; it partook of and was part of a discursive field concerned with the construction of a universal and homogeneous subject. This subject was held together by the annihilation of other subject-positions. The novel is an imperial genre, not in theme merely, not only by virtue of the historical moment of its birth, but in its formal structure – in the construction of that narrative voice which holds the narrative structure together. Charlotte Brontë's novels have to be read against this background [...].

Histories of the novel generally treat colonialism as a theme, reflected within the narrative terrain. The theme of colonialism is looked at from different perspectives. For example, Martin Green's *Dreams of Adventure*,

Deeds of Empire (1979), is celebratory, and appreciates novels such as *Robinson Crusoe* for the spirit of adventure, leading to the establishment of colonial rule and trade. The subject of the novel is outward-reaching, exploring and victorious. On the other hand, Patrick Brantlinger's *Rule of Darkness: British Literature and Imperialism* (1988) traces the development of the British novel from the early part of the nineteenth century to the twentieth century as reflective of the fluctuations of Britain's imperial history, which, from the initial adventurousness of Marryat's seafaring novels, progresses to the dark visions presented in Joseph Conrad's writings. I propose to carry this argument further, and to show that the translation of imperialism into the novelistic genre is not limited to its thematic concerns, but refers to the formation of the subjective positions of the coloniser and the colonised within the colonial terrain. The narration in the novel is also dependent on the centrality of the narrating subject. The notion of the centrality of this subject and of the homogeneity of its narration had also come into being within the colonising enterprise, as has the necessity of constructing a pedagogical subject out of the texts of English literature. The relationship between the novel and the imperialist project is many-faceted, and can be viewed from at least three vantage-points: of theme, of the formation of subject-positions, and of the formation of a pedagogical subject. [...]

Notes

1 See chapter 3.
2 This turn against realism is discussed on pp. 133–5 above.
3 G. C. Spivak, 'Three Women's Texts and a Critique of Imperialism', *Critical Inquiry*, 12 (1985): 243. For an extract from this text, see pp. 310–17 above.

Spivak inaugurated critical concern about the intersection between race and gender in Victorian fiction. This was developed by Sharpe's study but was the central focus of Deirdre David's influential *Rule Britannia: Women, Empire, and Victorian Writing* (1995). David, developing ideas about fiction's complicity with imperial ideology, asked how far Victorian women, consciously or not, served the cause of the empire. She considered *Jane Eyre*, Dickens's *Dombey and Son*, Wilkie Collins's *Moonstone*, and H. Rider Haggard's *She*. David mapped a change through the period, arguing that women moved to the heart of imperial ideology as self-sacrificing educators and civilizers to become, in the end, the focus of male anxiety about female authority and strength. According to David:

DEIRDRE DAVID, WOMEN AND THE EMPIRE

In the early-nineteenth-century nostalgia for a masculine spirit of adventure imagined as enfeebled by calls for moral improvement of the natives, women are tolerated as necessary but meddlesome; in the mid-Victorian Liberal emphasis upon the cares and duties involved in such imagined improvement, women are required, in historical actuality and in symbolic representations, to perform sacrificial roles, and in the late-nineteenth-century questioning of British engagement abroad, worries about empire and race are inseparable from patriarchal worries about female cultural assertion.[26]

The pattern that emerged from David's New Historicist study (see p. 162 above for the principles of New Historicism) was one in which not so much the whole novel but the female represented in it, and in related historical documents, was tightly bound in the logic of the empire. David ended her study with a consideration of Emilia Gould in Joseph Conrad's *Nostromo* (1904), suggesting that women in fiction at the end of the nineteenth century and the beginning of the twentieth began to critique the discourses of empire and to reverse their previous association with its ideology.

I have stressed an emphasis, though not an exclusive one, in postcolonial criticism of the 1980s and early 1990s, on the way novels were read as variously complicit with imperial ideology. The majority of critical texts so far examined interpreted Victorian novels as absorbing, to different degrees, ideologies of colonial possession or imperial expansion, or perceived them helping propagate such ideologies. Some critics, such as Perera, did suggest, often briefly, that the hegemonic ideology was ruptured in Victorian fiction – that, as Daniel Bivona put it, 'imperialist mentality [. . . was] pervasive but also challenged'.[27] But the implications of this understanding did not dominate the postcolonial debate. Deirdre David, indeed, argued that the critique of imperialism in fiction began, as far as female figures were concerned, only at the end of Victoria's reign. In the middle of the 1990s, however, Susan Meyer explored the challenge of the novel to dominant colonial ideology and her work represented a significant shift in emphasis.

MEYER AND FICTION'S DOUBLE RELATIONSHIP WITH COLONIAL IDEOLOGY

Meyer's *Imperialism at Home: Race and Victorian Women's Fiction* (1996) took issue with the notion of the Victorian novel's general collusion with imperial ideology, disagreeing with Deirdre David to suggest a complicated and contradictory relationship in women's writing. Meyer's sensitivity to the polyvocality of the relationship of fictional prose with ideology can be compared with Peter Garrett's work on Bakhtin, the multi-plot novel, and the indeterminacy of Victorian fiction discussed on pp. 219–24 above. Meyer's way of reorientating the postcolonial approach to Victorian fiction was, appropriately enough, to challenge Spivak's essay, discussed above, and its view of the ideological embeddedness of Charlotte Brontë's *Jane Eyre*. Meyer's chapter on *Jane Eyre*, an extract from which is reproduced below, argued that Brontë's work was in parts critical of the ideology of empire, suspicious of the British colonial project, and sympathetic in places to the oppressed races under British rule. The novel was not univocal in such criticism, Meyer claimed, and she was continually sensitive to the doubleness of its political position. Her understanding of the novel's complex relationship with the ideologies of empire may point to the future direction of postcolonial studies of nineteenth-century fiction.

Extract from Susan Meyer, *Imperialism at Home: Race and Victorian Women's Fiction* (New York and London: Cornell University Press, 1996), 60–66.

The colonies play an important metaphorical role in each of Charlotte Brontë's major novels. The heroines of *Shirley* (1849) and *Villette* (1853) are both compared to people of nonwhite races experiencing the force of European imperialism. Louis Moore and M. Paul, the men whom the heroines love, either leave or threaten to leave Europe for the colonies, and in each case the man's dominating relationship with a colonial people is represented as a substitute for his relationship with the rebellious heroine. In order to determine if Shirley loves him, Louis Moore tells her that he intends to go to North America and live with the Indians, where, he immediately suggests, he will take one of the 'sordid savages' as his wife.[1] Similarly, at the end of *Villette*, M. Paul departs for the French West Indian colony of Guadeloupe to look after an estate there instead of marrying Lucy. Such an estate would indeed have needed supervision in the early 1850s, as the French slaves had just been emancipated in 1848. Brontë suggests the tumultuous state of the colony by the ending she gives the novel: M. Paul may be killed off by one of the tropical storms that Brontë, like writers as diverse as Monk Lewis and Harriet Martineau, associates with the rage and the revenge of the black West Indians?[2] If M. Paul is a white colonist, Lucy is like a native resisting control: Brontë has Lucy think of her own creative impulse as a storm god, 'a dark Baal.' These metaphors make the novel's potentially tragic ending more ambiguous: it may not be entirely a tragedy if M. Paul is indeed killed by a storm and does not return from dominating West Indian blacks to marry the Lucy he calls 'sauvage.'[3]

The metaphorical use of race relations to represent conflictual gender relations is even more overt in Brontë's *The Professor* (1846). The novel begins as an unreceived letter, whose intended recipient has disappeared into 'a government appointment in one of the colonies.'[4] William Crimsworth's own subsequent experiences among the young women of a Belgian boarding school are represented as a parallel act of colonization. Crimsworth discreetly compares his Belgian-Catholic girl students to blacks whom he must forcibly keep under control. He likens one Caroline, for example, to a runaway West Indian slave when he describes her curling, 'somewhat coarse hair,' 'rolling black eyes,' and lips 'as full as those of a hot-blooded Maroon' (p. 86).[5] Even the atypical half-Swiss, half-English Frances Henri whom Crimsworth marries shows a potential rebelliousness against male domination that the novel figures using the imagery of race. Frances tells Crimsworth, with 'a strange kind of spirit,' that if her husband were a drunkard or a tyrant, marriage would be slavery, and that 'against slavery all right thinkers revolt' (p. 255). The metaphor is even more explicit when Frances tells Hunsden, who is matching wits with her in an argument about Switzerland, that if he marries a Swiss wife and then maligns her native country, his wife will arise one night and smother him 'even as your own Shakespeare's Othello smothered Desdemona' (p. 242). This imaginary wife's rebellion against women's subordination and against her gender role – she behaves like an angry man – precipitates her figurative blackness.

Even in the two existing chapters of Brontë's final and unfinished novel *Emma* (1853), race seems to be about to play an important figurative role: the heroine's suddenly apparent blackness suggests her social disenfranchisement due to gender, age, and social class. The two chapters are set in a boarding school and focus on a little girl, known as Matilda Fitzgibbon, who appears at first to be an heiress, but whose father disappears after leaving her at the school and cannot be located to pay her fees at the end of the first term. Matilda Fitzgibbon is revealed, at the end of the second chapter, to be of a race, or at least a physical appearance, that renders her susceptible to the following insult: '"If we were only in the good old times" said Mr Ellin "where we ought to be – you might just send Miss Matilda out to the Plantations in Virginia – sell her for what she's worth and pay yourself –"'[6] This revelation has been prepared for by several previous passages. Matilda, the narrator has informed us, has a physical appearance that makes her inadequate as a wealthy 'shew-pupil,' a physiognomy that repels the headmistress and causes her a 'gradually increasing peculiarity of feeling' (pp. 309, 312), and 'such a face as fortunately had not its parallel on the premises' (p. 313). Brontë has also given Matilda the name 'Fitz/gibbon,' one that suggests racist epithets when it is read in the context of the nineteenth-century scientific commonplace that blacks were low on the scale of being, closer to apes than to white Europeans: Matilda's last name is a patronymic that brands her the offspring of a monkey. Yet in a sense Matilda becomes black only at the moment in the novel in which she loses her social standing. Only then do any of those around her make any explicit references to her race or skin coloring, and only then does the reader become aware of what it is that is 'repulsive' in her 'physiognomy.' When Matilda becomes isolated, orphaned, unrooted, and poor – and more vulnerable and sympathetic – she is transformed by the narrative into a black child.

Brontë uses these references to relations between Europeans and races subjected to the might of European imperialism – in these instances, primarily native Americans and African slaves in the West Indies and the United States, although elsewhere in her fiction other peoples serve a similar metaphorical function – to represent various configurations of power in British society: female subordination in sexual relationships, female insurrection and rage against male domination, and the oppressive class position of the female without family ties and a middle-class income. She does so with a mixture of both sympathy for the oppressed and a conventional assertion of white racial supremacy: Matilda's apparently dark face is represented as repulsive, yet the situation that provokes Mr Ellin's harsh racism also evokes the reader's sympathy for Matilda. Lucy Snowe's strength of character is one of her most admirable traits – and yet to represent it Brontë invokes the Eurocentric idea of colonized savages. The figurative use of race relations in Brontë's major fiction reveals a conflict between sympathy for the oppressed and a hostile sense of racial supremacy, one that becomes most apparent in *Jane Eyre* (1847).

In the opening chapters of *Jane Eyre*, race is a controlling metaphor – the young Jane is compared to a slave both at Gateshead, as she resists John Reed's tyranny, and at Lowood where she argues the need to resist unjust domination and angrily states that she would refuse to be publicly 'flogged,' only later to find herself subjected to another form of public humiliation like 'a slave or victim.'[7] Although in a few of these references Brontë represses the recent and immediate history of British slaveholding by alluding in the same passages to a safely remote history of Roman acts of enslavement ('You are like a murderer – you are like a slave-driver – you are like the Roman emperors!' Jane cries out to John Reed in the opening chapter [p. 8]) the history of Britain's slaveholding, only nine years past at the time the novel was published, is inescapably evoked by such references. Indeed the novel will later hint at unflattering links between the British and the Roman empire. As the novel continues, the metaphor of slavery takes on such a central status that, although the novel remains situated in the domestic space, Brontë imports a character from the territory of the colonies (that territory also of her childhood writings) to give the metaphor a vivid presence. This realization of the metaphor through the creation of a character brings Brontë into a more direct confrontation with the history of British race relations. And Brontë's metaphorical use of race has a certain fidelity to the history of British imperialism. Brontë alludes to non-white races in the novel – primarily African slaves and Indians, though also Persians, Turks, and native Americans – in passages where she is evoking the idea of unjust oppression. But Brontë makes class and gender oppression the overt significance of these other races, displacing the historical reasons why nonwhite people might suggest the idea of oppression, at some level of consciousness, to nineteenth-century British readers. What begins then as an implicit critique of British domination and an identification with the oppressed collapses into merely an appropriation of the imagery of slavery, as the West Indian slave becomes the novel's archetypal image of the oppressed 'dark races.' Nonetheless, the novel's closure fails, in interesting ways, to screen out entirely the history of British imperialist oppression.

This complex metaphorical use of race explains much of the difficulty of understanding the politics of *Jane Eyre*. In an important reading of the significance of colonialism in this novel, Gayatri Spivak argues that 'the unquestioned ideology of imperialist axiomatics' informs Brontë's narrative and enables the individualistic social progress of the character Jane that has been celebrated by 'US mainstream feminists.' For her, Bertha, a 'white Jamaican Creole,' is a 'native "subject,"' indeterminately placed between human and animal and consequently excluded from the individualistic humanity that the novel's feminism claims for Jane.[8] While I agree with Spivak's broad critique of an individualistic strain of feminism, I find problematic her analysis of the workings of imperialist ideology and its relation to feminism, both in general and in *Jane Eyre*.

Spivak describes Bertha as at once a white woman and (as a native-born Jamaican white) a native, that is, as what she terms with little definition a 'native "subject."'[9] She is thus able to designate Bertha as either native or white in order to criticize both Brontë's *Jane Eyre* and Jean Rhys's *Wide Sargasso Sea* as manifestations of exclusive feminist individualism. *Jane Eyre*, she argues, gives the white Jane individuality at the expense of the 'native' Bertha; *Wide Sargasso Sea*, on the other hand, retells the story of *Jane Eyre* from Bertha's perspective and thus merely 'rewrites a canonical English text within the European novelistic tradition in the interest of the white Creole rather than the native' (p. 253). Bertha is either native or not native to suit Spivak's critique. Thus it is by sleight of hand that Spivak shows feminism to be inevitably complicitous with imperialism.

My own proposition is that the interconnection between the ideology of male domination and the ideology of racial domination, manifested in the comparisons between white women and people of nonwhite races in many texts in this period of European imperialist expansion, in fact resulted in a very different relation between imperialist ideology and the developing resistance of nineteenth-century British women to the gender hierarchy. *Jane Eyre* was written in an ideological context in which white women were frequently compared to people of nonwhite races, especially blacks, in order to emphasize the inferiority of both to white men. But as Brontë constructs the trope in *Jane Eyre*, the yoking between the two terms of the metaphor turns not on shared inferiority but on shared oppression. Although this figurative strategy does not preclude racism, it inevitably produces the suggestion that people of these 'other' races are also oppressed. While for the most part the novel suppresses the damning history of racial oppression and slavery, its ending betrays an anxiety that imperialism and oppression of other races constitute a stain upon English history and that the novel's own appropriation of nonwhite races for figurative ends bears a disturbing resemblance to that history. Thus although the ending of the novel does essentially permit the racial hierarchies of European imperialism to fall back into place, *Jane Eyre* is characterized not by Spivak's 'unquestioned ideology' of imperialism but by an ideology of imperialism that is questioned – and then reaffirmed – in interesting and illuminating ways. [. . .]

Notes

1   Charlotte Brontë, *Shirley*, ed. Herbert Rosengarten and Margaret Smith (Oxford: Clarendon Press, 1981), 613.

2   See Matthew Lewis, 'The Isle of Devils' (1815), in *Journal of a West India Proprietor* (London: John Murray, 1834), 261–89 and Harriet Martineau, *Demerara*, in *Illustrations of Political Economy* (London: Charles Fox, 1834), ii. 109–12.

3   Charlotte Brontë, *Villette*, ed. Herbert Rosengarten and Margaret Smith (Oxford: Clarendon Press, 1984), 456.

4   Charlotte Brontë, *The Professor*, ed. Margaret Smith and Herbert Rosengarten (Oxford: Clarendon Press, 1987), 14. Subsequent references are included in the text.

5   See Michael Craton, *Testing the Chains: Resistance to Slavery in the British West Indies* (Ithaca: Cornell University Press, 1982), esp. 61–7.

6   Charlotte Brontë, 'Emma,' appended to *The Professor*, ed. Smith and Rosengarten, 322–3. Subsequent references are included in the text.

7   Charlotte Brontë, *Jane Eyre*, ed. Jane Jack and Margaret Smith (Oxford: Clarendon Press, 1969), 63, 78. Subsequent references are included in the text.

8   Gayatri Chakravorty Spivak, 'Three Women's Texts and a Critique of Imperialism', *Critical Inquiry*, 12 (1985): 243–61. For an extract from this text, see pp. 310–17 above.

9   Here Spivak may be alluding to Homi Bhabha's notion of a unified 'colonial subject' that encompasses both the colonizer and colonized. Homi K. Bhabha, 'The Other Question...The Stereotype and Colonial Discourse', *Screen*, 24 (1983): 19.

Chapter Notes

1   Bart Moore-Gilbert, Gareth Stanton and Willy Maley, eds, *Postcolonial Criticism*, Longman Critical Reader (London: Longman, 1997), 1.

2   John McLeod, *Beginning Postcolonialism* (Manchester: Manchester University Press, 2000), 29.

3   Moore-Gilbert, Stanton and Maley, eds, *Postcolonial Criticism*, 9.

4   See Peter Widdowson, 'Hardy and Theory', in Dale Kramer, ed., *The Cambridge Companion to Thomas Hardy* (Cambridge: Cambridge University Press, 1999), 89.

5   I use imperialism and colonialism as more or less synonymous terms here as I don't want to open up a set of distinctions that are not central to the overall discussion. Clearly, however, colonialization is different from imperialism, and modern postcolonialists police their separation rigorously. See Young in the Further Reading Section.

6   Hugh Ridley, *Images of Imperial Rule* (London: Croom Helm, 1983), vii. Another work from the 1970s was Benita Parry's *Delusions and Discoveries: Studies on India in the British Imagination, 1880–1930* (1972). Parry's later work includes her *Conrad and Imperialism: Ideological Boundaries and Visionary Frontiers* (1983) and, most recently, Laura Chrisman and Benita Parry, eds, *Postcolonial Theory and Criticism, Essays and Studies*, 52 (Woodbridge: Brewer, 2000).

7   Ridley, *Images of Imperial Rule*, 2–3.

8   See Ngugi wa Thiong'o, *Homecoming: Essays on African and Caribbean Literature, Culture and Politics* (London: Heinemann, 1972). Ime Ikedden, in his 'Foreword' to this book, summarizes Ngugi's aims: 'Colonialism and capitalism are identified here as twin brothers whose mission is to exploit the material wealth of subject peoples, and who, in order to gain acceptability and perpetuation, enlist the services of their more sly but attractive first cousins, Christianity and Christian-orientated education, whose duty it is to capture the soul and the mind as well' (p. xii). Another important earlier study of the workings of colonialization was Octave Mannoni, *Prospero and Caliban: The Psychology of Colonization* (London: Methuen, 1956).

9   Edward Said, *Orientalism: Western Conceptions of the Orient* (Harmondsworth: Penguin, 1978), 3.

10   Moore-Gilbert, Stanton and Maley, for instance, rightly draw attention to the fact that Spivak makes Bertha Mason 'allegorically' the 'representative of the colonized woman, despite the fact that Bertha is "objectively" a member of the former slave-owning plantocracy', *Postcolonial Criticism*, 146.

11 Patrick Brantlinger, *Rule of Darkness: British Literature and Imperialism, 1830–1914* (Ithaca and London: Cornell University Press, 1988), 4.

12 Ibid., 8.

13 Martin Green, *Dreams of Adventure, Deeds of Empire* (London: Routledge and Kegan Paul, 1980; orig. pub. New York: Basic Books, 1979), xi.

14 Brantlinger, *Rule of Darkness*, 12.

15 Ibid., 102.

16 Patrick Brantlinger, 'Race and the Victorian Novel', in Deirdre David., ed., *The Cambridge Companion to the Victorian* Novel (Cambridge: Cambridge University Press, 2001), 160. Brantlinger did consider instances where texts do not transmit imperial ideology in a merely straightforward way. For instance, he suggested that Philip Meadows Taylor's *Confessions of a Thug* (1839) resisted one form of colonial ideology. 'In most British writing about the Empire,' he observed, 'English discourse and authority are imposed on imperialized peoples, often to the extent of denying them even imaginary voices [...] But in *Confessions of a Thug* the Sahib is entirely silent while the self-convicting Ameer Ali speaks on for three hundred pages' (88). Given that Ali, however, is a murderer and robber, this is not an entirely positive development.

17 Daniel Bivona, *Desire and Contradiction: Imperial Visions and Domestic Debates in Victorian Literature* (Manchester: Manchester University Press, 1990), viii.

18 Ibid., xii.

19 Suvendrini Perera, *Reaches of Empire: The English Novel from Edgeworth to Dickens* (New York: Columbia University Press, 1991), 7.

20 Ibid., 122.

21 Ibid. For another reading of *Edwin Drood* and imperial questions, see Tim Dolin's essay cited in Further Reading under Shearer West, ed., *The Victorians and Race*. See also David Faulkner, 'The Confidence Man: Empire and the Deconstruction of Muscular Christianity in "The Mystery of Edwin Drood"', in Donald E. Hall, ed., *Muscular Christianity: Embodying the Victorian Age* (Cambridge: Cambridge University Press, 1994), 175–93, and John S. DeWind, 'The Empire as Metaphor: England and the East in *The Mystery of Edwin Drood*' in John Maynard and Adrienne Auslander Munich, eds, *Victorian Literature and Culture* (New York: AMS, 1993), 169–89.

22 Jenny Sharpe, *Allegories of Empire: The Figure of Woman in the Colonial Text* (Minneapolis: University of Minnesota Press, 1993), 28.

23 Thomas Richards, *The Imperial Archive: Knowledge and the Fantasy of Empire* (London: Verso, 1993), 5.

24 Ibid.

25 This is suggested in Perera, *Reaches of Empire*, 6–7.

26 Deirdre David, *Rule Britannia: Women, Empire, and Victorian Writing* (Ithaca and London: Cornell University Press, 1995), 9.

27 Bivona, *Desire and Contradiction*, 8.

Further Reading

Source texts:
Diana Brydon, ed., *Postcolonialism: Critical Concepts in Literary and Cultural Studies*, 5 vols (London, New York: Routledge, 2000): a useful source book containing essays, many highly theoretical, on all aspects of postcolonialism by major contemporary theorists.

Introductions/histories of postcolonialism:
Elleke Boehmer, *Colonial and Postcolonial Literature: Migrant Metaphors* (Oxford: Oxford University Press, 1995): includes some initial discussion of Victorian fiction.
Peter Childs and Patrick Williams, *An Introduction to Post-colonial Theory* (London: Prentice Hall, 1997): fresh and accessible.
Robert J. C. Young, *Postcolonialism: An Historical Introduction* (Oxford: Blackwell, 2001): a challenging revisionist book that looks at the emergence of postcolonialism from anticolonial movements in Europe, Africa, Asia and Latin America. Good on the different genealogies of imperialism and colonialism.

Critical books on the Victorian novel and imperialism/colonialism:
Daniel Bivona, *British Imperial Literature, 1870–1940: Writing and the Administration of Empire* (Cambridge: Cambridge University Press, 1998): examines the gradual process by which the colonial bureaucratic subject, the figure whose work was rule, was constructed and celebrated in nineteenth and early twentieth-century Britain. Compare this argument with Thomas Richards's *The Imperial Archive* discussed above, pp. 320–1.
Robert H. MacDonald, *The Language of Empire: Myths and Metaphors of Popular Imperialism, 1880–1918* (Manchester: Manchester University Press, 1994): how the 'story' of the empire was shaped for the vast audience at home and in the colonies with an emphasis on how ordinary soldiers or adventurers represented the meaning of their lives at work in the empire.
Alan Sandison, *The Wheel of Empire: A Study of the Imperial Idea in Some Late Nineteenth and Early Twentieth-century Fiction* (New York: St Martin's Press, 1967): argues against the idea that action in the work of Rider Haggard, Kipling, Conrad, and John Buchan was always 'directed towards promulgating an imperial ideal': in Kipling, Buchan, and Conrad, the imperial idea was 'an expression of an individual's response to the fact of his own isolation'; for Rider Haggard, empire was a space in which he dramatized the ambiguity of man's place and purpose. Does not see novels as revealing the power politics of imperialism.
Brian Street, *The Savage in Literature: Representations of 'Primitive' Society in English Fiction 1858–1920* (London: Routledge and Kegan Paul, 1975): pioneering study by a social scientist of why 'particular aspects of "primitive" life were seized upon by many English writers in the later nineteenth and early twentieth centuries and taken as representative of the whole. The representations of alien peoples in much of this literature were based on now outdated scientific theory and on the limited experi-

ence of travelers, many of them unsympathetic to other ways of life. Such descriptions thus tell us more about the Victorians themselves than about the people they purport to describe.'

Essays and essay collections including discussion of the Victorian novel:

Jonathan Arac and Harriet Ritvo, eds, *Macropolitics of Nineteenth-century Literature: Nationalism, Exoticism, Imperialism* (Philadelphia: University of Pennsylvania Press, 1991): includes an essay on 'Private Property and the Oriental Body in *Dombey and Son*' by Jeff Nunokawa, and Susan Meyer's chapter on *Jane Eyre* (see above pp. 325–30).

Homi K. Bhabha, ed., *Nation and Narration* (London: Routledge, 1990): includes an essay on 'Telescopic Philanthropy: Professionalism and Responsibility in *Bleak House*' by Bruce Robbins (pp. 213–30).

Patrick Brantlinger, 'Race and the Victorian Novel', in Deirdre David, ed., *The Cambridge Companion to the Victorian Novel* (Cambridge: Cambridge University Press, 2001), 149–68.

David Dabydeen, ed., *The Black Presence in English Literature* (Manchester: Manchester University Press, 1985): contains two essays that include discussion of nineteenth-century fiction: Frances M. Mannsaker, 'The Dog that Didn't Bark: The Subject Races and Imperial Fiction at the Turn of the Century', and Brian Street, 'Reading the Novels of Empire: Race and Ideology in the Classic "Tale of Adventure"'.

Robert Giddings, ed., *Literature and Imperialism* (Basingstoke: Macmillan, 1991): includes an essay on race and empire in the novels of R. M. Ballantyne, and one on Lord Kitchener.

Nancy L. Paxton, 'Mobilizing Chivalry: Rape in Flora Annie Steel's *On the Face of the Waters* (1896) and Other British Novels about the Indian Uprising of 1857', in Barbara Leah Harman and Susan Meyer, eds, *The New Nineteenth Century: Feminist Readings of Underread Victorian Fiction* (New York: Garland, 1996), 247–75: novels about the 'Mutiny' explored the symbolic territory that Victorian history wanted to deny.

John Sutherland, 'Thackeray as Victorian Racialist', *Essays in Criticism*, 20 (1970), 441–5: 'With regard to what we should now call "racialist questions", [Thackeray] remained singularly unregenerate.'

Shearer West, ed., *The Victorians and Race* (Aldershot: Scolar, 1996): wide-ranging collection with an emphasis on visual arts and representations of race. Helpful first chapter on 'Race, Science and Culture: Historical Continuities and Discontinuities' by D. A. Lorrimer; also Tim Dolin, 'Race and Social Plot in *The Mystery of Edwin Drood*'.

Edward Said:

Culture and Imperialism (London: Chatto and Windus, 1993).

'Introduction' to Rudyard Kipling, *Kim* (Harmondsworth: Penguin, 1989).

Orientalism (Harmondsworth: Penguin, 1995 [*sic*], repr. with new Afterword): includes Said's 'Afterword' that concentrates on rebuffing those who thought the original text was anti-Western and supportive of Eastern nationalism. It was, he reminded his readers, a critique of power, 'not an affirmation of warring and hopelessly antithetical identities'.

'Orientalism Reconsidered', in Francis Barker et al., eds, *Europe and its Others* (Colchester: University of Essex, 1985), i. 14–27. Also in Bart Moore-Gilbert, Gareth Stanton and Willy Maley, eds, *Postcolonial Criticism* (London: Longman, 1997), 126–44.
The World, The Text, and the Critic (London: Faber, 1984).

Studies of Englishness:
Ian Baucom, *Out of Place: Englishness, Empire, and the Locations of Identity* (Princeton, NJ: Princeton University Press, 1999): examines how the empire influenced notions of Englishness, arguing that the empire was imagined as a place where England lost command of its own identity. Considers fiction including Kipling.
Simon Gikandi, *Maps of Englishness: Writing Identity in the Culture of Colonialism* (New York: Columbia University Press, 1996): examines the concept of Englishness during Great Britain's colonial period. Not focused on the novel, but does discuss Trollope's travel writing in chapter 3, 'Englishness and the Culture of Travel: Writing the West Indies in the Nineteenth Century'.

Index